Ethical Archaeologies: The Politics of Social Justice

More information about this series at
http://www.springer.com/series/7559

Cristóbal Gnecco • Dorothy Lippert
Editors

Ethics and Archaeological Praxis

Editors
Cristóbal Gnecco
Universidad del Cauca
Popayan, Colombia

Dorothy Lippert
Repatriation Office
National Museum of Natural History
Washington, DC, USA

ISBN 978-1-4939-1645-0 ISBN 978-1-4939-1646-7 (eBook)
DOI 10.1007/978-1-4939-1646-7
Springer New York Heidelberg Dordrecht London

Library of Congress Control Number: 2014951356

Cover illustration: @ photlook/22989368/Fotolia

Printed on acid-free paper

Springer is part of Springer Science+Business Media (www.springer.com)

Ethical Archaeologies: The Politics of Social Justice

Archaeology remains burdened by modern/Western values. Codified, these values harden into ethics with specific cultural and temporal foundations; indeed, ethics are contextual, shifting and negotiated entanglements of intent and practice that often conflict. Yet, archaeologists may uncritically mask these contexts unless they are adequately aware of the discipline's history and of their location in a globalised world order with its imprint of imperial, colonial and neocolonial values. A responsible and socially committed archaeology must historicise its ethical principles, showing how contingent they are and what kind of needs they are serving.

By adopting a global coverage that brings together academic activism for a historicised ethics, universally created lacunae surrounding disciplinary concepts, such as the archaeological record, stewardship and multivocality, as well as broader concerns of race, class and gender, can be discussed and acted upon. The four volumes comprising the *Ethical Archaeologies: The Politics of Social Justice Series* discuss historically based ethics in the practice of archaeology and related fields—anthropology, museology, indigenous and heritage studies, law and education—and highlight the struggle for social justice, in which the discipline can participate.

In this series we accept that social justice is broadly about equality and the right to freedom from any kind of discrimination or abuse. It is about seeking to transform the current order of the world, in which the hegemony of the Western cosmology still reigns with its ideas of individuality, linear time, development, competition and progress. Thus, social justice is also about the positioning in our research and disciplinary practices of non-modern values about life, time, past, place and heritage.

Hardened into reified principles, as they continue to be, ethical concerns have served to reproduce epistemic hierarchies and privileges. If archaeologists are content with what the ethical preoccupations of the last two decades have achieved, their trumpeted engagement with politics and justice is meaningless. If the ethics of archaeology continues to simply further embed disciplinary privileges, social justice is not a horizon of fulfilment. If ethics is just a disciplinary preoccupation, a way of better accommodating the discipline to changing times, social justice is an empty expression. For these reasons, this series aims to position the values of equality and freedom from all discrimination at the centre of archaeological thinking and practice. The four volumes are not toolkits or guides for standardised, universal, ethical conduct, but critically informed, self-reflective discussions of ethical problems and potentials.

Cristóbal Gnecco
Tracy Ireland

Contents

Contributors

Mitchell Allen Left Coast Press Inc., Walnut Creek, CA, USA

Jaime Almansa Sánchez JAS Arqueología S.L.U, Madrid, Spain

Terry P. Brock The Montpelier Foundation, Richmond, VA, USA

Rafael Pedro Curtoni Facultad de Ciencias Sociales, Universidad Nacional del Centro de la Provincia de Buenos Aires, Olavarría, Provincia de Buenos Aires, Argentina

Michael A. Di Giovine Department of Anthropology and Sociology, West Chester University, West Chester, PA, USA

Víctor M. Fernández Departamento de Prehistoria, Universidad Complutense de Madrid, Madrid, Spain

Neal Ferris Department of Anthropology, Western University, London, ON, Canada

Cristóbal Gnecco Departamento de Antropología, Universidad del Cauca, Popayán, Colombia

Lesley Green School of African and Gender Studies, Anthropology and Linguistics, University of Cape Town, Cape Town, South Africa

Alejandro Haber Escuela de Arqueología, Universidad Nacional de Catamarca & CONICET, Catamarca, Argentina

Carol McDavid Department of Anthropology, Rice University, Houston, TX, USA

Arkadiusz Marciniak Institute of Prehistory, University of Poznań, Poznań, Poland

Caroline Phillips The University of Auckland, Auckland, New Zealand

Anne Ross School of Social Science, The University of Queensland, Brisbane, QLD, Australia

Joe Watkins National Park Service, Washington, DC, USA

John R. Welch Department of Archaeology, Simon Fraser University, Burnaby, BC, Canada

Eldon Yellowhorn Department of First Nations Studies, Simon Fraser University, Burnaby, BC, Canada

Nicolas Zorzin The British School at Athens, Athens, Greece

About the Authors

Mitch Allen is Publisher of Left Coast Press, Inc., a publishing house based in the San Francisco region that specialises in scholarly and professional books on archaeology. He is also Visiting Professor of Anthropology at Mills College in Oakland, California. He was the founder and publisher of AltaMira Press, served as Executive Editor of Sage Publications and has taught archaeology at the University of Maryland, Santa Clara University and Diablo Valley College. Mitch has a Ph.D. in archaeology from UCLA. He was a recipient of a 2013 World Archaeological Congress Outstanding International Award for his sustained contributions to the organisation. Email: mitch@lcoastpress.com

Jaime Almansa Sánchez is founder and general manager of JAS Arqueología SLU, a commercial company based in Spain and devoted, as him, to public archaeology. His research focuses in the social image of archaeology and ethical, theoretical and practical models for the management of archaeological heritage. With one foot in Ethiopia and the other one in Spain, he struggles for a better archaeology through the public concern. Very active in the social media, he tries to bring debate to archaeology from different profiles in different platforms. More at about.me/JaimeAlmansa. Email: almansasanchez@gmail.com

Terry Peterkin Brock is a Ph.D. candidate in the Department of Anthropology at Michigan State University. He has worked at Historic St. Mary's City as a Special Projects Researcher, where his dissertation research is based. This research examines the transition from slavery to freedom at a nineteenth-century plantation in Southern Maryland. This research was recently featured as the topic of a digital exhibit, "All of us would walk together" (http://stmaryscity.org/walktogether), which Brock designed and curated. He also has served as the Campus Archaeologist in the Michigan State University Campus Archaeology Program (http://campusarch.msu.edu), where he conducted archaeological excavations on campus, and also designed and implemented their social media engagement programme. Brock is also an active member of the Society for Historical Archaeology, where he serves as their Social Media Coordinator (http://www.sha.org/blog). Brock has particular interest in the archaeology of Chesapeake Region, in particular the ways in which archaeology and digital tools can be used to better engage the public in understanding the past. You can learn more about him at his Web site (http://terrypbrock.com). Email: brockter@msu.edu

Rafael Pedro Curtoni is a Research Associate of CONICET and Dean of the School of Social Sciences, National University of Central Buenos Aires Province, Argentina. He also is a Lecturer in anthropology at the School of Natural Sciences and Museum, National University of La Plata. He has given several lectures and 11 postgraduate courses in different universities in Argentina and Colombia and has published more than 40 articles in books and specialised journals both nationally and internationally. His main research interests are landscape anthropology, heritage policy, indigenous communities, Latin American thought and social theory. Email: rcurtoni@soc.unicen.edu.ar

Michael A. Di Giovine is Assistant Professor of Anthropology in the Department of Anthropology and Sociology at West Chester University of Pennsylvania (USA), and an Honorary Fellow in the Department of Anthropology at the University of Wisconsin-Madison. Michael earned his Ph.D. from the University of Chicago with a dissertation examining pilgrimage, heritage and revitalisation associated with the Catholic cult of St. Padre Pio of Pietrelcina. A former tour operator, Michael's research in Italy and Southeast Asia (Vietnam and Cambodia) focuses on global mobilities (tourism/pilgrimage and immigration), heritage, development, foodways and comparative religious movements. The author of *The heritage-scape: UNESCO, world heritage and tourism*, as well as articles focused on the practices and the ethics behind the heritage and tourism fields, Michael has also co-edited *Edible identities: exploring food and foodways as cultural heritage*, *Astray: the seductions of pilgrimage* and *Tourism and the power of otherness: seductions of difference*. The book reviews editor of *Journeys: The International Journal of Travel and Travel Writing*, Michael sits on the academic board of the *Journal of Tourism and Cultural Change* and is a founding member and trustee of both the Tourism-Contact-Culture Research Network and the American Anthropological Association's Anthropology of Tourism Interest Group. Email: michael@michaeldigiovine.com

Víctor M. Fernández is Professor of Prehistory at the University Complutense (Madrid, Spain) and has directed archaeological research projects in Spain (1978–1991), Sudan (1978–2000) and Ethiopia (2001–2013). He is the author of *La cultura alto-meroítica del norte de Nubia* (Universidad Complutense 1985), *Teoría y método de la arqueología* (Síntesis 1989, 2000), *Arqueología prehistórica de África* (Síntesis 1996), *Una arqueología crítica. Ciencia, ética y política en la construcción del pasado* (Crítica 2006), *Prehistoria. El largo camino de la humanidad* (Alianza 2007) and *Los años del Nilo* (Alianza 2011), editor of *The Blue Nile Project. Holocene Archaeology in Central Sudan* (Complutum 2003) and co-editor of *Teoría arqueológica* (Complutum 2012). He is former director of the journal Complutum (2008–2012) and of the Department of Prehistory of the University Complutense (2010–2014). Email: victormf@ucm.es

Neal Ferris works with the people and archaeology of Ontario, Canada, including spending 20 years working as a Provincial Archaeologist, where his day to day consisted of regulating archaeology and land development. Those 20 years provided plenty of opportunities to experience and personally negotiate the full spectrum of ethical expression (positive and negative) in practice and how archaeology impacts and is impacted by its intersection with wider social values, corporate prerogatives and bureaucratic cultural logics. Twenty years was long enough to be stuck within the endless recycling of issues and head banging that is bureaucratic oversight of archaeology, so he retired from the civil service in 2006, to take up the Lawson Chair of Canadian Archaeology at the University of Western Ontario. This position is cross appointed between the Department of Anthropology and the Museum of Ontario Archaeology. There Neal directs Sustainable Archaeology, teaches the odd course and supports many graduate students researching applied and Ontario archaeology. He, too, happily gets to do research, as well as collaborate with colleagues and friends from across archaeology and across descendant communities, to try and make sense of a practice, community and way of seeing the world that continues to enthral his imagination. Email: nferris@uwo.ca

Lesley Green is Associate Professor of Anthropology in the School of African and Gender Studies, Anthropology and Linguistics at the University of Cape Town, where she leads the Contested Ecologies research initiative, and edited a book of that title (HSRC Press 2013). She and David Green have co-authored the volume *Knowing the Day, Knowing the World: Engaging Amerindian Thought in Public Archaeology* (University of Arizona Press 2013), and, with Uwet Manoel Antonio dos Santos, the volume *Waramwi: A Cobra Grande* (IEPE 2013). Email: lesley.green@uct.ac.za

Alejandro Haber is an Argentinian archaeologist and anthropologist from the National University of Catamarca and CONICET (National Council of Scientific and Technological Research). He is regionally focused in the Andes, and he is interested in coloniality as coded by academic disciplines. He is currently involved in un-disciplining archaeology as a no-methodology for cultural and social research. Email: afhaber@gmail.com

Arkadiusz Marciniak is Professor of Archaeology at Adam Mickiewicz University of Poznań. He also holds a position of Associate Professor in the School of Humanities at Flinders University. His expertise is in the development of early farming communities in western Asia and central Europe and their progression to complex societies. His other interests comprise zooarchaeology of farming communities, archaeological heritage and political context of practising archaeology as well as archaeological theory and history of archaeological thought. He has been a co-director of the Polish team at the Neolithic tell in Çatalhöyük, Turkey. He is currently directing a new project at Çatalhöyük in the previously unexcavated part of the mound. He has just completed a project on distance learning application in the domain of archaeological heritage. He has published extensively in peer-reviewed books and journals. Among his recent publications are *Placing animals in the Neolithic. Social zooarchaeology of prehistoric farming communities* and *Grahame Clark and his legacy* (with John Coles). He held a position of visiting professor at Stanford University (twice) and University College London. He is also a recipient of prestigious fellowships, including Fulbright, Humboldt, Mellon and Kościuszko. Email: arekmar@amu.edu.pl

Carol McDavid is the Executive Director of the Community Archaeology Research Institute in Houston, Texas. She also directs the Yates Community Archaeology Project, a programme of the Rutherford B. H. Yates Museum, Inc., in Freedmen's Town, Houston (www.publicarchaeology.org). She holds a Ph.D. degree in archaeology from the University of Cambridge and serves as adjunct faculty at Rice University and the University of Houston. She has also served or is serving on the Boards of several Houston history groups, the Levi Jordan Plantation Historical Society, the Society for Historical Archaeology (where she is currently Secretary) and the Board of the Archaeology Division of the American Anthropological Association. Her publications, community work and research focus on the archaeology of the African Diaspora and related justice issues. In particular, she is interested in finding ways to use historical archaeology to counter racist narratives and dismantle white privilege and to make it more accessible to diverse publics as a tool for community collaboration and reform. Email: mcdavid@publicarchaeology.org

Caroline Phillips is an Honorary Research Fellow at the University of Auckland and a consultant archaeologist. She has lectured in archaeology at the University of Auckland and Te Whare Wananga o Awanuiarangi. Caroline was a co-convenor of the Second Indigenous World Archaeological Inter-Congress and co-editor of the resultant book, *Bridging the Divide: Indigenous Communities and Archaeology into the 21st Century* (Left Coast Press 2010). Her studies of Maori settlements have involved the integration of archaeological fieldwork, geoarchaeological techniques and the rich material from Maori oral and post-European contact histories. Her research questions include how to identify dynamic settlement systems, small-scale cultural changes and issues of ethnicity and identity using landscape approaches, contextual archaeology and historical narratives. Caroline's involvement in the ethics of archaeological practice and resource management led to the development of the New Zealand Archaeology Professional Development Cell, which for the last 7 years has run a series of workshops aimed at up-skilling practising archaeologists. Email: phillips@orcon.net.nz

Anne Ross is Associate Professor in cultural heritage management at the University of Queensland. Her primary research interests are the relationships between indigenous peoples and their cultural landscapes. Annie works with Aboriginal Australians, mostly in south-eastern Queensland, and has documented the knowledge held by traditional owners regarding the management of a range of natural resources and their associated sites, both in the past and the present. Her recent co-authored book, *Indigenous Peoples and the Collaborative Stewardship of Nature: Knowledge Binds and Institutional Conflicts* (Walnut Creek, Left Coast Press), situates this research in a global context and incorporates a range of issues relevant to the review of the ethics of appropriation and codification of other peoples' knowledge. Recently Annie has undertaken research on the indigenous knowledge of peoples in parts of Solomon Islands and Tonga. This is a logical extension of her Australian research and covers many similar issues. Email: annie.ross@uq.edu.au

Joe Watkins has been involved in anthropology for more than 45 years. He became the Supervisory Anthropologist and the Chief of the Tribal Relations and American Cultures Program of the National Park Service in Washington, DC, in 2013. His current study interests are influenced by his Choctaw Indian background and involve the ethical practice of anthropology and the study of anthropology's relationships with descendant communities and aboriginal populations. He has published numerous articles on these topics as a means of trying to increase the conversation between indigenous groups and anthropologists. His book *Indigenous Archaeology: American Indian Values and Scientific Practice* (AltaMira Press 2000) is in its second printing. His book *Reclaiming Physical Heritage: Repatriation and Sacred Sites* (Chelsea House Publishers 2005) is aimed toward creating an awareness of Native American issues among high school students. He is co-author with Carol Ellick of *The anthropology graduate's guide: from school to a career* (Left Coast Press 2011), a student-oriented publication to help anthropology students to transition from college to the work force. Email: joe_watkins@nps.gov

John R. Welch is a Professor in the Department of Archaeology and the School of Resource and Environmental Management, Simon Fraser University (Canada). He is an applied archaeologist with research, teaching and outreach commitments that centre on collaborations with indigenous nations on projects at the interface of anthropology, archaeology and resource management. The points of departure for his work are indigenous peoples' sovereignty (rights and responsibilities derived from authority over people and territory) and stewardship (use of cultural and biophysical legacies grounded in altruism and sustainability). Since the mid-1980s, his work has involved partnerships with tribes in upland Arizona and First Nations in coastal British Columbia (BC). As constructive responses to indigenous scholars' critiques of extractive research and resource management, he has collaborated with diverse academic and community colleagues to develop partnerships premised on sovereignty and stewardship as a nexus for mobilising indigenous knowledge and advancing community goals as part of the current reassessment of what to conserve in the face of global change. His career is dedicated to aligning and advancing indigenous community and broader public agendas for sovereignty enhancement, applied archaeology and stewardship of cultural and biophysical legacies. Email: welch@sfu.ca

Eldon Yellowhorn is Associate Professor of Archaeology and First Nations Studies at Simon Fraser University. He grew up on the Peigan Indian Reserve, now the Piikani First Nation. He attended the day school on the reserve and completed his schooling in Fort Macleod, Alberta. He acquired his interest in natural history by exploring the countryside around the family farm. He obtained undergraduate degrees in geography and archaeology from the University of Calgary. His graduate studies began at Simon Fraser University, where he received a master's degree in archaeology. His doctoral work at McGill University brought together his interest in mythology and culture history. Using methods borrowed from archaeology and earth science, he examined the oral narratives of his Piikani ancestors to explain ancient cultural manifestations on the northern plains. His research continues to emphasise archaeological methods to better understand the lifeways of his Piikani ancestors. That interest formed the nucleus of his current research, which is a project of chronicling their historical experiences during their transition to their new life on an Indian reserve in the nineteenth century. This involved investigating farmsteads and institutional settings of that time, combined with archival data. Concurrent with the excavation, he is filming a video documentary about the history of the Piikani First Nation. Email: ecy@sfu.ca

Nicolas Zorzin is a Research Fellow at Kyushu University (Japan), where he is currently conducting a study on the archaeological heritage management system of Japan. He completed a B.Sc. and M.Sc. both in Anthropology from the Université de Montréal (Canada) specialising in archaeology, followed by a Postgraduate Diploma in Cultural Management from HEC Montréal. For his Ph.D. in archaeology (2011) from the University of Southampton (UK), his research focused mainly on the political economy of Western archaeologies. His work provided an analysis of archaeological practices through oral testimonies collected in Quebec (Canada), aiming to test the political-economic model in which archaeology is embedded and to interrogate both the social significance and ethics of archaeological outcomes. In 2011 he has taught Ethics in Archaeology at the Department of History of the Université Laval in Canada. In 2012, he received the Australian Endeavour Research Fellowship from the University of Melbourne followed by the JSPS Research Fellowship in Japan in 2013. Between 2001 and 2012 he was particularly active in two archaeological sites in Greece: Argilos (Proto-History and Antiquity) [http://www.argilos.net/home/] and Koutroulou (Middle Neolithic) Archaeological Ethnography Project [http://antiquity.ac.uk/projgall/hamilakis333/]. His recent publications tackle the developments of archaeology within heritage management following the global economic recession in Canada and Australia. Email: zorz66@hotmail.com

About the Editors

Cristóbal Gnecco is Professor in the Department of Anthropology at the University of Cauca (Colombia), where he works on the political economy of archaeology, the geopolitics of knowledge and the discourses on alterity. He currently serves as Chair of the Ph.D. Programme in Anthropology at his university and as a co-editor of the journals *Archaeologies* and *Arqueología Suramericana*. Email: cgnecco2001@yahoo.com

Dorothy Lippert is Choctaw and an archaeologist. She received her B.A. from Rice University and her M.A. and Ph.D. from the University of Texas at Austin. Dorothy has worked in the repatriation programme of the National Museum of Natural History, Smithsonian Institution, since 2001. She responds to repatriation requests from US tribes for human remains and sacred material. Dorothy served on the Executive of the World Archaeological Congress from 2005 to 2013 and is a past member of the Board of Directors for the Society for American Archaeology. Her research interests include the development of indigenous archaeology, repatriation, ethics and the archaeology and bioarchaeology of the Southeastern USA. Email: lippertd@si.edu

Chapter 1
An Entanglement of Sorts: Archaeology, Ethics, Praxis, Multiculturalism

Cristóbal Gnecco

Since their worldwide adoption some two decades ago, ethical principles/codes in archaeology have been subjected to a sustained critique. The main argument is that they have been naturalized. The moral *good*, always historical, has been reified, ignoring (or, perhaps, knowing full well) that what is *good* for a given society is context-dependent. For many archaeologists, ethical principles have frozen reflexivity and the will to change (if it ever existed). The preoccupation voiced by some (Tarlow 2001; Meskell and Pels 2005; Hamilakis 2007) about the reification of ethics (with the consequent elimination of any traces of historicity and happening) has now become a certainty.

To move beyond ethics as a reified set of principles history is needed. As a contribution to this end, the papers in this book seek to assess *ethics* in archaeology through *praxis* in the understanding that the two cannot (should not) be separated, ever. Ethics is not an absolute term. If considered as a set of principles of right conduct or a theory or a system of moral values, ethics entails a historical condition for it condenses the moral thinking of a society on specific times and places but not in others. Ethics is unavoidably nested in historical relations. Yet, it normally is reified, as if it were an anthropological universal. Restoring the historicity and plurality of archaeological ethics is a task to which this book is devoted; its emphasis on praxis mends the historical condition of ethics. In doing so, it shows that nowadays a multicultural (sometimes also called "public") ethics looms large in the discipline. By engaging communities "differently," archaeology has explicitly adopted an ethical outlook, purportedly striving to overcome its colonial ontology and metaphysics. In this new scenario, the respect for other historical systems/worldviews and

C. Gnecco (✉)
Departamento de Antropología, Universidad del Cauca,
Popayán, Colombia
e-mail: cgnecco2001@yahoo.com

C. Gnecco, D. Lippert (eds.), *Ethics and Archaeological Praxis*,
Ethical Archaeologies: The Politics of Social Justice 1,
DOI 10.1007/978-1-4939-1646-7_1

social accountability appear to be prominent. Being and behaving ethically in archaeological terms in the multicultural context has become mandatory, so much that most professional, international and national archaeological associations have ethical principles as guiding forces behind their openness towards social sectors traditionally ignored or marginalized by their practices.

Ethical concerns in archaeology were rare a few decades ago but became frequent in the last 20 years. The emergence of ethics in the discipline—a common preoccupation turned professional proscription and prescription—may have occurred some 40 years ago, but its popularity (which, at the same time, is a symptom) ripened alongside the transformation of national societies into multicultural ones. The entangled relationship between archaeology and the recent course of the West created new conditions for the discipline, which in due course activated mechanisms of adaptation; amongst them ethical principles stand out. What demanded their appearance? I hold that they are disciplinary responses to global changes associated with multiculturalism. Yet, to avoid *contextualism*—which implies the modern division between facts, power, and discourse—it is necessary to describe the links that allows politics and society to influence knowledge and ideas and vice versa. This can be the task: not understanding archaeological ethics in its context neither showing the operation of political pressures over it but showing how "a science, a context, and a demarcation between the two" (Latour 1993:16) became not only possible but *real*. In doing so, perhaps the first issue that comes to the fore is the parochialism of archaeological ethics and, at the same time, its violent universalism.

The papers in this book are symptoms of what archaeological ethics is nowadays as seen from praxis. While some papers express disappointment, some others believe that two decades of ethical discussions (and principles) have done well to archaeology by turning it more sensitive to contemporary issues, more accountable for its actions, and more responsible to the demands of different publics. The different assessments expressed in the papers are expressions of the political and academic positioning of their writers. These telling differences not only point to issues already debated, such as the need to go political and the need to overcome reification, but to another issue as well: archaeological ethics are mostly self-contained, disciplinary, and self-serving; they engage the world from within disciplinary limits and from within the cosmology of modernity. These issues do not amount to a putative lag between ethics as theory and ethics as practice, as if what was established in principles were summarily violated in action. The point is how a global ethics (which I will call *multicultural ethics*) shapes what archaeologists do; and what they do is what an assessment of their praxis tells us they do.

Have ethics in archaeology changed the discipline or hardened it? Has it worked towards social justice, a rhetorical horizon to where the discipline seemed willing to go since it became conscious of its modern/colonial origins and effects? Further, can archaeology have ethical principles committed to social justice if, at the same time, it strengthens its relationship with the market and development? Is this coincidence just mere haphazard or it obeys more structural rules? The papers in this book try to answer these questions by examining praxis-based contexts in which archaeological ethics unfolds. The book is about archaeological ethics today. That means that the papers bring into the picture the principal elements/changes that have shaped such a contemporary ethics: the global multicultural rhetoric and its local adoptions; the public (broadly including the grass-roots challenge and opposition to academic, positivist archaeology); and the widespread interventions of development.

Archaeological ethics has also had another effect: the creation and/or delimitation of archaeological values that were formerly vague and undefined—and some of which didn't even exist. Thus, commitment to a sound (fair, true) interpretation of the past, to sound disciplinary practices (swift publication, adequate curation of findings), to stewardship, to social responsibility, have emerged as the values the archaeologists must abide to. In this regard, two groups of (rarely interrelated) values have been formed: (a) disciplinary values, to which archaeologists seem to abide willingly (no wonder, since they strengthen and protect the profession); and (b) contextual values, which they address reluctantly because they have the potential to upset the discipline (as it has happened with repatriation, an unintended result of social accountability). For instance, the principles of archaeological ethics of the Society for American Archaeology (SAA 1996) are stewardship, accountability, commercialization, public education and outreach, intellectual property, public reporting and publication, records and preservation, and training and resources. Except for accountability, which expressly states the need to consult with affected groups in order to "establishing a working relationship that can be beneficial to all parties involved," all other values are disciplinary, based on the reified, undisputed existence of the archaeological record—perhaps the main actor in all ethical principles (see Hamilakis 2007:23)—and on the Enlightened, humanistic, and universal *nature* of the archaeological endeavor. As I will show further down, both groups of values are modern (but also multicultural) and unveil the ontology of which archaeology partakes.

Ethics is a liberating force: as far as the archaeologists comply with their basic precepts (mostly disciplinary), they are free (politically and psychologically) to go on with their usual trade, which more often than not entails a great dose of self-isolation. Ethics is an important part of the postmodern turn in archaeology. It "modifies" the relationship with the Other (I will sketch further down what this "modification" is all about) but it helps to keep intact the modern/colonial structuring of archaeological thought. Further, it helps to avoid thinking and acting reflexively and hinders actual transformations. It hinders, specially, a true different relationship with Otherness. As Michel-Rolph Trouillot (2003:28) noted about related events in anthropology:

> This recurring refusal to pursue further the archaeological exercise obscures the asymmetrical position of the savage-other in the thematic field upon which anthropology was premised. It negates the specificity of otherness, subsuming the Other in the sameness of the text perceived as liberating cooperation.

In this case, the Other is subsumed in the sameness of the ethical code, premised as a liberating cooperation. In the absence of a thorough discussion about power, capitalism, multiculturalism, and inequalities, that is, about contextual conditions (including, as I mentioned before, the conditions that permit the separation of discipline and context in the first place), ethics is meaningless, especially if social justice is at stake.

Multiculturalism, Archaeology, and Ethics

Archaeological discourses related to the creation and functioning of national societies have lost momentum and significance given the emergence of multiculturalism, which has the main tenets of modern societies crumbling, especially the construction of unified collectivities (national societies) in terms of culture, language, and history. In the last two or three decades multiculturalism has set in motion profound changes, especially regarding the organization of society, which is now premised upon the coexistence of diverse constituencies—conventionally referred to as *cultural diversity*. The multicultural idea of diversity hides differences and inequalities by eliminating historical specificities, processes of othering, asymmetries, and power relations.

Archaeology has been so shaped by this social order that a multicultural archaeology has emerged. In order to keep up with multicultural changes (which, by the way, archaeology has not promoted but to which it has to accommodate, often unwillingly), profound as they are, archaeology has basically done four things: (a) it has opened its practice to local actors; (b) it has widened the circulation of it discourse; (c) it has included other historical horizons in its interpretations; and, (d) it has given up the exclusive control of some disputed issues. Let me examine those four things. Firstly, the open practice it champions has only allowed local actors to be members of research teams or, the most, to be trained in the discipline. Such openness has normally been framed under the heading "collaboration" but power relations are rarely at stake. Most archaeologists are content to offer cultural crumbs to the communities (a local museum, a video, a booklet) while preserving the control of key issues (research designs, destination of findings, production and dissemination of narratives). Secondly, a widened circulation of archaeological discourses—which, along with collaboration, forms the backbone of public archaeology, part and parcel of a more comprehensive entity that I have chosen to call *multicultural archaeology*—has had two results: it reproduces the archaeological canon more widely and it furthers the reification and objectification of the past, such as in the case of local museums, which have sprouted everywhere. Thirdly, an expanded archaeological hermeneutics, achieved by incorporating non-Western conceptions (of the past, time, etc.), has doubtlessly enriched the explanatory potential of the discipline but has not engaged intercultural understandings. Such an interpretative expansion, many times resorting to alien cosmologies that produce curious argumentative hybrids (for instance: live objects, with agency, amidst rigid functional frames), deepens the logocentric gaze but does not aim to forge non-hierarchical relationships. And fourthly, relinquishing control over certain issues means precisely that: certain issues and under certain circumstances. This characteristic has been more commonly achieved through the selective repatriation of biological and cultural remains. Thus, a "reformed" archaeology is happy to share what it cherishes most with previously marginalized parties: disciplinary epistemic coherence. All in all, however, archaeology keeps spreading the fruits of Enlightenment and gets other (local) actors to participate in institutional spaces created to control the definition and management of disciplinary principles.

In line with multiculturalism (with its promotion of diversity alongside its condemnation of difference; with its promotion of political correctness); in line with what Moshenska (2008:160) called "neo-liberal self-congratulation," ethical preoccupations flourish in the discipline. A powerful, new multicultural ethics emanates from metropolitan centers, only to be adopted elsewhere. Although such an adoption is selective to suit local needs, a global ethical canon has been in place for quite a number of years. In this regard, two issues have not received due attention: (a) how that canon has been responded at local levels; and (b) how it articulates with the cultural logic of late capitalism, with development, and with the market. An answer to the former question must account for the fact that the discipline (along with its ethical principles) has not just been adopted widely (even by former contradictors) but has also been contested by grass-roots organizations, social movements, and academic militants. An answer to the latter must account for a temporal coincidence: at the same time that ethical codes were enacted in archaeology, the discipline tuned up its philosophical gear to accommodate to multicultural changes and to the growing needs of capitalist expansions—which usually engulf the frontiers where ethnic Others still live. In short, an answer to both questions cannot elude to record that a multicultural ethics does not destabilizes but strengthens archaeological tenets by providing the moral means by which they can accommodate to contextual transformations while remaining basically unchanged. In this accommodation the relationship with Otherness is salient. The contextual concerns of archaeological ethics aim to bring Others to share the benefits of the discipline while striving to banish confrontational dichotomies—such as indigenous peoples vs. archaeologists. Good intentions notwithstanding, banishing those dichotomies mostly serves to unify and solidify archaeology by making it more democratic.[1]

Accepting archaeology as is, especially through its promotion of a multicultural ethics, amounts to veiling conflicting views about history, the past, the ancestors, knowing. In a conspiring mood I could say that veiling differences and making discrepancies invisible has been a fulfilled aim of ethical principles; but given that so many good intentions are at stake, I could say that they were unintended consequences which, in the long run, only served disciplinary concerns—and thus, the modern cosmology. Indeed, archaeological ethics is modern and the promise of inclusion it delivers is also modern. The problem is that such an inclusion is violent and logocentric; further, it coexists with the utmost complicity with development and the market. These issues, and others, are addressed by the papers in this book.

[1] Contemporary democracy seeks to protect the rights of the minorities lest they are devoured by those of the majorities; yet, such a protection is mostly fulfilled by granting the disenfranchised access to dominant worldviews but rarely by protecting and respecting differences (ontological and otherwise). As Mario Blaser (2009:883) noted: "In the context of the encounters between diverse social formations and Euro-modernity, which is the historical milieu from which most contemporary claims of modernity arise, 'modernity' implied, first and foremost, a language of exclusion and, only then, a promise of inclusion—of course, always demanding that non-moderns reform themselves to be modern."

About the Arguments Set Forth in This Volume

The book is divided in two complementary sections, one devoted to address the first question posed above (how the global ethical canon has been received and responded locally) and the second to address the second question (how such a canon articulates with the postmodern, development, and the market). The first section (*Is there a global archaeological ethics? Canonical conditions for discursive legitimacy and local responses*) includes six papers, whose authors were asked to consider how a global (multicultural) ethical discourse affects their specific praxis, as seen from their situated, local perspectives. The results are disparate and show how their authors position themselves in the academic and militant arenas. The paper by Joe Watkins is truly emblematic in this regard. Ten years ago he wrote a paper for a volume on ethics (Watkins 2003), in which he reflected on the effects, that he deemed mostly positive, the new ethical principles could have on the relationship between archaeologists and Indigenous peoples. His tone was optimistic—in spite on some doubts regarding polarization and widening gulfs in some areas. Watkins (2003:132) even labeled some codes of ethics as "praiseworthy," specifically the SAA Code of Ethics and WAC's Vermillion Accord. In less than a decade that optimism has vanished:

> This is where North American archaeology falls short. Praxis—putting theoretical knowledge to work—should be part of the active cycle in the development of ethics in North American archaeology, but it has not been so. Perhaps there hasn't been an active movement to exclude Indigenous or "minority" populations from an active involvement with archaeology, but there has also not been an active welcoming of archaeology to those populations other than on individual cases until recently… the ability to change the ethical structures of North American practitioners seems unlikely (Chap. 2).

What has happened in the intervening years? Even a rapid glance will show reification and disciplinary hardening as the two main events that have occurred, one acting upon ethics and the other as its more profound consequence. And then we come to extant power structures, to privileges whose holders are not willing to relinquish:

> In the Principles, "interested publics" are considered to have relatively equal interest in the archaeological record, but in reality that interest does not equate to power, control, or ownership. It is highly unlikely that the members of the Society for American Archaeology who are currently privileged in the process will freely turn over control to non-academic communities, regardless of the intentions of those communities (Chap. 2).

Rafael Curtoni expresses similar concerns, especially as the current ethics arises from a conception of archaeology which is modern and thus disembodied, detached and instrumental. An ethics arising from a modern discipline could not be but modern—bringing along epistemic violence, distance and a fearful relationship with politics. Curtoni is specially critic of multivocality, with its neutralization of difference and its disdain of power structures. It is not surprising that both come from the geopolitical south, Watkins as a member of a subaltern minority in the USA and Curtoni as a citizen of country occupying a subaltern position vis-à-vis the metropolitan centers. Their subaltern perspectives, from which they fustigate current archaeological ethics, contrast with the positions of the other four contributors to this section—two from the Anglo world (Ferris/Welch and Phillips/Ross) and two from southern and eastern Europe (Fernández and Marciniak)—for whom ethics has pitfalls but is also promising. While Caroline Phillips and Annie Ross acknowledge ethics-related improvements in the relationship between archaeology and indigenous peoples in Australia and New Zealand (incorporation of indigenous knowledge into legislation, participation in community-based research and in decision-making) they also think that

> ...there is still a considerable distance for archaeological practice to travel to overcome the barriers of the imposed rationale for investigation, the underlying understandings of the past, and interpretations of the results of archaeological research, that remain almost solely with the archaeologists and administrators of heritage management in both countries (Chap. 3).

Ethical concerns in Central-Eastern Europe, a Arek Marciniak shows, are basically limited to disciplinary issues, especially as archaeology entered an unprecedented expansion in the contract arena in the current post-communist epoch; such concerns translate into ethical codes and regulations. Indeed, ethics is mostly geared to ensure the academic quality of contract-related archaeological products, as well as fostering what archaeologists consider an important duty, that is, targeting "illegal" practices (especially trade and looting of archaeological materials). Yet, unlike most preoccupations with contract or applied archaeology (generally expressed in terms of poor academic standards), Neal Ferris and John Welch think that it is a privileged field in which to put to test the concerns an ethics-led activist practice has positioned in the last two decades (multivocality, collaboration, commitment, authority decentring, and the like), especially as applied archaeologists vastly outnumber academic practitioners:

> The accumulated consequence of this trend, occurring across North America continually in applied contexts, is a re-alignment of archaeological ethics from being about advancing archaeological values and harvesting the material record before development impact, to being about servicing broad societal values that get variably asserted for the material past when encountered in the intersection of economic growth, capitalist endeavour, and community interest (Chap. 7).

Lastly, Víctor Fernández, writing from Spain but reflecting on what is going on in Western Europe ethics-wise, also shows that disciplinary preoccupations have taken the stage, not unlike the events accruing worldwide. Yet, he moves beyond describing what is currently happening to speak from a different morality, one that is still inexistent or fairly marginal. His call for taking seriously different publics and worldviews (not just those identified as "European" in mainstream parlance) articulates with his critique of modern archaeology:

> It is not an issue of undemanding tolerance from a superiority stand but of true equal rights to all parts, being well aware that the real danger to archaeology and heritage does not come today from different cultures and conceptions but from the same core of our western rationality, represented by the capitalist system.

These six different perspectives, situated as they are, see the glass half full or half empty regarding ethics. Mostly, they underscore that positioning and situatedness are key for understanding ethics through praxis; otherwise, reification will linger on unabatedly.

The second section (*Archaeological ethics in the global arena: emergences, transformations and accommodations*) includes eight papers also dealing with ethics and praxis. Yet, instead of writing from the places from which they work and write, the authors were asked to write from the specific topics in which they research and militate. The first paper, by Alejandro Haber, sets the tone of the section by addressing what it means to be an archaeologist doing archaeology (a modern discipline) within a modern matrix (the cultural logic of capitalism). The word *ethics* is almost absent from his paper, underscoring that the morality of archaeologists does not have to be mentioned in order to make it evident. It is just out there, waiting to be engaged. Once that occurs, archaeological ethics easily renders that it has been forged in the entanglement with modernity and capitalism. Development, Alejandro shows, is the master trope guiding the relationship, especially as its *absent plenitude* (taken as a natural given supported by universal laws) even dictates disciplinary agendas—such as the provision of epistemic arguments to suit its demands. Prominent in this regard is the role of contract archaeology, explored by Jaime Almansa and Nicolas Zorzin. Contract archaeology is not a minor thing: (a) it employs more than 90 % of acting archaeologists worldwide; (b) it has promoted profound curricular transformations (something achieved by no other event in the history of the discipline, not even by the advent of the scientific program in the 1960s)[2]; (c) it has abated the critical stance of archaeology towards the global order by an uncritical functionality with capitalism, agreeing with development projects that are negatively impacting human populations as well as the rights of nature; in doing so, it has led the discipline to an uncritical, unreflecting *cul-de-sac*, where social and political responsibilities are rare, to say the least; and (d) it has diminished the possibility for the discipline to rebuild its metaphysical and ontological apparatus, already clearly hierarchical and neocolonial. In contract archaeology the relationship of the discipline with development appears as an innocent instrumentality, as a mere technical service.

If we are to define what a multicultural ethics in archaeology looks like, no better place to look at that so-called public archaeology. In this point, McDavid and Brock (Chap. 11) are outright correct: "Over the course of the past century, public archaeology (however defined) and archaeological ethics have been mutually constituted." Public archaeology is the arena where archaeological ethics have been more clearly deployed. For them, "four of the most prominent approaches used in contemporary public archaeology practice" define what an ethical archaeology practice is today in contextual terms: activism, multivocality, collaboration, and community engagement. But as ethics, public archaeology is context-dependent and can have many readings.[3]

---

[2] New undergraduate programs—characterized by their short length (normally no more than 3 years) and their technical emphasis—are being created to mass-produce archaeologists to fulfill the contractual needs arising from capitalist expansions (transport infrastructure and mining are the most salient).

[3] See Green et al. (2003) for a different conception of public archaeology.

Archaeologists attach a great value to publishing, not only because it is the ace in career building but because ethical principles link a responsible relationship with the record to timely and accessible publications, as discussed by Mitch Allen. Yet, if this disciplinary value were considered in relation to contextual values, the possibility of archaeological research and practice not mediated by publication emerges. Publication may be *a must* for academic archaeology but that is not the case for other kinds of practice, especially those challenging the discipline's modernity. The urge of other archaeologies is not publication, which may or may not happen as a research result. But even if it happens, the material published (a booklet, for instance) bears no specific names, invisible behind the anonymous face of the collectivity.

Michael Di Giovine's discussion of ethics and heritage brings to the fore an important issue, usually overlooked: ethical concerns function in contested fields ("a clash of moralities") in which power and hegemonies are at stake, no matter how disguise they are by a naturalized professional morality. Conflict is bypassed through reification, especially as it unfolds in the hegemony of modernity. He also points out that "multicultural ethics, while frequently well-intentioned, create or perpetuate the very tensions it seeks to resolve." For that reason he proposes a *patrimonial ethics* centered "on a more robust understanding of the totality" of stakeholders as well as in the heritage object itself through its historicity, "pregnant as it is with myriad meanings."

The paper by Lesley Green describes "a participatory research ethic" which calls into question the extended multicultural goal of getting different worldviews to coexist without really trying to understand and respect each other[4]; it also questions the self-designated knowledge privileges of archaeology and anthropology. Her on-the-ground ethics takes Palikur ontology seriously. Her ethics is not modern-modeled and thus not archaeology-enforcing (excavation, for instance, was not even considered in the research she describes; and artifacts were not taken as givens but as "emerging in relation to particular interests and narratives and technologies"). At last, she posits that "The challenge is to move beyond matching perspectives, theirs to ours, to an engagement with the real challenges that are the challenges of 'the real': the possibility of different empiricisms; different 'cogitos'."

Once enacted, ethical mandates seem to establish themselves as unquestioned and ahistorical truths. They may be refined, amended, but their historicity is hidden. It is so for most professional archaeologists—for whom ethical principles are destined, after all, and who can be held accountable for their infringement. For others, however, ethics is a day-to-day matter more than a set of abstractions and can have lasting effects on different archaeologies. For Eldon Yellowhorn an ethical archaeology is tantamount to an archaeology serving indigenous needs and expectations. He feels that "I am doing a service to my community by appropriating the methods I need to pursue internally defined objectives."

---

[4] This is known in the West as *relativism*, widely performed in a power vacuum oblivious of ideologies and hegemonies.

The set of papers comprising the two sections of the book revolves around similar topics, two of which are the relationship of ethics with capitalism and politics. Indeed, a main actor portrayed in most papers in this collection is capitalism: they refer to it in one way or another; they assess its ultimate impact in the course archaeology has taken in the last three decades. Fredric Jameson (1984) noted that postmodern times were characterized by the capitalist assault on two realms untouched by modernity: mind and nature. The past has to be added to the list. Capitalism and the past have had a close and intimate, centuries-old relationship (especially as the latter provided the means for legitimating the former). Yet, the last decades have witnessed a significant shift: the past has become a commodity. Likewise, although the relationship of archaeology with capitalism may be as old as the discipline itself, it has changed in the last three decades: from being instrumental in the provision of empirical data for supporting a progressive temporality and a sense of identity (however defined) it has become "a commoditized form of practice, where material, knowledge, and heritage value are all translated into economic value" (Chap. 7).

The multiculturalism the discipline has come to embrace does not collide with the market but feeds it in several ways: transforming curricula to produce technical archaeologists eager to engage CRM/CHM projects; teaming up with the heritage business, either as a provider of cultural commodities (sites, contexts, exhibits) or by legitimizing market-controlled historical discourses; and helping to naturalize capitalist categories, such as development. The arising of ethical concerns in this scenario is not a fortuity: while the first ethical discussions in archaeology date from the 1960s, most date from the 1980s (including the principles adopted by main organizations), when the multicultural rhetoric had already transformed constitutions and legal systems worldwide.

And then there is politics. Ethical principles have become the way the discipline engages wider, non-disciplinary changes (especially multiculturalism), adopting corporate policies—such as social responsibility—while remaining at one side of politics. Indeed, talking politics while talking archaeology is a relatively recent practice that has been solved in several ways. One, the most widespread and common, is the multicultural way talked by academic archeology: it has turned to political correctness and the public arena to feel close to the others (and to the histories) that objectified and placed in the past, but without mixing too much, preserving privileges and the modern gaze. The multicultural policies adopted by archaeology has discovered the perfect recipe (*add local communities and stir*) to continue doing what the discipline has always done (esoteric academic research, usually with no relationship whatsoever with social needs in the present) but pretending that everything has changed[5] and that its changes turned it plural and open. To put it another way: archaeology has entered politics remaining strictly outside of it—its public turn satisfies its need to be political without questioning its disciplinary integrity. But politics are indeed needed if we really want transformations and if we really want to engage

[5] A well-known quote from *The leopard* (*Il gattopardo*), the novel by Tomassi di Lampedusa, depicts this process well: "Si vogliamo che tutto rimanga com'è, bisogna che tutto cambi" ("If we want that everything remains as it is, everything must change").

social justice and alternative social/historical worldviews. In the introduction to the book he edited with Philip Duke, Yannis Hamilakis (2007:15) stated:

> What makes this book different is its aim and ambition to reframe the discussion on ethics in archaeology by shifting the debate into the field of politics, showing that the ethical and sociopolitical arenas should not be treated as separate, as is often the case, and proposing that conundrums such as the tension between universal and context-specific ethics can be only dealt with through political praxis.

But after assessing what has happened in the last two decades Hamilakis (2007:20) was disappointed to find "bureaucratization and instrumentalisation of ethics, and these transformations have resulted in the depoliticisation of ethical debate in archaeology." This situation has not changed lately. To the contrary, it has hardened: instead of addressing pressing issues, such as social justice, ethical concerns in archaeology have locked themselves in a disciplinary agenda. A notorious absence in this utter disregard for wider issues is the relationship of archaeology *qua* modern discipline with other worldviews; this is surprising, though, because archaeologists are well aware of the colonial burden of their discipline. But, as Mario Blaser (2009:880) puts it:

> Because the contest with the non-modern manifests as ontological conflicts there is a strong tendency to misrecognize even the existence of this contest. In other words, the non-modern manifests itself as something that escapes the "radar screen" of modern categories.

If different ontologies are misrecognized and obliterated, there is not recognition of conflict either. As a result, hegemonies act in a power vacuum and disguise their violent character to become naturalized realities. Yet, if Hamilakis (2007:23) is right in that "ethics become the decoy that can rescue us from politics"; if ethics is the way archaeology armored itself against politics, then the price it has paid is excessively high for it has gone astray from engaging the very global issues that a anticolonial move coming from outside forced it to tackle. Instead of engaging politics head-on, an ethics-mediated archaeology is content with the de-politicization of its practice, especially as potential and ongoing conflicts with local communities (Indigenous and otherwise) are routinely attenuated by multicultural concessions (consultation, controlled participation, and the like).[6] But, as Pels (1999:103) noted, "ethics, with its impossible conceit of impartiality, only *masks* politics—the struggle between culturally specific and historically embedded interests." This masking of politics, this explicit de-politicization of ethics, is "built around the discursive oscillation between the absolute denial of politics that is implied by ethical standards and the absolute affirmation of politics that the necessarily partial use of these ethical standards brings with it" (Pels 1999:103).

[6]Consultation, for instance, is not a panacea in and of itself. When implemented in development projects in which great amounts of money are at stake (and, not surprisingly, transnational corporations are involved), consultation can be a simulation of respect and democracy while only being a formality besieged by corruption and threats. In this regard, it is worth recalling that the cultural project of multiculturalism is to "harness and redirect the abundant political energy of cultural rights activism, rather than directly to oppose it" (Hale 2002:498).

Ethics and the Future of Archaeology

Morality is constitutive of human actions (it is the horizon to where they go, so to speak), whether or not codified into ethical prescriptions. So, ignoring or bypassing moral/ethics in gauging the future of archaeology (not to say its very present) is pointless, if not irresponsible. Addressing them directly, as many have done, usually involves a good deal of historicization as a way of countering reification (that is, precisely, what most papers in this volume have done). It also involves *re-placing* them in the center of power struggles as a way of avoiding their masking of politics. It involves, at last, not opposing politics and ethics but reconciling them. It now seems clear that their re-entanglement requires that universal, naturalist pretensions are abandoned—indeed, it is naturalization that hinders any possible reconciliation.

At this important juncture in which archaeological ethics have become bureaucratized and instrumentalized by a brutal process of reification it is worth moving them into the political arena, as Hamilakis (2007) pleaded for, but we may also need a fresh bath of de-modernization. The ethical duplexity of archaeology—paraphrasing Pels (1999:102),—its oscillation between ethics and politics, is firmly entrenched by the modern matrix to which it clinches[7] and which posits two strict separations: between knowledge and power, and between nature and culture. It also posits the past as a nature to be known through highly ritualized disciplinary protocols (scientific and otherwise); the past as encrypted/codified in buried things; the archaeological record as an immanent nature; and the archaeologist and the knowledge she/he produces as neutral intermediaries for the appearance of the past in the present. This underscores that current archaeological ethics has not only been reified through principles but also that it builds up from reified "things" (stewardship, the record, excavation, the field, artifacts, just to name a few in a long list).[8] This process of double reification haunts archaeology and its ethics.

Yet, in spite of its obvious modernity, disciplinary practice usually proceeds by ignoring it. The disciplinary pretension that research procedures have become autonomous by technical means helps to hide that they are linked to the pervasive and powerful cosmology of modernity. It portrays them as just mere technical operations in a cultural vacuum. In this process, the archaeologist has lost any traces of ontological status by becoming a neutral intermediary instead of a creative mediator. However, no matter how much purification runs through archaeology and how skillful it is in getting round its relationship with modernity, the discipline and its practitioners have not escaped its ontology—it suffices to take even a glance at most

[7] Its universal/modern pretenses also shape its postmodern/multicultural morality—the righteous of archaeological knowledge (mostly science-inspired); the benignant character of archaeological stewardship; the Enlightened mission of most activist archaeologies.

[8] These "things" are what Bruno Latour (1993) called *hybrids*, neither fully natural nor fully social entities but socio-natural ones (half object and half subject). Archaeology operates with great numbers of hybrids that are presented as things-in-themselves—machines and artifacts as much as temporal/spatial structuring devices such as phases, types, horizons, and the like. They plague archaeological texts and curricula, yet are simultaneously denied, obliterated.

ethical principles to understand that they basically protect and enforce the modern tenets in which archaeology thrives. Indeed, an ethical perspective within the confines of one's ontology is, at the end, a reproduction of that ontology. But the appeal of some contextual (purportedly anticolonial) ethical principles—especially WAC's Code of Ethics and the Vermillion Accord—for disenfranchised groups is, justly, their potential to reach out to other ontologies (a move through which social justice can be finally realized), that is, their potential to hold modernity in abeyance in order to gauge and counter its intervention and its consequences. For that to happen we need more than simple ethical declarations. We need ethical bridges that account for and engage what Marisol de la Cadena (2008) called multi-ontologies, in which the negotiation and resolution of conflict is outstanding; a bridging that "focuses on the conflicts that ensue as different worlds or ontologies strive to sustain their own existence as they interact and mingle with each other" (Blaser 2009:877).

The "participatory research ethic" Lesley Green writes about in her paper in this volume is "an ethics of multiple perspectives." It is a relational ethics capable of taking archaeological morality out of political correctness, that invention that allows contemporary liberalism to have peace of mind, a cosmopolitan mood and a certain discursive coherence while feeding the old hierarchies of modernity. It is a relational perspective capable not of deparochializing current archaeological ethics but of rediscovering its parochialism, the violence of its universal operation. It is an alternative morality, a step beyond naturalized principles which have hardened archaeology *qua* modern discipline instead of promoting change and openness in an intercultural mood. It is a morality where the complicity of archaeology with capitalism and development can be challenged and alternatives can be offered.

An alternative archaeological morality is not only possible but ongoing. It emerges from genuinely engaging multiple perspectives, multiple ontologies, networking with those who have always been in an external condition, not in a place untouched by modernity (an ontological outside) but in an outside "that is, precisely, constituted as difference by the hegemonic discourse. With the appeal from the externality in which it is located, the Other becomes the original source of ethical discourse vis-à-vis a hegemonic totality" (Escobar 2005:36). Some archaeologists work to reunite knowledge and power (separated since the nineteenth century in the West, except in Marxism) and have turned political their disciplinary interventions. They have not framed their militancy in multicultural terms, from which they take distance, but have opened it up to different voices and ontologies. They are still marginal (for an apparatus that refuses to relax its monopolistic locks) but cannot be denied, despite the intolerance of the archaeologists who still believe in the benefits of modern knowledge and overlook the anti-systemic activism of a militancy that seeks allies on the people rather than objects of study. These archaeologies do not conceive of history as a linear chronological and teleological process but as a multi-temporal heterogeneity (García 1989) from where to talk about networks of local histories rather than to speak of grand narratives. (This change brings cultural differences to the field of colonial differences: it turns political the multicultural asepsis that seeks to deracialize and drain of power colonial relations through culturalism.) In sum, the relational morality they predicate is about freedom.

If we are to be free, "If we want to recover the capacity to sort that appears essential to our morality and defines the human, it is essential that no coherent temporal flow comes to limit our freedom of choice" (Latour 1993:141). That "coherent temporal flow" is what modernity imposed upon us and which the dominant archaeological ethics has so diligently served.

A relational ethics, an ethics of multiple perspectives, moves beyond critique and reflexivity and tackles the issue of (un)communication. Critical accounts of modernity, such as those espoused by some brands of activist archaeology and which some ethical principles imply, have established a one-way utterance (indeed, a one-way understanding). By only discussing the concepts that modernity created and mobilized, and by locking themselves in such a discussion, they have failed to open communicative and transformative understanding. Is this a *natural* consequence of the incommensurability of different perspectives? Not so. Eduardo Viveiros de Castro (2004:9) called *equivocation* "a type of communicative disjuncture where the interlocutors are not talking about the same thing, and know this." This would not be a problem[9] but the interlocutors often disregard this fact knowingly, especially when hegemonic positions are at stake—a colonial arrogance that repeats itself in the epistemic privileges academic knowledge so stubbornly holds to. Current ethical principles are not meant to reach out to incommensurable worldviews; they are meant to address commensurable things, concepts, and horizons. As a result, this kind of "communicative disjuncture" leads to blind alleys whereby intercultural understanding is curtailed—along with emancipation and freedom outside the walls of modernity. Indeed, (un)communication permeates the operation of most activist archaeologies and the ethics they promote. Concepts such as freedom, emancipation, openness, even democracy are all premised within the limits of modernity, that is, within its knowledge, its activism, and its subjectivity. Yet, those concepts are not explored (not to say enacted) in the terms of non-modern cosmologies, where *radical* transformations may occur. In the other hand, an alternative morality engages those issues from multiple perspectives. If archaeology is a liberation force for those who want and need *change*, it is worth considering the discipline as a locus where ontological struggles occur (only one of which revolves around *change*). While activist archaeologies do indeed foster collaboration and are open and respectful, building upon what contextual ethical principles propose, we cannot get round the predicament in which one of its related fields, public archaeology, has trapped itself (and which is a lesson all other related fields can learn from). As Richard Handler (2008:97) so aptly noted:

> Indeed, we might say that a concern for "public archaeology," while ostensibly a concern to "do the right thing," has become a new disciplining routine within anthropological archaeology.

[9] Indeed, as Viveiros de Castro (2004:10) noted "It is not merely a negative facticity, but a condition of possibility of anthropological discourse... The equivocation is not that which impedes the relation, but that which founds and impels it: a difference in perspective. To translate is to presume that an equivocation always exists; it is to communicate by differences, instead of silencing the Other by presuming a univocality—the essential similarity—between what the Other and We are saying."

> And as a routine that professionals adopt as part of their disciplinary identity, the practicing of public archaeology may lead away from the critical reflexivity (concerning both epistemological and political issues) it was intended to facilitate.

This timely assessment of what disciplining and reification can do to even the most engaged archaeologies brings to the fore the asymmetries that linger in a practice that is still hegemonic—even more so after its acceptance by "alternative" accounts, by virtue of which the ethnic other is no longer a nemesis but an ally. A good deal of such hegemony arises from one-way utterances and understandings, confusing the place where conflict unfolds: "These are conflicts that fester under the assumption that parties to the conflict agree on what is at stake, when actually that is not the case. In other words, what is at stake in these conflicts is precisely the differing 'things' that are at stake" (Blaser 2009:879). These "differing things" are, precisely, the *loci* from where an alternative archaeological ethics grows.

Can we be happy with what ethical principles have accomplished so far? It depends where you answer from. From the vantage point of mainstream, academic archaeology they have indeed been highly productive, especially as archaeologists are now more responsible to their professional duties than before. Public/community archaeologists would say that ethical principles have been instrumental in reaching out to the public and in forging a wide sense of accountability, formerly inexistent. Yet, from the point of view of radical transformations (including the struggle for social justice) they have done little else than solidifying archaeology's modern outlook. Further, there is a growing feeling that ethics has become a disciplinary routine that has numbed reflexivity. Indeed, the risk of ethical codes stifling ethical discussions should not be underestimated. If we couple the appearance of ethical codes in archaeology with its accommodation to multicultural changes, the possibility of ethics acting to mask, defer or ignore radical transformations should be considered seriously. As Pels (1999:101) suggested regarding his own discipline, ethical codes can be just "prophylactic against the uncertainties of questioning the anthropological self-image." More often than not, taking ethical codes for granted solidifies a discipline instead of getting it to change. Ethics becomes a deliberate violence when appealing to a universal definition that, by definition, cannot be universal because ethics refer to specific moral values and, thus, is always historically determined.

Before so many critiques the wary archaeologist asks: can archaeological ethics survive? But that is the wrong question because it universalizes ethics once more and implies that actions may exist without morality—a philosophical and political nullity. The question should be phrased differently: can a multicultural ethics in archaeology survive? My answer is that it won't—that it shouldn't. The answer of many others is not only that it will but also that it will help the discipline thrive. Obviously, these differing answers are function of the kind of archaeology they envision. Those content with current ethical principles are also content with an archaeology mostly devoted to address academic preoccupations (still linked to an enduring culture-historical agenda and still treating the *past as past*), basically disdainful of the contextual milieu—the networks of relationships in which the discipline is entangled. They are happy with archaeology confined within disciplinary limits and are unmindful of the events occurring outside the excavation trench. Those contesting the current ethical order do so thinking and acting contextually—which includes a rejection of *contextualism*,[10] that is, a rejection of the separation of ethics and context. The archaeology they envision engage other ontologies not for gaining hermeneutical power but for relating with them in a learning and transformative way. Theirs is a different archaeology with a different morality, whose current greatest challenge is to break free from the multicultural appeals to cultural diversity whereby differences (ontological and otherwise) are subdued by negating their specificities as mere cultural perspectives and whereby inequalities are veiled. Its greatest challenge is, at last, establishing a distance with diversity—which multiculturalism promotes: quiet and safe, exotic, organized, commoditized—while engaging differences in their occurrence and being.

This is, thus, the current situation in which the future of archaeology unfolds. An ethical struggle around ethics.

A matter of choice.

References

Blaser, M. (2009). Political ontology: Cultural studies without "cultures"? *Cultural Studies, 23* (5–6), 873–896.

De la Cadena, M. (2008). La producción de otros conocimientos y sus tensiones: ¿de una antropología andinista a la interculturalidad? In G. L. Ribeiro & A. Escobar (Eds.), *Antropologías del mundo. Transformaciones disciplinarias dentro de sistemas de poder* (pp. 241–270). Popayán: Envión.

Escobar, A. (2005). *Más allá del Tercer Mundo. Globalización y diferencia*. Bogotá: ICANH-Universidad del Cauca.

García, N. (1989). *Culturas híbridas: estrategias para entrar y salir de la modernidad*. Mexico: Grijalbo.

Green, L. F., Green, D., & Neves, E. G. (2003). Indigenous knowledge and archaeological science: the challenges of public archaeology in the Reserva Uaçá. *Journal of Social Archaeology, 3*, 366–398.

Hale, C. (2002). Does multiculturalism menace? Governance, cultural rights and the politics of identity in Guatemala. *Journal of Latin American Studies, 34*, 485–524.

Hamilakis, Y. (2007). From ethics to politics. In Y. Hamilakis & P. Duke (Eds.), *Archaeology and capitalism: From ethics to politics* (pp. 15–40). Walnut Creek, CA: Left Coast Press.

Handler, R. (2008). A dangerously elusive method. Disciplines, histories, and the limits of reflexivity. In Q. Castañeda & C. Matthews (Eds.), *Ethnographic archaeologies. Reflections on stakeholders and archaeological practices* (pp. 95–117). Altamira: Plymouth.

Jameson, F. (1984). Postmodernism, or the cultural logic of late capitalism. *New Left Review, 146*, 53–93.

[10] The effects of *contextualism* are far-reaching. It not just posits the separation of academic knowledge and context as absolute and given but it also posits their relationship as merely circumstantial. It is no wonder that contextual preoccupations are additive (and sometimes even dispensable) in academic settings. They are *added* to knowledge but are not treated as the creative conditions in which it occurs and in which it intervenes. Contextualism gets round the interdependence of context and knowledge.

Latour, B. (1993). *We have never been modern*. Cambridge, UK: Harvard University Press.
Meskell, L., & Pels, P. (2005). Introduction: embedding ethics. In L. Meskell & P. Pels (Eds.), *Embedding ethics* (pp. 1–28). Oxford, UK: Berg.
Moshenska, G. (2008). Ethics and ethical critique in the archaeology of modern conflict. *Norwegian Archaeological Review, 41*(2), 159–175.
Pels, P. (1999). Professions of duplexity: a prehistory of ethical codes in anthropology. *Current Anthropology, 40*(2), 101–114.
SAA. (1996). Principles of archaeological ethics. *American Antiquity, 61*(3), 451–452.
Tarlow, S. (2001). Decoding ethics. *Public Archaeology, 1*, 245–259.
Trouillot, M.-R. (2003). *Global transformations. Anthropology and the modern world*. New York, NY: Palgrave Macmillan.
Viveiros de Castro, E. (2004). Perspectival anthropology and the method of controlled equivocation. *Tipití, 2*(1), 3–22.
Watkins, J. (2003). Archaeological ethics and American Indians. In L. Zimmerman, K. Vitelli, & J. Hollowell-Zimmer (Eds.), *Ethical issues in archaeology* (pp. 57–69). Oxford, UK: Altamira.

Part I
Is There a Global Archaeological Ethics? Canonical Conditions for Discursive Legitimacy and Local Responses

Chapter 2
An Indigenous Anthropologist's Perspective on Archaeological Ethics

Joe Watkins

Archaeology in America has struggled with defining its ethical structure since the establishment of the Society for American Archaeology (SAA) in 1934. Its initial Constitution and By-laws set forth prohibitions against "securing, hoarding, exchanging, buying, or selling of archaeological objects…" for personal satisfaction or profit (Article I, Section 2). Article III, Section 10, gives the Society the right to drop from the rolls of the Society anyone who habitually commercializes archaeological objects or sites (Society for American Archaeology 1977:308–312). Additional statements provided by the SAA (Champe et al. 1961:137–138) offered SAA members ideas regarding accepted standards in delineating the field of archaeology, the methods of archaeology, ethics for archaeology, and recommendations for training in what may be considered right and wrong, at least in the eyes of the SAA, and provided guidelines to the Executive Committee relating to the expulsion of a member.

In 1977, the Society of Professional Archaeologists (SOPA) developed out of an ad hoc committee on standards appointed by the SAA to pursue the concept of certifying archaeologists (McGimsey and Davis 1977:97–105). SOPA allowed only those archaeologists meeting certain criteria to be admitted, required applicants to sign a Code of Ethics and Standards of Research Performance (Society of Professional Archaeologists 1976), and provided a detailed procedure for review of alleged violations. SOPA morphed into the Register of Professional Archaeologists (RPA) in 1998 with support of the major archaeological organizations (the Society for American Archaeology, the Archaeological Institute of America, the Society for Historical Archaeology, and the Society of Underwater Archaeologists). The RPA hopes to be the professional archaeological licensing organization in America, with the goal of establishing, supporting, and maintaining professional and ethical standards in all aspects of archaeological work. It offers a certification process

J. Watkins (✉)
National Park Service, 1201 Eye St NW, Washington, DC 20005, USA
e-mail: joe_watkins@nps.gov

C. Gnecco, D. Lippert (eds.), *Ethics and Archaeological Praxis*,
Ethical Archaeologies: The Politics of Social Justice 1,
DOI 10.1007/978-1-4939-1646-7_2

whereby professional archaeologists, students, teachers, amateur archaeologists, and all those interested in archaeological education and research can become registered archaeologists. In doing so, members agree to abide by a set of ethical codes and research standards. Registration allows the use of the distinction "RPA", much in the manner that Public Engineers are required to abide by certain rules and guidelines to gain the status of a Registered Public Engineer.

Since the 1990s, however, ethics in North American archaeology has revolved primarily around the Principles of Archaeological Ethics produced and adopted by the Society for American Archaeology in 1996 (Lynott 1997; Lynott and Wylie 2000), although the journey that the Society followed prior to the Code's establishment continues to have meaning as well.

This is the process of the SAA went through as it developed its body of ethical guidance, but the code should by no means be considered to have embraced "multicultural ethics", and the discipline (at least within the SAA) has only recently begun opening up or sharing some aspect of the disciplinary practice with local actors (in research-related activities and in decision-making). Only the SAA's Principle 2 (dealing with "Accountability") acknowledges that archaeologists have any sort of obligation to the public, to consultation (which theoretically includes notifying and working with the "public", and (implicitly) the people whose cultures are under study "with the goal of establishing a working relationship that can be beneficial to all parties involved". While the SAA's Principle 4 deals with public education and outreach, encouraging archaeologists to "reach out to, and participate in cooperative efforts with others interested in the archaeological record with the aim of improving the preservation, protection, and interpretation of the record", it does not in reality deal with particular aspects or cultural groups, but, rather, the general public, which can be interpreted to be broadly "American" but perhaps not really as multi-cultural as one might expect. In some ways, while the Principle suggests archaeologists should reach out to all cultures, in practice archaeologists reach out primarily to those who are educated or interested enough to grasp the effort.

As numerous authors have noted (cf. Colwell-Chanthaphonh 2010; Colwell-Chanthaphonh et al. 2010; McGhee 2008; Nicholas and Bannister 2004; Nicholas 2008; Zimmerman 2008), archaeologists in North America have been hesitant to relinquish control over contested topics, especially those topics that require sharing or handing over power to "marginalized" groups. The SAA encourages archaeologists to work towards increased dissemination of the results of their research "in accessible form (through publication or other means) to as wide a range of interested publics as possible" in its Principle 6, but this should not be confused with calling for increased involvement of marginalized groups in the process. While dissemination of information is important, it does little more than reinforce the archaeologist's opinion of what he or she believes to be "true". Nowhere does this principle create an ethical *requirement* to work with multiple publics rather than to publish in publically accepted form or format.

The Principles are either mute or somewhat antagonistic in relation to the sharing or relinquishing of control over contested topics and the inclusion or use of non-Western historical interpretations into archaeological hermeneutics. Rather than relinquishing control over such topics, the SAA's Principles are notably silent on repatriation or shared control of key biological and cultural remains. Its Principle 7 says only that "(a)rchaeologists should work actively for the preservation of, and long term access to, archaeological collections, records, and reports". This statement implicitly argues that it is the archaeologist's *obligation* to oppose actions which might result in lack of access to "archaeological collections, records and reports". Since repatriation of "key biological and cultural remains" affects "archaeological collections", support of repatriation might be seen to be somehow "unethical" and, therefore, against the principles to which archaeologists are responsible. Remarkably, the continued definition of human skeletal remains as "archaeological resources" included within "archaeological collections" creates a regulatory situation that can be openly antagonistic to the communities whose ancestral relations lie buried within museum collections.

Finally, further in relation to the inclusion or use of non-Western historical interpretations into archaeological hermeneutics, the formation and expansion of "Indigenous archaeology" has been influenced more fully by the codes of ethics proposed by the World Archaeological Congress (WAC): its First Code of Ethics; its Vermillion Accord; and the Tamaki Makau-rau Accord on the Display of Human Remains and Sacred Objects (each available online at http://www.worldarchaeologicalcongress.org/site/about_ethi.php#code1) than by any other codes of ethical responsibility. In many ways, WAC has been influential in trying to redistribute the power over Indigenous archaeologies in direct and indirect ways by providing alternative means of conducting and presenting archaeology to large numbers of Indigenous practitioners and by providing venues outside of more common Western locales where a wider variety of interested people can attend and interact with each other.

This Indigenous perspective on ethics cannot be explicitly labeled "public", rather the discipline as practiced (and espoused) by the SAA privileges the archaeologist rather than other groups who might have an active or intellectual interest in the practice and interpretation of the archaeological record as it relates to cultural heritage. While it is the "responsibility" of the archaeologist to include the public to some extent, the primary responsibility as implicit within the code is *to* the archaeological record and not to any living group or contemporary population other than the academic or discipline. Proceeding from the "prime directive" (Principle 1) that "(i)t is the responsibility of all archaeologists to work for the long-term conservation and protection of the archaeological record by practicing and promoting stewardship," the professional archaeologist is not only given control over the ways that "conservation and protection" is defined, practiced, and enforced, but is also required to do so in order to be considered "ethical". Only when that prime ethical responsibility has been met can such an archaeologist stoop to involve "interested publics" in the process.

This is where North American archaeology falls short. Praxis—putting theoretical knowledge to work—should be part of the active cycle in the development of ethics in North American archaeology, but it has not been so. Perhaps there has not been an active movement to exclude Indigenous or "minority" populations from an active involvement with archaeology, but there has also not been an active welcoming of archaeology to those populations other than on individual cases until recently. Colwell-Chanthaphonh (2010), Colwell-Chanthaphonh and Ferguson (2008), Silliman (2008), and Swidler et al. (1997), to name but a few, have actively written about and supported strengthening the voices and authority of under-represented minorities within archaeology to work within the existing structure to help modify the trajectory of archaeology. However, the ability to change the ethical structures of North American practitioners seems unlikely.

There has been a move by some individuals within archaeology to more fully address the concerns about the inequity between practitioners of archaeology and the descendant and interested communities involved with the archaeological heritages under examination. In October 2008, 12 archaeologists of diverse backgrounds, interests, and ages met at Indiana University, Bloomington, to discuss the Principles of Archaeological Ethics and their implications for archaeological practice in today's society. Proceeding from the position that collaborative practice is essential for quality archaeology, the group reviewed the Principles for possible revision and expansion. They also began developing ideas to improve interactions between archaeologists and affected groups, particularly Native American and Indigenous communities. The group solicited comments from archaeologists via an open letter published in the March 2009 edition of the *Record* (online at http://www.archaeology-ce.info/letter.html) as well as through other social media (Facebook). The group identified five major areas for discussion: consultation, reciprocity and partnership; collaborative stewardship; research practice and integrity; public engagement and responsiveness; and the global contexts of local collaborations.

However, only a handful of responses were received by the organizers. Such a lack of response can be interpreted in too many ways to be useful—it might be that a very small minority sees the need for revision of the Principles, that the majority of the SAA membership does not support the idea of sharing the enterprise with Native American and descendant communities, or that no one cares about the ethical practice of archaeology outside of the purely academic aspects of the discipline. But the action did serve as an impetus for the SAA to call for reflection.

In November 2010, the Board of Directors of the Society for American Archaeology charged the SAA's Committee on Ethics "to review the SAA Principles of Archaeological Ethics and recommend whether there are areas that may be in need of revision and further discussion, and report back to the Board by September 1, 2011". The Committee recommended that the SAA poll its members concerning the revision or visitation of the SAA Principles during the summer of 2012, especially in relation to the idea of stewardship and the role of the archaeologist to assume the primary role of "steward" to the apparent exclusion of others whose interests lie within the archaeological record.

While these might be seen to be positive steps in relation to the opening of archaeology to its many publics, including Indigenous and other "ethnic" groups described in the Principles as "interested parties", in reality those "interested parties" will still have a minority position of power when it comes to the interpretation and implementation of the various aspects of the archaeological enterprise. In the

Principles, "interested publics" are considered to have relatively equal interest in the archaeological record, but in reality that interest does not equate to power, control, or ownership. It is highly unlikely that the members of the Society for American Archaeology who are currently privileged in the process will freely turn over control to non-academic communities, regardless of the intentions of those communities. Those whose financial and professional livelihood depends on the practice archaeology as a profession are unlikely to turn over control to Indigenous groups and stakeholder communities without recognizing the changing face of archaeology as it is tied to social and political aspects of the cultures around it. WAC's strength lies in its wide reaching reliance on Indigenous practitioners to stay involved; it falls short, however, of having the true political power within the profession to initiate and create change rather than influencing the perspectives of a small subset of archaeologists within the United States. Still, it does continue to influence the writings and actions of people who are active members of the Society for American Archaeology at the Committee and Board levels of organizational governance.

External events in the broader American social and political spheres have had impact on archaeology in the United States. The passage of national legislation such as the National Museum of the American Indian Act in 1989 and the Native American Graves Protection and Repatriation Act of 1990 and the 1992 amendments to the National Historic Preservation Act reflect a growing awareness of the need for the discipline to work more fully with multiple stakeholders. But there continues to be legal challenges to the legislation—the court case over the Ancient One (Kennewick Man) and concerns over the 2012 passage of the regulations concerning the disposition of cultural unidentifiable human remains—that seem to indicate a growing movement towards more limited sharing of the past with contemporary cultures.

At this point in time it is uncertain what direction archaeological ethics in the United States will turn in the near future. There are very real consequences if the discipline chooses to focus more on the academic and business practices of archaeology than it does on the social aspects of archaeology's responsibilities to the people it studies. The discipline can choose to revert to the way it was before it became aware of its responsibilities to living contemporary cultures, or it can choose to move forward towards a more humanistic discipline that not only is aware of its responsibilities to living cultures but also embraces the opportunity to learn from and with those cultures. The choice is looming.

References

Champe, J. L., Byers, D. S., Evans, C., Guthe, A. K., Hamilton, H. W., Jelks, E. B., et al. (1961). Four statements for archeology. [Report of the Committee for Ethics and Standards]. *American Antiquity, 27*(2), 137–138.

Colwell-Chanthaphonh, C. (2010). *Living histories: Native Americans and Southwestern archaeology*. Lanham: AltaMira Press.

Colwell-Chanthaphonh, C., Ferguson, T., Lippert, D., McGuire, R., Nicholas, G., Watkins, J., et al. (2010). The premise and promise of Indigenous archaeology. *American Antiquity, 75*(2), 228–238.
Colwell-Chanthaphonh, C., & Ferguson, T. (Eds.). (2008). *Collaboration in archaeological practice: Engaging descendant communities*. Lanham, MD: AltaMira Press.
Lynott, M. (1997). Ethical principles and archaeological practice: Development of an ethics policy. *American Antiquity, 62*(4), 589–599.
Lynott, M., & Wylie, A. (Eds.). (2000). *Ethics in American archaeology*. Washington, WA: Society for American Archaeology.
McGhee, R. (2008). Aboriginalism and the problems of Indigenous archaeology. *American Antiquity, 73*(4), 579–597.
McGimsey, C., & Davis, H. (Eds.). (1977). *The management of archaeological resources: the Airlie House Report*. Washington, WA: Society for American Archaeology.
Nicholas, G. (2008). Native peoples and archaeology. In D. Pearsall (Ed.), *The encyclopedia of archaeology* (Vol. 3, pp. 1660–1669). Oxford: Elsevier.
Nicholas, G., & Bannister, K. (2004). Copyrighting the past? Emerging intellectual property rights issues in archaeology. *Current Anthropology, 45*(3), 327–350.
Silliman, S. (Ed.). (2008). *Collaborative Indigenous archaeology at the trowel's edge: Exploring methodology and education in North American archaeology*. Tucson, AZ: University of Arizona Press-Amerind Foundation.
Society for American Archaeology. (1977). By-laws of the Society for American Archaeology. *American Antiquity, 42*(2), 308–312.
Society of Professional Archaeologists. (1976). Code of ethics, standards of research performance and institutional standards. In C. Fluehr-Lobban (Ed.), *Ethics and the profession of anthropology: dialogue for a new era: Appendix E*. Philadelphia, PA: University of Pennsylvania Press.
Swidler, N., Dongoske, K., Anyon, R., & Downer, A. (Eds.). (1997). *Native Americans and archaeologists: stepping stones to common ground*. Walnut Creek, CA: AltaMira Press.
Zimmerman, L. (2008). Multi-vocality, descendant communities, and some epistemological shifts forced by repatriation. In T. Killion (Ed.), *Opening archaeology: repatriation's impact on method and theory* (pp. 91–108). Santa Fe, NM: School for Advanced Research.

Chapter 3
Both Sides of the Ditch: The Ethics of Narrating the Past in the Present

Caroline Phillips and Anne Ross

Introduction

Archaeology cannot be undertaken in a vacuum, with a lack of political and social awareness. Although archaeological sites and remains may have been produced in the past, they are understood and given meaning (narrated) in the present (Andrews and Buggey 2008; Meskell 2012). As a consequence, archaeologists and heritage practitioners need to recognise that all aspects of archaeological undertakings—theory, method, practice and interpretation—have a social context. Archaeological research and heritage consultancy must involve the consideration of ethical issues relating to Indigenous knowledge and intellectual property.

Ethical considerations in New Zealand and Australian archaeology largely revolve around relationships between descendants of the producers of Indigenous heritage and modern consumers—heritage managers, planners, tourists, etc. Recently both countries have witnessed an Indigenous renaissance of identity, often linked to moves for improved civil rights. Aboriginal Australians and New Zealand Maori have become increasingly involved in the practice of archaeology, changes in resource management legislation, and documents detailing ethical practice. Despite both legislation and ethics policies acknowledging the primacy of Indigenous owners of heritage in site management and heritage decision-making, and although there is now an unchallenged requirement for heritage practitioners and archaeological researchers to consult Indigenous groups when land is modified or research

C. Phillips (✉)
The University of Auckland, Post Box 60–230, Titirangi, Auckland 0642, New Zealand
e-mail: phillips@orcon.net.nz

A. Ross
School of Social Science, The University of Queensland, St Lucia, Brisbane, QLD 4072, Australia
e-mail: annie.ross@uq.edu.au

C. Gnecco, D. Lippert (eds.), *Ethics and Archaeological Praxis*, Ethical Archaeologies: The Politics of Social Justice 1,
DOI 10.1007/978-1-4939-1646-7_3

is undertaken, underlying issues of intellectual property, power and control, and integrity and intention remain. In this paper we unpack the similarities, subtle differences and changing opportunities Indigenous peoples have to be involved in archaeological policies and practice in the two settler/colonial nations on both sides of the Tasman Sea.[1]

Ethics and Legislation in Heritage Management

In 1769 and 1770, New Zealand and Australia (respectively) came to the attention of the British nation through the voyage of discovery undertaken by Captain James Cook. Subsequent British colonisation recognised New Zealand Maori as owners of land and resources, but Aboriginal Australians were regarded as having no land ownership or resource stewardship. Despite these different approaches to Indigenous land and resource management, remarkably similar methods of ethical archaeological and heritage management practices occur in both countries.

Ethics in New Zealand

In recognition of Maori land ownership the 1840 Treaty of Waitangi was signed between the Crown and Maori chiefs. Treaty principles granted Maori "full exclusive and undisturbed possession of their Lands and Estates, Forests Fisheries and other properties" and the full rights of British citizenship, In return, Maori ceded sovereignty or governorship[2] to the Crown (Wilson 2011). The Treaty still influences relationships between the Crown and Maori in many ethical documents and legislation today.

New Zealand archaeologists do not have a professional organisation, although most belong to the New Zealand Archaeological Association (NZAA). The Code of Ethics for NZAA members was adopted in 1993, based largely on the international World Archaeology Congress Code (New Zealand Archaeology 2009; pers. comm. Bulmer 2011). The principles of the WAC Code state that members have obligations to the discipline of archaeology, and to descendant communities, and should ensure the protection, preservation and conservation of the archaeological places and heritage objects.

---

[1] The Tasman Sea is affectionately known as "the ditch" by both Kiwis and Aussies, however this paper also uses "the ditch" to mean the gap between Indigenous heritage custodians and archaeologists in both countries.

[2] The English version of the Treaty used the term "sovereignty" to mean supreme or ultimate authority by the Crown. In the Maori translation, however, a word for "governorship" was used, which was understood by Maori to mean a more distant and limited power.

Curiously, in 1999 a separate professional code was adopted by NZAA, based on that of the Society for American Archaeology (SAA). The principles therein include stewardship of the archaeological record, accountability and professionalism, endorsement of public education and availability of information, and awareness of cultural sensitivity (New Zealand Archaeology 2009). Maori are not mentioned as having any particular status in this code, which reflects the absence of specific recognition of Native Americans in the SAA code.

The NZAA Code guides the work of those archaeologists working largely in the private consulting industry. Guiding principles for academic research in New Zealand are governed by institutional ethics committees that "ensure that the welfare, privacy, safety, health and personal, social and cultural sensitivities of participants are adequately protected" (University of Auckland 2010:1). A key aspect of institutional ethics guidelines is "informed consent," which can also be expressed in Memoranda of Understanding between academics and Maori tribal groups (Allen et al. 2002:322).

Ethics in Australia

Unlike New Zealand, Australia has never had a formal treaty between settlers and Indigenous land owners. In fact, British colonists believed that the Australian continent was *terra nullius*—a land devoid of people with legal forms of land ownership or land management (Banner 2005). This concept validated the British invasion and taking of Aboriginal land without treaty or compensation. *Terra nullius* as a concept was not overturned until 1992 when the High Court of Australia recognised Australian Indigenous attachment to land and resources in the native title decision known as Mabo (Stephenson and Ratnapala 1993). Native title recognises the prior ownership of the Australian continent by its original inhabitants, but the legislative parameters within which native title is situated limit Indigenous rights to land ownership and resources management (Ross et al. 2011).

Australian archaeologists have had a Code of Ethics for their dealings with Traditional Owners and custodians of heritage since the 1980s. Both the professional archaeological association (the Australian Association of Consulting Archaeologists Inc.) and the non-professional association (the Australian Archaeological Association Inc. or AAA) have Codes of Ethics that ensure Indigenous rights to heritage are enshrined in ethical and moral principles of practice.

Australian archaeological Codes of Ethics have recently been updated (2011) to ensure currency of principles and practice. The primary philosophies of the Codes—both based on the World Archaeology Code of Ethics and the guidelines for ethical research promoted by the Australian Institute of Aboriginal and Torres Strait Islander Studies—acknowledge that Indigenous peoples have a special relationship with their heritage places and, as a consequence, have the right to allow research, or otherwise, and also have the right to exercise control over the interpretation of heritage.

Despite the existence of strong moral codes of practice in both New Zealand and Australia, legislation on both sides of the Tasman has significantly lagged behind these disciplinary principles and practices.

New Zealand Legislation

The principal legislation relating to archaeological sites in New Zealand is the Historic Places Act 1993 (HPA)[3], which applies to land of all tenure throughout New Zealand (Allen 1998). The purpose of the HPA "is to promote the identification, protection, preservation and conservation of the historical and cultural heritage of New Zealand" (HPA 2008:10). Under this Act, an archaeological place is defined as any place that was associated with human activity before 1900 AD, and "may be able, through *investigation by archaeological methods*, to provide evidence relating to the history of New Zealand" (italics added). Any person intending to carry out work (including research investigation) that may damage, modify or destroy a site must apply for an authority to the New Zealand Historic Places Trust (NZHPT) which administers the HPA. Relevant Maori organisations must be consulted as part of the application, but only research applications necessitate the permission of tribal authorities. Nevertheless, archaeologists, developers and others are all required to abide by the "tikanga (correct procedure, custom[4]) Maori protocols" of the local tribal group.

Australian Legislation

In Australia, heritage management is the responsibility of each state. We outline the situation in Queensland. The purpose of the Queensland Aboriginal Cultural Heritage Act 2003 (ACHA) "is to provide effective recognition, protection and conservation of Aboriginal cultural heritage." The principles of the act incorporate: the centrality of Aboriginal knowledge in heritage management; the affirmation of Aboriginal rights and obligations to law and country; promotion of understanding of Aboriginal heritage; and the establishment of timely and efficient processes to manage activities that may harm heritage. These are all laudable aims and principles—unfortunately only the final principle is met by the provisions of the Act itself.

The ACHA defines heritage as including both sites and landscapes; it also recognises that heritage does not need to include material remains for heritage to exist (S. 12). However, in practice only tangible elements of the past can be included in

[3] Now *Heritage New Zealand Pouhere Taonga Act* 2014 and administered by Heritage New Zealand Pouhere Taonga, All other elements mentioned here remain the same.

[4] Maori words translated using the on-line Maori Dictionary. Retrieved from http://www.maoridictionary.co.nz.

heritage planning (Robins 2013; Ross 2010). Further, although "Aboriginal Parties" must be involved in the preparation of a Cultural Heritage Management Plan (CHMP). CHMPs are only necessary if a formal Environmental Impact Assessment is required, or as determined by the developer. Consequently, there are few opportunities for Indigenous Queenslanders to voice their desires for heritage protection, particularly if those desires relate to places whose values lie in a present narrative, rather than in scientific significance. Given that Queensland legislation has become the template for the revision of other legislation in Australia, the situation is worrying.

Legislation Versus Practice and Theory

Despite the stated role of Indigenous heritage legislation in both countries to protect heritage, the legislation is largely designed to facilitate development with the aim to recover the archaeological record prior to destruction (Godwin 2001; McFadgen 1966:98). Although well-argued cases can be reviewed through the courts to achieve some gains, these are usually in mitigation for losses elsewhere (Phillips 2010). This is contrary to the desire of Indigenous communities for the identification, protection, preservation and conservation of heritage (Maori Heritage Council 2009:4; Sullivan 2008).

Since the promulgation of new heritage legislation in both Australia and New Zealand, applications to modify, damage or destroy sites and heritage places in a development context have risen sharply (pers. comm. Kiri Peterson 2012; pers. comm. an officer with the Queensland regulatory authority 2011.)[5] This attests to the ongoing destruction of cultural heritage; the numbers of recorded archaeological sites (many already damaged) are reducing rapidly.

A significant limitation of legislation is that Acts deal with heritage places in isolation. The unit of assessment is the site, and although "landscapes" may be recognised in legislation, such areas tend to be identified as palimpsests of individual sites, rather than as cultural landscapes as defined in heritage discourse (e.g. Allen 2010; Allen et al. 1994; Brown 2008; Ellis 1994; Phillips and Allen 2006; Ross 1996).

Individual developments are similarly managed on a case by case basis, ignoring synergies between sites, landscapes, and development areas. Not only does this result in "death [of heritage places] by a thousand cuts" but it is contrary to Indigenous concepts that integrate both natural and cultural elements at the landscape scale (Allen 1998:37; Byrne 2008; Campbell 2005). Although it is difficult to quantify the effects of this provision, analyses undertaken by one Queensland local council found that over 80 % of known sites could not be relocated, as they had all been destroyed by development that had not been required to have a CHMP (AAA 2009).

To illustrate the ethical and legislative disconnects we outlined above, we now turn to a brief presentation of one case study from each jurisdiction.

---

[5] This officer prefers not to be identified.

Case Studies

New Zealand—Rangiatea

Rangiatea is a place name of great consequence to Maori, being the name of the island in Tahiti[6] on which the important ritual centre of Taputapuatea was located. Soil from that place was brought to New Zealand by founding ancestors and implanted as a life force for a new altar called Rangiatea (Robson and Rika-Heke 2011). Associated with the soil were fundamental sacred practices, ritual and practical knowledge known collectively as the "three baskets of knowledge" (Te Kenehi Teira pers. comm. 2011). Rangiatea was said to have been the location of a "house of learning" where practical and esoteric skills were taught. The name Rangiatea was originally applied to a location on the west coast of New Zealand, but the name was brought inland (with the associated soil, altar, rituals and traditions) by Turongo whose sons founded the major tribes of the area.

Archaeological records list 82 sites in the vicinity of Rangiatea. Of these there are eight fortifications which, together with Rangiatea, formed a prime defensive position (Phillips and Allen 2011) (Fig. 3.1). However, as a fortification Rangiatea looks unremarkable: it is less than the median size of Maori defensive sites (Walton 2006); the occupation area around it is also small; and it is not central to gardening lands or other key resources. Currently Rangiatea is located within five different pasture farm properties, so that fences and access tracks have damaged part of the site, and the surface features are not easily read. The surrounding environment has also changed, and the formerly productive swamps have largely been drained and converted to pasture.

Factors used by NZHPT (2006:8–9; see also Allen 1998:27) to assess archaeological values include site condition, rarity, contextual value, information and educational potential, and special cultural association. All, except the last factor, make Rangiatea only moderately significant. The legislation focuses on places that can provide evidence "through investigation by archaeological methods," which relates to tangible evidence. This contrasts greatly with the high intangible significance that sites like Rangiatea have to Maori.

Australia—North Stradbroke Island

North Stradbroke Island lies off the east coast of south-east Queensland in Moreton Bay (Fig. 3.2). The people of Quandamooka, the Traditional Owners of the land and waters that make up Moreton Bay, have managed their "country" for over 20,000 years (Neal and Stock 1986; Moreton and Ross 2011) until the arrival of European settlers in the 1820s. In the 1960s, sand mining became a significant industry on the island.

---

[6] Rangiatea is the Maori version of the Tahitian name Raiatea.

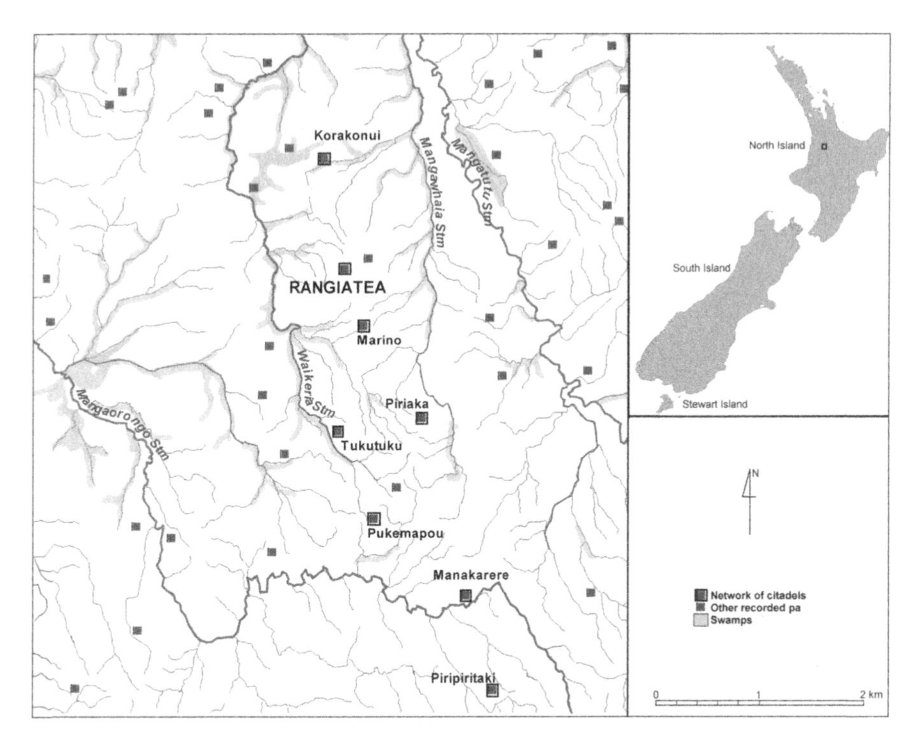

Fig. 3.1 Rangiatea pa, with its associated named citadels and other fortifications in the vicinity, former swamps and streams. Inset shows location in the North Island of New Zealand

Recently, expansion of sand mining was proposed, and in accordance with the ACHA the Quandamooka Aboriginal community was employed to negotiate a CHMP. Traditional Owners requested a cultural landscape approach to heritage assessment (Prangnell et al. 2010; Ross et al. 2010), which allowed both tangible and intangible components of heritage to be identified.

No archaeological sites were located during the heritage assessment, yet a number of significant cultural landscape elements were recognised:

- A significant origin story that linked the dunes to surrounding lakes;
- Two significant landforms, one of spiritual value to men and the other to women;
- Important food and other resource areas;
- Historic tracks across the dunes that facilitated human movement in the recent and distant past; and
- A landscape originally regularly modified by fire.

The environment of the sand mining lease is, therefore, a complex and interconnected web of stories and cultural landscapes of great significance to the people of Quandamooka. The proposed sand mine would destroy all these landscape elements. Yet, despite the aims and principles of the ACHA outlined above, none of

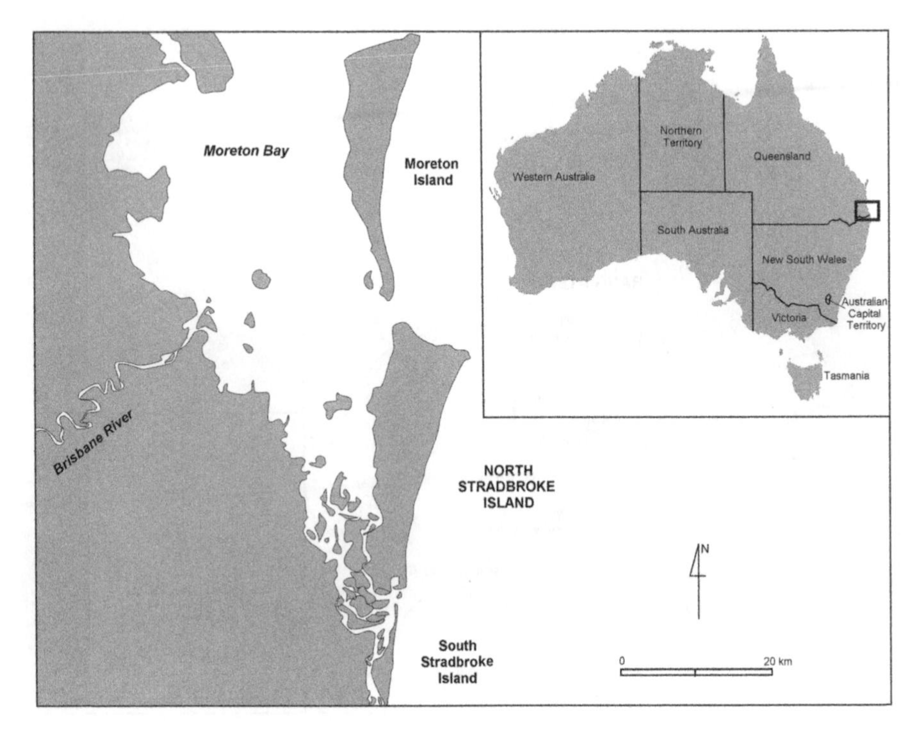

Fig. 3.2 The location of North Stradbroke Island and Moreton Bay, south-east Queensland. Inset shows location in Queensland, Australia

these landscape elements is protected under this Act. As a consequence, the documented cultural landscape was ignored in planning decision-making. Although the part of the development that would have impacted the women's site and associated dune did not proceed, this was not as a result of Aboriginal cultural significance, but because of the area's importance to tourism (Ross et al. 2010).

Discussion

Discussing this topic with Maori archaeologist Margaret Rika-Heke (pers. comm. 2012), it is clear that the layering of meaning in stories and history may not be adequately reflected, if at all, in the archaeological evidence. Often archaeologists employ more accessible accounts written by European historians, which can present a limited, rather shallow and Eurocentric view of the past (Barker 2006). As a member of a panel at the Second Indigenous Inter-Congress of the World Archaeological Congress in Auckland, New Zealand, in 2005 explained:

> Maori cultural research has a wide focus (based on language, environmental concerns, stories of sites, history, place names, taonga [prized possessions] *and the places*), but heritage

organizations have a narrow focus. The challenge to archaeology is to stop talking about archaeology and talk about how archaeology is going to integrate more fluidly with the rest of kaupapa [matters for discussion] that Maori commonly deal with (Phillips and Allen 2010:270; italics added).

Aboriginal archaeologist Shane Coghill (pers. comm. 2011; cf. Meskell 2012) agrees. For both Maori and Australian Aboriginal Traditional Custodians of heritage, an Indigenous-centred archaeology would start with oral accounts as the primary source of information, rather than archaeology, and would use traditions to identify patterns and pose questions (Clarke 2011). As a result, Rika-Heke argues that if Indigenous peoples were the academics doing archaeology, research questions, methodologies and the interpretation of results would be quite different from those posed by non-Indigenous investigators (cf. Allen 1998:52; Byrne 2002, 2005; Godwin and Weiner 2006; Ross 2010; Sullivan 2005, 2008).

Returning to Rangiatea, one tribal member, when asked what he wanted to know about the place, said he was keen to know more about the relationship of his ancestors with those already living in the district. Why did earlier people agree to Turongo setting up a house of learning? Was there an initial period of peace before warfare broke out? How did Turongo's people live and develop over time, and how did they ultimately achieve political dominance? Other questions revolved around the traditional accounts of structures such as carved houses, altars and houses of learning.

Similarly, in the Quandamooka case study Aboriginal questions relate as much to the present-day narrative of heritage places as to the past. What messages do the ancestors associated with past places of habitation bring to people in the present? What knowledge can archaeology bring to informing and supporting Indigenous science? How can archaeological data support native title claims? (Clarke 2011; see also Byrne 2002, 2003, 2005; Godwin 2005; Godwin and Weiner 2006; Greer 1999).

These questions are in sharp contrast to archaeological questions and interpretations which, without the benefit of oral traditions, might revolve around dates and changes to structures over time, or to economic pursuits and the importation of goods from other areas. Research themes in cultural heritage management tend to focus on establishing regional histories, or identifying the nature of early settlement, or interaction of people and the environment, a sense of place and defining identity (McGovern-Wilson 2008). The focus of these themes is to make archaeological research more accessible to the general public, and Indigenous concerns may not always be included (Allen 2010:164; Clarke 2011; Godwin and Weiner 2006; Phillips 2010:147–148). Consequently the data recovered, and the meanings attributed to them, are written from the point of view of the generally European archaeologist. Although there is now a strong movement in the discipline to avoid purely archaeological or academic approaches to cultural heritage management and to recognise, instead, the value and place of an Indigenous interpretation of the past; one that often incorporates the meaning of heritage in the present (Bradley 2008; Byrne 1991, 1996; Clarke 2011; Ellis 1994; McNiven and Russell 2005; Ross 2008; Smith 2006).

Despite an increasing opportunity to incorporate an Indigenous understanding of place in heritage management, particularly in heritage consultancies, this is not always the case in academic research. Academic research relies on funding bodies which in turn demand meaningful questions of interest in national and international science, which favours global, rather than local and tribal, topics and subsequent analyses (pers. comm. Ian Smith and Richard Walter 2012). This limitation is gradually changing with respect to Indigenous interests in resource and environmental management, particularly through the development of co-management agreements (Berkes 2009; George et al. 2004; Igoe 2004; Kennett et al. 2004; Kothari 2006; Robinson et al. 2006). However, there is still quite some distance to go in bridging this divide effectively (Pinkerton 1992; Ross et al. 2011; Stevenson 2006). This is largely due to contestations between Western, scientific epistemologies, which privilege logical positivist approaches to management, as opposed to Indigenous ways of knowing, which are holistic and therefore see little separation between cultural and natural heritage (Milton 1996; Ross et al. 2011): a situation that is exacerbated by the impoverished opportunities legislation provides to Traditional Owners of heritage (Rika-Heke 2010; see above).

So, although best practice heritage management principles and the stated aims of legislation are aimed at creating a situation that encourages researchers and heritage managers to relate ethically to Traditional Custodians, the issue of "informed consent," and assertions that Aboriginal people have "guardianship" of heritage, miss the point if control of the topics of investigation are governed by funding bodies, interpretation by international conventions in archaeology, and destruction of important places by pressure of development and the rights of property owners.

Bridging the Ditch

Over the last 30 years there have been major changes in New Zealand and Australian archaeology in response to Indigenous concerns. These changes have affected some aspects of practice and method, such as inviting Maori to bless a site prior to excavation, involving Aboriginal people in project and research design, and working with Maori and Aboriginal monitors whose role is to ensure that protocols are followed. A major departure from archaeological practice elsewhere is that relating to human remains which, having a special significance for both groups of Indigenous peoples discussed here, are on occasion recovered by Maori/Aboriginal people alone and reburied without the input of archaeologists (Phillips 2010:132).

Very significant advances have been made, as outlined in this paper, relating to Indigenous potential:

- to be involved in developments in archaeological and heritage practice;
- to be recognised in Codes of Ethics;
- to have Indigenous ways of knowing incorporated into principles of legislative frameworks;
- to be part of community-based archaeological research; and
- to be acknowledged as the primary source of decision-making about the management for human skeletal remains.

Despite these, there is still a considerable distance for archaeological practice to travel to overcome the barriers of the imposed rationale for investigation, the underlying understandings of the past, and interpretations of the results of archaeological research, that remain almost solely with the archaeologists and administrators of heritage management in both countries. To proceed beyond aspects of practice and method, more Indigenous people will need to engage with archaeology in order to have a better understanding of how archaeology can assist in the investigation of their past (Coghill in Clarke 2011; Rika-Heke 2010; Ross and Coghill 2000). For archaeologists, broader approaches to the past, such as in multi-disciplinary projects that incorporate Traditional Owners and custodians as equal partners in all aspects of project management, are seen as being better able to answer crucial questions, create new synergies and result in a sharing of information across different disciplines (pers. comm. Melinda Allen 2012; Allen and Phillips 2010:41). Archaeologists need to continue to find connections with Indigenous concepts, accept the primacy of Indigenous people in heritage, and work to overcome barriers to the integration of Indigenous knowledge in heritage management decision-making and Indigenous people as caretakers for their places (Allen 2010, p. 175). The dialogue has been initiated; it is time now to develop the practice.

Acknowledgements The authors would like to thank: Margaret Rika Heke, pouarahi (Maori heritage advisor), NZHPT for her thoughts on archaeology; Te Kenehi Teira, Kaihautu Maori (Senior Maori heritage advisor), NZHPT and Ngati Raukawa for permission to use Rangiatea as an example; Associate Professor Ian Smith and Professor Richard Walter, both at the Department of Anthropology and Archaeology, University of Otago and Associate Professor Melinda Allen, Department of Anthropology, University of Auckland for their insightful comments; Lynette Williams for proof-reading.

References

Allen, H. (1998). *Protecting historic places in New Zealand*. Auckland: University of Auckland.

Allen, H. (2010). The crisis in 21st century archaeological heritage. In C. Phillips & H. Allen (Eds.), *Bridging the divide: Indigenous communities and archaeology into the 21st century* (pp. 157–180). Walnut Creek: Left Coast Press.

Allen, H., Johns, D., Phillips, C., Day, K., O'Brien, T., & Mutunga, N. (2002). Wahi ngaro (the lost portion): strengthening relationships between people and wetlands in north Taranaki, New Zealand. *World Archaeology, 34*(2), 315–329.

Allen, H., & Phillips, C. (2010). Maintaining the dialogue: archaeology, cultural heritage and indigenous communities. In C. Phillips & H. Allen (Eds.), *Bridging the divide: Indigenous communities and archaeology into the 21st century* (pp. 17–48). Walnut Creek: Left Coast Press.

Allen, H., Phillips, C., Skipper, A., Te Moananui-Waikato, J., Reidy, C., & Cook, B. (1994). *Taskforce Green/University of Auckland archaeological project, Waihou River*. Auckland: University of Auckland.

Andrews, T. D., & Buggey, S. (2008). Authenticity in aboriginal cultural landscapes. *APT Bulletin, 39*(2/3), 63–71.

Australian Archaeological Association (AAA). (2009). *Submission to Review of the Indigenous Cultural Heritage Acts in Queensland*. Brisbane: Queensland government. AAA files.

Banner, S. (2005). Why Terra Nullius? Anthropology and property law in early Australia. *Law and History Review, 23*, 95–131.

Barker, B. (2006). Hierarchies of knowledge and the tyranny of text: Archaeology, ethnohistory and oral traditions in Australian archaeological interpretation. In B. David, B. Barker, & I. McNiven (Eds.), *The social archaeology of Australian indigenous societies* (pp. 72–84). Canberra: Aboriginal Studies Press.

Berkes, F. (2009). Evolution of co-management: role of knowledge generation, bridging organizations and social learning. *Journal of Environmental Management, 90*, 1692–1702.

Bradley, J. (2008). When a stone tool is a dingo: Country and relatedness in Australian Aboriginal notions of landscape. In B. David & J. Thomas (Eds.), *Handbook of landscape archaeology* (pp. 633–637). Walnut Creek: Left Coast Press.

Brown, S. (2008). Mute or mutable? Archaeological significance, research and cultural heritage management in Australia. *Australian Archaeology, 67*, 19–30.

Byrne, D. (1991). Western hegemony in archaeological heritage management. *History and Anthropology, 5*(2), 269–276.

Byrne, D. (1996). Deep nation: Australia's acquisition of an Indigenous past. *Aboriginal History, 20*, 82–107.

Byrne, D. (2002). An archaeology of attachment: Cultural heritage and the post-contact. In R. Harrison & C. Williamson (Eds.), *After Captain Cook: the archaeology of the recent indigenous past in Australia* (pp. 135–146). Sydney: Sydney University.

Byrne, D. (2003). The ethos of return: Erasure and reinstatement of Aboriginal visibility in the Australian historical landscape. *Historical Archaeology, 37*(1), 73–86.

Byrne, D., (2005). Messages to Manila. In I. Macfarlane, M. J. Mountain, & R. Paton (Eds.), *Many exchanges: archaeology, history, community and the work of Isabel McBryde* (pp 53–62). Canberra: Aboriginal History Monograph 11.

Byrne, D. (2008). Counter-mapping in the archaeological landscape. In B. David & J. Thomas (Eds.), *Handbook of landscape archaeology* (pp. 609–616). Walnut Creek: Left Coast Press.

Campbell, B. (2005). Changing protection policies and ethnographies of environmental engagement. *Conservation and Society, 3*(2), 280–322.

Clarke, A. (2011). *Narrating the past in the present: Gorenpul-Dandrabin understandings of the archaeological record on North Stradbroke Island and Peel Island, southeastern Queensland.* Unpublished BA Honours thesis, School of Social Science, The University of Queensland, Queensland.

Ellis, B. (1994). *Rethinking the paradigm: Cultural heritage management in Queensland.* Queensland: University of Queensland.

George, M., Innes, J., & Ross, H. (2004). *Managing sea country together: Key issues for developing co-operative management for the Great Barrier Reef World Heritage Area.* Townsville: CRC Reef Research Centre Ltd.

Godwin, L. (2001). *The bureaucracy, the law and blacks palace: A history of management of one site in the Central Queensland Highlands*. Queensland: University of Queensland.

Godwin, L. (2005). "Everyday archaeology:" Archaeological heritage management and its relationship to native title in development-related processes. *Australian Aboriginal Studies, 1*, 74–83.

Godwin, L., & Weiner, J. (2006). Footprints of the ancestors: The convergence of anthropological and archaeological perspectives in contemporary Aboriginal heritage studies. In B. David, B. Barker, & I. McNiven (Eds.), *The social archaeology of Australian indigenous societies* (pp. 124–138). Canberra: Aboriginal Studies Press.

Greer, S. (1999). Archaeology, history and identity in coastal Cape York. In J. Hall & I. McNiven (Eds.), *Australian coastal archaeology* (pp. 113–118). Canberra: Australian National University.

HPA (Historic Places Act). (2008). *Historic Places Act 1993.* Wellington: Department of Conservation.

Igoe, J. (2004). *Conservation and globalization: A study of National Parks and indigenous communities from East Africa to South Dakota*. Belmont: Thomson Wadsworth.

Kennett, R., Robinson, C. J., Kiessling, I., Yunupingu, D., Mununggurritj, M., & Yunupingu, D. (2004). Indigenous initiatives for co-management of Miyapunu/Sea Turtle. *Ecological Management and Restoration, 5*, 159–166.

Kothari, A. (2006). Community conserved areas: Towards ecological and livelihood security. *Community Conserved Areas, 16*, 3–13.

Maori Heritage Council. (2009). *Tapuwae: A vision for places of Maori heritage*. Wellington: New Zealand Historic Places Trust/Pouhere Taonga.

McFadgen, B. (1966). Legislative probes in the protection of New Zealand prehistoric sites. *New Zealand Archaeological Association Newsletter, 9*, 92–101.

McGovern-Wilson, R. (2008). New Zealand historic places trust research frameworks: Discussion paper. *Archaeology in New Zealand, 51*, 22–35.

McNiven, I.J., & Russell, L. (2005). Appropriated pasts: *Indigenous peoples and the colonial culture of archaeology*. Lanham, MD: AltaMira Press.

Meskell, L. (2012). *The nature of heritage: the new South Africa*. Boston: Wiley-Blackwell.

Milton, K. (1996). *Environmentalism and cultural theory: exploring the role of anthropology in environmental discourse*. New York, NY: Routledge.

Moreton, D., & Ross, A. (2011). Gorenpul-Dandrabin knowledge. In P. Davie (Ed.), *Wild guide to Moreton Bay and adjacent coasts* (pp. 58–67). Brisbane: Queensland Museum.

Neal, R., & Stock, E. (1986). Pleistocene occupation in the south-east Queensland coastal region. *Nature, 323*, 618–621.

New Zealand Archaeology. (2009). Members code of ethics – Principles of archaeological ethics. Retrieved from http://www.nzarchaeology.org.

New Zealand Historic Places Trust/Pouhere Taonga. (2006). Archaeological guidelines series No. 2: Guidelines for writing archaeological assessments. Wellington: New Zealand Historic Places Trust/Pouhere Taonga.

Phillips, C. (2010). Working together? Maori and archaeologists in Aotearoa/New Zealand today. In C. Phillips & H. Allen (Eds.), *Bridging the divide: Indigenous communities and archaeology into the 21st century* (pp. 129–156). Walnut Creek: Left Coast Press.

Phillips, C., & Allen, H. (2006). Damage assessment of Waihou River sites. *Archaeology in New Zealand, 49*, 82–93.

Phillips, C., & Allen, H. (Eds.). (2010). *Bridging the divide: Indigenous communities and archaeology into the 21st century*. Walnut Creek: Left Coast Press.

Phillips, C., & Allen, H. (2011). Archaeology in vicinity of Rangiatea Pa. Unpublished paper presented to Raukawa, 1 December 2011.

Pinkerton, E. (1992). Translating legal rights into management practice: Overcoming barriers to the exercise of co-management. *Human Organization, 51*, 330–341.

Prangnell, J., Ross, A., & Coghill, B. (2010). Power relations and community involvement in landscape-based cultural heritage management practice: an Australian case study. *International Journal of Heritage Studies, 16*(1–2), 140–155.

Rika-Heke, M. (2010). Archaeology and indigeneity in Aotearoa/New Zealand: Why do Maori not engage with archaeology? In C. Phillips & H. Allen (Eds.), *Bridging the divide: Indigenous communities and archaeology into the 21st century* (pp. 197–212). Walnut Creek: Left Coast Press.

Robins, T. (2013). *Intangible heritage, duty of care, and heritage legislation in NSW and Queensland*. BA Honours thesis, School of Social Science, The University of Queensland, Queensland.

Robinson, C. J., Ross, H., & Hockings, M. (2006). *Development of co-operative management arrangements in the Great Barrier Reef: an adaptive management approach*. Townsville: CRC Reef Research Centre Ltd.

Robson, D., & Rika-Heke, M. (2011). *Registration report for a wahi tapu Rangiatea Pa, Otorohanga*. Unpublished report. New Zealand Historic Trust/Pouhere Taonga, Auckland.

Ross, A. (1996). More than archaeology: New directions in cultural heritage management. *Queensland Archaeological Research, 10*, 17–24.

Ross, A. (2008). Managing meaning at an ancient site in the 21st century: the Gummingurru Aboriginal stone arrangement on the Darling Downs, southern Queensland. *Oceania, 78*, 91–108.

Ross, A. (2010). Defining cultural heritage at Gummingurru, Queensland, Australia. In C. Phillips & H. Allen (Eds.), *Bridging the divide: Indigenous communities and archaeology into the 21st century* (pp. 107–128). Walnut Creek: Left Coast Press.

Ross, A., & Coghill, S. (2000). Conducting a community-based archaeological project: anarchaeologist's and a Koenpul man's perspective. *Australian Aboriginal Studies, 1*(2), 76–83.

Ross, A., Prangnell, J., & Coghill, B. (2010). Archaeology, cultural landscapes, and Indigenous knowledge in Australian cultural heritage management legislation and practice. *Heritage Management, 3*(1), 73–96.

Ross, A., Sherman, K. P., Snodgrass, J., Delcore, H., & Sherman, R. (2011). *Indigenous peoples and the collaborative stewardship of nature: knowledge binds and institutional conflicts.* Walnut Creek: Left Coast Press.

Smith, L. (2006). *Uses of heritage*. New York, NY: Routledge.

Stephenson, M. A., & Ratnapala, S. (1993). *Mabo: A judicial revolution*. Brisbane: University of Queensland Press.

Stevenson, M. (2006). The possibility of difference: rethinking co-management. *Human Organization, 65*, 167–180.

Sullivan, S. (2005). Out of the box: Isabel McBryde's radical contribution to the shaping of Australian archaeological practice. In I. Macfarlane, M-J. Mountain & R. Paton (Eds.), *Many exchanges: archaeology, history, community and the work of Isabel McBryde*, (pp 83–94). Canberra: Aboriginal History Monograph 11.

Sullivan, S. (2008). More unconsidered trifles? Aboriginal and archaeological heritage values: Integration and disjuncture in cultural heritage management practice. *Australian Archaeology, 67*, 107–115.

University of Auckland. (2010). *Guiding principles for conducting research with human participants*. Auckland: University of Auckland.

Walton, T. (2006). How big are pa? *Archaeology in New Zealand, 49*, 174–187.

Wilson, J. (2011). Nation and government – the origins of Nationhood. In *Te Ara – the Encyclopaedia of New Zealand*. Retrieved from http://www.TeAra.govt.nz/en/nation-and-government/1.

Chapter 4
Against Global Archaeological Ethics: Critical Views from South America

Rafael Pedro Curtoni

Archaeology as a discipline has been largely formed as a nation-state's biopolitical device generating narratives and actions of control, management, classification, and ordering of people and objects, pasts and presents, their stories, relationships, and spaces from an Anglo-Saxon modern way of knowledge production. In this sense, hegemonic archaeology bears its colonial imprint and exhibits the principles of universality, objectivity, and rationalism that characterize modern Western science. Thus, archaeology has developed and expanded in close partnership with capitalism, generating a true industry and mercantilization of the past (Hamilakis 2007). Simultaneously, an attempt to globalize the vision of Western archeology and to install a monoculture of knowledge has been made in order to disqualify others' worldviews, reducing and contracting the present as well as eliminating those conceptions that do not fit with the scientific canons and principles (Santos 2006). The ideal of knowledge in modernity, also characterized by its objectivity and universality, is predefined as disembodied and ahistorical and by its atopy, namely by its possibility to ignore and transcend subjects, times, and places. This is linked to the ontological rupture between body and mind, the initial separation of the modern Western tradition, which places human beings in an external and instrumental position in relation to their environment (Lander 2003). This reinforces abstraction and detachment as main heuristics elements in the construction of knowledge. According to Maldonado-Torres, given the priority to scientific knowledge as the only model of knowing, the cognitive abilities in racialized subjects (the "other" colonized) are simultaneously denied, which provides the basis for their ontological negation and epistemic disqualification (Maldonado-Torres 2007).

R.P. Curtoni (✉)
Facultad de Ciencias Sociales, Universidad Nacional del Centro de la Provincia de Buenos Aires, Avda. del Valle 5737, 7400 Olavarría, Provincia de Buenos Aires, Argentina
e-mail: rcurtoni@soc.unicen.edu.ar

C. Gnecco, D. Lippert (eds.), *Ethics and Archaeological Praxis*, Ethical Archaeologies: The Politics of Social Justice 1,
DOI 10.1007/978-1-4939-1646-7_4

In its disciplinary history, much of South American archaeology has developed behind closed doors privileging a construction of knowledge from a modern "us," Western and white, based on evaluative neutrality, distancing, and objectivity. One could argue that this way of looking at archaeological practice in much of South America is a result of the theoretical and methodological influences of the historical–cultural school and processualism that predominated and still influence in this part of the Americas (Politis 2003). But not all is homogeneous in South American archaeology. Some complexities and differences characterize the practice of the discipline at continental level and even within each country. In the current scenario, the politics of knowledge in archaeology have begun to be subverted and thought from other horizons. Thus, it is possible to propose the timid, embryonic emergency of actions of reformulation or questioning of the modern Eurocentric colonial matrix of knowledge production and the beginnings of localized forms of considering the practice and generation of knowledge. Now, some of these initiatives have been framed within the multicultural and intercultural logic of knowledge production and management and others have begun different processes of reconfiguration of the archaeological practice from localized and multivocal areas (Gnecco and Ayala 2010; Jofré 2010; Haber 2009, 2011).

In general, discussions on the ethical dimensions of archaeological practice have been activated indirectly through the ideas of multivocality, multiculturalism, and related issues such as repatriation, cultural resource management, impact assessments, mercantilization of knowledge, and so on and so forth. Thus, demands concerning participation and involvement of the indigenous peoples in archaeological research projects (understood in multiple ways) are now being presented by local groups, such as indigenous and peasants, in specialized congresses. Conflicts arising from territorial dispossession, encroachments of sacred places, destruction of sites, and claims for restitution of human remains and associated materials are being dealt with. However, although these minority trends are emerging, they have failed to overcome the multicultural rhetoric and thus continue reproducing conditions of epistemic control, distance, and inhibition of politics. Therefore, the uncritical applications of the Anglo-Saxon idea of "multivocality" imply the consideration that the "academics" should provide a wider vision among many possibilities and, in most cases, adopt a stance of self-suspension of judgment so as not to confront or contradict the voices of the "other". The criterion of allowing it to flow, the idea that we are all equal, and the absence of criticisms implicit in the notion of "multivocality" approach it to the multicultural ideal declared as a constitutive principle of the modern nation-state (Gnecco 1999; González-Ruibal 2010). Advocates of "multivocality" reproduce the attitude of "epoche" of the Greek skeptics, namely suspension of judgment, neither denying nor affirming anything, thus activating the "ataraxia" or imperturbability and indifference to everything (Curtoni and Chaparro 2008). Hence, the inhibition of political questioning and the lack of criticism to the power structures (e.g., multinational companies, agricultural pools, hegemonic science, editorials, political systems, and so on), and the possibilities of contradicting the narratives of the "others," tend to neutralize the transformative potentiality and subversion inherent in the situated praxis committed with local interests (Curtoni and Paredes Mosquera 2012). By contrast, archaeologists that support the idea of "multivocality" have been concerned with the integration of different viewpoints in disagreement proposing a reflexive and symmetrical dialogue but taking as reference the disciplinary standards and practice forms of archaeological ethic committed with global heritage (Silberman 1995; Hodder 1999; Webmoor 2005). Consequently, some have argued that engagement and participation of local communities revolve around their visits to the archaeological sites, for some interventions in academic events and for partial control in the steps of the research (Marshall 2002; McNiven and Russell 2005). At this point, it is appropriate to question the usefulness of the concept of "multivocality" or rather, who benefits from it. Undoubtedly, these stances reproduce disciplinary power relations which tend to neutralize the implications of others' voices and their interests, subjecting and controlling them under structures of academic power-knowledge, predefined and globalized.

Also, the formal adoption in different South American countries of codes of ethics that seek to regulate the practice of archaeology reflects, in some way, the neocolonial global logic that characterizes modern scientific production. That is the idea of the professionalized individual, apolitical and constrained by disciplinary practices and subjected to conditions of productivity, efficiency, and rationality. In most South American countries, there have been reflections over the ethical turn occurred in the 1990s in the Anglo-Saxon hegemonic archaeology that displaced the concerns about the political issues and minority rights characteristic of the 1980s towards ethical issues related to the regulation of the professional practice and global heritage (Hamilakis 2007). In that turn, in South America a scientific archaeological ethic could emerge primarily concerned with defining the professional performance in the light of scientific standards and rules. In most of the codes of ethics of the South American countries the concerns have revolved around codifying and regulating archaeological practices, establishing duties and obligations in relation to the profession, to the archaeological heritage, with colleagues, with citizenship, with publishing, and with local communities. In this sense, encoding archaeological practices through codes of ethics has contributed to deepening scientific internalization given that disciplinary criteria of rigor and professionalism were the most developed. By contrast, the social and political interests of local communities (e.g., indigenous, rural) are not enough contemplated in the codes of ethics, having just statements of intention such as promoting positive interactions and respect to their concerns, customs, beliefs, and values. Neither are specifics criterions' serving as guidance for professional action in conflicting situations or encroachments on the rights of local people founds in ethical codes (Endere and Ayala 2011). For instance, in recent decades and in various South American countries, the expansion of the agricultural frontier, the brutal deforestation of native forests, the usurpation and violent occupation of large areas previously considered marginal and unproductive land due to the action of agricultural consortia, mining, and the development of tourism have been activated (Torterolo 2005). These situations generated the dispossession and violent expulsion of indigenous groups and peasants who had occupied these ancestral lands for generations. The sale, of questionable legality, of thousands of state hectares to private hands and the absolute commodification of land, its products, and people, implies an inexorable process of dehumanization and destruction of landscapes, identities, and human lives. The complicity of the state or its inefficiency and, in some cases, its absolute absence contribute to the lack of commitment and the demarcation of responsibilities that legally belong to it.

All these processes and phenomena are not only negatively impacting in the livelihood of peasants and indigenous peoples from diverse regions, but they are also putting into question the role of science and professionals (specially considering the claims to participate carried out by indigenous people involving their interests and the deterioration of the "landscapes" in areas of archaeological research). This situation expresses, in general, some tension within the social sciences between those who postulate a necessary involvement with the actors and daily problems and those who maintain academic distance. Thus, archaeology as a modern discipline and its practice always carry its inherently political mark and reflect in very different ways and intensities the complex and dynamic relationships between interest groups, archaeologists, and sociopolitical contexts. In this sense, one might ask how the continuous claims made by indigenous groups and the daily problems that rural communities face are academically considered. Also, is it possible to find complete disengagement, disinterest, and imperturbability (ataraxia) in these problems daily faced by the actors living in landscapes chosen as research areas? Is it possible to neglect the direct claims of interest groups (whether indigenous or peasant) in relation to their land and/or in relation to their need to participate in research programs? In South America, the cases of participation and involvement of local nonacademic actors (indigenous and/or peasants) in archaeological projects have not been very numerous in the history of the discipline. In this decade it seems that this trend is reversing due mainly to the increased presence of archaeologists concerned about their relationships with the communities of reference. However, considering the long-term projects, the proposed opening of archaeology, and the effective participation of other stakeholders in research, it seems to be the exception rather than the rule (Gnecco and Ayala 2010, Jofré 2010).

In the present context, it is possible to suggest that in South American archaeology, at a discursive level, a multicultural ethic prevails that promotes disciplinary openness, participation, and involvement of local actors; encourages multivocal developments; and enables discussion and returning of human remains and associated materials. In practice and represented through the codification of professional conduct, the scientific ethic emerges as part of the multicultural rhetoric that not only reproduces relations of knowledge-power but simultaneously inhibits any assessment and emission of judgment by the archaeologist and thereby overrides any political project of social critique and emancipation. It is also reflected by the maintenance of the narrative control (oral, textual, and enunciative locus) of archaeology, which supports the belief in the preeminence of archaeological discourse as a product of scientific knowledge above other different ways of doing and knowing such as the so-called epistemologies "others." Furthermore, one consequence of the above is the limited presence and representation of nonacademic voices, including indigenous and peasants, both in archaeological textuality and in specific areas of discussion (e.g., conferences, workshops, and meetings). The scientific ethic encodes the behavior of archaeologists in order to guide and to evaluate their performance in relation to the profession and to establish one's responsibility of ensuring the conservation and protection of the archaeological heritage. It further states that scientific studies of the past are of interest to all mankind, regardless of nationality, origin, and religion, thereby establishing the right and legitimacy to carry out research elsewhere. Thus, scientific ethics constitutes an expression of multiculturalism; on the one hand, it declares the obligation of scientists to obtain the free and informed consent from indigenous peoples, and their rights to participate in research projects and to decide on the management of heritage; and on the other, it defines the role of the professional under scientific standards that predefine evaluative neutrality, distance, and exclusivity. Scientific ethics contributes to deepen the disciplinary self and hence excludes professionals from their social context, exempting them from the vicissitudes and external concerns which are not part of the academic agenda. Thus, scientific ethics reflects the sense of coloniality of archaeology as discipline which leads to different strategies of knowledge construction such as the separation between fact and value, the "denial of contemporaneity," the primacy of the object, the objectification, and externality in the definition of its subject of study. These aspects are consequences of the configuration and development of archaeology under the principles and canons of the modern Western science. Therefore, archaeology as discipline can be characterized as part of a technology of power or hegemonic biopolitical device whose narratives construct and control histories, places, subjects, and their social relationships and materiality from a modern and Eurocentric way of knowledge production. The disciplinary structure of archaeology presupposes objectivity, universality, and disincorporated ways of knowing that tend to place human beings in an external and instrumental position with their surrounding. Furthermore, archaeology as a modern discipline defines its own standards of validation and legitimization that tends to regulate and structure the right ways of practice, prescribing in that process all the external views and meaningful opinions.

Thus, as far as we are not able to overcome the sense of coloniality of knowledge as the main model of science and the coloniality of archaeology, it will not be possible to generate knowledge "others" coproduced and sustained in ways of knowing which are located and plural. This involves promoting actions that tend towards decolonization of archaeology as a scientific discipline and contribute to "expand the present" (Santos 2006). In this context, there is no doubt that archaeology is politics and its disciplinary practices inscribe relations of power-knowledge both at micro- and macro-political levels. Similarly, dealing with ethics means dealing with politics; and therefore, the discussion on ethics cannot be conceived without referring to its political implications. That leads directly to the location of the political dimensions of ethics and their temporary space contextualization, revealing the contingent and situated nature of the political aspects. This position contradicts the idea of global archaeological ethics, which by definition disables the political and contributes to replace specific problems by abstract axioms. By contrast, this chapter proposes that the ethical discussions about archaeological practices must be considered from an ethics of relationships, which is basically sociopolitical, localized, and positioned in line with the needs of the interest groups involved in investigations. Thinking about an ethics of relationships in its sociopolitical dimension means that the criteria of regulation of archaeological practice will be the emergent of an interrelation horizon of interests activated by the involvement of local actors, popular knowledge, the community, and archaeologists. The ethics of relationships implies the acceptance that in sociopolitical relatedness there is no place for neutrality, since that engaging through praxis contributes to activate specific interests, conflicts, critical positions, differences, and negotiations. At this point it is clear that the situated relatedness does not mean that there should be symmetry and equality of conditions. On the contrary, the social encountering tends to activate the emergence of the valuations and interests of each actor and the possibilities of antagonisms. Such an ethics of relationships is dynamic, participative, changing, and subject to the problems and conflicts that arise, so it is contingent, open, and always susceptible to transformation and redefinition. Assuming a localized ethics of relationships generates implications related to academic decentralization; the denaturalization of canonical and disciplinary forms of knowledge; the staging of our own interests, scopes, and limitations; and the understanding of the historical nature of knowledge and the plurality of voices. Thus, the exchange of opinions and valuations contributes both to the encounter of knowledge and interests in common, encouraging the ethical discussions about situated archaeological practices from and with the difference and from alternative geo-chrono-political positions.

Acknowledgments This work is part of INCUAPA, UNICEN, and CONICET (PIP 275).

References

Curtoni, R., & Paredes Mosquera, A. (2012). Arqueología y multivocalidad en la encrucijada. Aportes críticos desde Sudamérica. In press in M. C. Rivolta, M. Montenegro & L. Menezes Ferreira (Eds), *Multivocalidad y Activaciones Patrimoniales en Arqueología: Perspectivas desde Sudamérica*. Buenos Aires: Universidad Maimónides & Facultad de Ciencias Sociales, Universidad Nacional del Centro.

Curtoni, R., & Chaparro, M. G. (2008). El espejo de la naturaleza y la enfermedad histórica en la construcción del conocimiento. *Intersecciones en Antropología, 9*, 213–227.

Endere, M. L., & Ayala, P. (2011). Normativa legal, recaudos éticos y práctica arqueológica. Un estudio comparativo de Argentina y Chile. *Chungara, 4*, 39–57.

Gnecco, C. (1999). *Multivocalidad histórica. Hacia una cartografía postcolonial de la arqueología*. Bogotá: Universidad de los Andes.

Gnecco, C., & Ayala, P. (Eds.). (2010). *Pueblos Indígenas y arqueología en América Latina*. Bogotá: FIAN-Universidad de los Andes.

González-Ruibal, A. (2010). Contra la pospolítica: arqueología de la guerra civil española. *Revista Chilena de Antropología, 22*, 9–32.

Haber, A. (2009). Animism, relatedness, life: Post-western perspectives. *Cambridge Archaeological Journal, 19*(3), 418–430.

Haber, A. (2011). Nometodología payanesa: Notas de metodología indisciplinada. *Revista Chilena de Antropología, 23*, 9–49.

Hamilakis, Y (2007). From ethics to politics. In Y. Hamilakis & P. Duke (Eds), *Archaeology and Capitalism: From ethics to politics* (pp 15–40). Walnut Creek: Left Coast Press.

Hodder, I. (1999). *The archaeological process. An introduction*. Oxford, UK: Blackwell.
Jofré, I. C. (Ed.). (2010). *El regreso de los muertos y las promesas del oro. Patrimonio arqueológico en conflicto*. Córdoba: Encuentro-Editorial Brujas.
Lander, E. (2003). Ciencias sociales: Saberes coloniales y eurocéntricos. In E. Lander (Ed.), *La colonialidad del saber: eurocentrismo y ciencias sociales. Perspectivas latinoamericanas* (pp. 11–40). Buenos Aires: CLACSO.
Maldonado-Torres, N. (2007). Sobre la colonialidad del ser: Contribuciones al desarrollo de un concepto. In S. Castro & R. Grosfoguel (Eds.), *El giro decolonial. Reflexiones para una diversidad epistémica más allá del capitalismo global* (pp. 127–167). Bogotá: Iesco-Pensar-Siglo del Hombre.
Marshall, Y. (2002). What is community archaeology? *World Archaeology, 34*(2), 211–219.
McNiven, I., & Russell, L. (2005). *Appropriated pasts. Indigenous peoples and the colonial culture of archaeology*. Oxford, UK: Rowman AltaMira.
Politis, G. (2003). The theoretical landscape and the methodological developments of archaeology in Latin America. *American Antiquity, 68*(2), 247–272.
Santos, B. S. (2006). *Renovar la teoría crítica y reinventar la emancipación social*. Buenos Aires: CLACSO.
Silberman, N. (1995). Promised land and chosen peoples: The politics and poetics of archaeological narrative. In P. Kohl & C. Fawcett (Eds.), *Nationalism, politics, and the practice of archaeology* (pp. 249–262). Cambridge: Cambridge University Press.
Torterolo, M. K. (2005). La expansión de la frontera agrícola, un acercamiento desde el punto de vista climático. *Apuntes Agroeconómicos*, 4 (3). Facultad de Agronomía, UBA. Versión digital: http://www.agro.uba.ar/apuntes/, (23 de junio de 2006).
Webmoor, T. (2005). Mediational techniques and conceptual frameworks in archaeology: A model mapwork at Teotihuacan, Mexico. *Journal of Social Archaeology, 5*(1), 52–84.

Chapter 5
Archaeology and Ethics: The Case of Central-Eastern Europe

Arkadiusz Marciniak

Introduction

Archaeology practiced in Central-Eastern Europe was and remains to be distinct from the rest of Europe. This peculiarity has been developing through years as a consequence of a range of different and intertwined processes. These included intellectual traditions, geographical position, political circumstances and turbulent history. Its distinct character was evident already in the beginning of the twentieth century.

These developments led to the emergence of what is often being referred to as Central European tradition (see Marciniak 2006). It is composed of a number of distinct national schools including that of Austria, the Czech Republic, Denmark, Germany, Hungary, the Netherlands, and Poland, which however retained a certain degree of distinctiveness. It is dominated by German archaeology, but should certainly not be equated with it despite the fact that the German language has dominated its discourse (Härke 1991, 2000).

The most distinct similarities comprise the objectives of archaeological enquiry, the explanatory schemes and applied methods. The archaeology of Central-Eastern Europe is believed to be characterised by "empiricist work; a preference for description over interpretation; technical excellence, but little reflection on basic questions; hierarchical attitudes; an absence of lively debate; and self-imposed isolation from the intellectual mainstream" (Bloemers 2002:381).

As a consequence of the turbulent history of the region, itself composed of countries from both sides of the Iron Curtain, after the WII, the archaeology of Central-Eastern Europe began to be deliberately defined as a purely academic and objective endeavour, devoid of any theoretical deliberations and neglecting any social role

---

A. Marciniak (✉)
Institute of Prehistory, University of Poznań, św. Marcin 78, 61-809 Poznań, Poland
e-mail: arekmar@amu.edu.pl

C. Gnecco, D. Lippert (eds.), *Ethics and Archaeological Praxis*,
Ethical Archaeologies: The Politics of Social Justice 1,
DOI 10.1007/978-1-4939-1646-7_5

that all were supposedly to deprive it from its scientific character (Marciniak 2011). The reluctance to engage in any theoretical debate in this period is striking but it can be explained by a number of interconnected historical, political, sociological and academic circumstances. In particular, archaeology was misused to meet nationalistic goals by the Nazis in Germany. At the same time, the overwhelming dominance of an orthodox Marxist doctrine in the countries under the Soviet dominance in the years following the end of the WWII necessitated in making a constant compromise with the communist rule. Numerous archaeologists on both sides of the divide more or less deliberately and to different degree served both regimes. A significantly ideologised archaeology began to be seen with disrespect, in particular when the grips of both totalitarian systems ceased. This resulted in the search for a secure position of the discipline. This goal was soon achieved through an escape into supposedly "objective" scholarship, which guaranteed political security refrained from any involvement in political struggle. A passive collection of data was conducted in hopes that a mass of "pure facts" will be transformed into objective knowledge about the past. As archaeology was regarded as a purely scientific discipline, its practitioners found themselves in "ivory towers", satisfied from their academically sanctioned positions and exempt from any kind of public engagement. The general public was not thought of as any reliable partner as archaeologists regarded themselves as sole stakeholders of archaeological heritage. The fact that archaeology was fully founded by the state and served its goals further fossilised this situation. Not surprising then, ethical concerns beyond the academia themselves were deemed irrelevant and unimportant.

Developments and Challenges of the Post-1989 Period in Central-Eastern Europe

The archaeology of Central-Eastern Europe changed dramatically in the period following the end of communism in the years 1989–1990 and a steady integration of these countries with the European structures. The transition to market economy affected all aspects of archaeological practice, which underwent changes in virtually all its domains in a pace unparallel to the rest of Europe.

The second half of the twentieth century has been marked by a number of international charters and conventions dealing with the conservation and preservation of cultural heritage. They provided guiding principles and adequate responses to appealing conservation and heritage issues of the time. One of the most important conventions that shaped the character of archaeology of Europe in the last two decades of the twentieth century was the *European Convention for the Protection of Archaeological Heritage* adopted by the Council of Europe in Valetta, Malta, in 1992. It was adopted and ratified in the very period in which countries of Central-Eastern Europe struggled to join the European Union. Not surprisingly, the Malta Convention had a profound influence upon almost all facets of archaeology in this part of Europe.

The *European Convention for the Protection of the Archaeological Heritage* confirmed and codified the foundational role of archaeological heritage for the reunited Europe. It rightly and timely identified efficient means to the threats it faced in the period of unprecedented large-scale investments. It established new legal standards to be met by national policies for the protection of archaeological assets as sources of scientific and documentary evidence along with the principles of integrated conservation. When the Malta Convention was ratified by the Council of Europe it became an undisputable guide and point of reference for different initiatives in the field of archaeological heritage as it rightly captured the soul and challenges of the time.

For almost two decades, the Malta Convention laid down foundations for the management and protection of archaeological heritage across Europe. The major challenge archaeology had to face in the 1990s was the upsurge in spatial development and urbanisation across Europe, in particular huge infrastructure projects such as gaslines, pipelines, the network of highways and expressways, canals and airports. They have brought about large-scale destruction of numerous archaeological sites and cultural landscapes. Awareness of threats to the substance of the archaeological heritage and the fast pace of its destruction became much more common than earlier and archaeologists themselves became more aware of their own responsibility to protect this heritage (Kobyliński 2001a:19). The Malta Convention induced legal and administrative regulations applied during these large-scale projects.

Archaeology in Central-Eastern Europe began to face these new developments to an unprecedented scale, in particular a rapid destruction of the archaeological heritage due to large-scale developments, intensive agriculture, commercialisation and the need to get engaged with the general public (Kobyliński 2001a:17; see also Lozny 1998). Archaeologists began to recognise their new role as stewards of rapidly disappearing heritage and had to redefine the existing *status quo* of the discipline. This led to a fundamental shift in understanding archaeological substance from its purely academic content to the recognition of cultural and social dimensions of archaeological sites and objects (Kobyliński 2001b:77). Consequently, the archaeologist is no longer seen as a discoverer of the past, but situates himself or herself as a member of the larger community concerned with the degradation of the heritage and the management of its finite "resources". Consequently, practicing archaeology means now a public service to many and archaeological expertise is to serve the relationship between the producer and consumer of archaeological data (Marciniak 2011). Not surprisingly, it soon became clear that many developments advocated by the Malta Convention triggered significant ethical concerns.

The new developments in archaeology in Central-Eastern Europe of the last two decades brought about different unforeseen consequences. One of the most profound outcomes was the commercialisation of the discipline. A reaction to numerous rescue projects in relations to large-scale investments was the emergence of private archaeological firms and consequently the rapid creation of a new professional group on the archaeological market characterised by high efficiency in conducting large-scale, long-term excavation projects. As a result, this kind of archaeological fieldworks in some countries of the region, such as Poland, is almost exclusively carried out by private firms, including survey, evaluation, recording and excavation before the planned infrastructural projects are implemented.

The dynamic and largely uncontrolled commercialisation of archaeological practice had understandably profound consequences upon different facets of the discipline. It led to the fragmentation of the archaeological process, as marked by a departure from the standardised methodology for excavations and for the recording and analysis of archaeological finds. The new situation required also to set up and define the relationship between investors and contractors, which should require a compromise of free market rules with the obligations for monument protection. The contractual nature of these kinds of projects, often financially very profitable, was a particularly difficult and contentious issue and was a matter of constant struggle resulting in different solutions and regulations implemented across the region.

Mitigation Strategies and Ethical Solutions

The Malta Convention put into the fore the importance of the general public for archaeology. This in turn required redefining a new role of the discipline in contemporary society, which has to recognise concerns of other stakeholders and come to terms with the destructive nature of archaeological practice. In particular, the debate was focused on previously unimportant and unnoticed issues such as treatment of human remains, looting and illicit trade of antiquities, ownership of artifacts, use of metal detectors, preservation of archaeological sites, commercialisation and tourism, the character of excavation practices and responsibility for future generations. These issues required appropriate legal measures and accompanying organisational and administrative solutions. However, the European archaeological milieu stressed from the very beginning a need of abiding by appropriate ethical standards. This was well manifested by the adoption of important codes and principles of conduct.

A particularly significant role in this respect was played by the European Association of Archaeologists. The Association was created in the early 1990s as an explicit attempt to address emerging concerns of the then European archaeology and to facilitate the reunification of the European archaeological communities following the collapse of the Iron Curtain.

One of the first major documents adopted by the EAA was the EAA *Code of Practice*, approved in 1997. In its preamble, the Code provides a definition of archaeological heritage as the heritage of humankind, by explicitly referring to Article 1 of the 1992 *European Convention on the Protection of the Archaeological Heritage*. The Code makes it clear that archaeology is the study and interpretation of that heritage for the benefit of society as a whole and archaeologists are the interpreters and stewards of that heritage on behalf of the general public. Its major objective is to establish standards of conduct for the members of the EAA, who need to meet the expectations of both the community and their peers.

The Code further referred to the character of archaeological practice, including illicit trade of antiquities, and relationship to the public. Archaeologists are obliged to ensure the preservation of the archaeological heritage by every legal means. Where preservation is impossible, they shall ensure that investigations are carried out to the highest professional standards. They need to make use of the newest methods and methodological protocols from their fields of specialization as well as the best techniques of fieldwork, conservation, information dissemination and related areas. Archaeologists are also obliged not to engage in any form of activity relating to the illicit trade in antiquities and works of art. They also need to refrain from any activity that impacts the archaeological heritage and is carried out for commercial profit.

The Code of Practice was further expanded by the EAA *Principle of Conduct for Archaeologists Involved in Contract Archaeological Work* adopted in 1998. The document aimed to define the role of archaeologists involved in large-scale rescue projects. It stressed a need of avoiding conflicts of interest between the role of giving advice in a regulatory capacity and undertaking work in a contract capacity. It further reiterated that archaeologists should not offer to undertake contract work for which they or their organisations are not suitably equipped, staffed or experienced. It is required that they adhere to recognised professional standards for archaeological work. The Principle then obliged archaeologists to make the results of contract works publicly available. It is also required they demonstrate the benefits of support for archaeological work both to the developers and the public at large.

These documents rightly recognized potential problems triggered by the redefined role of archaeology in the public domain but largely failed to prevent them from materialising. The archaeological community at large was aware of potential pitfalls, shortcomings and disfunctionalities of Malta archaeology, which were already pretty evident around the middle of the first decade of the 2000s, however articulated differently in different European countries. They all have been amplified and accelerated by the global crisis that hit the world in 2008. The wild commercialisation of archaeological practice and the introduction of commercial relations between the investor and the developer made heritage protection to become too much of a business and not surprisingly became recognised and treated as such. Hence, the solutions advocated in the Malta convention were no longer seen as feasible and in accord with new strategies of sustainable development in the continent, especially in Central-Eastern Europe. The national governments have recently implemented different mitigation measures significantly reducing effectiveness and efficiency of existing solutions. The new situation marks a departure from the hitherto accepted status quo and indicates the beginning of a new era in heritage archaeology and the role of heritage in contemporary European society (see Marciniak 2013).

Ethical Issues in the Practice of Central-Eastern European Archaeology

The move of funding responsibilities from the state to private developers in Central-Eastern brought about new concerns to archaeology regarding professional standards and accountability. Managerial decision-making regarding the aims and means of attaining certain goals, selection of priorities and a holistic approach to the research process introduced a complete new way of handling the archaeological process.

These developments caused numerous problems and required a rapid implementation of satisfactory mitigation strategies. These mainly comprised new legal regulations, introduction of efficient organisational schemes and application of appropriate methodological standards (see more Marciniak 2011), differently articulated across the region. However, in due course archaeologists of Central-Eastern Europe turned also more explicitly their attention to ethical aspects of archaeological practice. Interestingly, it became particularly pronounced in the period when large-scale investment projects started to decline. However, in a majority of instances, this discussion was focused more on good practices rather than on ethics to avoid the unnecessary axiological controversies it may have caused (Kobyliński 2012:158). This tendency is well manifested by the adoption of codes of practice in some countries of the region.

Zbigniew Kobyliński—an eminent Polish archaeologist—has recently identified a range of major ethical issues that need to drive contemporary archaeologists (Kobyliński 2012; see also Wróblewska 2000). They are required in order to provide efficient conditions for the preservation and protection of irreplaceable archaeological heritage. An important set of issues concerns the character of archaeological fieldwork. In particular, Kobyliński argues that it is not recommended to excavate archaeological sites that are not endangered, and their study should be carried out using non-invasive methods, whenever possible. All rescue excavations need to be directed by qualified staff and be conducted according to the best professional standards, and their results properly studied, documented and published.

Another important set of issues postulated by Kobyliński concerns the destruction of archaeological heritage and illegal trade. He postulates that archaeologists should refrain from any illegal trade of antiquities and objects of art. Referring to the Polish situation, he strongly discourages archaeologist from any cooperation with metal detectors, whose activities need to condemn.

The other major ethical dimension of contemporary archaeological practice involves relations between archaeologists and the public at large. Different social groups should be granted rights to receive competent and updated accounts about the past, as produced by archaeologists. Kobyliński further stresses that archaeological materials be properly stored and made available to other scholars and the general public. Archaeologists should also respect the rights of indigenous people while working on their territories.

The final set of issues comprises political and non-scientific misuse of results of archaeological works and their interpretation. Moreover, it is postulated that archaeologists refer, respectively, to their peers, conduct their research to the highest standards and make the acquired archaeological materials available to others.

First attempt to codify ethical issues in Polish archaeology was the document *Rules of conduct and ethical norms of Polish archaeological milieu*, prepared in 2003 by Bolesław Ginter and Michał Kobusiewicz on behalf of the Committee for Pra- and Protohistorical Sciences Polish Academy of Sciences—the major and most influential professional body of Polish academic archaeologists (Ginter and

Kobusiewicz 2003). The document is directed to all practicing archaeologists in the country. It was adopted as an explicit reaction to increasingly negative tendencies in Polish archaeology. These rules of conduct and ethical norms are defined in six thematic blocs: (a) research procedures, (b) scientific publications, (c) documentation and protection of archaeological materials, (d) dissemination, (e) didactic process and (f) legal framework. More particularly, the document postulates a professional preparation of any field project and application of the highest scientific standards of archaeological works. It further obliges archaeologists to carefully document all materials and their context. The works must be conducted by respecting the contribution of all team members. Those involved in contract projects need to cooperate with the investor to facilitate a smooth and competent completion of fieldwork. As regards publications, the document obliges archaeologists to make results of their work available in the shortest possible time and presented at the highest level. Archaeologists retain the right to publish results of his works during 10 years following their completion. The document explicitly condemns the so-called honorary co-authorship, namely adding the authors that have not contributed to the production of an archaeological work. It further explicitly protests against any form of plagiarism. Furthermore, the document obliges archaeologists to carefully store both materials and field documentation in such a way that access to them is granted to all interested parties. It further obliges them to be actively engaged in different forms of dissemination strategies. The academic archaeologists are expected to provide the highest standard of education, both at the theoretical and practical levels. In terms of legal frameworks, the document condemns any links to illegal trade of antiquities and holding any private archaeological collection.

Numerous issues identified by the *Rules of conduct and ethical norms of Polish archaeological milieu* and in the Kobyliński's (2012) overview can be identified in the *Code of Conduct of members of the Association of Polish Archaeologists* (Stowarzyszenie Naukowe Archeologów Polskich), adopted in 2010. As specified in the preamble to the Code, members of the Association are obliged to fulfill four major duties: (a) preserve archaeological heritage for current and future generations, (b) conduct professional archaeological works, (c) disseminate their work to make them widely available, (d) provide non-destructive access to archaeological heritage.

The Code further identified their three major responsibilities to (1) archaeological heritage, (2) society and (3) fellow archaeologists. As regards the responsibility to archaeological heritage, the Code imposes an obligation to the members to convey a message on significance of archaeological heritage to the decision-making bodies, both governmental and local. It is required that the archaeological heritage be preserved in situ. Rescue archaeological works need to be conducted according to the highest professional standards and it is recommended to avoid excavations whenever possible and replace them by other methods, mainly non-invasive and archive. Archaeologists are obliged to produce a thorough and detailed documentation of all elements of archaeological heritage. They cannot be involved in any illegal trade of antiquities and non-scientific acquiring of archaeological data. They should also actively react to any illegal trade of antiquities and illegal excavations and should not create private collections of archaeological materials. The Code also expects the members of the Association to treat human remains recovered during excavations with due respect.

As regards the responsibility to society, the member of the Association is obliged to provide competent information about the results of archaeological projects using all possible media. He needs to be engaged in relations with local community and duly respects culture, tradition and religion of these groups.

The longest is the list of Code's obligations to fellow archaeologists. It is required that archaeological works are conducted at the highest level and apply the newest methods and techniques. Archaeologists should not get involved in any project not in accord with their competences and specialisations. While doing contract excavations, they should not enter into any conflict of interest; in particular they cannot play a double role of an expert involved in contracting the works and the excavator. Archaeologists are explicitly obliged to systematically carry out fieldwork and carefully document them, be responsible for storage of archaeological materials and field documentation and have the preliminary results of the works available not later than 6 months after their completion. They need to fully respect appropriate legal conditions and regulations during contract archaeological works. The Code makes it clear that it is unethical to steal ideas and discoveries from others and use unpublished MA dissertations and grant applications. The members working at universities are obliged to provide students with the most recent knowledge.

A similar situation took shape in Hungary. The Budapest History Museum was the first institution that addressed ethical issues in Hungarian archaeology. It developed a code of practice for contract archaeology in Budapest already in the 1980s. Archaeological recovery was deliberately integrated within the process of investments. The document advocated a need of completing a thorough documentation and obliged archaeologists to publish reports after each excavation (Wollak and Raczky 2012:117).

The major document regulating ethical issues in Hungarian archaeology is the *Code of Ethics of the Association of Hungarian Archaeologists* (Magyar Régész Szövetség) adopted in 2006 and enforced in 2007. It obliges the members of the Association to abide by professional ethical standards. The first bloc of issues stresses a significance of archaeology for the public. It makes the members aware of consequences of their work in terms of the impact upon both archaeological community and the general public. Archaeological heritage is non-renewable resource, so any work needs to take into account sustainability criteria and be properly documented, and its results are widely available. The contract works need to meet high criteria and be transparent, predictable and verifiable. Archaeologists need also to be aware that the interpretation of the archaeological heritage has impact upon different segments of the public. Furthermore, they are obliged to treat heritage of different groups with due respect and without any prejudices.

The second major bloc comprises recommendation to heritage. The document requires the members of the Association be well aware of the significance of archaeological heritage. Hence, they need to limit excavations as a destructive technique to the minimum and are obliged to properly store archaeological materials. They should not be in a possession of any archaeological finds and collections.

The next set of issues tackles professionalism of archaeological work. The document expects archaeologists to constantly improve their skills and quality of professional performance. They need to behave professionally as regards relations with the co-workers, and timely produce excavation reports and required analyses. They are also obliged to maintain proper relations with archaeological heritage institutions and cooperate without any prejudges with all individuals otherwise involved in the work with archaeological heritage.

The Code reiterates that archaeologists should respect needs of their peers and make the results of their work available to them. Those involved in contract works need to establish good relations with the investors. They should make their work sustainable and in coordination with activities of other professional groups. They must also comply with contractual obligations and no compromises and concessions with the client may impact the quality of works.

The Code also explicitly stresses importance of relations with society. It requires making all the works available to the public, which needs to be regularly informed about the progress of them. More generally, archaeologists are expected to work closely with other stakeholders to protect archaeological heritage.

The other Central-Eastern European country that deliberately and explicitly tackled issues of ethics in archaeological practice is Romania. The *Code of Conduct for Archaeology in Romania* was approved by the National Commission for Archaeology (Comisia Naţională de Arheologie) in 2000. It is a special legal body with advisory role in cultural heritage for the Ministry of Culture and works under the umbrella of the Romanian Academy. The document specifies a range of obligations archaeologists have to the public and professional community (see Musteaţă 2009).

The Code explicitly refers to the regulations and recommendations specified in the ICOMOS *Charter for the Protection and Management of the Archaeological Heritage* from 1990. It obliges archaeologists to preserve archaeological heritage using all legal means. Their works need to meet the highest professional standards and they are obliged to keep the general public informed about them. Before the beginning of any fieldwork, archaeologists are obliged to make the prior environmental and social assessment on local communities. Archaeologists should not be involved in any form of illicit trade of antiquities and should not be pursing a profit obtained directly from archaeological heritage. They are obliged to inform the component authorities about any thread to archaeological heritage.

A special section of the Code deals with the profession. The document obliges archaeologists to work at the highest professional level and constantly improve their skills and competences. They should not engage in any work for which they are not properly trained. They are also obliged to professionally publish results of their works. All unpublished materials can be published following a written permission from the author.

Important part of the Code comprises the contract archaeology-related issues. It obliges archaeologists to abide by legal regulations, and have a good understating of the organizational structure, responsibilities and role of different institutions.

They should not be in any conflict of interest and refrain from getting involved in any works if they feel incompetent. They need to be aware of their obligations as contractors of archaeological works. The document obliges archaeologists to meet adopted standards for archaeological research and make the results of their work available to the public.

Final Remarks

Ethical concerns in contemporary archaeology of Central-Eastern Europe have hardly been debated to date. Hence, their numerous facets remain largely unexplored and can only be grasped intuitively and implicitly. As there is no explicit record of any in-depth debate, publications or controversies, it is unclear what ethical mandates actually mean. The fiasco of the Malta Convention in delivering archaeology as a public service further blurred the potentially emerging ethical concerns of archaeological practice beyond the conduct of fieldwork.

Archaeology of Central-Eastern Europe has been practiced in the circumstances in which both its practitioners and the public originate from the same cultural milieu. Hence, both major stakeholders of archaeological heritage share similar values and worldviews originating from common ontology and metaphysics. Hence, no major clash between competing positions is on play and archaeology is communicated to the public in an expert mode and any feedback from potential stakeholders of archaeological heritage is not heart, assuming such a voice at all exist. Hence, we deal with pretty standardized ethical concerns and there is hardly any multicultural ethics, maybe except for Gypsies in Slovakia and Hungary.

This peculiar cultural situation is then responsible for a limited impact of broad ethical concerns, which are largely limited to disciplinary issues. In particular, they clearly refer to how highly commercialised conditions of practicing archaeology impact a quality of archaeological works and their ability to properly and correctly reconstruct the past. This is manifested by a range of relatively similar codes of practice adopted across the region.

These circumstances have been shaping a character of archaeology in Central-Eastern Europe having far-reaching consequences for different facets of archaeological practice. They have manifested themselves in different formats and intensity. Such issues as illegal trade, reckless excavations, damage to archaeological heritage and inefficient legal frameworks have been identified and firstly tackled in terms of administrative and organisational regulations, penalisation and access to contact works (e.g. Gediga 2012; Michalik 2012). They were mainly approached from the legal, administrative and organisational standpoints trying to improve contracts on rescue works, and standardise procedures, documentation protocols, storage facilities, etc. (e.g. Marciniak 2011; Bozóki-Ernyey and Pasztor 2012; Wollak and Raczky 2012).

In subsequent years, some countries of Central-Eastern Europe, like Hungary, Poland and Romania, went on to adopt codes of conduct and codes of ethics while others, like Slovakia (Michalik 2012, personal communication), had chosen not to follow this path. The major ethical concern was professional standards to be met amidst increasing pressures of extensive fieldwork (see Wollak and Raczky 2012:115).

The analysis of existing codes from three Central-Eastern countries revealed striking similarities between them. They clearly refer to *the EAA Code of Practice* and the *Principle of Conduct for Archaeologists Involved in Contract Archaeological Work.* They echo these documents by addressing major issues triggered by uncontrolled commercialisation of archaeological profession, rapid increase of fieldwork, corruption, lack of good-quality excavations and increasing role of public engagement. They all stress a need of preserving archaeological heritage amidst the large infrastructure works and intense agriculture, conducting archaeological works at the highest level, disseminating the results to the peers and different segments of the general public as well as explicitly condemning illegal trade of antiquities and objects of art.

In general, an investigation of broader ethical facets of archaeology and archaeological practice in Central-Eastern Europe is badly needed. It would require systematic and long-lasting projects, which by no means is an easy and straightforward task. The region, which may look homogeneous from outside, is in fact very diverse with complex historical trajectories and different intellectual traditions. Last but not least, a number of different languages spoken will not make such a task easier.

References

Bloemers, J. H. F. (2002). German archaeology at risk? A neighbour's critical review of tradition, structure and serendipity. In H. Härke (Ed.), *Archaeology, ideology and society. The German experience* (pp. 378–399). Frankfurt am Main: Peter Lang.

Bozóki-Ernyey, K.,& Pasztor, E. (2012). *Preventive archaeology in Hungary. Authentic development of foreign model without adaptation.* Unpublished manuscript.

Gediga, B. (2012). *Badania archeologiczne związane z budową autostrad to skandal na skalę europejską.* Gazeta: Pomorska.

Ginter, B., & Kobusiewicz, M. (2003). Zbiór zasad postępowania i norm etycznych środowiska archeologów w Polsce. http://www.archekom.pan.pl/index.php?option=com_content&view=article&id=68:zbior-zasad-postpowania-i-norm-etycznych-rodowiska-archeologow-w-polsce&catid=32:aktualnoci-i-wydarzenia&Itemid=46.

Härke, H. (1991). All quiet on the Western front? Paradigms, methods and approaches in West German archaeology. In I. Hodder (Ed.), *Archaeological theory in Europe. The last three decades* (pp. 187–222). London: Routledge.

Härke, H. (Ed.). (2000). *Archaeology, ideology and society. The German experience.* Frankfurt: Peter Lang.

Kobyliński, Z. (2001a). Quo vadis archaeologia? Introductory remarks. In Z. Kobyliński (Ed.), *Quo vadis archaeologia? Whither European archaeology in the 21st century?* (pp. 17–20). Warsaw: Institute of Archaeology and Ethnology Polish Academy of Sciences.

Kobyliński, Z. (2001b). Archaeological sources and archaeological heritage. New vision of the subject matter of archaeology. In Z. Kobyliński (Ed.), *Quo vadis archaeologia? Whither European archaeology in the 21st century?* (pp. 76–82). Warsaw: Institute of Archaeology and Ethnology Polish Academy of Sciences.

Kobyliński, Z. (2012). Etyka w archeologii. In S. Tabaczyński, A. Marciniak, D. Cyngot, & A. Zalewska (Eds.), *Przeszłość społeczna. Próba konceptualizacji* (pp. 178–189). Poznań: Wydawnictwo Poznańskie.

Lozny, L. (1998). Public archaeology or archaeology for the public? In W. Hensel, S. Tabaczyński, & P. Urbańczyk (Eds.), *Theory and practice of archaeological research. Volume III. Dialogue with the data. The archaeology of complex societies and its context in the '90s* (pp. 431–459). Warsaw: Institute of Archaeology and Ethnology Polish Academy of Sciences.

Marciniak, A. (2006). Central European archaeology at the crossroads. In R. Layton, S. Shennan, & P. Stone (Eds.), *A future for archaeology. The past in the present* (pp. 157–171). London: UCL Press.

Marciniak, A. (2011). Contemporary Polish archaeology in global context. In L. Lozny (Ed.), *Comparative archaeologies. A sociological view of the science of the past* (pp. 179–194). New York: Springer.

Marciniak, A. (2013). *Heritage archaeologies of the united Europe*. Unpublished manuscript.

Michalik, T. (2012). Archaeology in Slovakia. *Materials for the 18th Annual Meeting of European Association of Archaeologists in Helsinki.*

Musteaţă, S. (2009). Etica şi deontologia profesională în archeologie. Tyragetia, III(XVIII)/1:353–360.

Wollak, K., & Raczky, P. (2012). Large-scale preventive excavations in Hungary. In J. Bofinger & D. Krausse (Eds.), *Large-scale excavations in Europe: Fieldwork strategies and scientific outcome.* EAC Occasional Paper No. 6, Proceedings of the International Conference, Esslingen, (pp 115–136).

Wróblewska, L. (Ed.). (2000). *Etyka w archeologii.* Poznań: Instytucie Prahistorii Uniwersytetu.

Internet Resources

Code of Ethnics, Hungarian Association of Archaeologists: http://www.regeszet.org.hu/a-szovetseg/etikai-kodex/.

EAA Code of Practice. http://www.e-a-a.org/EAA_Code_of_Practice.pdf.

EAA Principle of Conduct. http://www.e-a-a.org/EAA_Princ_of_Conduct.pdf.

The Code of Conduct of Members of the Association of Polish Archaeologists. http://www.snap.org.pl/kodeks-postpowania-czonka-snap.

The Code of Conduct for Archaeology in Romania. http://www.cimec.ro/Arheologie/cod_deont_arh.htm.

Chapter 6
Europe: Beyond the Canon

Víctor M. Fernández

Undoubtedly the best approach to the common normative practice in European archaeology is to examine the "codes of practice" produced by the various associations of European archaeologists. Following a review of a few of them (European Association of Archaeologists, those of UK and Spain, as well as a comparison with the US code) a number of general principles can be drawn that make up the ethical "canon" of what we might call the mainstream "Western archaeology."[1]

In most cases, archaeological activity includes scientific research, protection, conservation, restoration, assessment, and dissemination of the archaeological heritage. Archaeologists are the "stewards" of the archaeological record, acting both as "caretakers" to preserve and "advocates" to defend (Lynott and Wylie 1995a, b). Other principles that appear as indisputable in the codes are to control and finish the work once started; to get informed about it before beginning; to delegate to specialists when a subject is not mastered; to have independence of judgment; to serve the community and maintain confidentiality; to avoid corruption (e.g., using insider information or paying commissions for getting employment contracts); to avoid trading or purchasing illicit artifacts; to respect the intellectual property in the publications; to keep safely the documentation from the fieldwork; and to protect the sites and the surrounding environment.

The codes also link professional ethics and scientific quality, recommending the latest methodology and techniques, as recognized currently by the pairs of the profession (or its mainstream). It is also advised to choose, from among several alternative research methods, the one that is less destructive to the site. Given the fast

[1](http://e-a-a.org/codes.htm; http://new.archaeologyuk.org/best-practice; http://www.ceab.es/divulgacion/codigo-deontologico-del-profesional-de-la-arqueologia-2.html; http://www.saa.org/AboutTheSociety/PrinciplesofArchaeologicalEthics/tabid/203/Default.aspx; all accessed august, 2014)

V.M. Fernández (✉)
Departamento de Prehistoria, Universidad Complutense de Madrid, 28040 Madrid, Spain
e-mail: victormf@ucm.es

C. Gnecco, D. Lippert (eds.), *Ethics and Archaeological Praxis*,
Ethical Archaeologies: The Politics of Social Justice 1,
DOI 10.1007/978-1-4939-1646-7_6

progress in excavation and analysis methodology, there are strong recommendations to preserve a substantial part of the archaeological record for future study. The more difficult is the preservation, the more complete will be the excavation. The US code goes so far as to recommend the excavation of a nonthreatened site only when it is expected to yield special information or nonexistent in other threatened sites or museum records from previous excavations (Lynott and Wylie 1995b:30).

Related to the previous issue is the question of preventive archaeology. In recent years, companies, mostly private, have carried out a high percentage of archaeological fieldwork and consequently the public research organizations are responsible for increasingly fewer sites (Cumberpatch and Blinkhorn 2001).

A case in which there is also general agreement is the reference to the publication of the results, which must be "diligent" ("with the minimum delay" in the European code, "within a reasonable time" in the American). The American code treats the awkward question of intellectual property of the data and information by the archaeologists, which is acknowledged for a "reasonable period." The European code is much more specific on this issue, admitting an initial period of confidentiality for 6 months, after which the term of the obligation to make public the results starts to run, up to a deadline 10 years after that marks the end of the right of the archaeologists on their findings.

The codes also address the relations of archaeology and society, a subject where most often appear the conflicts considered by postmodern/multicultural criticism. In general, the codes claim that archaeological work is not only for the benefit of scientific knowledge but also for the sustainable development of the community and the economic empowerment of the area where the research is performed. However, the problems begin with the diversity of social concepts, which do not always coincide with the archaeological position. Thus we have the idea proposed by M. Parker-Pearson for the code of ethics of the British Institute of Archaeologists, i.e., to respect the wishes of the public, where known, in the handling of human remains. For example, in the case of Christian graves, whose bones belonged to believers in their future resurrection, a minimal disruption to them should be guaranteed (Parker-Pearson 1995). This recommendation relates, however, to the sensitivity of current populations, and not the past which often is unknown; for example, when people living near the site somehow feel themselves the descendants or related to the archaeological population (Marshall 2002; Atalay 2012). It must be understood that these feelings are not essential but historical and changing: when I begun to excavate in Sudanese Nubia in the 1980s I was prompted by the central Heritage authorities to dig the supposed grave of a Muslim saint—in the hope to find an important ancient grave underneath. Yet when I continued investigating in Central Sudan in the 1990s, just after the radical Islamic coup of 1989, we could not even make superficial survey in any area where recent graves were noticeable (Fernández 2011:42–44).

The previous paragraph introduces us to the key issue in any ethical code. They are universal by definition, and this is one of their greatest merits. They have undoubtedly contributed to increase the quality of archaeological research, both in scientific and ethical terms. But from that same uniformity come their main problems, for as general rules the codes are based on a single universal notion of ethics, which in turn comes from an idea of society as a homogeneous whole

(Tarlow 2001). However, society is intrinsically divided and can never be spoken of as a single entity. As Sarah Tarlow aptly put it: "the dependence of ethics on shared cultural beliefs also gives rise to problems in negotiating between groups in the present whose expectations of ethical practice arise from different beliefs" (Tarlow 2006: 215).

In Europe, the division cuts principally through social classes, but ethnicity issues are being raised with greater force. With respect to archaeology, I think an "advanced" ethics should take into account that the "scientific-rational" stance that "cares and represents" what we call the "archaeological record" needs not be necessarily exclusive of other approaches, some of them very old but also a few recent ones. Different viewpoints about archaeology can be found among us, e.g., in local and farmer people, religious groups (among them not the less important are the "pseudoarchaeologists" or the "new agers"), private collectors (and their necessary correlate, the looters), immigrants, etc.

The conflicts with local populations living near the archaeological sites can be more frequent than normally expected in our "modern" countries. The novel *El Tesoro* (*The treasure* 1983) by Spanish writer Miguel Delibes describes humorously the tensions aroused in a local farming community on the occasion of the discovery and excavation of a Bronze Age rich hoard, based on actual events. The problem, of course, is the local widespread feeling that foreign robbers deprive them of their ancestors' riches. Increasingly less anyway, the newspapers inform of similar clashes for the same or related reasons (e.g., *El País*, December 10, 1987). My guess is that these problems are more acute in the developing countries than in Europe. Curiously, just before writing this paper I had a similar difficulty while excavating a Catholic mission site from the seventeenth century in Central Ethiopia. The village administrator reported to the regional capital government that we were robbing the hidden treasures of the Ghimb Giyorgis site (the ancient mission of Sarka). The result, after 1 day of bureaucratic mess, was a new official representative joining the team, coming from the local level, which added to the already present two persons from the federal and regional ranks.

This issue clearly refers to the thorny debate about who are the real owners of the archaeological findings (Young 2006). The well-known Iberian sculpture of the "Lady of Elche" (fifth to fourth centuries BC) is a paradigmatic illustration of these problems. Found and appreciated first by Spanish workers and specialists at the end of the nineteenth century, it was legally acquired by the Louvre Museum in Paris, where it remained until it was exchanged for other artworks with the Vichy regime during the German occupation of France. Due to its cultural significance to the whole country, it remained in the National Archaeological Museum in Madrid, but in 2006 there was a sharp debate between the central government and the Elche municipality, which reclaimed its presence in the local museum. The Lady's is not an isolated case, far from it. Gathered again from my poor personal experience, when I dug in an Iberian site in the central Mancha region south of Madrid in the 1980s, we found the broken pieces of two big painted jars, more than 1 m in height. After their restoration, they were proudly exhibited at the entrance of the local town hall. However, as soon as the finding was noticed in the province capital, the pieces were forcefully transferred to the provincial museum. When I spoke with the museum director to try moving back the vessels to the small town, he replied that by law they should be in there.

Archaeologists' ethical norms must also include our attitudes towards those archaeological "fantasies" derogatorily called pseudoarchaeology (Fagan 2006). We must acknowledge that an important part of the "public," even the educated one (Feder 2006), feels more attracted to those stories of alien and disappeared civilizations, UFOs, crop circles, pharaoh's curses, and other supposedly bizarre events, than to our serious and well-argued articles and textbooks. Maybe the main reason for that is that pseudoarchaeologies are presented in a more narrative and exciting style, and probably a great percentage of actual archaeology students and practitioners were first attracted to the topic when reading those stories (irrespective of the fact that many of their authors are probably moved by unethical goals).

As it has been signaled (Feder 2006: 94–95), a usual posture of archaeology professionals is to ignore the pseudoscientific claims and leave them unaddressed in the classroom and the scholar papers, letting this task to a few willful popularizers of the discipline, and this is most surely a mistake. It is our responsibility to share with the students and the general public the results of our research in a way as open and democratic as possible. Also to understand the hunger for mystery inherent to the human mind (and not infrequently fostered by our own, sensationalist, way of presenting some "great discoveries," cf. Reece 2006: 104) and exploit it, replacing contempt and elitism for collaboration for the sake of a true popular undertaking of archaeology (see the nuanced analysis of the "Mother Goddess" cultists and the site of Çatalhöyük in Meskell 1998). Here we do not need belief but tolerance, "tolerance as a deliberate position that we take up and tolerance that proceeds from our disbelief" (Byrne 2009:88).

Another key ethical issue in archaeology refers to its relations to the illegal antiquities market and the looting of archaeological sites. As we saw before, the position of professional archaeology towards this question is of outright rejection, even to decline the scientific study of any object coming from the illegal market and whose context is unknown. However, the illegal antiques traffic shows no signs of abating, and large sections of society seem to have at least a sympathetic attitude towards it. Is there anything we can do from our scientific position to improve the situation?

A few studies have dealt with the looters' topic trying to understand it from an "ethnographic" point of view, e.g., in Alaska, Sicily, or Greece (Hollowell 2006; Migliore 1991; Antoniadou 2009). An argument acceptable by some archaeologists would be "that a person has a 'right to loot' and to sell artifacts for subsistence purposes if other alternatives for livelihood are not available" (S. Hardy, in Hollowell 2006:73). Even though in most European countries the subsistence excuse does not seem very pertinent at first look, in some cases the illegal traffic appears as one of the few alternatives to unemployment and even hunger. The biggest capture of archaeological looters in Spain took place in 2007, with more than 300,000 pieces recovered. Among the private collectors were "doctors and businessmen" from Seville, Barcelona, and Madrid, and the looters lived an apparent honest life in Andalucian villages where most of the youngsters are unemployed (*El País*, February 8, 2007).

Understandably, nothing is said about the ethnic or religious affiliation of the delinquents, but personally, I've been informed that Roms could be connected to the traffic in other parts of Spain (see Tijhuis 2011: 93 for a related instance in France). This would be a curious case of "acquaintance" with the past of a people without or endorsed with very scant material heritage (Bánffy 2013). Anyway, the biggest looter of ancient, especially religious, art in Spain was René Alphonse van den Berghe, known as "Erik the Belgian," who was very active since the 1970s and after his stay in prison wrote a book cynically entitled "For the art's sake" (van den Berghe 2012).

From a multicultural ethical view, we must acknowledge that looters can be "people who sought more intimate and personal meanings from the 'distant' past" and that "they choose to approach the material past outside official preferences and agendas" (Antoniadou 2009: 251–252). In addition, "collectors argue that artifacts lie unseen in locked dark basements and reports are never published, and feel that they are better stewards and give objects more care and exposure than most museums" (Hollowell 2006:87). As it is the case with other sectors considered in this paper, here too the need for us archaeologists to open to other societal stances appears quite clear.

We come now to the most intricate problem, and one that probably will go worse in the next years, for heritage in Europe: the increasing presence of population migrated from other parts of the world. As Cornelius Holtorf very aptly expressed: "What challenges and changes the role of heritage management in Europe in our age is not oppression by immigrants of indigenous minorities but, if anything, an oppression of immigrants by indigenous majorities" (Holtorf 2009:672). For many of these people, who "now occupy multiple frames, the in-between or 'third spaces'—the homes-away-from-homes—of the post-colonial metropolis" (Hall 2008:225), their original heritage lies in another part of the world except in the cases when is presented here, with its derogative aura of exoticism, in the ethnographical museums. That heritage plays an important role in their lives can be assessed by the occasional presence in the immigrants homes of pictures that immediately recall it, be it photographs of Mecca for Muslims or paintings or their gods or religious leaders in the case of Hinduists.

In Spain, there is the interesting case of Muslim immigrants from Northern Africa living in the same area of the important Muslim kingdom of Al-Andalus during the Middle Ages. Even though the importance of this original and rich heritage has been occasionally exploited by andalusian politicians to mark a difference of their autonomous region with respect to the central government (Dietz 2004), the dominant culture there, as in the rest of Spain, is eminently Christian, and two recent examples will suffice to illustrate it. During the last decades, there have been extensive archaeological excavations in the central part of the city of Granada, where a big part is occupied by an enormous Muslim cemetery from the times of the Nazari kingdom. Even if the number of Muslims living in the province approaches 20,000 (including not only Maghrebians but also local people recently converted), the local authorities ignored the formal request by this community that the recovered human bones were transferred to a new Muslim cemetery in the outskirts of the town (http://www.webislam.com, March 2, 2006).

Another problem arose in 2010 when a group of Muslims were forbidden to pray in the ancient mosque of Cordoba (a World Heritage site of exceptional historical and artistic importance). The local authorities considered that the mosque had been converted to a Catholic church soon after the Christian conquest and thus the use by other religions should not be allowed (Monteiro 2010). Following the recent turn towards a more conservative position by the Spanish Catholic church, the city's bishop has tried also to change the building's name (usually "mosque-cathedral") to be only "cathedral" (El País, October 12, 2010). That all this trouble has hardly affected and even being known by the mass of Spanish population is just another evidence of the sheer subaltern position suffered by African immigrants in many parts of Spain and the rest of Europe.

There seem to be two extreme possibilities for a modern state to create a minimum of shared cultural values among its residents, exemplified by Holtorf (2009:676–678) in Denmark and Sweden. The first has created a national historical canon that all immigrants must know before acquiring the nationality, the immigrant's own heritage being often overlooked, while the second acknowledges the need to integrate the heritage of foreign residents in order to build a true multicultural society. The reasons for the second option are not only ethical but also historical: the past of Sweden, and indeed of the whole Europe, is composed of a long list of cultural changes and migrations of peoples. Also, as K. Kristiansen aptly perceived (cit. in Holtorf 2009:674), "There are fewer similarities between a Danish Iron Age farmer and a present day farmer than there are between a present day Danish farmer and a Pakistan immigrant."

The resulting ideas from this paper could be concentrated in only one: as archaeologists we need to take into account and to address intellectually and personally the whole of European society, composed of even more varieties of "public" that those identified more than two decades ago by McManamon (1991). Now that the economic crisis has dreadfully affected the archaeological activity (as a result of the sudden halt in construction activity, especially in southern Europe), many of us have lamented not having made the most of the previous "bubble" period to communicate more intensively with local and general public, which in turn would surely be more sympathetic with our activity in the current lean years (cf. the contributions in Almansa Sánchez 2011).

However, the core of this paper goes beyond the scope of the "general" to concentrate on the "particular," represented by the fringe groups and ideologies outside our mainstream canon. The reasons to this "leap forward" are eminently ethical (since those groups frequently represent the disenfranchised locales in our continent), but also epistemological: in order to deepen and productively renovate our way of research we need to deal with different forms of knowledge, including the nonacademic one (Appadurai et al. 2001).

Obviously the final end is to move towards a multicultural society, but not the one model that converts the "other" in a half-tolerated "exotic" whose unpleasant features have been erased from the picture, as criticized by Žižek (1997; see an archaeological counterpart in Gnecco 2012). It is not an issue of undemanding tolerance from a superiority stand but of true equal rights to all parts, being well aware that the real danger to archaeology and heritage does not come today from different cultures and conceptions but from the same core of our western rationality, represented by the capitalist system. Making "good" use of the economic depression, ultraliberal politicians are unashamedly dismantling the European welfare state (the same that a few years ago was considered a substantial part of our identity as a social group); in which affects to the cultural heritage, for example the new law prepared for parliamentary approval in my region, Madrid, will gravely reduce the protection of sites and monuments, for the sake of "free economic growth." It is my opinion that an epistemological extension of the scope of archaeology, in the "cosmopolitan" sense advocated by this paper (Meskell 2009), would put us in a better position to resist the hard assaults that we are to confront in the next years.

References

Almansa Sánchez, J. (Ed.). (2011). *El futuro de la arqueología en España*. Madrid: JAS.

Antoniadou, I. (2009). Reflections on an archaeological ethnography of "looting" in Kozani, Greece. *Public Archaeology, 8*(2–3), 246–261.

Appadurai, A., Chadha, A., Hodder, I., Jachman, T., & Witmore, C. (2001). The globalization of archaeology and heritage. A discussion with Arjun Appadurai. *Journal of Social Archaeology, 1*(1), 35–49.

Atalay, S. (2012). *Community-based archaeology. Research with, by, and for Indigenous and local communities*. Berkeley: University of California Press.

Bánffy, E. (2013). The nonexistent Roma archaeology and nonexisting Roma archaeologists. In P. F. Biehl & C. Prescott (Eds.), *Heritage in the context of globalization. Europe and the Americas* (pp. 77–83). New York: Springer.

Byrne, D. (2009). Archaeology and the fortress of rationality. In L. Meskell (Ed.), *Cosmopolitan archaeologies* (pp. 68–88). Durham: Duke University Press.

Cumberpatch, C., & Blinkhorn, P. (2001). Clients, contractors, curators and archaeology: Who owns the past? In M. Pluciennik (Ed.), *The responsibilities of archaeologists. Archaeology and ethics* (pp. 39–55). Oxford: British Archaeological Reports, International Series 981.

Delibes, M. (1983). *El tesoro*. Barcelona: Destino.

Dietz, G. (2004). Frontier hybridisation or culture clash? Transnational migrant communities and sub-national identity politics in Andalusia, Spain. *Journal of Ethnic and Migration Studies, 30*(6), 1087–1112.

Fagan, G. C. (Ed.). (2006). *Archaeological fantasies. How pseudoarchaeology misrepresents the past and misleads the public*. London: Routledge.

Feder, K. L. (2006). Skeptics, fence sitters, and true believers. Student acceptance of an improbable prehistory. In G. Fagan (Ed.), *Archaeological fantasies. How pseudoarchaeology misrepresents the past and misleads the public* (pp. 71–95). London: Routledge.

Fernández, V. M. (2011). *Los años del Nilo. Arqueología y memoria de Sudán y Etiopía*. Madrid: Alianza.

Gnecco, C. (2012). Arqueología multicultural. Notas intempestivas. *Complutum, 23*(2), 93–102.

Hall, S. (2008). Whose heritage? Un-settling "The Heritage", re-imagining the post-nation. In G. Fairclough, R. Harrison, J. H. Jameson, & J. Schofield (Eds.), *The heritage reader* (pp. 219–228). London: Routledge (Orig. publ. in Third Text, 46, 1999).

Hollowell, J. (2006). Moral arguments on subsistence digging. In C. Scarre & G. Scarre (Eds.), *The ethics of archaeology. Philosophical perspectives on archaeological practice* (pp. 69–93). Cambridge: Cambridge University Press.

Holtorf, C. (2009). A European perspective on indigenous and immigrant archaeologies. *World Archaeology, 41*(4), 672–681.

Lynott, M. J., & Wylie, A. (Eds.). (1995a). *Ethics in American archaeology: Challenges for the 1990s*. Washington: Society for American Archaeology.

Lynott, M. J., & Wylie, A. (1995b). Stewardship: The central principle of archaeological ethics. In M. J. Lynott & A. Wylie (Eds.), *Ethics in American archaeology: Challenges for the 1990s* (pp. 28–32). Washington: Society for American Archaeology.

Marshall, Y. (2002). What is community archaeology? *World Archaeology, 34*(2), 211–219.

McManamon, F. (1991). The many publics of archaeology. *American Antiquity, 56*(1), 121–130.

Meskell, L. (1998). Oh my Goddess! Archaeology, sexuality and ecofeminism. *Archaeological Dialogues, 5*(2), 126–142.

Meskell, L. (Ed.). (2009). *Cosmopolitan archaeologies*. Durham: Duke University Press.

Migliore, S. (1991). Treasure hunting and pillaging in Sicily: Acquiring a deviant identity. *Anthropologica, 33*, 161–175.

Monteiro, L. (2010). The mezquita of Córdoba is made of more than bricks: Towards a broader definition of the "Heritage" protected at the World Heritage Sites. *Archaeologies, 7*(2), 312–328.

Parker-Pearson, M. (1995). Ethics and the dead in British archaeology. *The Field Archaeologist, 23*, 17–18.

Reece, K. (2006). Memoirs of a true believer. In G. Fagan (Ed.), *Archaeological fantasies. How pseudoarchaeology misrepresents the past and misleads the public* (pp. 95–106). London: Routledge.

Tarlow, S. (2001). Decoding ethics. *Public Archaeology, 1*, 245–259.

Tarlow, S. (2006). Archaeological ethics and the people of the past. In C. Scarre & G. Scarre (Eds.), *The ethics of archaeology. Philosophical perspectives on archaeological practice* (pp. 199–216). Cambridge: Cambridge University Press.

Tijhuis, E. (2011). The trafficking problem. A criminological perspective. In S. Manacorda & D. Chappel (Eds.), *Crime in the art and antiquities world. Illegal traffic in cultural property* (pp. 87–97). New York: Springer.

van den Berghe, R. ("Erik el belga") (2012). *Por amor al arte. Memorias del ladrón más famoso del mundo*. Barcelona: Planeta.

Young, J. O. (2006). Cultures and the ownership of archaeological finds. In C. Scarre & G. Scarre (Eds.), *The ethics of archaeology. Philosophical perspectives on archaeological practice* (pp. 15–31). Cambridge: Cambridge University Press.

Žižek, S. (1997). Multiculturalism, or, the cultural logic of multinational capitalism. *New Left Review, 225*, 28–51.

Chapter 7
New Worlds: Ethics in Contemporary North American Archaeological Practice

Neal Ferris and John R. Welch

Introduction

The challenge to writing a summary of archaeological ethics for North America is that we feel thoroughly unqualified to do so, as, we suspect, any other archaeologist caught in a reflexive moment might also. From where we sit, as academic archaeologists perched on either side of the vastness of Canada, and collectively engaged in practice, research and the archaeological communities of eastern and western Canada, the southern USA, and global discourses surrounding contemporary archaeological practice, we feel only marginally qualified to speak to broad trends occurring across all of Canada, never mind the multipliers of diversity and scale that complicate our ability to comprehend the range of practices occurring across the USA.

And yet, perhaps this is our first point: being an archaeologist situated in Canada and engaged with North American archaeology invites a certain reflexivity about relevancy, marginality, categories of practice and place in the profession. It is certainly the case, for example at Society for American Archaeology meetings, within American publications and so on, that while Canadian-based practitioners tend to be intimately aware of the range and breadth of research and issues coming out of American contexts, it is not uncommon to find that many of our colleagues on the other side of the border are somewhat or mostly unaware of relevant Canadian archaeological research occurring, in some cases, within a few miles of that border.

N. Ferris (✉)
Department of Anthropology, Western University,
SC 3331, 1151 Richmond Street, London, ON, Canada
e-mail: nferris@uwo.ca

J.R. Welch
Department of Archaeology, Simon Fraser University,
8888 University Drive, Burnaby, BC, Canada, V5A1S6
e-mail: welch@sfu.ca

C. Gnecco, D. Lippert (eds.), *Ethics and Archaeological Praxis*,
Ethical Archaeologies: The Politics of Social Justice 1,
DOI 10.1007/978-1-4939-1646-7_7

Canadian archaeology and research seem to be beyond the pale in a fair bit of American literature. Indeed, it is not uncommon to see archaeological cultural zones or regions in the USA depicted on maps in publications as ending where national borders exist today, with only blank space or grey shaded areas depicted north of that contemporary border.

It is also not unheard of to have conversations with well-meaning American colleagues, only to experience the border between these two countries conceptually erased in the course of inclusive discussions about "American Archaeology" or having to explain that NAGPRA and other Federal US archaeological regulations do not operate in Canada. Or, in one rather surreal occasion, hearing an American colleague complaining that the Society for Historical Archaeology had not hosted a meeting in a "foreign" country for too long (while sitting at a planning meeting during their conference hosted in central Canada at the time).

It also bears mentioning that similar issues pertain to Mexican archaeology, though one might argue that the linguistic, cultural and institutional divides along the USA-Mexico border are sharper (not to mention the "border fence" and other impediments to institutional and intellectual exchange). And, finally, it is also the case that regional specialisations within North American archaeology also breed borders, communities and limits to awareness and conceptual understandings. These insular communities and conceptual framings of what archaeology is can be difficult to overcome when entering from elsewhere, as Welch has found negotiating research interests and career development that has joined the American southwest with the Canadian northwest.

These observations are not offered to exorcise nationalistic or even regional insecurities (or perhaps not entirely) over the slight chaffing this gentle and unintentional imperialism can engender, but because this captures one of the challenges in writing about how the global/multicultural ethical discourse affects specific praxis in North America. At a general level, and while there are many, many individual archaeologists who are exceptions to this rule, it can seem that North American practice tends to be fairly insular—regionally and nationally—to broader, global discourses (but note specific counter-examples such as Altschul 2010; Atalay 2012; MacEachern 2010; and various authors in King 2011b; Messenger and Smith 2010; Nicholas 2010b; Nicholas and Wylie 2009; Trigger 1980, 1984, 2006; and in Rockman and Flatman 2011).[1] This is not to say North American discourse does not engage with broader, global trends in archaeology; just that such engagements tend to be filtered through emphatically local discourses, and then manifest as internalised discussions germane to a largely domestic and regional North American archaeological form of praxis.

It also tends to be the case that "global" trends tend to be mostly extracted from the largely, readily accessible English language places of the world, such as the UK, and especially from similar, descendant colonial states (e.g. Australia, New Zealand, South Africa). Global thus tends to mean the largely "English-speaking" archaeological

[1] It is also worth pointing out that Bruce Trigger (e.g., 1980, 1984, 2006) pioneered the adoption of a global perspective on archaeological practice, and many others (e.g., Atalay 2012; McGuire 2008; Nicholas and Wylie 2009) regularly frame praxis within global contexts.

community the world over, and engagement is more for domestic consumption, rather than participatory at that global level ("they do things differently there", being a kind of end to the discussion of thinking beyond national borders).

What this means, at least to us, is that in North America ethical issues generally arise within a localised and distinct set of sensibilities and challenges, especially around notions of descendant or community group access to regional or national archaeological heritage. For example, the concept of "indigenous" is rarely problematised the way it has been elsewhere in the world (e.g. Gnecco and Ayala 2011; Holtorf 2009; Lane 2011; Trigger and Dalley 2010; but note Echo-Hawk 2010; Echo-Hawk and Zimmerman 2006; Nicholas 2010a; Watkins 2004). We would also argue we're only beginning to see in North America the conceptual unpacking and problematising of the differences between archaeology and heritage (e.g. King 2009, 2011b; Smith et al. 2010; Welch et al. 2009, 2011), which is a critical distinction between the internal act of doing archaeology and the external place where archaeological information beyond archaeology is variably made into a heritage of meaning and value for communities and descendant groups (cf. Harrison 2012; Smith 2004, 2006). In the absence of critically understanding the difference, archaeologists often mistakenly envision dialogue with publics beyond archaeology as necessary in order to convince these non-archaeologists why archaeology is important … to archaeologists. In other words control and authority dominate archaeological conceptions of archaeological heritage value, something others should appreciate, even embrace and promote, but never contest.[2] This sets up a fairly substantial "fail" if archaeologists seek to engage communities differently and inclusively but nonetheless operate under the assumption that it is their own, internal values that are shared beyond archaeology, and are what bring people to the archaeological heritage in the first place (see for example Carman 2005; Skeates 2000; Smith and Waterton 2009, 2012).

Another challenge to defining ethical trends in North American archaeology is that there really is no "North American archaeology", at least in a singular sense. Rather, and as is increasingly typical globally these days, archaeology is a fragmented enterprise. This includes the usual diversity of forms of practice, from scholarly research to government regulation, to commercial enterprise and to avocational pursuit. But there is also a palimpsest of conceptual framings over what archaeology is supposed to do in the act of making knowledge about the material past, ranging from regional cultural historical description to hard science analytics and multidisciplinary, lab-based studies, to interpretive, contextual narratives, to inclusive, multi-vocal participatory and collaborative practices, to educational and public engagements and to resource conservation and management. This diversity means that any kind of definitional inclusiveness implied in the word "archaeology"

[2] This is reflected in the development of ethical principles developed by the Society for American Archaeology in the 1990s (Lynott 1997; Lynott and Wylie 1995a) that embraced stewardship as a central, abiding principle of ethical conduct (Lynott and Wylie 1995b). This was challenged subsequently as simply reaffirming the archaeologist as authority and gate-keeper to the archaeological heritage (e.g., Groarke and Warrick 2006; Hamilakis 2007; Wylie 2005).

is sorely put to various tests across the breadth of the discipline. And likewise, within that fragmented imagining of the study of the material past, the concepts of "ethics" and "praxis" are highly variable and certainly contested.

Academic Ethics

Within academic settings, there has been a broad advancement in North America over the last couple of decades of what could be called an activist practice. For those who have embraced a focus on this contemporary form of archaeology, legacies of antiquarian impulses to collect are left behind, epistemological and moral limits to studying the past are engaged with and basic cultural historical inventory and description become as foreign to these practitioners as research on contemporary practice is to their more materially focused colleagues. Well intentioned to be sure, this activist practice tends to be on behalf of causes and communities and typically adopts multi-vocality in the form of community, collaborative, engaged, activist, public or indigenous archaeologies as the means of defining and undertaking archaeological research, and more critically, of sharing or re-centering authority beyond archaeology (e.g. Atalay 2006, 2012; Baram 2011; Bilosi and Zimmerman 1997; Blakey 2010; Colwell-Chanthaphonh 2012; Colwell-Chanthaphonh and Ferguson 2008; Dawson et al. 2011; Derry and Malloy 2003; Dongoske et al. 2000; Ferguson 1996; Ferris 2003; Hart 2011; Hodgetts 2013; Hollowell and Nicholas 2009; Kerber 2006; Killion 2008; LaRoche and Blakey 1997; Little and Shackel 2007; McDavid 2002; Nicholas 2005; Nicholas and Hollowell 2007; Nicholas and Andrews 1997; Sabloff 2008; Shackel and Chambers 2004; Silliman 2008; Stottmann 2010; Swidler et al. 1997; Watkins 2000, 2003, 2005; Welch and Ferguson 2007; Zimmerman 2005; Zimmerman et al. 2003). This work seeks to explore the role of archaeology as a broad social engagement in and with contemporary societies over the material past. Much of it is overtly revisionist to more conventional academic practices that situate archaeology as an internal, authorised investigation of intellectual curiosity driven by a "science-like" prerogative, and whose accountability is limited only to academic peers and institutions. Revisionist practice seeks to be inclusive, redresses colonial legacies embedded in archaeological conventions and is quick to acknowledge the broader implications of practice in contemporary society, and the overtly political nature of making meaning from the past in the present (e.g. Hamilakis 2007; McGuire 2008; Zimmerman et al. 2010).

A clear focus of this research is a reflexive understanding of the implications of archaeology as the contemporary act of engaging with the material heritage of place. This trend mirrors a growing dimension of global perspective that frames archaeology as heritage, reconsiders what is an "ethical" practice, engages the past as something made relevant in the present, undertakes ethnographies of practice, supports alternative archaeologies and postcolonial conceptualisations of archaeology and seeks to make space for multi-vocality otherwise missing in archaeological discourse (e.g. Castañeda and Matthews 2008; Edgeworth 2006; Habu et al. 2008;

Hamilakis 2011; Liebmann and Rizvi 2008; Lydon and Rizvi 2010; Mortensen and Hollowell 2008; Nicholas et al. 2011; Scarre and Scarre 2006; Schmidt and Patterson 1996; Silverman and Ruggles 2007).[3]

The research arising from these various inquiries makes the practice of archaeology, not the findings of archaeology, a central focus of study, and seeks to make overt the colonial legacies in practice, deconstructing Western intellectual epistemologies and institutional privileges that can subvert other ways of knowing the past and making meaning of the past for the present. However, a reflexive, activist archaeology is also found in more conventional knowledge-making research endeavours in North America. A notable example of this is the archaeological research arising from the material record of the last 500 years, encompassing the rise of a global colonialism and capitalism. This scholarship offers revisionist interpretations and practical tools for deconstructing the conventional narratives that had marginalised indigenous experiences in descendant colonial national histories and had previously framed indigenous experiences within a master or negative narrative of decline and ruin as the inevitable outcome of interaction with Europeans (Jordan 2008, 2009; Wilcox 2009). Revisionist archaeologies of the colonised demonstrate the vital role archaeology can and does play in re-centering that colonial legacy, and in engaging the contemporary, ongoing consequences of that history (e.g. Ferris 2009a; Ferris et al. 2014; Liebmann and Murphy 2011; Loren 2008; Martindale 2009; Oland et al. 2012; Oliver 2010; Orser 2012; Rubertone 2000; Silliman 2005, 2010). Likewise, the archaeologies of others marginalised from dominant narratives have also been recovered and re-situated as a result of this kind of reflexive research (e.g. Beaudoin et al. 2010; Chidester and Gadsby 2009; Mullins 1999, 2008; Ogundiran and Falola 2010; Singleton and Orser 2003).

A common thread across this activist practice and research on contemporary archaeological practice is a rejection of singular narratives in archaeological interpretations, especially those interpretations built on trait description, uncritical acceptance of historical accounts and models of cultural behaviour derived from earlier twentieth-century anthropological sensibilities. There is also an acceptance of contextual, interpretative frames in conceptual models, and a willingness to work with non-archaeological conceptions of the past to generate more robust and multivalent understandings of archaeological histories that reach beyond the marginalisation of those voices from dominant histories to better reflect the multiplicities of the past that were and are negotiated by both coloniser and colonised.

[3] This is also visible in various large scale research projects that have been funded over the last decade in Canada in particular, including the Intellectual Property in Cultural Heritage (IPinCH) project, which is exploring practices and prospects for the protection and culturally appropriate use of traditional knowledge and other IP issues embedded in the archaeological record and other sources of heritage (www.sfu.ca/ipinch/). Also, projects like the Reciprocal Research Network (www.rrnpilot.org/), Plateau Peoples' Web Portal (www.plateauportal.wsulibs.wsu.edu/), The Great Lakes Research Alliance (https://grasac.org/gks/gks_about.php) and Sustainable Archaeology, where the amassing and digitization of a region's archaeological collections provides the means of facilitating a change in practice and engagement in commercial and academic archaeology (sustainablearchaeology.org/).

It is fair to say that this kind of research and the broader revisionist studies of archaeology that engage in a de-centered, multicultural ethics can be and are perceived by some in the academy as de-stabilising to conventional academic orientations and ways of making meaning in North American archaeology. Indeed, efforts to re-align contemporary archaeological practice within a multicultural, multi-vocal, global ethical frame have been regularly dismissed as service, not research, in the academy, and have been aggressively challenged as a scholarship lacking "rigour"—the touchstone, legacy and defensive rebuttal of processualist calls for archaeology to be objective, science-like and resistant to other standpoints. Certainly some archaeologists perceive the inclusiveness of multiple perspectives within revisionist archaeological ethics as a kind of opening of the gates, facilitating an assault on the primacy of archaeology as the authoritative truth teller and sole interpreter of the material past (e.g. Fagan and Feder 2006; Mason 2006; McGhee 2004, 2008, 2010). While revisionist forms of practice in North America can be seen as embracing the kind of global, public ethics and praxis explored in this volume, other scholars see themselves as stewards or gatekeepers of the scientific integrity of archaeological meaning making, and assert an ethical imperative and praxis policing against loss of control, of ownership, of exclusive access to the record and of scientific validation.

Of course, there are also many practitioners who are largely content to pursue cultural historical description and normative analysis in North America today, and see little of relevance in discussions about archaeology at an intersection beyond archaeology, or feel the need to engage with debates around the political and philosophical fragmentation of what it means to be doing archaeology in the early twenty-first century. But in the exchanges between those who see archaeology as science under siege, and archaeology as an activist practice that has to be engaged beyond archaeology, there is a significant divide in even basic core understandings of what archaeology is and does, and what its role is or should be in contemporary society (compare, for example, McGhee 2008, 2010, to Colwell-Chanthaphonh et al. 2010; Nassaney 2012). While abstract theoretical wars over what archaeology is and how it makes meaning may have waned in the last decade, this more fundamental difference makes it difficult to contemplate imagining the ability to bridge or find some common ground … with fellow practitioners, let alone those outside archaeology.

Beyond Academic Archaeology

Ironic to the foregoing, however, is the readily recognised but rarely considered reality that the fragmented discourse and conceptual divide within academic archaeology is actually a relatively minor sideshow to what has come to dominate archaeological representations of practice across North America today. Currently, the vast majority of all archaeology practiced in North America—80–90 % are the figures typically quoted—is within commercial consultant or contract forms of practice, often referred to as cultural resource management (CRM), or more specifically, archaeological resource management (ARM; see Welch and Ferris 2014; see also Altschul and

Patterson 2010; Cleere 1984; Ferris 1998; Fox 1986; King 2002, 2008, 2011b; La Salle and Hutchings 2012; McGimsey and Davis 1977; McKay 1977; McManamon and Hatton 2000; McManamon et al. 2008; Messenger and Smith 2010; Roberts et al. 2004; Schiffer and Gumerman 1977c; Sebastian and Lipe 2009; Smith and Ehrenhard 1991; Stapp and Longenecker 2009; Williamson 2010; Zorzin 2011). The vast majority of this work occurs as a result of government-defined, -imposed, and -regulated development processes that require archaeological fieldwork to be undertaken before land impacts tied to these development projects can occur (e.g. Ferris 2002; Fowler 1995; King 2008; Neumann et al. 2010). And it is within this applied form of practice where archaeology is much more regularly and routinely negotiated and engaged with by society beyond academic corridors. As such, the implications ARM practice has for public and government perceptions of and support for archaeology are substantial, and far greater than the implications of academic practice.

The expense of ARM archaeology is typically absorbed by the proponent, which is a dynamic mix of development agents, ranging from federal, state/provincial and municipal entities to industrial resource harvesters, commercial/residential land developers and, in some jurisdictions, private landowners. The process followed by this mix of development proponents varies considerably from state to province, city to rural municipality and whether the development will impact public or private lands. In some regions ARM activities are only carried out for a small portion of the overall development impact footprint occurring in that region year to year, while in other parts of the USA and Canada ARM is part of most of if not all regulated land development activity.

The particular practices, standards and procedures followed by ARM archaeologists vary, to be sure, especially around expectations over the amount of the archaeological record to be documented, recovered and sampled. But in general these procedures aim, first, to identify archaeological sites present on lands scheduled for development impact, usually achieved through a combination of screening out lands that have a greater chance or "potential" for containing sites, and then having those lands physically surveyed by an archaeological crew (or partially surveyed to identify a representative range of sites present). Sites identified are then evaluated for value or significance—measurements typically defined as contributing to scientific archaeological knowledge, or heritage appreciation. Those sites deemed to be of value, either by arbitrarily imposed standards or individual professional judgements, are preserved while development occurs away from the locale, or much more commonly are excavated in part or whole prior to land alteration. While the cost of archaeological studies can range from a few thousand to a few million dollars, depending on the scale of the undertaking and development agency leading the work, typically these are relatively "modest" costs, representing a few percent or less of the overall investment to complete the undertaking and translate those costs into profit or social worth for the proponents and beneficiaries (see Altschul and Patterson 2010; Ferris 2004).

In effect, this process of conservation "works" because site management consists of screening, selecting, recovering and removing archaeologically relevant information and material from a given locale before that land is converted into whatever new use is planned. In other words, archaeological management enables regulated development planning by simply making archaeology one more item on the rote checklist of tasks to be accomplished in order for development to proceed. In effect, in this context archaeological ARM practice *is* development (Ferris 2000, 2002; Zorzin 2011).

And by dint of regulated definition or self-asserted criteria, all this archaeological work needs to be done by individuals who in some way are deemed qualified to serve the archaeological development process in these contexts. Professional organisations such as the Register of Professional Archaeologists define professionalism as consisting of a combination of field experience and academic achievement, the latter determined by the completion of a thesis MA.[4] Some governmental jurisdictions formally define these as minimums required to obtain full professional certification (e.g. Province of Ontario archaeological license qualifications), or set broad definitions of professional standards (for example, the US Secretary of the Interior's Standards and Guidelines for Archaeology and Historic Preservation, subject to interpretation by particular state historic preservation offices [SHPOs]).[5]

These variably regulated or self-defined and profession-based standards of qualification have meant that archaeologists carry the weight of state sanction and "official" authority: an authorised expertise by dint of regulated qualification, operating "on behalf of" the archaeological record to ensure conservation of that record—for archaeology and on behalf of a public heritage trust (e.g. Knudson and Keel 1995; Skeates 2000). This has significant ramifications for the position of the archaeologist in society, especially as the quantity of ARM activities has increased exponentially over the last several decades. Archaeologists in applied contexts are not just another informed opinion related to heritage; by state acknowledgement they are *the* experts in a theatre of contested heritage values that play out over the archaeological record between development proponents/landowners and their economic enterprise, on the one hand, local communities or others objecting to development plans and change, on the other, descendant groups that draw value and association from the archaeological heritage encompassed within developable parcels of land, on yet another hand, and even state regulatory regimes that provide oversight, as a fourth hand in this contestation. As McGuire (2008) aptly points out, while archaeology in North American society is trivial to economic and social development, given the imperative to enable economic growth, and state marginalisation of fiduciary responsibilities to First Nations over that decision making, archaeology thus can become a tool for communities and marginalised groups to engage the state over protection of archaeological and geographic heritage that in turn facilitates addressing broader societal issues these groups seek to change. The pivot point for this engagement is the authorised archaeologist, often by default tasked with mediating these contested interests, and as such expected to do much more than just find sites, identify them and excavate them in advance of construction.

---

[4] ROPA's standards can be accessed through their application form, accessible at: www.rpanet.org/displaycommon.cfm?an=4

[5] Ontario licensing qualifications: http://www.mtc.gov.on.ca/en/archaeology/archaeology_licensing.shtml; U.S. Federal standards: http://www.cr.nps.gov/local-law/Prof_Qual_83.htm

The imposition of these expectations on commercial, consultant archaeologists was never a dimension of practice envisioned when archaeologists initially sought to avoid development destruction in the 1960s and 1970s (e.g. Byrne 1976; Cleere 1984, 1989; Davis 1972; Lipe 1974). From the vantage of the early twenty-first century, the staggering growth of ARM in just a few decades (e.g. Altschul and Patterson 2010; Ferris 1998; La Salle and Hutchings 2012; Tainter 2004; Wheaton 2006) has been a largely unanticipated consequence of seeking to reduce the scale of site destruction occurring across North America in the 1950s and 1960s. Likewise, the eventual consequence of needing to care for and make use of all the accumulated outcome of this practice, though in hindsight a patently obvious challenge to the massive scale of harvesting conservation facilitated, was not an anticipated issue at the time. At this point in the early twenty-first century, many of the first generation of archaeologists who perhaps initially entered ARM as a short-term diversion along an intended academic career path are now veteran ARM practitioners who can look over careers marked by a much larger footprint on archaeological practice as a result—harvesting hundreds, even thousands of sites more than a typical academic, who conventionally may only undertake investigations on a few dozen sites or collections (or less) over a typical career (e.g. Ferris 1998, 2009b; Metcalf and Moses 2011; Peacock and Rafferty 2007; Whittlesey and Reid 2004; Williamson 2010).

For subsequent generations of archaeologists, the rise of applied commercial practice has become the overwhelming, and most viable, career option to pursue, far outpacing academic employment, and offering a permanent livelihood for many, although there is significant disparity in salary, security and benefits depending on employer (e.g. Cumberpatch and Roberts 2011; Everill 2007, 2009; Ferris 2002, 2004; La Salle and Hutchings 2012; Zorzin 2010). Unlike other forms of archaeological practice, however, commercial archaeologists negotiate a direct link between their compensation and the archaeological activities they do. This means the consequences of decisions, and ethical preferences, translate immediately into quality and quantity of personal compensation, as well as quality of satisfaction for "properly" managing the archaeological record. This central fact of applied commercial practice has invited, internally and from colleagues in academic settings, a continual ethical critique and question about ARM "worth" and value of contribution since its inception.

Applied Ethics

Not surprisingly, ethical issues have long been a thread in the critical analysis of ARM (e.g. Byrne 1976; Ferris 2000; Green 1984; King 2002, 2009; Noble 1982; Schiffer and Gumerman 1977c), beginning with the birth of the practice and the need to "price out" the methodological and analytical procedures of practice, along with judgements of meaning, value, significance and knowledge made over the record being managed in this context. Initially, this tension played out in the form of a rift between private, for-hire archaeologists, and their academic colleagues who were some of the first to actually undertake archaeological management contracts. A critique raised at the time was that applied practice was not archaeology if that work lacked research designs, sampling strategies or a clear aim to contribute, project by project, to archaeological science (e.g. Dunnell 1984; Lipe 1974; Pokotoylo 1982; Schiffer and Gumerman 1977a, b; Schiffer and House 1977; see also Wheaton 2006). Additionally, as the applied practitioner operated as a fee for service contractor, often with an MA or less serving as the "terminal" degree to launch their career, critiques arose that consultant archaeologists were more accountable to their clients than to the discipline, and were under-qualified to direct complex project management without aide of academic oversight, vision or ethical parameters (e.g. Finlayson 1986; Fitting and Goodyear 1979; King 1979; see also Ferris 1998; Green and Doershuk 1998).

This form of critique, at least in retrospect, can appear as little more than reactionary academic contempt for the tawdriness of archaeology so directly linked to capitalist enterprise and an outrage that ARM work was decidedly not being driven by academic priorities but by salvage priorities. Importantly, this distain and dismissal of commercial practitioners as not doing "real" archaeology also served to isolate and "silo" applied from academic practice, despite the fact that commercial firms quickly became the primary consumers of academic output: graduate and undergraduate students trained in the university to be scholarly archaeologists and subsequently re-trained as applied archaeologists when entering employment with consultant firms (e.g. Biehl 2013; La Salle and Hutchings 2012; McCarthy and Brummitt 2013; Tainter 2004; Wheaton 2006). These silos persisted into the last decade, and differences in methodological and philosophical understandings between academic and applied fields remain. This divide still exists despite the fact that applied practice has matured and become much more than any kind of place for "those who could not find success as academics".

The rapid growth of ARM over the latter part of the twentieth century did create a range of ethical issues that applied practitioners, and bureaucratic archaeologists providing oversight of practice, variously attempted to address. Most obviously, these emerged from having to balance archaeological requirements and cost efficiencies; proper documentation and boiler-plated reporting; livelihood, competitiveness and underbidding; and a professionalism asserted and measured; and self-censuring as a conscious strategy to be more palatable in a marketplace and development community context archaeologists had only limited experience negotiating (e.g. Barker 2010; Bergman and Doershuk 2003; Brink 1982; Cumberpatch and Roberts 2011; Fitting 1984; Fowler 1984; Metcalf and Moses 2011; Peacock and Rafferty 2007; Valentine and Simmons 2004; Whittlesey and Reid 2004). These issues, especially around perceptions of cost and capital driving the appropriateness of methodological expediencies (e.g. Ferris 2004, 2007), facilitated a degree of second guessing, angst and cynicism that has tended to sustain both external assumptions of an ARM practice driven by money and a lack of ethical commitment, and internally a malaise fueled by an awareness of individual incidents of dubious ethical practice undertaken by others, and a continual barrage of questionable outcomes and second guessing by clients, reviewers, colleagues and various publics (e.g. Adams 1994; Ferris 1998, 2009c; King 2002, 2009, 2011a; Williamson 2000).

While certainly commercial archaeology operates overtly as a commoditised form of practice, where material, knowledge and heritage value are all translated into economic value, this is simply the most explicit expression of what is more broadly an entrenched capitalist formation of archaeology, arising from neoliberal Western values of the later twentieth century (Hamilakis 2007; Patterson 1999; Zorzin 2011). The rise of an applied, commercial ARM practice and its focus on accumulating more and more of the record in advance of development impact simply encapsulate what arguably has been a core philosophy of a globalising cultural historical archaeology over much of the nineteenth and twentieth centuries, i.e. the extraction and consumption of the things and sites of archaeology: objects, fragments, bits and remains that are classified, analysed and stored away for a continued, archaeological need to re-access those material collections. At this point, with applied archaeology dominating practice worldwide, so internalised and normalised has this extractive-consumptive approach become that we generally have convinced ourselves, in research and resource management contexts, that this way to access the past is the *only* correct means of doing so. Certainly this is the explicit authorised message within resource management regulation, standards and formal language around why archaeological remains are important, and why others are expected to pay for that archaeological work. But, at the scale applied archaeology operates at, both overconsumption and under digestion, i.e. increasing site excavation leading to incomplete analysis and publication, subverts claims that archaeology in the early twenty-first century is anything other than rote compliance and harvesting of the record for livelihood and personal intellectual curiosity (Ferris and Welch 2014; Welch and Ferris 2014).

Conceits such as that the record recovered is rescued from destruction; that applied archaeologists represent and care for the interests of that record and undertake "good" forms of site alteration (as opposed to developer or looter-based alterations); that this work "preserves the past for the future" and that future generations of archaeologists will come along to study and make sense of this accumulated output may all embody good intents and certainly could become true consequences of the rise of commercial archaeology. But these notions are also increasingly suspect in light of the lack of consistent or sufficient standards for documentation and conservation during and after extraction. Moreover, these sentiments don't change the fact that, as archaeology practiced in North America is currently envisioned in applied practice, the primary function of the commercial archaeological industry is to aid in the alteration and commoditisation of land and resources through mitigation and removal of the archaeological heritage of those places, by means of a fee-for-service utilisation of government- and profession-sanctioned expertise and privileged right to alter that record.[6]

[6] The denial of this self-evident truth regarding the primary role of capitalism in applied practice, and the implications that has for archaeological conservation ethics and the rhetoric of preserving the past, can be profound. Orthodox and heterodox reactions, for example, of a World Archaeological Congress sponsored Inter-Congress on Contract Archaeology in 2013 took as its critical focus the consequences arising from contract archaeology engaging in capitalism. Reaction to the critical tone of the announcement led to a heated exchange on the WAC online forum, with some decrying the critique as "casting aspersions" on applied practitioners and "demagoguery," while others applauded the call to explore this critical dimension of practice, and offered up examples of various unethical practices in North American commercial archaeology – a perfect illustration of the angst that constantly runs through self-reflexive considerations of applied practice.

However, it is also important to underscore that ARM is borne from general archaeological practice in North America, not somehow corrupted subsequently in the face of a (more) overt link between practice and personal financial gain than academic colleagues may have to experience.[7] As such, ARM outcomes, and the ethical issues they raise, are really just supersized government- and industry-financed expressions and a continuation of the long-standing priority in archaeology of wanting to accumulate the record for archaeology's sake.

A New Ethics for Applied Practice

ARM platitudes such as preserving the past for tomorrow and advancing our knowledge of the past are insufficient ethical validations for the scale and intensity of harvesting going on across the continent. Indeed, appeals to scholarly advancement are dubious, given the disjuncture between applied and academic fields, and the fact that the accumulated output of applied practice, while to a small extent has contributed to scholarship, mostly remains inaccessible and in a perpetual state of collection management crisis (e.g. Childs 1995; Childs et al. 2010; Childs and Sullivan 2004; Marquardt et al. 1982; Trimble and Marino 2003; Williamson 2009).

But applied archaeology itself has begun to transform over the last couple of decades, shifting significantly from a sole intent of getting archaeological stuff "out of the way" of development, towards the servicing of a complex and complicated nexus of contested heritage values that come to bear over the management of archaeology. This role is not articulated in academic training, regulatory regimes or accreditation standards, but is nonetheless implicit in state sanctioning of archaeologists as "experts" of archaeological heritage, and the inherent structural framing within statutory development processes that require some effort to accommodate mediation of contested values in the decision-making and approval of development projects, if only to create a "defensible record" thereof (King 2009). To be sure, archaeologists can simply insert their own interests and agendas into these contexts, often assuming that others inherently share and understand the archaeologist's values and expectations as to why a site needs to be managed in a particular way. However, the state increasingly has sought to incorporate other voices, especially descendant voices,[8] into the decision-making of ARM work, including around

[7] Though personal financial benefits are clearly linked to performance in academics, and breed the same levels of differential entitlement between tenured faculty, sessional instructors, post-docs and grad students. But these similarities are regularly unexplored in the critique of applied practitioners.

[8] This need has emerged from the initial engagement of NAGPRA and emergence of State equivalents, as well as from Tribal directed management programs in the USA (e.g., Anyon et al 2000; Kerber 2006; Stapp and Burney 2002), and from defined and asserted rights affirmed through a raft of upper court decisions, especially coming out of Canada (e.g., Bell 2000; Bell and Napoleon 2008; Ferris 2003). This has led to a number of federal and Provincial/State jurisdictions requiring differing formal or informal levels of consultation or engagement with First Nations in the planning and outcome of applied archaeological work on Indigenous archaeological heritage in those

whether or not sites should be preserved or excavated, methodologies to be used and ultimate disposition of collections and information generated by that work (e.g. Brickerman 2006; Budhwa 2005; Dent 2012; Ferris 2007; King et al. 2011; Klassen et al. 2009; Williamson 2010). These consultative engagements can be restricted to reserve/reservation lands, wider traditional territories and increasingly, in relation to indigenous archaeological sites of value, regardless of where located.[9] The complexities, on the ground, of resolving contested issues of heritage have required applied practitioners to explore solutions and seek mediations that go far beyond anything to do with local cultural history, simply to satisfy the consultation requirement and to get the job done.

This extra-to-archaeology dimension to the role applied practitioners play has injected a new dynamic into their relationship with and on behalf of clients, the state, communities, research colleagues and descendant groups who draw value from the archaeological heritage being "managed". In particular development contexts this dynamic creates a unique reflexivity, and an immediacy to that reflexivity, rarely experienced by other forms of archaeologist—and certainly not at chronic scale that characterises an applied practitioner's day to day. Effective resolution is the goal of the process from the point of view of those practitioners mediating these contested values, so there is an expediency that requires the applied archaeologist to confront not what archaeology is to archaeologists studying the past, but rather what it is in the present to people who struggle to have their voice and values accounted for in decisions that affect them. This forces the applied archaeologist to communicate and participate, willingly or otherwise, in the global/multicultural ethical discourse that others bring to archaeology. Negotiated outcomes, whether one-off solutions to particular contexts, formulaic response or emergent "best management practices" accumulate, while recurring discussions forces that dialogue past assumptions and stereotypical assumptions of the various people at the table. Over time a repertoire of engagement tools and solutions have emerged that seemingly work for the archaeologists, their clients and descendant communities—or at least expedite resolutions so that everyone can move on. Ultimately, solutions that do indeed "get the job done" have begun to revise applied practice and practitioners, giving rise to a praxis of accommodation and mediation, albeit still within the confines of capitalist consumption of land and resources, that nonetheless regularly redresses issues of marginalisation in the decision-making around the archaeological heritage, as well as affects broader development outcomes.

Critically, this emerging role the applied archaeologist plays, well or begrudgingly, underscores that the spectra of values embedded in archaeological sites and objects is cultural heritage, not archaeology, and that archaeology really only

---

jurisdictions. This has also included First Nation community members serving as monitors on ARM crews, has led to collaborative training undertaken by communities/applied archaeologists, teaching each other development, research, and community values, preferences, and processes (e.g., Hunter 2008; Kapyrka 2010), and has also given rise to Indigenous CRM firms that specialize in bridging community representation with archaeological management (e.g., Nicholas 2010b).

[9] For example: www.mtc.gov.on.ca/en/publications/AbEngageBulletin.pdf.

becomes cultural heritage at the point when diverse perspectives access and engage with the record *beyond* archaeology (e.g. Carman 2009; Harrison 2012; Skeates 2000; Smith 2006; Smith and Waterton 2009). Emerging from applied archaeology, ironically in the rather focused rush to complete a job, is an ethical, conceptual shift from pursuing archaeology-centric values, to servicing this spectrum of broader based societal contested values that converge where heritage is made and carried forward (Ferris and Welch 2014).

In this role, applied practitioners become enablers and facilitators of marginalised groups to negotiate and assert a role for themselves in the decision-making around the management of land and archaeological heritage. This occurs through the routine need to consult with First Nations and other descendant groups on archaeological matters, ensuring that high-quality consultative communications occur throughout a project, by training and enabling the hiring of community members as monitors on ARM projects, and by working directly for descendant groups to investigate places or issues of community importance. This occurred, for example, in Caledonia, southern Ontario, where a commercial archaeology firm was hired to reassess a development property in 2006 that had been successfully occupied and reclaimed by the Six Nations Iroquois (Devries 2011). This reclamation was over whether or not the lands in question were ever formally surrendered to the Crown. But the issue quickly encompassed much more, with indigenous and non-indigenous communities squaring off over whether the actions taken were lawful or not, creating for all intents and purposes a police state for protesters and surrounding residents alike. That archaeology emerged as one of a host of high-profile issues ultimately negotiated by the First Nations sovereign, Canadian and Ontario Crown, underscores that it isn't about archaeology as archaeologists conventionally understand the term, but about contemporary values playing out over this material heritage.

The archaeological firm, in the case of Caledonia, was hired by the Six Nations community to address community member suspicions and concerns that previous ARM work had intentionally or otherwise failed to document important archaeological sites, or colluded with the development proponent to cover up and destroy evidence of ancient burials. The firm hired by Six Nations was required to negotiate barricades, suspicion about their allegiances and hostility from all sides, the rejection of established ethical and professional standards of archaeological practice that were deemed not "good enough" in this context, provincial regulatory oversight and the lack thereof and an anti-archaeology sensibility to archaeologists' values and preconceptions of the material record. This messy process consultant and bureaucratic archaeologists engaged with over the Caledonia reclamation aptly reflects the common experiences of applied practitioners who find themselves operating beyond intra-disciplinary comfort zones. Applied practice, especially good applied practice, like any other form of public resource planning or management, involves trade-offs. ARM has emerged as the context for negotiating the protection and treatment of the archaeological record as it transforms into a cultural heritage meaningful to others. From this reality, applied archaeological practice can only function by servicing that wider, contemporary relevance, not the archaeologist's agenda.

This broader relevance situates applied practitioners in a contested borderland between archaeology and other conceptions and uses of the material record, the past and the making of heritage. Decision and meaning making here occurs entirely in an interactive, sometimes collaborative, sometimes combative frame where the archaeologist seeks accommodation between disparate valuations of the archaeological record played out over a particular locale (e.g. state regulations, transitory landowner needs, descendant values), none of which, strictly speaking, mirrors the archaeologist's own values and concerns for the "knowledge potential" of that archaeology. While this accommodation is often a source of frustration for practitioners, who decry that their work is no longer about the archaeology, that, in fact, is the point (Ferris 2007). The accumulated consequence of this trend, occurring across North America continually in applied contexts, is a realignment of archaeological ethics from being about advancing archaeological values and harvesting the material record before development impact to being about servicing broad societal values that get variably asserted for the material past when encountered at the intersection of economic growth, capitalist endeavour and community interest. The loss of the exclusive power archaeology has over the archaeological record as a result of this shift from servicing archaeological values to heritage values is transformative, enabling the beginnings of an ethical practice to emerge in some portion of ARM that at the very least mitigates the degree otherwise of (real or imagined) tendencies towards collusive capitalist expediencies when oversight is limited to client and consultant. But at the very most, this shift in what applied archaeology is about has the potential to deconstruct the dominant paradigm in archaeology, and some few practitioners today have begun to see their role as enabling a social relevance and even social justice into archaeological practice that two centuries of advancing a narrower, archaeological sensibility has failed to achieve (e.g. Atlay et al. 2014).

Bridging the Divide

This shift in the dynamic and role the applied archaeologist plays, the maturing of ARM, meaningful partnerships that have emerged between applied and academic researchers and institutions and a generational shift in the academic archaeological community have all contributed to a rapprochement between academic and applied dimensions of archaeology over the last decade. Those academic archaeologists who embrace an activist ethic and research focus on the contemporary practice of archaeology can find themselves seeking the experiences and contexts that forward-thinking applied practitioners find themselves operating within on a daily basis. Through the necessity of revising practice to accommodate regulated and expected external accountabilities and collaboration, shared decision-making around archaeology in ARM is exactly engaging with theoretical dimensions of multi-vocality, praxis, collaborative archaeology and the de-centering of archaeological values that activist researchers are exploring in their own work. There is much that these academics and these commercial archaeologists can talk about to each other, as they are all directly participating in the emerging global/multicultural ethical discourse that is increasingly redefining what archaeology is about in North America.

Moreover, the dominance of applied archaeology in North America today is overwhelmingly defining the role archaeology plays in contemporary society. As a result, changes and the changed expectations of descendant groups, government and communities over what archaeology is supposed to be and do in society emerge primarily from the applied context. But those changes, in turn, feed back onto academic archaeology, and create differing expectations in that practice, too. After all, if in commercial contexts First Nation communities now have an expectation of participating in the decision-making over whether and how a particular site should be excavated and documented in advance of development, or what will happen to the collection accumulated afterwards, it shouldn't be a surprise that at least that level of input and direction will be expected of academic endeavours, especially around research-driven excavations and accumulation.[10] There is little chance, too, that academic archaeology can fortify the wall between themselves and their activist academic colleagues, applied practitioners, the state and descendent groups with a mortar made up of cries to protect their intellectual freedom, scientific rigour and continued exclusive access to the material and interpretive space of archaeology. The "rigour" of this stance is dubious given the legacy of the consumption of the archaeological record by archaeologists for archaeology, the state of the accumulated result of that harvesting and the clear intellectual and practical debts archaeologists owe to collaborators (and resisters) hailing from local and indigenous communities who perhaps view the "emergence" of a reconfigured role for archaeology in contemporary society as little more than an overdue archaeological backfilling of retrospectively obvious moral gaps.

While those who may wish for archaeology to remain the exclusive and state-sanctioned, authorised domain of archaeologists worry about the infusion of a global multicultural ethics and praxis into their practice, those that embrace this reorientation know that an archaeology and archaeological interpretation arising from this engagement and collaboration make for good archaeology—research arising from the spaces created in those collaborations, or from the collections generated over the last half century. But this reorientation in North American archaeological ethics also affords an opportunity for archaeology, especially archaeology in the service of broader heritage values, to encompass a much wider relevance, as archaeology aids in a discourse across society redressing colonial legacies, enabling marginalised communities to access the state, reassert their voice in social decision-making and initiate wider discussions over sovereign rights, fiduciary responsibilities and how these need to play out in the management of land, the environment and redistribution of wealth arising from those development projects led by latter day neoliberal capitalist initiatives.

---

[10] Indeed, given the massive accumulation of the archaeological record as a result of ARM harvesting tens of thousands of sites across North America over the last 50 years and available for value added academic research endeavours, and the fact that students now gain most of their field experiences working for consultant firms seasonally, it seems ethically dubious for academic archaeologists to insist on excavating archaeological sites that are not otherwise threatened with alteration and destruction by non-archaeological means and not otherwise community-consented beforehand.

Acknowledgements We'd like to thank our many colleagues who have offered us the chance over the last many years, separately or together, to reflect on the contemporary practice of North American archaeology, especially our compatriots participating in and thinking about an activist archaeology, and colleagues helping to work towards a sustainable archaeology. As well, opportunities to frame and explore the concept of a sustainable archaeology, separately or together, have been supported through funding by the Social Sciences and Humanities Research Council, Canada Foundation for Innovation, Ontario Research Fund and our respective institutions.

References

Adams, N. (1994). Gnawing gently on the metacarpals. *Arch Notes, 94*(1), 9–15.

Altschul, J. (2010). Archaeological heritage values in cross-cultural context. In G. Smith, P. M. Messenger, & H. Soderland (Eds.), *Heritage values in contemporary society* (pp. 75–85). Walnut Creek: Left Coast Press.

Altschul, J., & Patterson, T. (2010). Trends in employment and training in American archaeology. In W. Ashmore, D. Lippert, & B. Mills (Eds.), *Voices in American Archaeology* (pp. 291–316). Washington: SAA Press.

Anyon, R., Ferguson, T. J., & Welch, J. (2000). Heritage management by American Indian tribes in the Southwestern United States. In F. P. McManamon & A. Hutton (Eds.), *Cultural Resource Management in contemporary society* (pp. 120–141). New York: Routledge.

Atalay, S. (2006). Indigenous archaeology as decolonizing practice. *American Indian Quarterly, 30*, 280–310.

Atalay, S. (2012). *Community-based archaeology: Research with, by, and for Indigenous and local communities*. Berkeley: University of California Press.

Atlay, S., Clauss, L. R., McGuire, R., & Welch, J. R. (Eds.). (2014). *Transforming archaeology: Activist practices and prospects*. Walnut Creek: Left Coast Press.

Baram, U. (2011). Community organizing in public archaeology: Coalitions for the preservation of a hidden history in Florida. *Present Pasts, 3*, 12–18.

Barker, P. (2010). The process made me do it or, would a reasonably intelligent person agree that CRM is reasonably intelligent? In L. Sebastian & W. Lipe (Eds.), *Archaeology and Cultural Resource Management* (pp. 65–90). Santa Fe: SAR Press.

Beaudoin, M., Josephs, R., & Rankin, L. (2010). Attributing cultural affiliation to sod structures in Labrador: A Labrador métis example from North River. *Canadian Journal of Archaeology, 34*, 148–173.

Bell, C. (2000). Protecting Indigenous heritage resources in Canada: Kitkatla v. B.C. *International Journal of Cultural Property, 10*, 246–263.

Bell, C., & Napoleon, V. (Eds.). (2008). *First Nations' cultural heritage and the law: Case studies, voices and perspectives*. Vancouver: University of British Columbia Press.

Bergman, C., & Doershuk, J. (2003). Cultural Resource Management and the business of archaeology. In L. Zimmerman, K. Vitelli, & J. Hollowell-Zimmer (Eds.), *Ethical issues in archaeology* (pp. 85–98). Walnut Creek: AltaMira Press.

Biehl, P. (2013). Teaching and researching cultural heritage. In P. Biehl & C. Prescott (Eds.), *Heritage in the context of globalization. Europe and the Americas* (pp. 45–50). New York: Springer.

Bilosi, T., & Zimmerman, L. (Eds.). (1997). *Indians and anthropologists: Vine Deloria Jr. and the critique of anthropology*. Tucson: University of Arizona Press.

Blakey, M. (2010). African Burial Ground Project: Paradigm for Cooperation? *Museum International, 62*, 61–68.

Brickerman, I. (2006). Tribal consultation in Pennsylvania: A personal view from within the Pennsylvania Department of Transportation. In J. Kerber (Ed.), *Cross-cultural collaboration. Native Peoples and archaeology in the Northeastern United States* (pp. 183–196). Lincoln: University of Nebraska Press.

Brink, J. (1982). Riverrun: An appraisal of contract archaeology in Alberta. In P. Francis & E. Popli (Eds.), *Directions in archaeology. A question of goals* (pp. 37–46). Calgary: University of Calgary.
Budhwa, R. (2005). An alternative model for First Nations involvement in resource management archaeology. *Canadian Journal of Archaeology, 29*, 20–45.
Byrne, W. (1976). The resource question and rescue archaeology. *Canadian Archaeological Association Bulletin, 8*, 109–121.
Carman, J. (2005). *Against cultural property: Archaeology, heritage and ownership*. Oxford: Duckworth.
Carman, J. (2009). Where the value lies: The importance of materiality to the immaterial. In E. Waterton & L. Smith (Eds.), *Taking archaeology out of heritage* (pp. 192–208). Newcastle: Cambridge Scholars' Publishing.
Castañeda, Q., & Matthews, C. (Eds.). (2008). *Ethnographic archaeologies: Reflections on stakeholders and archaeological practices*. Lanham: AltaMira Press.
Chidester, R., & Gadsby, D. (2009). One neighborhood, two communities: The public archaeology of class in a gentrifying urban neighborhood. *International Labor and Working-Class History, 76*, 127–146.
Childs, T. (1995). Curation crisis—What's being done? *Federal Archaeology, 7*(4), 11–15.
Childs, T., Kinsey, K., & Kagan, S. (2010). Repository fees for archaeological collections. Trends and issues over a decade of study. *Heritage Management, 3*, 189–212.
Childs, T., & Sullivan, L. (2004). Archaeological stewardship: It's about both sites and collections. In T. Childs (Ed.), *Our collective responsibility: The ethics and practice of archaeological collections stewardship* (pp. 3–21). Washington: SAA.
Cleere, H. (Ed.). (1984). *Approaches to the archaeological heritage*. Cambridge: Cambridge University Press.
Cleere, H. (1989). Introduction: The rationale of archaeological heritage management. In H. Cleere (Ed.), *Archaeological heritage management in the modern world* (pp. 1–19). London: Unwin-Hyman.
Colwell-Chanthaphonh, C. (2012). Archaeology and Indigenous collaboration. In I. Hodder (Ed.), *Archaeological theory today* (pp. 267–291). Cambridge: Polity Press.
Colwell-Chanthaphonh, C., & Ferguson, T. J. (Eds.). (2008). *Collaboration in archaeological practice: Engaging descendant communities*. Lanham: AltaMira Press.
Colwell-Chanthaphonh, C., Ferguson, T. J., Lippert, D., McGuire, R., Nicholas, G., Watkins, J., & Zimmerman, L. (2010). The premise and promise of Indigenous archaeology. *American Antiquity, 75*, 228–238.
Cumberpatch, C., & Roberts, H. (2011). Life in the archaeological marketplace. In M. Rockman & J. Flatman (Eds.), *Archaeology in society. Its relevance in the modern world* (pp. 23–44). New York: Springer.
Davis, H. (1972). The crisis in American archaeology. *Science, 175*, 267–272.
Dawson, P., Levy, R., & Lyons, N. (2011). Breaking the fourth wall: 3D virtual worlds as tools for knowledge repatriation in archaeology. *Journal of Social Archaeology, 11*, 387–402.
Dent, J. (2012). *Past tents: Temporal themes and patterns of provincial archaeological governance in British Columbia and Ontario*. Unpublished Master's thesis, Department of Anthropology, University of Western Ontario, London.
Derry, L., & Malloy, M. (Eds.). (2003). *Archaeologists and local communities: Partners in exploring the past*. Washington: Society for American Archaeology.
DeVries, L. (2011). *Conflict in Caledonia: Aboriginal land rights and the rule of law*. Vancouver: University of British Columbia Press.
Dongoske, K., Aldenderfer, M., & Doehner, K. (Eds.). (2000). *Working together: Native Americans and archaeologists*. Washington: Society for American Archaeology.
Dunnell, R. (1984). The ethics of archaeological significance decisions. In E. Green (Ed.), *Ethics and values in archaeology* (pp. 62–74). New York: Free Press.
Echo-Hawk, R. (2010). Working together on race. *The SAA Archaeological Record, 10*(3), 6–9.
Echo-Hawk, R., & Zimmerman, L. J. (2006). Some opinions about racialism and American archaeology. *The American Indian Quarterly, 30*, 461–485.
Edgeworth, M. (Ed.). (2006). *Ethnographies of archaeological practice: Cultural encounters, material transformations*. Walnut Creek: AltaMira Press.

Everill, P. (2007). British commercial archaeology: Antiquarians and labourers, developers and diggers. In Y. Hamilakis & P. Duke (Eds.), *Archaeology and capitalism: From ethics to politics* (pp. 119–136). Walnut Creek: Left Coast Press.

Everill, P. (2009). *The invisible diggers: A study of commercial archaeology in the UK*. Oxford: Oxbow Books.

Fagan, G., & Feder, K. L. (2006). Crusading against straw men: An alternative view of alternative archaeologies: Response to Holtorf (2005). *World Archaeology, 38*, 718–729.

Ferguson, T. (1996). Native Americans and the practice of archaeology. *Annual Review of Anthropology, 25*, 63–79.

Ferris, N. (1998). I don't think we're in Kansas anymore…: The rise of the archaeological consulting industry in Ontario. In P. Smith & D. Mitchell (Eds.), *Bringing back the past Historical perspectives on Canadian archaeology* (pp. 225–247). Museum of Civilization: Ottawa.

Ferris, N. (Ed.). (2000). Steep grade ahead: Current issues in the governance of archaeology in Canada [Special issue]. *Canadian Journal of Archaeology, 24*(2).

Ferris, N. (2002). Where the air thins: The rapid rise of the archaeological consulting industry in Ontario. *Revista de Arqueología Americana (Journal of American Archaeology), 21*, 53–88.

Ferris, N. (2003). Between colonial and Indigenous archaeologies: Legal and extra-legal ownership of the archaeological past in North America. *Canadian Journal of Archaeology, 27*, 154–190.

Ferris, N. (2004). Guess who sat down to dinner? Archaeology in laws. In W. Lovis (Ed.), *An Upper Great Lakes archaeological odyssey: Essays in honor of Charles E. Cleland* (pp. 199–214). Detroit: Wayne State University Press.

Ferris, N. (2007). Always fluid: Government policy making and standards of practice in Ontario Archaeological Resource Management. In W. Willems & M. van der Dries (Eds.), *Quality management in archaeology* (pp. 78–99). Oxford: Oxbow Books.

Ferris, N. (2009a). *The archaeology of native-lived colonialism: Challenging history in the Great Lakes*. Tucson: University of Arizona Press.

Ferris, N. (2009b). From crap to archaeology: The CRM shaping of nineteenth-century domestic site archaeology. *Ontario Archaeology, 83/84*, 3–29.

Ferris, N. (2009c). Fear and loathing in applied archaeology, or, befuddled bureaucrats & contemptible consultants—Lies my career taught me. Online paper retrieved from http://uwo.academia.edu/NealFerris/Talks

Ferris, N., Harrison, R., & Wilcox, M. (2014). *Rethinking colonial pasts through archaeology*. Oxford: Oxford University Press.

Ferris, N., & Welch, J. (2014). Beyond archaeological agendas: In the service of a sustainable archaeology. In S. Atalay, L. R. Claus, R. McGuire, & J. R. Welch (Eds.), *Transforming archaeology: Activist practices and prospects* (pp. 215–238). Walnut Creek, California: Left Coast Press.

Finlayson, W. (1986). Archaeological contracting and consulting in southern Ontario. In W. A. Fox (Ed.), *Archaeological consulting in Ontario: Papers of the London Conference 1985* (pp. 107–114). London: Ontario Archaeological Society.

Fitting, J. E. (1984). Economics and archaeology. In E. Green (Ed.), *Ethics and values in archaeology* (pp. 117–122). New York: Free Press.

Fitting, J., & Goodyear, A. C. (1979). Client-oriented archaeology: An exchange of views. *Journal of Field Archaeology, 6*, 352–366.

Fowler, D. (1984). Ethics in contract archaeology. In E. Green (Ed.), *Ethics and values in archaeology* (pp. 108–116). New York: Free Press.

Fowler, J. (1995). The legal structure for the protection of archaeological resources in the United States and Canada. In R. Knudson & B. Keel (Eds.), *The public trust and the First Americans* (pp. 75–86). Corvallis: Oregon State University Press.

Fox, W. (Ed.). (1986). *Archaeological consulting in Ontario: Papers of the London conference 1985*. London: Ontario Archaeological Society.

Gnecco, C., & Ayala, P. (Eds.). (2011). *Indigenous peoples and archaeology in Latin America*. Walnut Creek: Left Coast Press.

Green, E. (Ed.). (1984). *Ethics and values in archaeology*. New York: Free Press.

Green, W., & Doershuk, J. F. (1998). Cultural Resource Management and American archaeology. *Journal of Archaeological Research, 6*, 121–167.

Groarke, L., & Warrick, G. (2006). Stewardship gone astray? Ethics and the SAA. In C. Scarre & G. Scarre (Eds.), *The ethics of archaeology: Philosophical perspectives* (pp. 163–177). Cambridge: Cambridge University Press.

Habu, J., Fawcett, C., & Matsunaga, J. M. (Eds.). (2008). *Evaluating multiple narratives: Beyond nationalist, colonialist, imperialist archaeologies*. New York: Springer.

Hamilakis, Y. (2007). From ethics to politics. In Y. Hamilakis & P. Duke (Eds.), *Archaeology and capitalism. From ethics to politics* (pp. 15–40). Walnut Creek: Left Coast Press.

Hamilakis, Y. (2011). Archaeological ethnography: A multi-temporal meeting ground for archaeology and anthropology. *Annual Review of Anthropology, 40*, 399–414.

Harrison, R. (2012). *Heritage: Critical approaches*. London: Routledge.

Hart, S. (2011). Heritage, neighborhoods and cosmopolitan sensibilities: Poly-communal archaeology in Deerfield, Massachusetts. Present Pasts 3. Retrieved March 15, 2013 from http://www.presentpasts.info/article/view/pp.42/74

Hodgetts, L. (2013). The rediscovery of HMS Investigator: Archaeology, sovereignty and the colonial legacy in Canada's Arctic. *Journal of Social Archaeology, 13*, 80–100.

Hollowell, J., & Nicholas, G. P. (2009). Using ethnographic methods to articulate community-based conceptions of Cultural Heritage Management. *Public Archaeologies, 8*(2–3), 141–160.

Holtorf, C. (2009). A European perspective on Indigenous and immigrant archaeologies. *World Archaeology, 41*, 672–681.

Hunter, A. (2008). A critical change in pedagogy Indigenous Cultural Resource Management. In S. Silliman (Ed.), *Collaborating at trowel's edge: Teaching and learning in Indigenous archaeology* (pp. 165–187). Tucson: University of Arizona Press.

Jordan, K. (2008). *The Seneca restoration, 1715-1754: An Iroquois local political economy*. Gainesville: University Press of Florida.

Jordan, K. (2009). Colonies, colonialism, and cultural entanglement: The archaeology of post-Columbian intercultural relations. In T. Majewski & D. Gaimster (Eds.), *International handbook of historical archaeology* (pp. 31–59). New York: Springer.

Kapyrka, J. (2010). With true spirit and intent: Williams Treaty First Nations and the Association of Professional Archaeologists break new ground. *Arch Notes, 15*(4), 11–14.

Kerber, J. (Ed.). (2006). *Cross-cultural collaboration. Native peoples and archaeology in the northeastern United States*. Lincoln: University of Nebraska Press.

Killion, T. (Ed.). (2008). *Opening archaeology: Repatriation's impact on contemporary research and practice*. Santa Fe: SAR Press.

King, T. (1979). Preservation and rescue challenges and controversies in the protection of archaeological resources. *Journal of Field Archaeology, 6*, 351–352.

King, T. (2002). *Thinking about Cultural Resource Management: Essays from the edge*. Walnut Creek: AltaMira Press.

King, T. (2008). *Cultural resource laws and practice: An introductory guide*. Walnut Creek: AltaMira Press.

King, T. (2009). *Our unprotected heritage: Whitewashing the destruction of our cultural and natural environment*. Walnut Creek: Left Coast Press.

King, T. (2011a). Public archaeology is a menace to the public—And to archaeology. *AP: Online Journal in Public Archaeology, 2*, 5–23.

King, T. (Ed.). (2011b). *A companion to Cultural Resource Management*. Malden: Wiley-Blackwell.

King, A., Lepofsky, D., & Pokotylo, D. (2011). Archaeology and local governments: The perspectives of First Nations and municipal councillors in the Fraser Valley, BC. *Canadian Journal of Archaeology, 35*, 258–291.

Klassen, M., Budwa, R., & Reimer/Yumks, R. (2009). First Nations, forestry, and the transformation of archaeological practice in British Columbia, Canada. *Heritage Management, 2*, 199–238.

Knudson, R., & Keel, B. C. (Eds.). (1995). *The public trust and the First Americans*. Corvallis: Oregon State University Press.

La Salle, M., & Hutchings, R. (2012). Commercial archaeology in British Columbia. *The Midden, 44*(2), 8–16.

Lane, P. (2011). Possibilities for a post-colonial archaeology in sub-Saharan Africa: Indigenous and useable pasts. *World Archaeology, 43*, 7–25.

LaRoche, C., & Blakey, M. L. (1997). Seizing intellectual power: The dialogue at the New York African Burial Ground. *Historical Archaeology, 31*(3), 84–106.

Liebmann, M., & Murphy, M. S. (Eds.). (2011). *Enduring conquests: Rethinking the archaeology of resistance to Spanish colonialism in the Americas*. Santa Fe: SAR Press.

Liebmann, M., & Rizvi, U. Z. (Eds.). (2008). *Archaeology and the postcolonial critique*. Lanham: AltaMira Press.

Lipe, W. (1974). A conservation model for American archaeology. *The Kiva, 39*(3–4), 213–245.

Little, B., & Shackel, P. A. (Eds.). (2007). *Archaeology as a tool of civic engagement*. Lanham: AltaMira Press.

Loren, D. D. P. (2008). *In contact: Bodies and spaces in the sixteenth- and seventeenth-century Eastern Woodlands*. Lanham: AltaMira Press.

Lydon, J., & Rizvi, U. Z. (Eds.). (2010). *Handbook of postcolonial archaeology*. Walnut Creek: Left Coast Press.

Lynott, M. (1997). Ethical principles and archaeological practice: Development of an ethics policy. *American Antiquity, 62*, 589–599.

Lynott, M., & Wylie, A. (1995a). Stewardship: The central principle of archaeological ethics. In M. Lynott & A. Wylie (Eds.), *Ethics in American archaeology: Challenges for the 1990s* (pp. 35–39). Washington: Society for American Archaeology.

Lynott, M., & Wylie, A. (Eds.). (1995b). *Ethics in American archaeology: Challenges for the 1990s*. Washington: Society for American Archaeology.

MacEachern, S. (2010). Seeing like an oil company's CHM programme: Exxon and archaeology on the Chad Export Project. *Journal of Social Archaeology, 10*, 347–366.

Marquardt, W., Montet-White, A., & Scholtz, S. C. (1982). Resolving the crisis in archaeological collections curation. *American Antiquity, 47*, 409–418.

Martindale, A. (2009). Entanglement and tinkering: Structural history in the archaeology of the northern Tsimshian. *Journal of Social Archaeology, 9*, 59–91.

Mason, R. (2006). *Inconstant companions: Archaeology and Native American Indian oral traditions*. Tuscaloosa: University of Alabama Press.

McCarthy, J., & Brummitt, A. (2013). Archaeology in the "real world": The training-practice disconnect in North American consulting archaeology. In J. Jameson & J. Eogan (Eds.), *Training and practice for modern day archaeologists* (pp. 145–151). New York: Springer.

McDavid, C. (2002). Archaeologies that hurt; descendents that matter: A pragmatic approach to collaboration in the public interpretation of African-American Archaeology. *World Archaeology, 34*, 303–314.

McGhee, R. (2004). Between racism and romanticism, scientism and spiritualism: The dilemmas of New World archaeology. In B. Kooyman & J. Kelley (Eds.), *Archaeology on the edge: New perspectives from the Northern Plains* (pp. 13–22). Calgary: Canadian Archaeological Association.

McGhee, R. (2008). Aboriginalism and the problems of Indigenous archaeology. *American Antiquity, 73*, 579–598.

McGhee, R. (2010). Of strawmen, herrings, and frustrated expectations. *American Antiquity, 75*, 239–243.

McGimsey, C., & Davis, H. A. (Eds.). (1977). *The management of archeological resources: The Airlie House Report*. Washington: Society for American Archaeology.

McGuire, R. (2008). *Archaeology as political action*. Berkeley: University of California Press.

McKay, A. (Ed.). (1977). *New perspectives in Canadian archaeology*. Ottawa: Royal Society of Canada.

McManamon, F., & Hatton, A. (Eds.). (2000). *Cultural Resource Management in contemporary society: Perspectives on managing and presenting the past*. New York: Routledge.

McManamon, F., Stout, A., & Barnes, J. A. (Eds.). (2008). *Managing archaeological resources: Global context, national programs, local actions*. Walnut Creek: Left Coast Press.

Messenger, P. M., & Smith, G. S. (Eds.). (2010). *Cultural Heritage Management. A global perspective*. Gainesville: University Press of Florida.

Metcalf, M., & Moses, J. (2011). Building an archaeological business. In M. Rockman & J. Flatman (Eds.), *Archaeology in society. Its relevance in the modern world* (pp. 89–96). New York: Springer.

Mortensen, L., & Hollowell, J. (Eds.). (2008). *Ethnographies and archaeologies. Iterations of the past*. Gainesville: University Press of Florida.

Mullins, P. (1999). *Race and affluence: An archaeology of African America and consumer culture.* New York: Springer.
Mullins, P. (2008). Excavating America's metaphor: Race, diaspora, and vindicationist archaeologies. *Historical Archaeology, 42*, 104–122.
Nassaney, M. (2012). Decolonizing archaeological theory at Fort St. Joseph, an eighteenth century multi-ethnic community in the Western Great Lakes Region. *Midcontinental Journal of Archaeology, 37*, 5–24.
Neumann, T., Sanford, R., & Harry, K. (2010). *Cultural resources archaeology: An introduction.* Lanham: AltaMira Press.
Nicholas, G. (2005). The persistence of memory; the politics of desire: Archaeological impacts on aboriginal peoples and their response. In C. Smith & H. Martin Wobst (Eds.), *Indigenous archaeologies. Decolonizing theory and practice* (pp. 75–98). London: Routledge.
Nicholas, G. (2010a). Seeking the end of Indigenous archaeology. In C. Phillips & H. Allen (Eds.), *Bridging the divide. Indigenous communities and archaeology into the 21st century* (pp. 232–252). Walnut Creek: Left Coast Press.
Nicholas, G. (Ed.). (2010b). *Being and becoming Indigenous archaeologists.* Walnut Creek: Left Coast Press.
Nicholas, G., & Andrews, T. D. (Eds.). (1997). *At a crossroads archaeology and First Peoples in Canada.* Burnaby: Simon Fraser University.
Nicholas, G., & Hollowell, J. (2007). Ethical challenges to a postcolonial archaeology: The legacy of scientific colonialism. In Y. Hamilakis & P. Duke (Eds.), *Archaeology and capitalism: From ethics to politics* (pp. 59–82). Walnut Creek: Left Coast Press.
Nicholas, G., Roberts, A., Schaepe, D. M., Watkins, J., Leader-Elliot, L., & Rowley, S. (2011). A consideration of theory, principles and practice in collaborative archaeology. *Archaeological Review from Cambridge, 26*(2), 11–30.
Nicholas, G., & Wylie, A. (2009). Archaeological finds: Legacies of appropriation, modes of response. In C. Brunck & J. O. Young (Eds.), *The ethics of cultural appropriation* (pp. 11–54). Malden: Wiley-Blackwell.
Noble, W. (1982). Potsherds, potlids and politics: An overview of Ontario archaeology during the 1970s. *Canadian Journal of Archaeology, 6*, 167–194.
Ogundiran, A., & Falola, T. (Eds.). (2010). *Archaeology of Atlantic Africa and the African diaspora.* Indianapolis: Indiana University Press.
Oland, M., Hart, S., & Frink, L. (Eds.). (2012). *Decolonizing Indigenous histories: Exploring prehistoric/colonial transitions in archaeology.* Tucson: University of Arizona Press.
Oliver, J. (2010). *Landscapes and transformations on the Northwest Coast: Colonial encounters in the Fraser Valley.* Tucson: University of Arizona Press.
Orser, C. (2012). An archaeology of Eurocentrism. *American Antiquity, 77*, 737–755.
Patterson, T. (1999). The political economy of archaeology in the United States. *Annual Review of Anthropology, 28*, 158–174.
Peacock, E., & Rafferty, J. (2007). Cultural Resource Management guidelines and practice in the United States. In W. Willems & M. van der Dries (Eds.), *Quality management in archaeology* (pp. 113–134). Oxford: Oxbow Books.
Pokotoylo, D. (1982). Contract archaeology and academic research: Crisis, what crisis? In P. Francis & E. Poplin (Eds.), *Directions in archaeology. A question of goals* (pp. 5–14). Calgary: Archaeological Association of the University of Calgary.
Roberts, H., Ahlstrom, R., & Roth, B. (Eds.). (2004). *From campus to corporation: The emergence of contract archaeology in the southwestern United States.* Washington: Society for American Archaeology.
Rockman, M., & Flatman, J. (Eds.). (2011). *Archaeology in society: Its relevance in the modern world.* New York: Springer.
Rubertone, P. (2000). The historical archaeology of Native Americans. *Annual Review of Anthropology, 29*, 425–446.
Sabloff, J. (2008). *Archaeology matters: Action archaeology in the modern world.* Walnut Creek: Left Coast Press.

Scarre, C., & Scarre, G. (Eds.). (2006). *The ethics of archaeology: Philosophical perspectives*. Cambridge: Cambridge University Press.
Schiffer, M., & Gumerman, G. J. (1977a). Cultural Resource Management. In M. Schiffer & G. Gumerman (Eds.), *Conservation archaeology. A guide for Cultural Resource Management studies* (pp. 1–17). New York: Academic.
Schiffer, M., & Gumerman, G. J. (1977b). Assessing significance. In M. Schiffer & G. Gumerman (Eds.), *Conservation archaeology. A guide for Cultural Resource Management studies* (pp. 239–247). New York: Academic.
Schiffer, M., & Gumerman, G. J. (Eds.). (1977c). *Conservation archaeology. A guide for Cultural Resource Management studies*. New York: Academic.
Schiffer, M., & House, J. (1977). Cultural Resource Management and archaeological research: The Cache Project. *Current Anthropology, 18*, 43–68.
Schmidt, P., & Patterson, T. (Eds.). (1996). *Making alternative histories: The practice of archaeology and history in non-Western settings*. Santa Fe: SAR Press.
Sebastian, L., & Lipe, W. D. (Eds.). (2009). *Archaeology and Cultural Resource Management: Visions for the future*. Santa Fe: SAR Press.
Shackel, P., & Chambers, E. (Eds.). (2004). *Places in mind: Public archaeology as applied anthropology*. New York: Routledge.
Silliman, S. (2005). Culture contact or colonialism? Challenges in the archaeology of Native North America. *American Antiquity, 70*, 55–74.
Silliman, S. W. (Ed.). (2008). *Collaborating at trowel's edge: Teaching and learning in Indigenous archaeology*. Tucson: University of Arizona Press.
Silliman, S. (2010). Indigenous traces in colonial spaces: Archaeologies of ambiguity, origin, and practice. *Journal of Social Archaeology, 10*, 28–58.
Silverman, H., & Ruggles, F. (Eds.). (2007). *Cultural heritage and human rights*. New York: Springer.
Singleton, T., & Orser, C. E. (2003). Descendant communities: Linking people in the present with the past. In L. J. Zimmerman, K. D. Vitelli, & J. Hollowell-Zimmer (Eds.), *Ethical issues in archaeology* (pp. 143–152). Walnut Creek: AltaMira Press.
Skeates, R. (2000). *Debating the archaeological heritage*. London: Duckworth.
Smith, L. (2004). *Archaeological theory and the politics of cultural heritage*. New York: Routledge.
Smith, L. (2006). *The uses of heritage*. New York: Routledge.
Smith, G., & Ehrenhard, J. (Eds.). (1991). *Protecting the past*. Baton Rouge: CRC Press.
Smith, G. S., Messenger, P. M., & Soderland, H. A. (Eds.). (2010). *Heritage values in contemporary society*. Walnut Creek: Left Coast Press.
Smith, L., & Waterton, E. (2009). There is no such thing as heritage. In E. Waterton & L. Smith (Eds.), *Taking archaeology out of heritage* (pp. 10–27). Newcastle: Cambridge Scholars' Publishing.
Smith, L., & Waterton, E. (2012). Constrained by commonsense: The authorized heritage discourse in contemporary debates. In R. Skeates, C. McDavid, & J. Carman (Eds.), *The Oxford handbook of public archaeology* (pp. 153–171). Oxford: Oxford University Press.
Stapp, D., & Burney, M. S. (Eds.). (2002). *Tribal Cultural Resource Management: The full circle to stewardship*. Walnut Creek: AltaMira Press.
Stapp, D., & Longenecker, J. G. (2009). *Avoiding archaeological disasters: A risk management approach*. Walnut Creek: Left Coast Press.
Stottmann, J. (Ed.). (2010). *Archaeologists as activists: Can archaeologists change the world?* Tuscaloosa: University of Alabama Press.
Swidler, N., Dongoske, K., Anyon, R., & Downer, A. (Eds.). (1997). *Native Americans and archaeologists: Stepping stones to common ground*. Walnut Creek: AltaMira Press.
Tainter, J. (2004). Persistent dilemmas in American Cultural Resource Management. In J. Bintliff (Ed.), *A companion to archaeology* (pp. 435–453). New York: Wiley-Blackwell.
Trigger, B. (1980). Archaeology and the image of the American Indian. *American Antiquity, 45*, 662–675.
Trigger, B. (1984). Alternative Archaeologies: Nationalist, Colonialist, Imperialist. *Man, 19*, 355–370.
Trigger, B. (2006). *A History of archaeological thought*. Cambridge: Cambridge University Press.
Trigger, D., & Dalley, C. (2010). Negotiating indigeneity: Culture, identity, and politics. *Reviews in Anthropology, 39*, 46–65.

Trimble, M., & Marino, E. (2003). Archaeological curation: An ethical imperative for the 21st century. In L. Zimmerman, K. Vitelli, & J. Hollowell-Zimmer (Eds.), *Ethical issues in archaeology* (pp. 99–112). Walnut Creek: AltaMira Press.
Valentine, D., & Simmons, A. (2004). A gray literature whitewash. In H. Roberts, R. Ahlstrom, & B. Roth (Eds.), *From campus to corporation: The emergence of contract archaeology in the southwestern United States* (pp. 126–182). Washington: Society for American Archaeology.
Watkins, J. (2000). *Indigenous archaeology: American Indian values and scientific practice*. Walnut Creek: AltaMira Press.
Watkins, J. (2003). Beyond the margin: American Indians, First Nations, and archaeology in North America. *American Antiquity, 68*, 273–285.
Watkins, J. (2004). Becoming American or becoming Indian? NAGPRA, Kennewick, and cultural affiliation. *Journal of Social Archaeology, 4*, 60–80.
Watkins, J. (2005). Through wary eyes: Indigenous perspectives on archaeology. *Annual Review of Anthropology, 34*, 429–449.
Welch, J., Altaha, M., Hoerig, K., & Riley, R. (2009). Best cultural heritage stewardship practices by and for the White Mountain Apache Tribe. *Conservation and Management of Archaeological Sites, 11*(2), 148–160.
Welch, J., & Ferguson, T. (2007). Putting Patria into repatriation: Cultural affiliations of White Mountain Appache Tribe Lands. *Journal of Social Archaeology, 7*, 171–198.
Welch, J., & Ferris, N. (2014). We have met the enemy and he is us: Transforming archaeology through sustainable design. In S. Atalay, L. Clauss, R. McGuire, & J. Welch (Eds.), *Transforming archaeology: Activist practices and prospects* (pp. 91–114). Walnut Creek, California: Left Coast Press.
Welch, J., Lepofsky, D., Caldwell, M., Combes, G., & Rust, C. (2011). Personal foundations for effective leadership in northern coast Salish heritage stewardship. *Heritage & Society, 4*, 83–114.
Wheaton, T. (2006). Private sector archaeology: Part of the problem or part of the solution? In L. Lonzy (Ed.), *Landscapes under pressure. Theory and practice of Cultural Heritage Research and preservation* (pp. 185–205). New York: Springer.
Whittlesey, S., & Reid, J. (2004). Money for nothing: Ethical issues in contemporary Cultural Resource Management. In H. Roberts, R. Ahlstrom, & B. Roth (Eds.), *From campus to corporation: The emergence of contract archaeology in the southwestern United States* (pp. 114–126). Washington: Society for American Archaeology.
Wilcox, M. (2009). *The Pueblo revolt and the mythology of conquest: An Indigenous archaeology of contact*. Berkeley: University of California Press.
Williamson, R. (2000). Trends and issues in consulting archaeology. *Canadian Journal of Archaeology, 24*(2), 158–162.
Williamson, R. (2009). An historic mess: The government is charged with protecting Ontario's historical artifacts on behalf of the people of Ontario. So why is so much of its cultural patrimony being thrown away? Retrieved May 26, 2009 from www.themarknews
Williamson, R. (2010). Planning for Ontario's archaeological past: Accomplishments and continuing challenges. *Revista de Arqueología Americana (Journal of American Archaeology), 28*, 7–45.
Wylie, A. (2005). The promise and perils of an ethic of stewardship. In L. Meskell & P. Pels (Eds.), *Embedding ethics* (pp. 47–68). Oxford: Berg.
Zimmerman, L. (2005). First, be humble: Working with Indigenous peoples and other descendant communities. In C. Smith & H. Martin Wobst (Eds.), *Indigenous archaeologies. Decolonizing theory and practice* (pp. 284–296). London: Routledge.
Zimmerman, L., Singleton, C., & Welch, J. (2010). Activism and creating a translational archaeology of homelessness. *World Archaeology, 42*, 443–454.
Zimmerman, L., Vitelli, K., & Hollowell, J. (Eds.). (2003). *Ethical issues in archaeology*. Walnut Creek: AltaMira Press.
Zorzin, N. (2010). Archéologie au Québec: portrait d'une profession. *Archéologiques, 23*, 1–15.
Zorzin, N. (2011). Contextualising contract archaeology in Quebec: Political-èconomy and economic dependencies. *Archaeological Review from Cambridge, 26*(1), 119–135.

Part II
Archaeological Ethics in the Global Arena: Emergences, Transformations, Accommodations

Chapter 8
Archaeology and Capitalist Development: Lines of Complicity

Alejandro Haber

Coming of Age in Buenos Aires

The city, that world beyond the bounds of the family house, turns increasingly interesting as one abandons childhood. The mystery and variety appeal anxious explorer of the surrounding world. In the late 1970s and early 1980s the world outside the house in suburban Buenos Aires was militarized, and the first steps by one own in the social forest of dangers and unknowns were also the first steps in a war-like landscape. I wonder if growing up at the hottest side of the cold war prepared myself in some way to the changes to overcome. As the public scars of 1970s' guerilla's action were progressively being effaced from the city streets and walls—and, as I would learn as part of the same process of growing up, were correspondingly concealed in clandestine jails of torture and death managed by the government—increasing voices of dissent managed to be heard here and there. "Open Theatre", an un(anti)official cultural festival that started in 1981 and eventually had its theatre set on fire by repressive irregular forces, was one of the more visible signs that people would not remain in silence. Every Thursday afternoon the Madres de Plaza de Mayo continued, almost solitary, moving round, silently but visibly claiming for their missing daughters and sons, a walk that had the effect of a drop that manages to drill the stone. Finally, the labor syndicates, whose consequent members "supplied" thousands of victims of the clandestine jails, decided to organize their first public demonstration against the government.

In the early 1980s, as one began to be bored of repeating at school the goodness of Western Christian Civilization, and as the stupidity of official censorship became more and more obvious (Eric Clapton's song *Cocaine* and Discépolo's tango

A. Haber (✉)
Escuela de Arqueología, Universidad Nacional de Catamarca & CONICET,
Salas Martínez 464, 4700 Catamarca, Argentina
e-mail: afhaber@gmail.com

C. Gnecco, D. Lippert (eds.), *Ethics and Archaeological Praxis*,
Ethical Archaeologies: The Politics of Social Justice 1,
DOI 10.1007/978-1-4939-1646-7_8

Cambalache red-listed among thousands of books, songs, and people), a general distrust on whatever discourse came from official means (the government, the school, TV, books) grew up as part of one self's bodily composition.

Those were the early days of neo-liberalism. Reagan and Thatcher, but more decidedly Videla and Pinochet, prepared the scene for a new account on the roundness of the world. In Argentina, the 1978 Football World Cup-time fear for "the image of the nation in the world" was suddenly but consistently replaced by the fear for investment capital not coming to the country. "If capitals don't come to Argentina", it was once and again explained in the TV show interestingly called *New Time* (*Tiempo Nuevo*) "we won't have possibilities of production, the economy would remain paralyzed, and we won't have even the technology to produce insulin for diabetes treatment". In those days there was not real chance to learn from an engaged discussion of these prophecies and, probably as an enduring consequence in political culture, the need of capital ended being assumed by the general public opinion for at least a couple of decades. Argentina was said to be neither a developed nor an underdeveloped country, but "developing". Someway we were on the mood for change, and while we saw ourselves as becoming something else, at the same time we were defined as lacking something. While in the early 1970s the most popular political aims were liberation and socialism, in the early 1980s we needed capitals. In between, terror came from the state.

Thirty years later, the capitals have finally come in. We are, more than ever, on the way to development. Extraction of natural resources, depletion of fuel reserves, poisoning of water and land, dispossession of peasants, greater urban poverty and violence, commoditization of politics, collapse of public education, and reappearance of epidemics inexistent for a century time are several of the effects of foreign capital investment. At the same time that the blood of this country is still being sucked, I finally became an established archaeologist. Capital, blood, and archaeology seem to be completely unrelated things.

Capital, it is said, is about putting economy into movement; blood is about circulation of necessary elements for bodily well-being and life; archaeology is a science that studies the past through its material remains. This chapter is about the non-obvious relationships between capital, blood, and archaeology. It is about my live, my history, and my place. It is about the world I live in, and about my living in the world. Made through contexts of repression and resistance, to be an intellectual has to deal with the consequences of repression and resistance, that is, colonialism, coloniality, and decoloniality. As an archaeologist, this also means developing decolonial ways of understanding archaeology, the broader world, and myself.

Welcoming Capital: A Farewell to Land

As the Cold War was said to come to an end in 1989, the next decade would undergo major transformations. While a secular underdevelopment was the official diagnosis for third-world countries, their chance to become "emergent economies" came together with their extreme receptiveness of foreign capital investment. In practical terms, this meant opening up of financial barriers, reduction of royalties for non-renewable resource exploitation, greater flexibility of the labor relations, and disposition of juridical resources at the service of great capital. State investment in health, education, social infrastructure, and care diminished continuously, while different sorts of repression contained social unrest. The active role of multilateral finance organizations as the World Bank and the International Monetary Fund in shaping these transformations along the decades of 1980 and 1990 was always justified by the assumed lack of financial capital. The cleansing terror of the military dictatorship was indeed coupled to a pedagogy terror: "we needed capital to develop ourselves, we needed development to survive".

In 1989 I moved from Buenos Aires to Catamarca while a known wall was being smashed to portable tourist's souvenirs in Berlin. Aside from implying a shift in personal lifestyle from a megalopolis to a provincial marginal town, that move made it possible for me to observe the face of the approaching edge of the reactivated colonial border. I also learned to see my own face reflected on the edge of that border. In those days the urban gaze saw the Catamarca valley lowlands as wild bush and unproductive land. I remember not knowing what to answer to the questions about what did people in Catamarca do. Those questions were marked by the expectation for a particular kind of answer: life is to be measured by its relative inclusion in the marketplace. What really matters when accounting for dwelling in one's place is the market-oriented production, even better if the global market is targeted. In those days the desert-like bush interrupted by huge mountains where I moved in while the world was becoming a hamlet produced not too many things more than its very dwellers.

In 1990 I began an archaeological research project in the Coneta-Miraflores area immediately south of Catamarca city, starting with an intensive archaeological survey of the foothill and the alluvial plains, what gave me the opportunity to know local people. In El Bañado hamlet, a tiny place in the dry bushy plains, I looked in vain for different ways of engaging local people with the past I was bringing to light. Instead, I learned from local people's stories. They told me how their production of charcoal from cut-wood which they sold on horse-driven carts in the city streets came to an end a decade before when a police checking point was set at the city entrance. Then they lived from the cattle they had in the bush and from several dispersed and small agricultural plots when they managed to withdraw water from the concrete-irrigation canals built in the 1950s for carrying water from a distant dam to the government-planned agricultural colonies immediately north and south of El Bañado. After a couple of years I left that research area. At the mid-1990s they began to be surrounded by fenced olive plantations, as the government promoted developmentally driven policies, including subsidies and tax deferral schemes. Land acquisition by olive entrepreneurs was never clear, neither clarified by the government. Most of the lowlands were remnants of communal lands of former indigenous nearby towns or disappeared haciendas, and consequently local people had no perfect titles but owned land customarily. Taking advantage of the land tenure legal status, real estate speculators intervened through mendacious actions obtaining and transferring titles to agri-business companies.

Twenty years later, the landscape of the valley lowlands has changed from wilderness to modernity. Olive plantations can be seen everywhere, while their water pumping from the always lowering subterranean streams remains unseen. Also the process of dispossession of local population remains invisible. Their lands were reduced so as to make cattle raising almost unviable, and many of the locals have migrated to the outskirt settlements around Catamarca city. As olive oil is produced for its exportation from Catamarca to overseas markets, the companies involved in the business multiply their incomes. At the end, capitals came in and the valley lowlands were developed. In the process local people were dispossessed of their land; as a result people grow more and more poor. As the local climatic conditions proved to be unsuitable for premium-olive oil production, capitals began to fly away to other valleys. Dried-out plantations where bushy woods used to grow, a couple of employees where rural communities used to make a living, dispossession and poverty, is the landscape left after the colonial boundary cycle passed.

My research project eventually came to an end just before the main changes happened to occur; I wrote three papers about settlement in the area some ten centuries before (Haber 1994, 1996; Haber et al. 1997), and one on the process of political organization and cultural mobilization of the local population that described local people as in the process of elaborating their identity as local villagers (Pizarro et al. 1995). I was unable to link social memory with land history, people's voice with the matter of my research. My archaeological finds, as I saw them, were old and mute, and the words of people, as I listened to them, were about a shallow time. A conception of lineal time was implicit in my idea of history; my idea of archaeological remains was focused on materiality. I thought of myself as talking and writing separately about both local history and people's telling of local history. I couldn't see, though, up to which point I was intervening in (un)doing local people's history. Now that time has gone and land has almost gone, history hurts.

Exactly what is hurtful for me as an archaeologist? Even feeling myself in solidarity with local people, the way that the archaeological discipline equipped me with the means to obtain knowledge placed me on the colonialist side of the border. I was looking for knowledge in the countryside. I was interested in long-term history, and I looked for archaeological finds in an extensive area of alluvial lowlands covered with xerophytic bush and open woods. I found several sherd-scatters, tested several of them, and finally excavated one that seemed to have a plastered house floor (Haber 1994). Local people were not so interested in my research as in my presence, but were reluctant to identify themselves with the indigenous people that I admitted were responsible for the remains (Pizarro 2006). They talked about their own history in the area, and they told stories about the "Indians", but I wasn't able to listen to those stories as history. My faith in my privileged capacity to access old history in some way pervaded myself of learning local memory as history in itself. It is not that I feel responsible for recent colonial expansion in the area; I know that it was (and still is) a process that has its own impulse. But I also acknowledge my personal contribution to epistemic and historic violence on local people. My archaeological data were themselves a predatory construction that mined local culture and history, both in material and epistemic terms. Materially, I took away things from the soil. Epistemically, I conducted myself as if the metaphysical conditions of my discipline were universal and natural, as if my conception of time, materiality, and knowledge were naturally correct. My own constitution as an expert in the locality was a direct function of my predation on the local constitution.

Epistemological predation is, in fact, a corollary of an epistemic predation (de Castro 2010) or, even better, an ontological predation incorporated through the formative years at university. Western episteme needs to feed itself from the destruction of others' epistemes; the Western being lives through the transformation of its other. The West exists only in its border. And the border of the West is always warlike. In postcolonial times, archaeology turned to be one more of the weapons used in the battlefield. Once you are inside the battle with a weapon in your hand, you can be hurt if you don't know which side you should point at. This chapter is about remaking decisions, considering the ways archaeology, history, and knowledge are already weapons in the "cool" war.

Living at the Colonial Border

One of the main features of the current renewed cycle of colonialism is the appearance of huge amounts of capital available for venture investments. Financial fluidity makes possible the collection of capital from diverse sources and its investment in equally diverse ventures. It also fosters the everywhere appearance of developers, a new kind of people specialized in the transformation of knowledge into commodities.

In the case of the Catamarca valley lowlands, for instance, a combination of different pieces of knowledge were transformed by developers: agronomical engineering of olive plantations, olive oil processing and commercialization, arid land irrigation techniques, legal situation of local land tenure, juridical particularities of land appropriation, and financial prospecting. A mix of agronomy, laws, and business made able the expansion of the colonial border. Knowledge was transformed into commodity. Why is capital so voracious in poor countries? Why seems postcapitalism to have renewed the pace of colonial borders around the darker side of the globe? Economic causes, such as the oversupply of capital, are part of the explanation. But the culture of colonialism is also a central part of the understanding of the current border reactivation. The reorientation to poor countries of industrial extractive activities, which are also energy demanding and/or polluting, has been called "environmental racism", which has been seen intimately coupled to an "ecological imperialism" (Machado 2009). Those industries are technologically driven and huge in scale, and imply very high capital investments and global markets. For the sake of maintaining high their revenues, these postcolonial investments imply ecological liabilities. The management of these is much cheaper to deal with in poor countries than in countries where the capitals come from. Metropolitan countries also tend to benefit much more from the colonial products. For instance, olive oil, paper, soy for oil and bio-fuel, and metals are goods mostly consumed in the north but mostly (and increasingly) produced in the south. Together with such an imbalance in the terms of exchange, the depletion of freshwater resources even in already arid dry areas, the pollution of water reservoirs with cyanide and land with glyphosate and other dangerous chemicals, and the consumption of huge amounts of energy with further ecological consequences are the main effects that remain within the colonies. At the same time goods and revenues flow to northern metropolis.

The peoples from the global south have our land and water polluted and depleted, our mountains milled to powder-size particles, our natural reserves emptied, and our people poisoned and dispossessed. Southern people are worthless than others from the perspective of global capital. Colonialism is always about land, its resources, and people. And it is always basically racist. This is the way post-capitalism—globalization by other name—recapitulates colonialism. Even while both Western leaders and thinkers are very eloquent about their ideas against racism and Western intellectuals and scholars are often very much committed in the same direction, the Western episteme, with its set of ideas about development, history, and charity, cannot avoid being a continuation of colonialism and racism in all its forms.

The remaining question is how is that colonial expansion is possible with a minimum of social resistance in the Catamarca valley plains. This question is not related to the contents of the pieces of knowledge combined in the development process, but on the fact that those—and other—pieces of knowledge were enacted in situ as hegemonic knowledge. In other words, it is not the semantics of knowledge what explains development a.k.a. colonial expansion in the absence of physical violence, but the performativity of expertise. This epistemic violence does not make its appearance at the very moment of colonial expansion, but is already disseminated by disciplining institutions (school, law, science). Thus, colonialism has, also in postcolonial contexts, a double-edged contribution of academic knowledge. On the one hand, it provides the content that produces, appropriately combined, the convenient commodities that justify the revenue expectancies of capital investment. On the other hand, scientific and academic knowledge already exerted epistemic violence on local knowledge, increasing credibility of its effectiveness and superiority in accounting for the world. Colonial expansion acts on the basis of hegemonic relationships already contributed upon by science and academic disciplines.

The place as intellectual against colonialism is the same place where I live in. It is my land, my air, my water, my people, my children, myself as person and as collective and as the place I am writing from and for. This is my political determination; it implies that this writing may be relevant for ones and irrelevant for others. But the place as intellectual is double: I'm also, as disciplined intellectual and willingly or not, an agent of epistemic violence. The border is not a line to be seen out there, but a relational difference that constitutes us.

I'm not in this place because of an intellectual fashion; I have no choice but to be here. I inhabit this land and this land inhabits me. And this writing is from this land and towards this piece of land. This writing is not only about colonialism but it is also about archaeology. How is archaeology involved in colonialism? I've already said something in this short introduction. I'll now be more systematic in the exposition. Archaeology is involved in colonialism in different layers. I'll proceed with an excavation of those layers, from the topsoil to the deep bottom, that is, from active orientations to epistemic and metaphysical understandings.

Archaeology and Colonialism I: Archaeology as Developer

As an undergraduate student in the late dictatorship and early post-dictatorship years in Argentina (mid-1980s), a central discussion in university was about the role of anthropologists and archaeologists. This discussion was bounded in the "applied" vs. "academic" knowledge debate, or, in other words, helping vs. knowing others. In the early 1990s, once in Catamarca, I met several colleagues that argued for the transformation of archaeological knowledge into a commodity for the tourism market, and thus transforming academic research into a strategy for development. At that time every single research-funding agency began to include "development" within the factors for asserting relevance for research proposals. Archaeologists moved massively to the idea of tourism development, albeit the great majority of them as a formal justification for their proposals, and only few of them designing programs for presenting sites and/or artifacts as tourist attractions.

At least since mid-twentieth century tourist industry is largely based on archaeological attractions in some countries as México, Perú, and Egypt. There, state investment in archaeological research is probably more related to tourist development than in other countries. It was nevertheless not until the 1990s that tourism was transformed into a global industry. With the aid of UNESCO-designed devices such as the World Heritage list, archaeological sites (and a bit later also landscapes) gained the potential of being transformed into commodities to be sold to national and/or international tourists coming in to see, touch, picture, and buy. Tourists "make" these sites as much as they visit them. Archaeologists intervene in supplying the material remains and the basic narrative fabric into which the remains are inserted so as to build them as a tourist experience. Archaeological knowledge is directly transformed into commodity. Tourist narratives couple an exploitation of the exotic, the passage of time, and the irretrievable otherness of the ruins, together with an explanation of the basics of archaeological discipline, its aims, its subject matter, and its methods. The other is built at a distance from the tourist, and the archaeologist is himself/herself placed as the necessary intermediate between the tourist and the attraction, between the present and the past, but also between the urban and the rural, the West and the indigenous, the modern and the precolonial. Archaeology is present in the content of the narrative and in the content of the ruins, but it is also present as the way—the correct way—of transcending the distance.

Several consequences arise from tourist development in peasant/indigenous areas apart from market place expansion. Only some of them are relevant at this stage. The irruption of the capitalist market in previous peasant and/or indigenous areas has many disastrous consequences for local people. The development of a tourist resource implies many associated businesses. Tourists pay for transportation, accommodation, meals, information, handicrafts, and a whole of further services, each one of these providing an opportunity for capital investment from outside the locality. Because local peasant communities' economies are often at least partially based on self-subsistence, it is usually the case that local people have less available capital than outsiders to compete in equal conditions with them.

Given such imbalances local people usually end allocated in the lowest echelons of the tourist industry, as cheap handicraft manufacturers, or as low-paid employees of outsiders' businesses.

An even more dramatic consequence of tourist development is related to the commoditization of land, a process triggered as soon as the tourist development proves to be a real opportunity for venture capital investment. Local people's relationship to land is usually regulated by customary law, and is rarely recognized by state bureaucracies. The pressure of real estate speculation, even sometimes through not entirely legitimate procedures, often results in the dispossession of local people from their land. The case of Tilcara and other towns in the Quebrada de Humahuaca area (Jujuy, Argentina) is quite eloquent of this process. Tilcareño people has been virtually dispossessed from their urban and semi-urban plots as soon as the inclusion of the Quebrada in the UNESCO World Heritage list as a cultural landscape began to show its effect in tourist development. The inclusion of their area in an international showcase fostered tourism and had the immediate effect on land prizes. The irony is that local dwellers, that is, the very reason for the Quebrada de Humahuaca being included in the UNESCO list, are the first victims of that inclusion. Tourism pushes the colonial border, and as it does so, it spoils its former attractiveness. Simulacra of the other are always preferred at the end, because the other, already transformed in the victim of tourism, is no more attractive once it displays the scars of violence.

It is not that archaeologists need to be directly involved in dispossession to make archaeology responsible of colonial consequences as those commented above. Archaeologists involved in development-oriented research are usually highly committed to the welfare of local people. It is highly probable that the dispossession of local peoples' lands was never in the mind of the archaeologists researching in the Quebrada de Humahuaca area, including those who reconstructed the Pucará de Tilcara archaeological site, and lived in the area as personnel of a locally based research institute and museum. Colonialism need not to exclude good intentions or good practice; on the contrary, it is more often than not that the colonial border is driven by good intentions of helping others.

Archaeology is only one piece of knowledge mobilized in tourist development, others being the juridical status of land, tourist business and marketing, and many others. It is rare that archaeologists market tourism themselves, but archaeologists do intervene in marketing their own discipline by coupling it to development aims, as tourism. Archaeological discipline already builds its knowledge as a matter of expertise, distancing archaeological narratives from local people's ones. The expertise of archaeology disjoins the knowledge that it produces about the past from local knowledge. The intervention of archaeology usually implies the exclusion of local knowledge, making it easy for archaeology to intervene in tourist development projects as expert knowledge—that is, autonomous from the people who are subject to the consequences of that knowledge and projects. It is often the case that tourist developers use archaeological narratives to build tourist commodities by their own. In these cases, the intervention of archaeology is indirect: having produced public texts about certain peoples and places, archaeologists do not retain control on them, exposing in public information and narratives that are used by third parties with their own aims.

The tourism market, once arrived, imposes its own dynamic. Tourism, being one of the main areas of market global expansion during the last couple of decades, is always looking for new formerly unknown destinies, always more distant and exotic, in order to feed the need of Western public consumption of its otherness. Once tourism market enters local communities, it is almost impossible to contain, local people being the first victims. "Community," "sustainable," "indigenous," and other so-called strands of soft-brand "ecological" tourism have been developed in order to manage sad consequences of tourist expansion. It is never easy enough to know whether these tourisms are local communities' initiatives in conditions of secured relationship to land and resources and local management of tourist services, or if on the contrary these labels are marketing make-ups seeking for ecologically minded shares of the tourist market. And even if the socio-economic consequences of tourism are locally controlled and managed, it remains to be seen which the sociocultural consequences would be, and how would these impact in locally sustained relationships to land.

Being the more important and visible, tourism is not the only development orientation of archaeology. Reactivation of largely abandoned agricultural technologies using archaeological data is a conspicuous trend alongside the Andes. Archaeologists intervene in these projects unburying supposedly forgotten technologies and planning and executing its reconstruction and reactivation. In a recent field survey of the present situation of formerly published reactivations, Alex Herrera (2011) has shown the overall unsuccessfulness of that strategy after two decades, and the superficiality of the views of technologically driven developmental change that inspired many of those reactivation projects. In the majority of the cases major external disturbances have not been observed in local communities, but it should be reminded that these are generally unsuccessful projects.

After many decades of development-oriented policies, an evaluation of the appropriateness of development as an aim is needed. As Escobar (2005) aptly poses, it is more probable that development policies are responsible for the worsening of social and economic conditions of the targeted populations than having fulfilled its purported aims. Development itself has been so much criticized as a concept and as a policy that it remains to be a mystery why it is so much recapitulated by its qualification as local, ecological, appropriate, sustainable, etc. The mystery seems to be focused on the fact that development is something that ends being desired but never accomplished or, even worse, because it is never accomplished it continues to be an object of desire (Žižek 2003).

When development consolidates as an object of desire, it becomes empty of meaningful content. It is attractive as a sign, not as a meaning. Development works as an empty significant placed at the arrow of a vector line. This unaccomplished (always-not-yet-accomplished) desired place is in some way close to the place of utterance of the rhetoric of development. The underdeveloped/developing world is uttered as if oriented towards the vector's end; the South is uttered as yet lacking development, as oriented to it. Blending Aristotelian metaphysics of substance together with Judeo-Christian metaphysics of messianic time, the very idea of unfolding transmitted by the word development, implies that something is folded in some way. Certain possibilities are within something in a folded, latent, way, and these possibilities can be unfolded, actualized. In some sense, development is the shadow of the West as projected on the other.

The Pristine Other and the Gone Past, which are so appealing for the tourism industry, are related to the wide popularization of the vectorial theory of time in the West. While the orientation towards development cannot be proved, and except for the capitals involved the state of plentitude is never achieved, the vectoriality of time can at least be supplied with a sense of materiality and truth when doing archaeological tourism. Both pastness and otherness are conjoined in the personal experience of tourism, an experience that relationally places the person of the tourist in a progressive point of the vectorial timeline. Tourism need not be a true experience, for it is already experienced as truth. Visiting a ruin beside a peasant indigenous village provides the means to transform the tourist in a direct witness of vectorline time.

Archaeology and Colonialism II: Archaeology Licensing Development

Archaeology is increasingly implied in licensing development projects rather than actively intervening as developer itself. CRM legislation is quite different alongside the world, going from mandatory high-coverage impact assessment for every kind of soil movement in any kind of land to virtually inexistent pertinent legislation. Even in these latter cases, archaeological impact assessment is done when development projects are financed by multilateral agencies or when certain kinds of industries are to be established. Roadway building (and other lineal layout projects for transport infrastructure) and large-scale mining are among the projects usually demanding assessments. In Argentina, for instance, the mining industry has a singular environmental law that includes archaeological assessment, while large-scale agro-business, usually implying the modification of extensive tracts of land, does not. Archaeology intervenes researching the potential effects on archaeological remains of the actions to be executed by the project. In contexts where state governments are interested in the projects themselves, or even when mining companies have such a gigantic financial power that they virtually decide the orientation of governmental decisions, state control for professional impact assessment is quite limited. But even if impact assessments were not a matter of venial practices, the structure of archaeological intervention is what deserves to be analyzed here.

When included in impact assessments, archaeology is included in an administrative procedure already conceptualized for the licensing of a previously targeted project. The aims and general actions of the investment projects are not in question when archaeology is called to intervene. Archaeological remains are already defined as a specific segment of the material landscape to be acted upon, and archaeology is already defined as the expert knowledge to deal with it. Local knowledge regarding the same matter that matters archaeology is unworthy for the administrative procedure. In turns to be the case that archaeology quantifies and qualifies the impacts on cultural heritage, and even tries to maintain the entirety of the historical and cultural heritage. While archaeology acts on behalf of a cultural heritage to be potentially impacted by a project, it is usually the case that the very same project seriously challenges the continuity of the lives and culture of the heirs to that same heritage. While the heritage is already disjoined from its heirs, archaeology comes to intermediate between both of them. CRM places archaeology within that disjuncture. But the intermediation of archaeology is not balanced; archaeology, seen as a discipline specialized in the archaeological record, faces the heritage while neglecting the heirs' relationship (territorial inheritance) to it.

This is particularly the case with large-scale mining, often but not always of the open-pit kind, usually including chemical procedures for mineral processing. Large-scale mining projects, rapidly expanding all along South America and Africa as soon as metropolitan nations prefer to get rid of such polluting industries, consume and pollute gigantic amounts of freshwater (even in desert areas), destroy significant aspects of the landscape, pollute the air, the soil, and the subsoil, corrupt local state bureaucracies in order to make them defend their interests, and introduces deep social divisions within local communities (Svampa and Antonelli 2009). Archaeology intervenes assessing the impact of these investment projects on the archaeological record, quantifying the impacts so that they can be included within the costs of the project. The scale of investment of large-scale mining projects tends to be so big that archaeological impacts don't amount to the regulation of the project. Impact assessment is one of the most clear post-disciplinary devices for capitalist expansion, replacing political regulation through public governmental decisions by technical modulation through expert knowledge intervention (Lazzarato 2006). Large-scale mining projects' feasibility is usually not precluded because of archaeological impacts, but local dwellers' feasibility usually is. Nevertheless, what is the sense of managing the impacts on cultural heritage if mining challenges the life of local heir populations? A heritage without heirs is difficult to conceive if not as a symbol of the disappearance of cultural inheritance. Archaeological impact assessment seems to imply the replacement of inhabited inheritance by archaeological identity.

Archaeology and Colonialism III: Coloniality of Time

Modernity is, basically, a theory of history. It says that tradition withholds the human potential for mastering the world; liberating itself from tradition the full human potential could be actualized. Disease, famine, ignorance, poverty, and other evils will be overcome through the modern intervention controlling nature and tradition. History, within modern theory, moves from evil past to good future. Rational planning and intervention fuel the movement of history. Modernity is a theory of power over primary nature, and a practice of power over a second nature, that is, society. Domination of nature is always the domination of someone's lands, usually being peasants and non-Western peoples. Modernity was always the theory of power of ascent social classes, being low nobility, bourgeoisie, conquerors, adventurers, and every kind of speculator. In the present time modernity is the theory of developers.

Western theory of time has at least two main components. One of them is linearity. Time passes from past to present to future along a timeline; and the timeline is the easiest representation of historic time. Events happen, one after the other. But the line of time is not just a line; it is also a vector. A vector is particular kind of straight line, which has magnitude and direction. The magnitude of time is the distance to a departure point, and the direction is its orientation in space. As a vector, history has a point of origin and a direction. Within Western tradition, the point of origin is sometimes overtly metaphysical, as in the case of the biblical creation, or the arrival of the Son of God to the human world. Within the modern recapitulation of Western tradition, another origin point is set in the onset of history, the knowledge about history as a period in time—a period that starts when historical knowledge does.

Within the West, res gestae begin when historia rerum gestarum departs: the (relevant) history of humankind begins when the (Western) discipline of knowledge of that history is invented. History—the events—is understood as a magnitude of time, that is, a length of the line from the metaphysical departure to the present. History, as viewed from the Western theory of time, consists in the history of the West. The history that happened and matters (that is, history of the West and its expansion on the other) has its origins in the invention of the device for codifying Western knowledge as superior (history as what it is told about what has happened). The origin point in Western version of history is coupled, thus, to its self-understanding as a superior civilization and at the same time to the consideration of the superiority of its own means for considering itself superior. The metaphysics of (Western) history is objectified in the timeline (in objective history), producing the effect of a metaphysical point of origin, being at the same time a naturalized place of knowledge. Such a point of origin marks the origin of the self (the West as civilization as a project of knowledge and intervention). The birth of Jesus in Nazareth is the main origin point in the time line, and marks the origin of the Christian self. Jesus' life (what has happened) is narrated in the gospels (the tale of what has happened), and the correct knowledge of the sacred history is obtained through the reading of the sacred texts that codify history. In European countries, history is usually considered as having its origin when the first written historical sources through which they can be known appeared, usually from Roman conquerors, on particular places where they expanded. The resistant and dominated peoples, as named by those sources, become the ancestors of the now national selves. Before those peoples there was not history but prehistory. In the Americas, the arrival of Columbus is a second point of origin, marking the transplantation of the self to the New World, and separating history (known) from prehistory (unknown). Archaeology is devoted primarily to obtaining knowledge of pre-historic times, expanding Western coding and rules for knowing history over the periods lacking written sources. It remains clear that the place from where history is classified as known (or knowable) and unknown (or unknowable) is the same place from where the conquest is practiced and theorized. History as the representation of the Western self embodies the West as a discourse of knowledge and a project of domination.

As every metaphysical origin point that marks the onset of a project (moralizing, civilizing, purifying), Western timeline is also projected towards the future. For the Iberian conquerors in the Americas during the first modernity, the future was thought as a greater proximity to Christ. For the European conquerors during the second modernity, and the European descendants in the politically independent countries, and evolutionary anthropology, the future was thought as civilization (understood as Western civilization). For present-day developers and Western common sense in general, the future consists of development. Western time is always a vector, with a magnitude and a direction. This fundamental spatial orientation of Western time, hard wired in its founding metaphysics, is the way both space and otherness are collapsed in time. Western time connotes time and denotes domination. The West is a theory of history where history consists in the direction towards increasing domination of man over nature, of modernity over tradition, of the West over the other.

The idea of development is based on the vector kind of time, as it is understood by Western metaphysically based theory. This is why development need not be demonstrated to be a powerful significant: it is deeply rooted in Western metaphysics.

Archaeology is not innocent regarding the strengthening of Western notions of time. It expands the Western tradition of history to times when, and places where, that tradition is not directly applicable. Being archaeology a project of knowledge codified in Western ideas on time and history, it expands on "prehistoric" times and "oral" peoples the means for objectifying Western metaphysics. Archaeology awards Western time to non-Western peoples by transporting to their worlds the metaphysical conditionings of Western historiography. In this way, it can be said that the West feeds itself on histories-other-than-itself. Archaeology has a central role in this particular predatory process.

The West needs its other for fulfilling its core project of expansion. But the other needed by the West should not manifest itself as other-in-itself, that is, cannot manifest in its own terms, for those terms are unbearable for the West. When faced to the other-self, the West suffers being confronted to its own predatory self. Thus the other is represented as excessive, animal-like, governed by emotions and needs, repulsive, in other words, non-representable. The other must be tamed, already apprehensible by Western discourse even as other (that is, other-than-West). The other in Western discourse is already the shadow of the West; it cannot speak by itself, as Spivak (1988) argues, because it is already a shadow, not a self. The history of the other written by archaeology is already a history in Western terms, in the sense that the West has already awarded to the other its own metaphysics (Western time in the first hand).

Development is based on Western metaphysics of time. It implies a straight line with magnitude and a direction. As every people can be placed in a point on the timeline, each one's development has a magnitude. That magnitude admits the comparison between any two societies in terms of relative development. As the core assumption is not just lineal but vector-like, it is implied that there are certain societies more developed than others, and that those who are underdeveloped should move along the vector in the direction already represented by developed societies, thus collapsing space and otherness in the representation of time. Development is an appeal to move forward in the line, usually said backwards: "come to this direction", "develop yourselves", "let us help you", "let us show you the way", "move forward". Because of the kind of cultural colonization exerted by the West that consists in considering Western knowledge a superior kind of knowledge, what has been called the coloniality of knowledge (Quijano 2000), it can also be a discourse of the (already tamed) Other: "let us develop ourselves", "let us be as them", "let them help us and show us the way".

Archaeology provides the means to naturalize and objectify the linearity of time and its vector-like orientation towards the future. Archaeology places its subject matter on lineal time, aligns each fact along the line, one after the other. The technical manipulation of time through chronometry has been a central preoccupation of archaeology because chronology is the objectification of the Western cultural ideas on time. Also, the strong emphasis of archaeology on evolution and/or process provides directionality to the timeline. Because archaeology has become the means to bridge the unbridgeable relationship with the "gone time", it is archaeology itself the field that embodies the conveyance of an objective reality of Western time. The stratification of layers in an archaeological excavation is the most potent image of linearity and directionality, moving Western metaphysics from objectification to naturalization. Symbols based on Western lineal and vector time are not really known, but "felt" as natural. Thinking of the past as being in front of us, or living today, sounds unnatural, and saying such things can imply be considered insane. The naturalness of development owes much to archaeology's provision of a material nature for Western metaphysical time.

Archaeology and Colonialism IV: Archaeology as Epistemic Violence

The metaphysical hard wiring of Western history is built within its own foundations and definitions of object and method. Within its historiographical frameworks Western metaphysics couples both, history as facts happening along the line of time and historiography as a set of rules and codes for privileging sight and alphabetic writing over memory and other textual traditions. Other historiographical traditions, based on oral devices, textiles, ritual, and performance, are ruled out from the methods accepted as correct. At the same time history becomes the self-narration of the West as superior civilization. Western history as res gestae and Western history as historia rerum gestarum, that is, history as what has happened and history as what is told about what has happened become, thus, one and the same thing with the West. The West is at once the subject matter of history and the agent of historiography (Trouillot 1997).

In fact, the founding of Western historiography is related to a double operation of domination of the other being and exclusion of other knowledge. In the fifth century B.C. Herodotus, the so-called Father of (Western) History, established a classification of knowledge in order to write a narrative about what has happened in the war the Greeks fought against the Medes. On the one hand, Herodotus coined the word barbaroi to nominate the cultural other, in fact, the enemies or would-be enemies of the Greeks. The epithet, coming from the repetition of the particle bar which, meaning nothing but a vocal sound, gives the idea that the other, not speaking the writer's language, lacks a proper one. At the same time history, that is, the tale about what has happened, was to be written based on a classification of sources of information, a gradation of knowledge, from falseness to truth. The superior sources of information are for Herodotus those given to him directly by eyewitnesses, while social memory and legend were considered as polluted by imagination and falseness. Thus, already in the founding moments of Western historiography there was a coupling of the subject matter of history (what has happened) and the basic method for writing confident tales about what has happened. Linguistic (and cultural) competence on the historian's language and eye witnessing complement each other to bound the writing of history about the self-relationship with the others within a cultural intimacy (Abercrombie 1998).

The classical Greek historiographic footprint was inherited by future expansionist organizations, such as the Roman Empire and the Christian Church. Roman writers described European barbarians, that is, their actual or potential enemies, as the other. In Renaissance times and after, those texts were to be considered the demarcations of the local divides between history and prehistory. When Iberian colonial expansion unfolded over the Americas in the fifteenth and sixteenth centuries, writing of history became a central imperial strategy of justification of invasion. Native peoples of Tawantinsuyo, while having their own textual traditions, lacked alphabetic writing. As a result, the European divide between history and prehistory was transported to the Americas. What was to evolve as "archaeology" in Europe for knowing times before alphabetic-writing sources was to be applied in the Americas to the study of the Other. The closer relationship of archaeological discipline to History in Europe and to Anthropology in the Americas, says a lot more about the first person of archaeological discipline than about any other fact.

Archaeology differs from history in a number of basic features. It, nevertheless, shares history's foundational coupling of the metaphysical divide in its object and method. In fact, archaeology is, much more that it is usually acknowledged, an extension over the other of Western metaphysics of history. Archaeology introduces the language with which other's relationship with ancestors, things and gods is collapsed within a discipline of knowledge (Haber 2012). This discipline is framed in a singular metaphysics that is transported as if it were universal, not as a planned aim, but in its very frameworks and fundamental definitions.

Back to the example drawn from my own brief research in the Catamarca valley alluvial plains, the archaeological discipline equipped me with a particular set of ideas about time and history. These ideas were coined in the Western belief in a lineal, dimensional, measurable time, and that history consists on accounting for what happened along that time. Even if interested on local oral references to local history, occupation of the area, and cultural and political identities, I was unable to recognize the constitutive differential link between archaeological data and social memory. I was disciplined to count only material remains as data for archaeology, and implicitly to exclude what remains in its non-material character. Focused on material remains from what I understood as a distant past (pre-Columbian, at least), I was almost implicitly equipped with the means to ignore the remaining consequences of colonialism in the area, and present local cultural mobilization in their silenced struggle to remain themselves.

Because of the involvement of the archaeological team with local population, local people visited us a couple of kilometers from El Bañado village where I excavated an area of 25 m^2. One-half meter below the surface I found a plastered house floor delimited by lines of postholes (Haber 1994). This was the first (and the only one as far as I know) archaeological find for built settlement in the alluvial plains area (while on the contrary in the surrounding piedmont and hills there is plenty of visible remains of occupation) (Haber 1996; Haber et al. 1997). I thought that this find could be interesting for local people's claims regarding traditional relationship to land, but their disinterest on my account (as apparently my own disinterest on their's) proved that things were being thought otherwise. A boy came almost every day from El Bañado with the group of students to the excavation spot. When invited to participate of the excavation, he politely refused. Instead, he dug his own excavation just by ours. Happy to provide him with tools and plastic bags at his demand, he handed me a bag full of sherds at the end of the day. As I understood things happening, he was trying to engage as subject of research while he refused (as generally the local community did) to engage with the subject matter of the research. What was my research about was probably uninteresting for El Bañado people; the importance of the research was focused on who was spelling history out. It is evident now that local processes demanded at that time something different from archaeological surveying and excavation. But what wasn't in that time as clear as now is that the sole presence of a "qualified" utterance exerts epistemic violence over local vocality. While one feels oneself equipped with a powerful instrument of knowledge as archaeology, one ends being instrument of the discipline. Researching archaeology in that context was an intervention that diminished local vocality. A parallel excavation dug by a boy was one local resistance, but it could not be assembled within the disciplinary framework put to work by a research design. There is an unacknowledged differential relationship between archaeological objectification and local subjectification.

The sole idea of expertise regarding the other's place, culture and history, is violent to the difficult intercultural workings of symbolic expression and the concomitant collective subjetivation. As a banner in an archaeological museum in Antofagasta de la Sierra village (Catamarca, Argentina), explaining the exhibition assembled by the archaeological team that researches in the area, ends:

> We have traveled as briefly as a breeze through 10,000 years of history of the man of Puna region. Antofagasta de la Sierra and its people go on living every day that difficult romance between the man and the desert. Lonely and beautiful landscapes, proud camelids, powerful winds, freezing winters and the burning summer sun, are part of the quotidian experience of Puneño people, today as they were thousands of years ago. They, men and women, continue to be here, serene, humble and proud. Maybe they know that they are heirs to a lineage that knew how to conquer the mountain and approximate the sky. Many people of this nation

ignore all about the Puna, its inhospitable and heady beauty, its people's silent hospitality, its thousands of years of history. Antofagasta de la Sierra walks towards the future trying to climb to the benefits of new technology, but without discarding its millenarian traditions. In order to do that it tries to recognize itself in it's past and offer it to its conationals. If archaeologists are retrievers of memory, the people are the owner and custodian of that retrieved memory.

The role of archaeology seems to be to intermediate between the subjects of memory and memory itself. Any challenge to that intermediate position is felt as a challenge to the discipline as a whole. I received closed resistance from my colleagues as I commented the El Bañado boy case at the university department, as is the case every time other's vocalities are listened. Once listened, local vocalities say: "we can deal with our history too, we don't need you".

My research in the El Bañado area came to an end in a couple of years from its starting date. A great deal had to be done in order to dismount epistemic violence from archaeological discipline.

Capital, Blood, and Archaeology

This chapter introduces a cultural contextualization of archaeological discipline in post-colonial times. Firstly, it was shown here how is the culture and practice of capital expansion as it is seen, not from the metropolis, but from the colonial border. This has implied depicting the border, both as a place of cultural and ideological production and a place of colonial friction. It was shown here how the construction of cultural hegemony concerning capitalism is an ongoing process, and that this process is often linked to intense forms of political violence, including diverse forms of state-commanded pedagogy. At the same time, the ways in which capitalism culture is based on broader Western metaphysics, prominently within this a singular theory of history, were described. The aim of this discussion is to depict capitalism as, apart from an economic and social system, a culture. The consequence of this discussion is a move of the view of capitalism as a political option to a cultural bond. Epistemically speaking, the border is the counterpoint of globalization. But in economical terms they are no counterpoints but structurally linked: the border is reactivated under the conditions of globalization capitalism.

As seen from the other side of globalization, the colonial border of capitalist expansion is shown under the banner of blood. Here, blood is to be understood as the necessary constituent for life. In Eduardo Galeano's famous book (1971) given as a Trojan gift to the US President Obama by the Venezuelan President Chávez, blood includes the lives of the people, its land and resources, and the violence exerted over local resistances. Galeano rewrote the postcolonial history of Latin America through the description to what he called "the open veins", that is, the mechanisms and instruments for sucking the blood of Latin America all along its history. Blood is a strong image, and is purposely so. Blood means, thus, not just the object of colonial sacking, but the place where I'm related to history not just as researcher, but also as inhabitant. Blood means that history hurts me, and that I consciously place myself in that place for relating with history.

I'm archaeologist. Archaeology is what I do, and what I do for a living. This chapter showed how is that archaeology places me on the other side of the colonial border concerning capital and blood (the "other" side here means the opposite side from where I would prefer to be). So, this is my explanation of my discomfort with archaeology and my point of departure from archaeology as it is. To depart does not imply to abandon, to forget neither to neglect. I'm seriously committed to understanding the place of the discipline in our world. I don't share the common understanding of archaeology (often self-understanding) as a secondary or unimportant endeavor. I think that, albeit often unrecognized, archaeology is entangled at the very focus of postcolonial world and that postcolonial contexts are usually implicated at the trowel's edge (Shepherd 2002). This text is a contribution to the theory of those postcolonial contexts and the roles that archaeology plays in them. The ethical contexts for archaeological practice are at the same time the political contexts of social practice and the epistemic contexts of subjectivity. If one thinks of layers of complicity, it should be said that the ethical discussion of archaeological practice should be informed by the relationships among the different layers, even cultural constituencies and ontological taken-for-granted. Once the role as agents of coloniality is clearly seen, openness to subjective change in intercultural conversation can be a desired aim (Haber 2011). But such an issue falls beyond the end of this text.

References

Abercrombie, T. (1998). *Pathways of memory and power: Ethnography and history among an Andean People*. Madison: University of Wisconsin.

De Castro, E. V. (2010). *Metafísicas caníbales. Líneas de antropología posestructural*. Buenos Aires: Katz.

Escobar, A. (2005). *Más allá del tercer mundo: globalización y diferencia*. Bogotá: ICANH.

Galeano, E. (1971). *Las venas abiertas de América Latina*. Buenos Aires: Siglo XXI.

Haber, A. (1994). La Aguada en el Valle de Catamarca. Detección y caracterización de sitios en la cuenca inferior de Coneta-Miraflores (Huillapima, Capayán, Catamarca, Argentina). *Boletín Del Museo Regional de Atacama, 4*, 71–83.

Haber, A. (1996). Paisaje y asentamiento. Investigaciones arqueológicas en la cuenca del Río Coneta-Miraflores (Huillapima, Capayán, Catamarca). *Revista Del Museo Municipal de Historia Natural, 25*, 123–139.

Haber, A. (2011). Nometodología payanesa. Notas de arqueología indisciplinada. *Revista Chilena de Antropología, 23*, 9–49.

Haber, A. (2012). Severo's severity and Antonlín's paradox. *E-Flux, 36*, 1–6.

Haber, A., Ferreyra, J., Granizo, G., Quesada, M., & Videla, F. (1997). Construcción de categorías de paisaje en Capayán. *Shincal, 6*, 83–100.

Herrera, A. (2011). *La recuperación de tecnologías indígenas. Arqueología, tecnología y desarrollo en los Andes*. Bogotá: Uniandes.

Lazzarato, M. (2006). *Políticas del acontecimiento*. Buenos Aires: Tinta Limón.

Machado, H. (2009). Minería transnacional, conflictos socioterritoriales, y nuevas dinámicas expropiatorias. El caso de Minera Alumbrera. In M. Svampa & M. Antonelli (Eds.), *Minería transnacional, narrativas del desarrollo y resistencias sociales* (pp. 205–228). Buenos Aires: Biblos.

Pizarro, C. A. (2006). *"Ahora ya somos civilizados". La invisibilidad de la identidad indígena en un area rural de la Provincia de Catamarca.* Córdoba: Universidad Católica de Córdoba.

Pizarro, C. A., Haber, A., & Cruz, R. (1995). Diálogos en el Bañado. Relaciones socioculturales en la construcción científica y popular del pasado. *Revista de Ciencia y Técnica, 2*, 43–63.

Quijano, A. (2000). Colonialidad del poder, eurocentrismo y América Latina. In E. Lander (Ed.), *La colonialidad del saber: eurocentrismo y ciencias sociales. Perspectivas latinoamericanas.* Buenos Aires: CLACSO.

Shepherd, N. (2002). Heading south, looking north. Why we need a post-colonial archaeology. *Archaeological Dialogues, 9*(2), 74–82.

Spivak, G. (1988). Can the subaltern speak? In C. Nelson & L. Grossberg (Eds.), *Marxism and the interpretation of culture* (pp. 271–313). Urbana: University of Illinois.

Svampa, M., & Antonelli, M. (Eds.). (2009). *Minería transnacional, narrativas del desarrollo y resistencias sociales.* Buenos Aires: Biblos.

Trouillot, M.-R. (1997). *Silencing the past. Power and the production of history.* Boston: Beacon.

Žižek, S. (2003). *El sublime objeto de la ideología.* Mexico: Siglo XXI.

Chapter 9
Archaeology and Capitalism: Successful Relationship or Economic and Ethical Alienation?

Nicolas Zorzin

A New Ethical Perspective on Archaeological Practices: A "Political Ethic"

In the last three decades, ethics in archaeology have been more intensely debated (Scarre and Scarre 2006; Vitelli 1996; Wylie 1996; Zimmerman et al. 2003), and especially after the capitalist acceleration at the end of the 1970s, characterised by growing privatisation, which lead to the creation of commercial archaeology (Lynott 1997:589–590).

As a result of an increasing pressure on archaeological remains incurred by economic growth, and paired with an increasing interest of populations in heritage protection (Lowenthal 1999), a large number of codes of ethics and codes of deontology have been promulgated and applied worldwide since the 1980s (Society for American Archaeology 1996; World Archaeological Congress 1990; The Institute for Archaeologists (UK) 2010—revised; European Association of Archaeologists 2009—revised) also called "normative ethics" (Wylie 2003:4). In these codes, not only the ethical obligation of archaeologists towards the record of archaeological data and the obligation towards the scientific community were considered, but they combined with new ethical obligations towards the public as well as policies aiming at the protection of the material remains themselves.

However, a satisfying answer towards ethics in archaeology cannot be a fixed and universal one (Wylie 2003:13). Codes of ethics should be continuously challenged and revised to avoid the danger of stagnation, and of the "bureaucratisation" and "instrumentalisation" of ethics (Hamilakis 2007:20–22). The term "ethics" should be applied to fields of practice where the norms and the rules of behaviours have to

N. Zorzin (✉)
The British School at Athens, 52 Souedias, 10676 Athens, Greece
e-mail: zorz66@hotmail.com

C. Gnecco, D. Lippert (eds.), *Ethics and Archaeological Praxis*,
Ethical Archaeologies: The Politics of Social Justice 1,
DOI 10.1007/978-1-4939-1646-7_9

be endlessly negotiated and reinvented. The definition of ethics for archaeology should be then based on a thoughtful collective consideration of its outcomes and on its significance for groups of people in their specific spatio-temporal and socio-economic context.

To practice an archaeology following this basic ethical statement, it is essential to understand the context of production of archaeological outcomes and the very nature of those outcomes. To do so, archaeologists need to have a better idea of who wants what from archaeology, and for what motives, because archaeologists deal necessarily with the present and not only with the past (Holtorf 2005:159). To this end, archaeologists need to place archaeological projects permanently in arenas of political debate, to scrutinise power relationships between the actors involved, and to fully understand socioeconomic dynamics.

I suggest here that the process of contextualising archaeology in modern society constitutes an ethical approach to the discipline in itself. As such, the practice of an ethical archaeology could be defined as: the combination of both: (1) a practice conforming to the basic definitions of ethical/standard behaviours in every archaeological community while remaining critical of these standards, applying them to each specific situation while explaining how and why this critical process should be achieved. The first step in practicing an ethical archaeology is thus a reflexive process; (2) a production of archaeological outcomes fully connected to the present realities, i.e. not only based on accumulating and managing data, but involving archaeologists in a close commitment to the present. The second step is thus an active process.

From this perspective, a new project for archaeology has emerged, defined by the idea of the "political ethic" (Hamilakis and Duke 2007) or "political action" (McGuire 2008), which could be both described as a new praxis for archaeology, and which could be implemented in order to produce ethical archaeological outcomes. As suggested by Hamilakis and McGuire, this new praxis in archaeology could be achieved by:

- Criticising the practice of a commodified archaeology as a potential device of the late capitalist logic.
- Scrutinising archaeological organisations, their networks and their socio-economic environment, which could generate an archaeological product that will justify and sustain this device (Hamilakis 2007:33–34).
- Eventually, combating capitalist alienation by reconnecting the subjective past created by archaeologists with the realities of the present world in order to promote social justice through contestation, education through the dissemination of knowledge and consultation and collaboration with the populations primarily concerned (McGuire 2008:7–8).

To this end, the way to engage in "political ethic" has been for me to explore the political-economy of the commercial archaeological practice, with a case-study conducted in the province of Quebec (Canada) between 2008 and 2010. The "political-ethical approach" (Hamilakis 2007:35) applied in the case of contract archaeology allows us to (1) explore the political economy of archaeology units and deconstruct their internal and external sociological, political and economic dynamics and (2) test the capacity of commercial-archaeological entities to produce an ethical outcome as defined above.

Contract Archaeology and the Neoliberal Paradigm

Contract archaeology—the result of the transformation of archaeology within the neoliberal paradigm—as governed by a capitalist economic system, has fundamentally altered how the contributions of archaeology are brought about and disseminated. As defined above, the objective of this paper is to contribute to current criticisms of capitalist market logic by posing the following questions: does the implementation of a neoliberal economy in archaeology sustain the accomplishment of a meaningful and ethical (Cf. definition in previous section) archaeological activity?

Part of this paper was presented for the first time in a conference in Halifax (Nova-Scotia, Canada), in 2011, during the CAA annual symposium, and the contents are drawn from my doctoral thesis. Consequently, this paper focuses on how archaeology articulates itself within capitalist logic, and the impact of that logic on the practice of archaeology and on the professional lives of those who participate in its political economy. The central idea developed here is that the use of the capitalist logic in archaeology seems to lead to different levels of alienation of archaeological work from society, and also to the alienation of its practitioners.

Archaeology should not be perceived solely as a technical profession but as a socio-political actor in itself; a social actor that is an integral part of modern communities. This position necessitates a critical analysis of the construction of the archaeological product and most importantly its outcomes in those communities. As suggested by some archaeologists, archaeology could be seen as a philosophy seeking justice, and aiming at a better shared future for struggling communities (Hamilakis 1999:74; McGuire 2008: xi; Shanks and McGuire 1996: 85–86; Zimmerman et al. 2003: xi–xvi). Perceiving archaeology as such implies that it might not gain from its integration into the neoliberal economic system because social values and "community ethic" (Wylie 2003:4) are simply not encouraged within a neoliberal framework. As suggested by Bourdieu, the logic of profitability creates competition between commercial entities and between individuals within the companies, destroying all values of solidarity and humanism, and reducing relationships to the violence of the all against all (Bourdieu 1998:98). Moreover, even the archaeology practiced in academia (Gill 2009; Hamilakis 2004; Rainbird and Hamilakis 2001), and in centralised public organisations (Coppens 2003:20; Lauzanne and Thiébault 2003:25–27; Ralite and Jack 2003) appears to be currently at risk by following this economic logic.

To contextualise my argument on the recent capitalist conversion of archaeology against a solid background related to archaeological realities, I use a case study in Quebec (Canada), where contract archaeology represents almost 75 % of all archaeological activities (Zorzin 2010:7). I intend here to deconstruct how the alienation of work is extant within archaeological communities (i.e. the people involved with activities related to archaeology, heritage management and most of all the archaeologists themselves).

The alienation of humankind was defined by Marx, in the fundamental sense of the term, as the loss of control, but he separated the concept of alienation into four different aspects: the alienation of human beings from (a) each other; (b) nature; (c) their "species being" as members of the human species and (d) their own productive activity (Mészáros 2005: 360). It is essentially the last aspect of this traditional Marxist definition of alienation that I will develop here, but some facets of the three other aspects percolate throughout the analysis.

In this paper, alienation within archaeology refers primarily to the undermining of any attempt by archaeologists to assume their role as researchers, as producers of knowledge about the past, and, by extension, their critical and reflexive role as social scientists and intellectuals (Hamilakis 1999:74), which should constitute the bases for the practice of an ethical work. Through this definition I argue that the product of archaeological labour is not a measurable economic and material output, but is instead an abstract set of productions, based on a long term construction of knowledge and understanding of the past interrelated with the present.

Social responsibility is now perceived as essential by some part of the global archaeological community (e.g., Duke and Saitta 1998; Hamilakis 2003; Hamilakis and Duke 2007; Little and Shackel 2007; Sabloff 2008); however, until recently archaeology showed no interest in its consequences for modern populations. Since the 1930s, and as suggested by Stout (2008:4–5, 10–11), archaeologists adopted a certain disdain for communicating the results of their research to the masses. This practice has evolved, particularly after the processualist period at the end of the 1980s, and archaeological representations and communications are now a focal point of concern for many archaeologists (Moser 2001:262–263). Since then, many archaeologists have chosen to place social responsibility and implications at the core of their archaeological work and research activities.

What Is Contract Archaeology?

An Ethnography of Commercial Archaeology

The main methodological tool used during my doctoral research was ethnography. I interviewed 52 individuals involved in archaeology from a total estimated population of around 300 individuals within the province of Quebec (Zorzin 2010:4–5). Most were archaeologists, but some were individuals who had opted out of archaeology, and others were representatives of First Nations peoples. The sampling process was based on the relative proportions represented by each category of workers in the population: that is to say, a majority of people selected were working in contract archaeology (56 % of my sample, representing 20 % of Quebec archaeologists working in the private sector), of which I interviewed managers, senior archaeologists, assistants and technicians. To have a more accurate vision of archaeological realities in the Canadian Province, I also obtained interviews with government representatives, company employees charged with archaeological obligations, archaeologists involved in non-profit activities, and various academics. The interviews were semi-directed, that is to say they were conducted without a rigid structure and without a predefined questionnaire. The overall goal of these interviews was to make archaeologists freely express their perceptions and expectations about work. The encounters had an approximate duration of two and a half hours and a large range of subjects in line with the interests and experiences of the interviewees were broached. To study how contract archaeology was articulated and shaped by the current dominant political-economy, I interpreted the results of my studies mostly within the framework of a new reading of Marx's theory of alienation (Fischbach 2009; Haber 2007).

Contract Archaeology: A "Modernisation" of Archaeology?

Since the 1980s, the process of "modernisation" (Thomas 2004) forced a separation of a rational, technical and rigorous archaeology from society, which eventually, according to Shanks and McGuire (1996:83), could lead to an alienation of archaeological work. In the last three decades, archaeology—which is still mostly perceived by developers as a source of disturbance in the process of development (Demoule 2010:14; Joukowsky 1991:16)—has been then addressed by the solutions formulated by technology.

As such, archaeology was perceived by promoters, managers or some civil servants as a technical problem within the planning process, and the solutions proposed by archaeologists were technical and technological. Instead of focusing on producing meaning, archaeologists started to produce quantifiable records, and, in the end, technical reports in accordance with clients' expectations and needs. This commodified and standardised method of practicing archaeology operates today within the primacy of an unregulated market, which privileges these technological answers that are, according to Harvey (2005:68), the fundamental principles of neoliberalism: "This drive becomes so deeply embedded in entrepreneurial common sense, however, that it becomes a fetish belief: that there is a technological fix for each and every problem". In the end, this technological answer has established a collective of professional archaeologists, for whom activities were shaped by the neoliberal framework, and resulted in the creation of the first archaeological companies conceived as businesses.

Contextualisation: A Case Study in Quebec (Canada)

In the Quebec system, the primary client of archaeological services is the developers, essentially because they have to comply with specific laws protecting material heritage. Thus, developers hire the services of archaeologists, not because they really need this service within the building process, but because of legal requirements. Archaeological interventions performed by firms are now embedded within this process of development, and consist in the removal or preservation in situ of all material traces of the past before potential destruction or disturbance. One of the main clients of private archaeological firms is the government (Ministries of Culture, Transport or Environment, and public corporations such as the electricity producer Hydro-Quebec) which pays for most fieldwork activities (Zorzin 2011:123), and tries to establish or maintain high standards for the practice of a professional archaeology through the control of permits, released by the Ministry of Culture (Zorzin 2011:124).

The number of individuals active in Quebec archaeology is estimated by the archaeological community as being between 100 and 150 individuals (Lord 2011). However, according to my research the archaeologist population of Quebec could be estimated at around 300 individuals involved at various levels of competences and lengths of employment, in a territory of 595,391 sq. miles (Fig. 9.1). It should be noted here that the tendency to underestimate the number of people active in archaeology within the community is a latent problem and is not limited to Canada. This results from, as emphasised by Everill (2007:126–127) for the UK, a complete denial of the existence of many diggers, whom he called "invisible diggers," and which literally constitute an archaeological proletariat or "labourer class" within private archaeology firms. According to Everill, they are invisible mostly because they are interchangeable individuals, underestimated and paid no more than a "labourer" (not in the negative sense, but in the sense of an unqualified manual worker). These are mostly students working on occasional contracts, young graduated students accumulating short contracts with various companies, and professional diggers (in the long term) alternating periods of fieldwork activities and periods of unemployment in a ritualised/seasonal year schedule.

Some Results Based on a Quantitative Analysis

A fundamental characteristic of the current situation in the archaeological profession was revealed in studying the entire population in detail: the radical disengagement from archaeology of numerous individuals in their early thirties. Archaeologists and apprentice archaeologists are relatively young, and women dominate the profession for the age group between 20 and 34, but participation in the archaeological work force diminishing radically after age 35. The figure here graphically illustrates the dramatic drop in all staff numbers for persons in their early thirties (Fig. 9.2).

This situation is not unique. A comparison between the Quebec case and the British case for the same periods (2007–2008) reveals the following (Figs. 9.2 and 9.3): in both contexts the employee population falls for those in their early thirties, though results were markedly different in Quebec compared to England (Everill 2007:127). In Quebec, both male and female archaeologists almost disappear from the roster, which means that Generation X has almost no presence in Quebec's

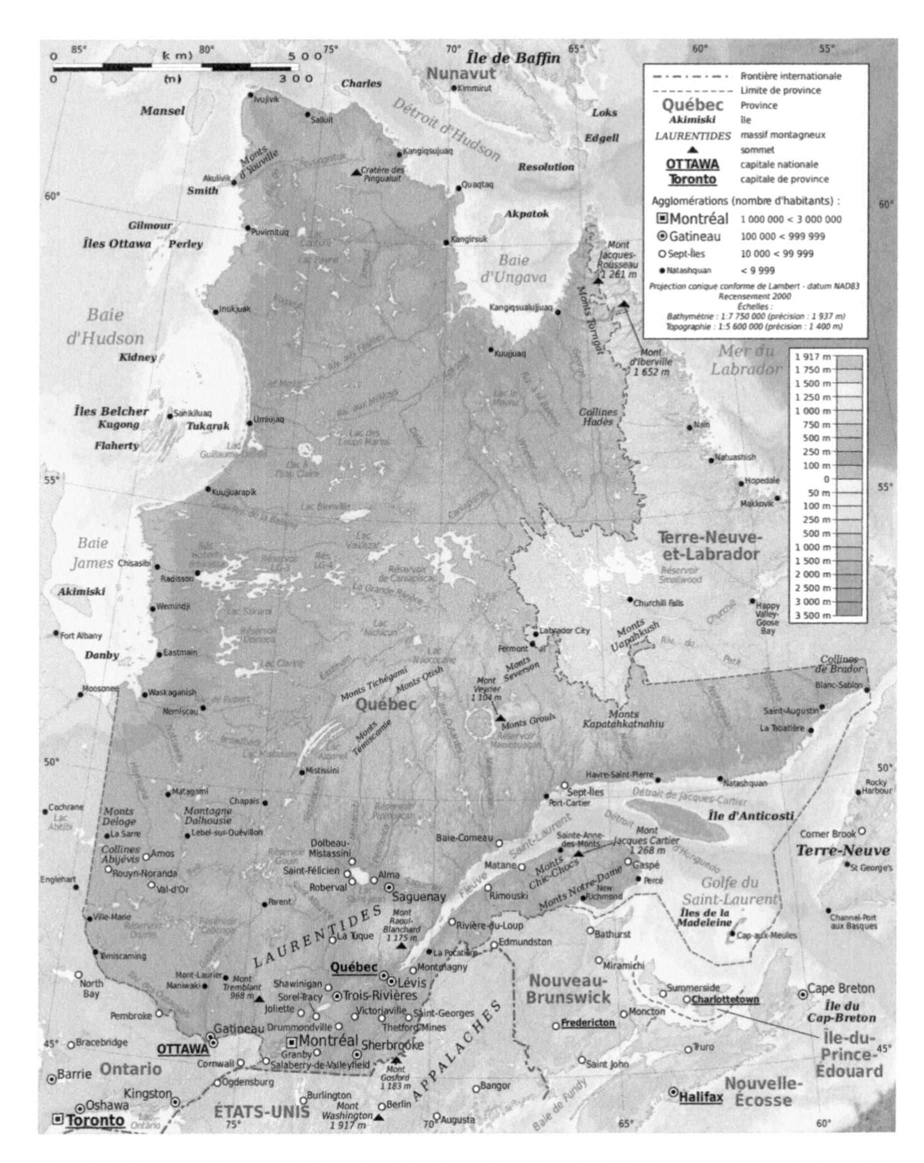

Fig. 9.1 Topographic map in French of Quebec, Canada, with 2000 census cities. Author: Eric Gaba—Wikimedia Commons user: Sting, Source for Boundaries: Canadian GéoBase (2009). URL: http://fr.wikipedia.org/wiki/Fichier:Quebec_province_topographic_map-fr.svg

archaeology. In England, the scenario is the same, but the big difference is that the fall in population numbers only affects women. The male population remains perfectly stable until the forties bracket, while the female population loses approximately 60 % of its representation by the time it reaches this age bracket.

The results of my survey illustrates that over the last three decades one of the most immediate consequences of the systematic implementation of neoliberal policies in

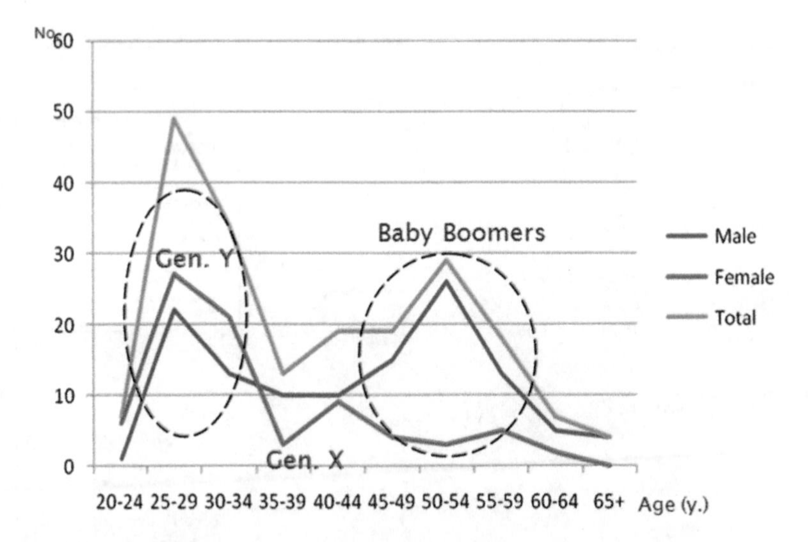

Fig. 9.2 Age and gender of archaeologists in Quebec in 2008

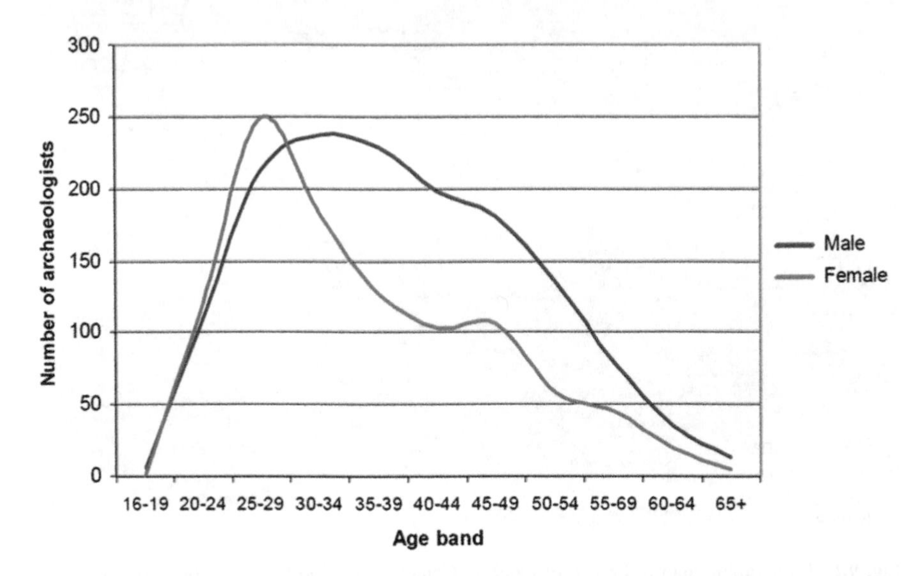

Fig. 9.3 Age and gender of archaeologists in England in 2008 (Aitchison and Edwards 2008:49)

all sectors of the economy has been, according to Bourdieu (1998), a "generalisation of precariousness". This phenomenon can be defined by the systematisation of short-term contracts which have become the new intermediary redefining the relationship between employees and employers (Bourdieu 1998:96–98) This form of precariousness has had the following consequences on people's lives: the disintegration of existence through dispossession of lifetime aspirations (e.g. generational or progression of professional or social status), and destroying any possibility of rational hope for the future.

Table 9.1 Sector distribution of the main actors in Quebec archaeology

In 2008	Commercial archaeology	Governmental and para-governmental	Academic and museums	Others	Total
Number of archaeologists	143	64	47	10	265
% of Employees by sector (%)	54	24	18	4	100
% of permits by sector (%)	73	7	15	5	100

Sources: Personal data collection & Tableau du suivi administrative des demandes de permits de recherché archéologique, *Ministere de la Cultire, des Communications et la Condition Feminine, Quebec,* 2008, 8p

Table 9.2 Distribution of full time, part-time, and contract work, all staff

	Full-time		Part-time		Contracts (short term)		Total	
All staff in Quebec	100	39 %	17	7 %	136	54 %	253	100 %

In Quebec archaeology today, the precariousness of jobs seems to have become the rule, particularly for the contract sector. In 2008, the data collected shows that 73 % of archaeological field activities in Quebec were conducted in the contract archaeology sector, which accounts for 54 % of all jobs in Quebec archaeology (Table 9.1). Also, 54 % of the jobs occupied by archaeologists over all sectors were short-term contracts (Table 9.2); that is to say without any guaranty of continuity on an annual, monthly or weekly basis. This young and precarious population has de facto become a "reserve army" (to use an expression from Bourdieu 1998:96), considering that the large majority is employed only on short-term or part-time contracts.

This "proletarianisation" has contributed to the instillation in every digger and archaeologist of the sense that he or she is dispensable, that his or her right to work is a privilege and a fragile and permanently threatened one to say the least. Furthermore, the effect of out-casting part of the workers in archaeology has been amplified by the surplus production of graduates, which means that highly educated and well-trained individuals can be found at the lowest level of competences and technical qualifications in units. Thus, the currently prevailing precariousness of working conditions in archaeology means that archaeologists do not have any way of perceiving a potential future within the profession. The ability to visualise future possibilities is, however, the condition per se for making rational life choices. Without options, archaeologists are not in a position to challenge the present system of organisation, nor to take any ethical decisions on the fieldwork. Here, ethical decisions could consist of, for example, challenging the legitimacy of a development project based on their archaeological expertise and their critical point of view as citizens, thus conflicting with corporate obligations, which in turn could potentially threaten their position in units and compromise their career.

Jason [25, digger in Contract Archaeology]:

> Listen, I need to eat. If it only depended on me, the River [Name] won't be diverted. The problem is that [Corporation Name] ... their development project ... they will do it anyway. At this level, I am neither a politician nor a lobbyist, and I have no means to challenge them

> or make them change their mind. So, in this imposed framework ... yes, I have no choice to go and do the archaeological excavation.

Furthermore, and in contrast to the actual situation described above:
Michael [54, no-longer working in archaeology; retrained]:

> At the end of the 1970s ... we had the space to have an ethical questioning, i.e.: "Do we accept to do that?" According to the projects, we contested how it was negotiated with the First Nations. We were also often dissatisfied with the fast pace of work because we could not conduct any serious in depth scientific studies both for the environment and for the archaeology. We were constantly debating if we should participate into the creation of a false representation.

Today, simply, out of this professional catalepsy, ethical void and long-lasting precariousness, most archaeologists are demotivated, and opt out of the profession. The risk is that, in the case of the Quebec scenario, when all the baby-boomer generation retires (around 2020), and with the non-participation of Generation X in the workforce, 40 years of competence, knowledge and know-how will be lost within the space of a few years. This phenomenon could pose a direct threat to the existence of archaeology itself if the profession is not supported, rethought and reorganised in depth. Indeed, the 2012, the federal government decision to move Quebec province's Park Canada services in Ottawa and to reduce drastically the numbers of employees, illustrates the threat of impoverishment of the archaeological community. During this process, out of 27 federal archaeologists and specialists, 26 were moved or simply dismissed from Quebec offices.

Archaeology: A Non-alienated Vocation?

What does the privatised version of archaeology mean for archaeologists? Is contract archaeology able to bring satisfaction or to produce an archaeological product that can give meaning to their existence as practitioners of their craft? In search of an answer to this question, this section examines the interviews with archaeologists conducted during winter 2007/2008.

For most of my interviewees, archaeology was not described as a job, but was seen more as a philosophy of life: sometimes a voluntary decision to live on the margins of society, a rejection of the global ideological dogma, a political choice, an identity seeking process, a passion converted into a livelihood, or simply a self-fulfilling experience. Whatever the reasons for choosing archaeology, the aspirations of those currently involved in the field appear to correspond to the definition of a non-alienating activity. As a result, I suggest here that there is a clear dichotomy between the goals of practicing archaeology and the actual conditions of the labour.

According to the neo-Marxist philosopher Haber, non-alienated work could be defined by the following two characteristics: (1) A bond exists between the worker and the "concrete object" of his work. (2) The worker can take responsibility for his/her professional activity. Work becomes a tool for an individual to achieve personal goals and a means to access happiness within a form of completeness. A human being can recognise him/herself in their daily environment, and can attribute meaning to his/her life (Haber 2007:239). Are these characteristics present in the contract archaeology practiced today?

Based on the testimonies of my interviewees, something happened after the 1980s, which transformed the profession from being the practice of a craft to an alienated job; but what exactly happened? I would like to deconstruct the socio-economic signs of alienation of the work using five major characteristics which emerged during my interviews. Excerpts from some of the testimonies I collected will be used, though names have been changed to preserve anonymity, and authorisation for this use was obtained from all the individuals concerned.

Experiencing the Void: A Dead End Job

Chloe [30, no-longer working in archaeology; retrained]:

> There are major reasons why I gave up on contract archaeology: there were almost no analyses and publications because of budget constrictions. Almost every winter, I was unemployed. I had almost no opportunities to work all year, unless I agreed to clean artefacts or do inventories. Some archaeological companies do a little more analysis but, as a general rule, no analysis is performed! The person in charge of the project makes his report and that is all. Nothing is really developed in any great depth, and thoughts go no further. It is also almost impossible to integrate research teams. I was under the impression that my brain was totally unexploited. I even managed to forget my cultural sequences ... i.e., I was no longer able to recognize the different types of artefacts because I was not using any of my competencies! [angry tone] I was almost ashamed to say I was an archaeologist. I did not feel my work was rewarding in any way. Also, the work environment was extremely competitive and people would do anything to demean each other. Between assistant archaeologists and technicians [i.e., diggers], the game was ugly! They were bitching all the time, it was ridiculous! [furious].

The inability to articulate archaeological activities within a scientific and social picture could be a strong indication that work has lost most of its meaning. What Chloe's discourse illustrates here in the way she accomplishes her work is that the aim of her activity had become unintelligible for her. Instead of deriving any satisfactory meaning from what she does, her work is performed mechanically. The contrast between the rigour of the standardised archaeological fieldwork operations and the futility of its aims makes the situation unbearable. Workers are unavoidably plunged into a crisis in their search for a purpose and meaning for the excavation. Today, the fragmentation of the production process and specialisation of work has made this kind of damage commonplace (Shanks and McGuire 1996:77).

Another important fact within neoliberal structures emphasised in Chloe's testimony, is that competition for work appears to be accompanied by competition within the workplace. This internal competition seems to be the basis for permanent battling between employees, which destroys any form of solidarity or human values. As a result, cynicism towards work is directly related to the political-economic choices which facilitate it, impose it and even reward it (Bourdieu 1998:98).

Lack of Means and Time Does Not Allow Archaeologists to Perform Well

Edward [40, Archaeologist/Digger in Contract Archaeology]:

> It was a week-long contract. I was supposed to make an archaeological inventory on the location of approximately a hundred pools of a mining company [the client] … To find the remote location of the future drilling spots, I had no satellite telephone, and no GPS. When I arrived, the spots had still not been officially defined. Equipped only with a map, I found some spots where the land had been cleared. As soon as the mining company employees realised I was able to find the drilling locations without their assistance, they stopped the clearing activities, waiting for me to go ahead. [This means that a decision was made to undermine the archaeologist's work, apparently judged as harmful for the mining company] … I think the mining industry tried to obstruct the location of finds as much as possible and tried to obtain the widest possible permit for a zone considered free of archaeological material. In the report, I wrote that the zone had a lot of potential but I had only been asked to do a technical report … I ended up sending an e-mail to the archaeological unit saying that I no longer wanted to continue working as an archaeologist.

According to Eltchaninoff (2010:48), the lack of means for accomplishing a task in the long term, and the lack of moral, technical and legal support from the archaeological employer, client or state, inhibits the production of any sort of satisfying archaeological product for the archaeologist. In the case of contract archaeology, flexible hours, periods of inactivity combined alternatively with periods of intense activities, and the necessity to adapt to multiple changes of positions and changes of companies, weaken the idea of the attainment of a valuable craft. It is then impossible to perceive archaeological work in long lasting terms.

According to Marx (1996 [1844]:8–9; 23–28), work can be an external and material expression of the self: you are what you make. Thus, in the case of contract archaeology, if the product of work is perceived as incomplete or compromised, the archaeologist will then feel dissatisfied, careless, poorly talented, or will see himself/herself as imperfect, unethical or simply as a failure. The feeling experienced here by Edward, describes well the issue of having no means to accomplish a task, seen as part of the long-term archaeological process. The first step of the archaeological process, consisting in preserving the past and recording it, is only the beginning of a long process aimed at understanding a complex human phenomenon. In the end, this lack of time and means undermines one's self-esteem and could lead to deep dissatisfaction.

Finally, the archaeological unit is partially responsible for this situation, because its main obligation is to satisfy the needs of the clients, not to formulate long-term research queries. Clients pay for archaeological expertise, but their decision to hire an archaeological unit depends on the rules of market competition, so their decision is based on the minimisation of expenses, not on the quality of the work and its potential results and dissemination of knowledge among communities. This characteristic of free-market competition automatically reduces the time and the means given to archaeologists to accomplish their work, as the pressure for them is simply to obtain contracts and assure perenniality.

Proletarianisation

James [32—Digger/Assistant Archaeologist in Contract Archaeology and NPO]:

> Today, my goal is to retrain professionally as a school teacher, essentially because of the major financial problems encountered in archaeological units. I also want to free myself from the actual professional [i.e., contract] framework, to be able to dig, and only dig for fun! I am not into analyses or impact studies ... I know it is important ... but it's absurd because all artefacts will end up uselessly on shelves anyway without any research or any publications. The work is done purely because it has to be done, but nobody uses it. We work in a void, a one-way street to nowhere! I just want to be able to dig once in a while, even for free! I just want to dig out 'things' ... The truth is that I am in a relationship now, and we need to make a living at some point!

James, obviously disenchanted with professional archaeology, has now prioritised a good standard of living. From his point of view, archaeology should be relegated to a simple hobby if personal happiness and family life could be jeopardised by being involved within the profession. Among the individuals I interviewed from the Generation Y, I felt the same initial desire for adventure and mysteries in archaeology as older generations, but they were much more rational, realistic and cynical, mostly because of different economic realities.

David:

> Because we want to be paid, the older generation tends to look on us as lousy fellows! ... What is paradoxical is this common idea that the older ones are fighting for better recognition of the profession, while the young ones are just looking to make more money ... But for us, nothing is easy and we have to fight to survive, with our debts, with everything getting more expensive, and with a social system in decline ... it is thus understandable that we should be more 'interested' in money!

In this case, the dispossession of the work process results in alienation from work for the workers, enacted by diverting energy from the primary task to attaining the productivity defined by capitalist rules (e.g., quantifiable reports), and towards an obligation for archaeologists to make enough money to sustain themselves.

Under these conditions, there is no space for them to understand the projects to which they contribute (or even to be interested in it). This process is perceived as one of proletarianisation, which corresponds to a loss of know-how, a divorce from what is done at work, and the comprehension of what is accomplished through this work. Today, the economic struggle for survival and permanent economic instability are preventing archaeologists from focusing serenely on their work, developing a long-standing and transferable know-how, and this in turn threatens the future of the practice.

As a result, we can see in archaeology what Harvey (2006:31) qualified as a "deskilling" phenomenon, when skills are eroded and when a theoretically intellectual work is emptied of its complexity to become a technical and manual task. The competitive system in which archaeology has been embedded has created a certain type of productivity of labour, which it has at the same time devalued and depreciated (reduced to time/price values). In addition, during this process archaeologists have lost their dignity, their sense of control over their work process, and have had to adapt to the dictates of the client's needs.

The "Narrative of Merit"

Nowadays, the "narrative of merit", generally accepted in fully converted neoliberal societies, validates the false idea that one's status in society is related to the "intrinsic qualities of individual" (Kingwell 2011:20). By "fully converted" neoliberal societies, I refer here to societies where all human actions are brought—or attempts are made to bring them—into the domain of the market (Harvey 2005:3), in the belief that the well-being of mankind can best be advanced through privatisation, deregulation, and withdrawal of the state. Societies could be defined as such when strong private property rights, free markets and free trade become common sense for all, and specifically in the way individuals conceive, live in and interpret the world on a daily basis (Harvey 2005:2–3). The precursors and most advanced examples are the UK, the USA, Australia and until recently Argentina and Chile, but new "fully converted" societies have also emerged in Asia.

Currently, knowing the precarious situation of most active archaeologists, the belief in the "intrinsic qualities of the individual" is highly problematic and sensitive in contract archaeology. It is even worse knowing that this "narrative of merit" is more and more common in young generations of archaeologists who have grown up with it, including myself as an early representative of Generation Y. This generation is trapped between two contradictory messages: first, archaeology is often seen as a professional and social failure if we refer to the capitalist symbolic that encourages and reveres economic success, self-help and a normative individualism as the only respectable and responsible ways to lead a successful life (Bourdieu 2001:28). Yet, archaeology, as a profession, can barely sustain the current high standards of living, or cope with the material standards of success expected by society from graduated, highly skilled, working individuals. Inspired by Fussell's analysis of the American classes, archaeologists might belong to the upper-middle class (Fussell 1983:27), together with engineers or highly qualified technicians. However, low incomes, precariousness and absence of social protections irremediably disqualify archaeologists socio-economically from the current vision of success. In complete contrast, archaeology can also be seen by many as socially meaningful work, a philosophy of life and an intimately fulfilling profession.

As we have seen, when the second message is blurred by an actual void in archaeological production, archaeologists feel that they do not generate anything other than their own spectacle. As asserted by Ibáñez, when the "why?" and the "what is the point?" brutally appear, the impossibility to give a semblance of answer provoke: "a sort of nausea of disgust and of lassitude, which constitute the fall into a state of absurd conscience" (2011:19, my translation). Thus, when archaeologists start asking themselves what an archaeological unit produces, for whom, and for what, the answer often leads them to an aversion towards the profession. Other archaeologists will answer that "saving" the past from destruction by protecting and preserving it is the ultimate and valuable goal for archaeology. My first reaction to this answer is acquiescence; however, some fundamental components of archaeology seem missing from this definition. Again, by accepting the idea of being the stewards of the past, archaeologists reduce themselves to a very technical—but rudimentary—task of saving and preserving ... but for whom? For what? And even for when? Without a clearly defined social outcome, I see this function as problematic and closely related to what neoliberal doxa prepare individuals for: i.e. to give a simple technical answer to every single problem/action in society.

Archaeologists also hear other interpretations of the meaning of their activities, provided by their clients, answers that mainly define archaeology as unimportant, a pointless constraint or costly whim which only hinders development. For example, in 2006, a municipality in France accused archaeology of "curbing development" and "acting against the community's interests" (Aubigny (Mairie de) 2009). The last line of defence for the workers, who choose to ask themselves these questions, is to admit that "there is no point to what is being done, but it must be done anyway" (Kingwell 2011:20).

The result of such logic can be summarised as follows. For those still working in contract archaeology, the most common option is to choose not to challenge or fight capitalist logic by accepting the "narrative of merit". In doing so, individuals are trying to shadow the globally accepted perception of a productive, respectable and profitable private firm. Such logic results in the adoption of technicalisation and the application of the sacrosanct concepts of "quality assurance" or "quality control", which are broad programs of planned and systematic controls for maintaining established standards, and for the measurement and evaluation of performance according to these standards. This approach is in complete opposition to the intellectual flexibility required by archaeologists to master the archaeological process from conception to analysis, from interpretation to dissemination.

Thomas [in his 50s, out/retrained as an archivist]:

> In contract units, I think archaeology is no longer fun. I was very disappointed by this. Minimal publication of materials following excavations was even more disappointing. At the time, I was motivated to work and even to work for free to produce better and more consistent reports. The only way to produce a quality job was to do it in your free time, at night or during the weekend, and, without pay ... indeed. Nonetheless, nobody was really interested in the results. It was painful to produce a quality product, which did not serve any purpose ... Following the logic of the Ministry of Culture, and of the contract units following clients' injunctions, the idea was more: 'pick up the stuff, write descriptions' and, that's it!

I am not saying here that the systematisation of controls and implementation of rigorous work on excavations are wrong, but only that the application of such standardisation without consideration distorts the definition of archaeological work by removing any opportunity for thought and reflection. Instead, work is controlled by a simple ticking of boxes, which in the end, completely relieves archaeologists of all their responsibilities, apart from the obligation to "clean" the site in an appropriate, rigorous and technical way.

In the interviews, other archaeologists had chosen what could be defined as a cynical approach, which consists of them being aware of all the above, but choosing to give up on the original aims they had when they first started their job. They choose to transform the profession into no more than a banal economic activity:

Edward [40, archaeologist/digger in Contract Archaeology]:

> As soon as I became distanced from my initial dream of archaeology, I saw my archaeological activities just as a task to be performed. It acquired a purely financial aspect. If I want to

> continue in archaeology, I will have to maintain this financial and food security vision to avoid disappointment.

According to this testimony, the only way to survive in professional archaeology is to decrease expectations from work and to learn to respect even the most humble and absurd tasks, or to recognise the potential intrinsic value of any work. Furthermore, this approach enables archaeologists to protect themselves morally by conceiving the future hypothetical usefulness of their work as serving others. However, these processes clearly amount to alienation from work when:

1. The external requirements (i.e. those of the clients) are absurd, by only serving specific interests.
2. Archaeology is used as a commodity without any production and dissemination of knowledge (due to the lack of activities such as interpretation and synthesis, publication, conferences or public exhibitions).

A common reaction, as demonstrated in this chapter, is to opt out of the profession altogether (Fig. 9.2). Unable to deal with the two contradictory messages transmitted by society about archaeology and archaeologists, and unable to cope with the realities of work, archaeologists simply abandon the profession to do something more fulfilling in their early thirties.

Thomas [in his 50s, out/retrained as an archivist]:

> … It is nice to have fun at work, but on $20,000 CDN per year, with kids, student debts, and a doctorate, it sounds terrible! It is alright when you are in your twenties and single, but, later, it becomes far too difficult and everyone starts looking for something different. In fact, at around 30 the pressure increases and radical decisions must be taken.

In the end, other archaeologists simply retain their positions in the profession while suffering in silence because they no longer recognise or see any value in their work:

Henry [ca. 50, archaeologist consultant] (in an email to the author)

> Unfortunately, I have to refuse your request [for an interview] because nowadays I am extremely wary about archaeology. I do not think you will learn anything interesting from me! I want something new, and I don't feel like talking about the situation in contract archaeology at all. I don't have any opinions anymore! This really annoys me and if I talk about it, it will depress me even more …

Colonisation of Terminology

According to Kingwell (2011), one of the major problems encountered in resisting the changes enforced by capitalist logic is the colonisation of work vocabulary. This has resulted in the adoption of what he qualifies as "meta-bullshit". For Kingwell (2011:21), "the victory of work bullshit is that, in addition to having no regard for the truth, it passes itself off as innocuous or even beneficial".

A typical example in the case of contract archaeology is the use of the term "report". The term initially engendered a certain respect, as the ultimate, legitimate and useful contribution of archaeology to society. The contribution of a report per se is now questionable. In reality, a report is the acknowledgment that an activity has taken place, which justifies payment for services to clients. This term "report" is then little more than a sweeping under the rug of the intellectual void of this minimalist operation, consisting mostly of the packaging and standardisation of the so-called preservation by records (Hamilakis and Aitchison 2009 April 4th, Radio 4—UK, online). The term "report" was then chosen and used to make the archaeological activities look beneficial in technical and professional terms. Some archaeologists have chosen to believe in this reassuring self-prophecy, but others have preferred to face the truth:

Thomas [ca. 50, no-longer working in archaeology—retrained]:

> [In units] work was done in a minimalist fashion, without ever going further into research studies. We were doing work, which was almost identical every time. In the end, I found it pretty depressing.

Again, and crucially, I am not accusing contract archaeology and the managers of the archaeological units of being directly responsible for this situation. I consider the effective practice of contract archaeology more as collateral damage within the systematic application of neoliberal doxa to this specific sphere of activities. As a matter of fact, contract archaeology as part of that doxa, works in a small way to perpetuate it. It would be presumptuous to assume that archaeologists chose willingly, knowing where the neoliberal economic system had taken the profession, to embark on this type of self-destructive transformation. Indeed, professionalisation was and still is perceived as the only way to gain respectability, recognition and perenniality for archaeology.

Ethics and Fieldwork Archaeology in a Commercial Environment

The Process of Reduction of Archaeological Ethical Responsibility Towards the Quantifiable

In this chapter, we saw how the economic context of the competitive market in which archaeology is now conducted does not allow archaeologists to produce a satisfactory outcome for any party. We saw that the frustrations, the disillusionment and the degraded work conditions often encouraged archaeologists to leave the profession. Now, another fundamental problem exists in this professional community that is ignored: the importance—in archaeologists' decision to give up archaeology—of the failure in applying ethical codes defined by the archaeological community itself, and of the ethical void or incompatibility of archaeological ethics with the obligations of a commodified archaeological practice. On that matter, the following testimonies illustrate the perceptions of some individuals who left the profession, took some distance from it or were planning to do so in a near future because of its ethical failures:

Alexander [50, Archaeologist—Independent consultant]:

> From an ethical point of view, what do I do when I have a project with a 4 weeks excavation deadline (and, if I am lucky, 8 weeks to write the report), and suddenly I have to extend the fieldwork, but the budget and the deadline stay the same? In height weeks, I have just enough time to do a limited analysis… so if the report has to be cut further, what do I do with the archaeological interpretations? If I overlook it, the data is simply lost. It is a serious ethical problem in commercial archaeology. How many times I had to go over the dates of my contract… one week, two weeks to finish properly my report. Of course, this is an unpaid and voluntary work, financially unsustainable on the long term, but it is the only ethical answer I found for me.

Benjamin [ca. 40, Archaeologist—Independent consultant]:

> In Quebec, we discovered and excavated thousands of archaeological sites at the James Bay. However, the artefacts and the reports coming from these digs ended up in boxes at the Ministry of Culture and there will never be any or hardly any studies done whatsoever. We all know very well that, within the excavation process and the archaeological analysis, an archaeologist likes to control his own data. It is illusory to believe that archaeologists will study material collected by others. This is an aberration and a clear misunderstanding of the archaeological process! … It is an aberration because the reports we produce are read by the developer-funder corporations whereas the reports should be evaluated by senior archaeologists at the Ministry of Transport or at the Ministry of Culture, who could give their informed approval for the continuation of a development project [reports are actually evaluated in ministries by trainees using preformatted forms]. Unfortunately, the ministries have nothing to say, and they have got completely disengaged from their social responsibilities, trusting the market to take care of the archaeology for them, supposedly professionally and ethically.

In such work configuration, the developer possesses the economic power as well, as explained here by Benjamin, to have the right of inspection on work accomplished by archaeologists. In such a situation, the developer ends up in a particularly inappropriate position by being both judge and jury. Here, it seems inevitable that the "quality" criteria of archaeological work will irremediably concern time and cost reduction, and that change in archaeological practice will be imposed through a multitude of managerial and legal policies, with the support of governmental entities (Zorzin 2011).

As underscored by Andrews et al. (2000:526): "Practical and managerial procedures separate excavation recording from post-excavation interpretation". This process is a fundamental characteristic of the neoliberal doctrine aiming to impose fragmentation within professional communities, in order to dissolve critical thought and prevent resistance towards economic growth and generation of profit. Furthermore, the fragmentation process leads to the generation of a discourse of "aimlessness," that is to say, a so called "apolitical" discourse, to be deemed socially meaningless, apart from the "narrative of the extreme" (e.g. the largest, the tallest, the oldest, etc.) (Mizoguchi 2006:135):

Laura [29, archaeologist/digger in Contract Archaeology]:

> Budget and time is missing most of the time, and because of this, in archaeological units we often make not very ethically correct decisions. I think it is becoming true for academia as

well. Nowadays, to have money, you need to demonstrate that a site is old and it has to be already popular somehow, or related to a well-known popular story!

As such, a new praxis has been de facto imposed for archaeology, but a praxis in complete dissonance with the praxis suggested by many contemporaneous archaeologists, as defined in the beginning of this chapter. The inclusion of archaeology within the competitive market creates the conditions for precariousness and instability. Fear of unemployment isolates, atomises, individualises, demobilises and strips away any forms of solidarity (Bourdieu 1998:98); solidarity which could lead to resistance and a will to implement a praxis that conforms to the ethical obligations defined by the archaeologists, in close collaboration with each community they are working with.

The irony of this situation is that the policy of "preservation by records"—which converts remains into records and archives—presents the archaeological practice as highly ethical. In reality, this policy enables the destruction of the archaeological remains and refutes completely the crucial importance of research, analyses, interpretations, dissemination and social involvements. In such situations, the main objectives of archaeology are definitively lost (Andrews et al. 2000:527).

The emphasis in archaeology's practices and outcomes has been on the record of archaeological data, which is the only ethical obligation that can really be measured in the short term. As such, ethics have been rendered compatible with management practices, and consisting of the constant evaluation of the "quality" of the work and the generation of evidence that "normative ethical" work is being conducted. The others ethical obligations defined in the introduction of this chapter are simply ignored or it is often suggested that they could always be postponed (See Benjamin). However, in certain cases, these obligations will be implemented, but they might serve some specific corporate interest as we will now scrutinise in the next section.

How Codes of Ethics Can Be Alienated to Legitimise the Neutralisation of Archaeological Practice: The "Ethics-Washing" Process, or the Failure of Normative Ethics

Embedded into a client-customer relation with both developers and governments (Zorzin 2010), I suggest that commercial archaeology is now involved into a process comparable to "ethics-washing" (based on the expression "green-washing": "disinformation disseminated by an organisation so as to present an environmentally responsible public image"—Oxford Dictionaries 2012, online). Ethics-washing could be defined as a form of public relations in which ethical principles are deceptively used to promote the perception that an organisation's activities are driven by morally superior principles. Whether it is to increase profits or gain political support, ethics-washing may be used to manipulate popular opinion to support questionable aims.

A Quebec Case: A Corporation as a Client/Employer

Jason [25, digger in Contract Archaeology]:

> Somehow, we [archaeologists] clean the image of [H Corporation]. In their corporate ads, it said: "our work is made in collaboration with First Nations". Hey! What exactly is this collaboration? In reality, in the morning, you pick up a member of a first nation group and someone explains him how to dig. Yet, in the evening, he is nagging about the job and he will never come back … Is this the collaboration [H Corporation] is bragging about? I think this is false advertising! We hire first nations peoples, well [sigh …] we only buy them to ease our conscience … To ease the pain, I tell myself that, at least, I do my part of the job, because if all archaeologists refuse to do the digging and the recording for ethical reasons … well, in the end, the [H Corporation] will flood the site anyway!

In the corporate environment, the terms "green-washing" or "ethics-washing" are indeed not used publically, but the concept of "corporate environmental social responsibility" certainly is. This concept could be defined as "initiatives that corporations undertake to improve their regulatory compliance or go beyond what regulations require either to reduce [social or environmental impacts] below mandated levels or limit their activities in areas that are not currently regulated" (Babcock 2010:21). As underscored well by Jason here, collaboration as it stands is not in fact particularly fruitful for anybody, but it does set up a positive image for the corporation towards both First Nations from which lands will be confiscated, and for Quebecers, consumers and international shareholders who will be able to believe that the dispossession was done ethically. The particular nature of this ethics-washing process, and the guarantee of its efficiency, consists precisely of making the ones implementing it, firmly believe in its fair-mindedness (for example, towards First Nations populations). As described previously, fragmentation of work considerably helps this process, by separating the various actors in fieldwork, limiting their tasks to technical operations and preventing anyone being able to get a glimpse of the broader context; context which might cause people to question the very existence of development projects.

Joshua [53, Archaeologist]:

> If [H Corporation] hires you; you cannot go against the interests of the company. You cannot even be neutral.

Archaeologists are well aware that their archaeological outcomes are often disregarded or undesirable to corporations. Their activities are only tolerated for a certain time and within certain areas as long as they do not put development and economic growth into jeopardy. In these conditions, archaeological ethics are rendered entirely ineffective, by being both politically and socially systematically neutralised to protect clients' interests. Through the demonstration of the so-called collaboration with First Nations, for example, the corporation can then legally address issues of "social responsibility" and present itself as a group taking ethical and thoughtful decisions.

Edward [40, Archaeologist/Digger in Contract Archaeology]:

> [H Corporation] uses archaeology as a colonial agent, like any other company which wish to polish its image in the eyes of First Nations … In the end, it is not a land colonisation by

> planting a Quebec's flag everywhere, but instead it is a form of colonisation by imposing a neoliberal society style. Nowadays, the way of proceeding is to place the archaeological data/archives on the side … and wait that someone, some sort of Cree Messiah, turns into an archaeologist and makes good use of these data. However, even if in 100 years a Cree nation really emerges, the data would have lost already its potential political meaning because the capitalist system and its values will prevail.

This testimony illustrates another level of the process of "ethics-washing" implemented by corporations in close collaboration with government entities. Colonisation continues under the illusion of a fair and "ethical dispossession" (which is an oxymoron), made acceptable by so called environmental and archaeological "sustainable strategies", and financial compensation for anything that will be lost. Dispossession is compensated by money, short term local employment, archaeological reports and collections of artefacts. Still, land dispossession in Northern-Quebec remains a hardly justifiable process of appropriation of natural resources, highly questionable, and comparable to a form of internal neo-colonialism (Harvey 2003:32). Edward's testimony here demonstrates how simple it is to use the argument of preservation by records to postpone research and yet forestall potential conflicts with First Nations emerging from the archaeological outcomes.

Finally, despite the chart of ethics in Quebec archaeology, its vibrant and engaged archaeological community, and government entities overseeing the—all too limited—ethical obligations, I believe that the economic system within which commercial archaeological units are embedded today has deeply alienated the ethics defined by the archaeological community of Quebec. This process of alienation has developed even further by the use of "quality control" in archaeological activities seen as evidence of "ethics" itself. I see this purported parallel as effectively a protection of unethical corporate interests and behaviours, and define it as "ethics washing".

Conclusion: Taking a Distance from Contract Archaeology

Through privatisation and the organisational changes accompanying the process of economic transformation which came with neoliberalism, archaeologists began to lose control over their production and eventually ceased to be autonomous entities. The advent of contract archaeology seems to have contributed mainly to dispossessing archaeologists of both their initial way of life and their archaeological production, restricting their activities to mere technical operations. As it is configured, archaeology does not provide the means to proceed with the analysis or interpretation of data, which should normally lead to the fruitful production of a critical and complex set of thoughts. As such, archaeology has been alienated.

Moreover, as emphasised by the archaeologists themselves, another dimension of alienation has been the social exclusion of archaeologists through a combination of constant social and financial indignities. Through privatisation, many archaeologists were expecting to see a general increase in their income and improvement in work conditions. Instead, archaeologists were rewarded with a double penalty: the alienation of their profession and no observable improvement in work conditions.

Nowadays, the alienation of work has given archaeologists good reason to opt out of archaeology. In fact, there is a huge contrast between the renewed visions that archaeologists had of their discipline in the 1990s through the postprocessual turn—which had presented archaeology as a craft serving society—and the present commodified practice in units. This contrast probably makes the alienation even more difficult to deal with. In these circumstances, archaeologists are only producing a commodified representation of their profession. Shadowing the neoliberal narrative of productivity, the production of archaeologists only makes sense now if it is orientated towards exchange and profit (Fischbach 2009:203), perceived as fundamentals and obvious outcomes for the archaeological "product."

Looking at the present situation, I suggest that the French concept of "cultural exception" (*l'exception culturelle*, see Regourd 2004) could apply to the future development or rethinking of archaeology. This expression was primarily formulated to protect French/francophone cultural production from Anglo-Saxon domination. The idea could easily be applied to archaeology to combat its recent systematic capitalist conversion. If treated as extraneous to the competitive system, archaeology could be preserved as a "cultural exception", and as a result, be sustained financially by the state, patronage or local sponsorships (depending on the traditions of each country). If we pursue this logic even further, archaeology would, in certain cases, do better to re-integrate a national structure through public archaeological services, as suggested by Everill (2007:135) for the UK.

Nevertheless, what I suggest here for archaeologists, as a substitute to both the capitalist structure and the state model, is to adopt an alternative model based on an associative or cooperative structure oriented towards communities' socio-economic interests, and leaded by them. Such orientation choices are developing in Quebec (Corporation Archéo-08; Coopérative Artefactuel; Institut culturel Avataq, Grand Conseil des Cris), and are sometimes designated as "collaborative archaeology" (Colwell-Chanthaphonh and Ferguson 2008). The idea that I am particularly sensitive to in this approach is that the archaeological process of removing the material traces of the past and obtaining intellectual outcomes from it should primarily benefit populations, instead of corporate clients' interests as contract archaeology tends to be forced to do lately. To be able to accomplish this, a form of economic independence will have to be obtained from business relationships, and it constitutes one of the major challenges that archaeologists will have to face in the near future. The very existence of archaeological units is not a problem in itself, but the issue here is moreover the economic structure in which is it embedded. The problems for the archaeological industry have become the obligation to profit and the facilitation of the development processes—the intrinsic objectives in the current capitalist system, as demonstrated. These problems might be greatly counterbalanced by giving units the resources and legal tools as well as the obligations to practice an archaeology of which the product will be satisfactory for both archaeologists and communities.

Nowadays, reality dictates that archaeologists generally tolerate or integrate the fundamental ideas of capitalism (Matthews 2010). However, as demonstrated throughout this chapter, this situation arises ethical issues which still need to be addressed: (1) Archaeologists are not in a position to consider the modern political-economy framework in which archaeology is produced to ensure a critical distance from an archaeology serving market interests and logic. (2) Some opportunities of resistance exist, notably with the development of an ethical based "collaborative archaeology". This is however only if this collaboration is not only serving the interests of those who initiated the collaboration (developers/corporations), and not when it has the tendency to operate as an "ethics-washing" device aiming to facilitate processes of dispossession. Finally, in order to produce an ethical outcome within a new praxis for archaeology, archaeologists might have to work outside the influences of capitalist logic (Matthews 2010:196). Presently, the work configuration within which commercial archaeology lies is preventing this from being possible.

Acknowledgements I wish to thank Yannis Hamilakis most sincerely for his full support during my doctoral research. I am also grateful to the University Laval for its financial support through a postdoctoral fellowship at the Faculty of Letters, and funding from Les Laboratoiresd'Archéologie de l'Université Laval (Groupe de Recherche en Archéométrie).

References

Aitchison, K., Edwards, R. (2008). *Discovering the archaeologists of Europe: United Kingdom. Archaeology labour market intelligence: profiling the profession 2007/08*. Reading: Institute of Field Archaeologists.

Andrews, G., Barrett, J., & Lewis, J. (2000). Interpretation not record: the practice of archaeology. *Antiquity, 74*, 525–530.

Aubigny (Mairie de) (2009). Actualités: lancement des travaux de la ZAC de la Belle-Etoile. http://www.mairie-aubigny.fr/developpement/actualites/659-lancement-des-travaux-de-la-zac-de-la-belle-etoile.html. Online resource, accessed 16 Jul 2011.

Babcock, H. M. (2010). Corporate environmental social responsibility: corporate "greenwashing" or a corporate culture game changer? *Fordham Environmental Review, 21*, 1–78.

Bourdieu, P. (1998). *Contre-feux. Propos pour servir à la résistance contre l'invasion néo-libérale*. Paris: Éditions Raison d'Agir.

Bourdieu, P. (2001). *Contre-feux 2. Pour un mouvement social européen*. Paris: Éditions Raison d'Agir.

Colwell-Chanthaphonh, C., & Ferguson, T. (2008). *Collaboration in archaeological practice: engaging descendant communities*. Lanham, MD: AltaMira.

Coppens, Y. (2003, May 29). L'archéologie sort de l'exception culturelle. *Le Figaro*, p. 20.

Demoule, J.-P. (2010). The crisis: economic, ideological and archaeological. In N. Schlanger & K. Aitchison (Eds.), *Archaeology and the global economic crisis* (pp. 13–18). Tervuren: Culture Lab Editions.

Duke, P., & Saitta, D. (1998). An emancipatory archaeology for the working class. http://www.assemblage.group.shef.ac.uk/4/4duk_sai.html. Online resource, accessed 15 July 2011.

Eltchaninoff, M. (2010). Vouz avez dit aliénations? *Philosophie Magazine, 39*, 48–55.

Everill, P. (2007). British contract archaeology: antiquarians and labourers; developers and diggers. In Y. Hamilakis & P. Duke (Eds.), *Archaeology and capitalism: from ethics to politics* (pp. 176–205). Walnut Creek, CA: Left Coast.

Fischbach, F. (2009). *Sans objet: capitalisme, subjectivité, aliénation*. Paris: Vrin.

Fussell, P. (1983). *A guide through the American status system*. New York, NY: Touchstone.

Gill, R. (2009). Breaking the silence: the hidden injuries of neo-liberal academia. In R. Ryan-Flood & R. Gill (Eds.), *Secrecy and silence in the research process: feminist reflections* (pp. 228–244). London: Routledge.
Haber, S. (2007). *L'aliénation: Vie sociale & expérience de la dépossession*. Paris: Presses Universitaires de France.
Hamilakis, Y. (1999). La trahison des archéologues: archaeological practice as intellectual activity in postmodernism. *Journal of Mediterranean Archaeology, 12*(1), 60–79.
Hamilakis, Y. (2003). Iraq, stewardship and "the record:" an ethical crisis for archaeology. *Public Archaeology, 3*, 104–111.
Hamilakis, Y. (2004). Archaeology and the politics of pedagogy. *World Archaeology, 36*(2), 287–309.
Hamilakis, Y. (2007). From ethics to politics. In Y. Hamilakis & P. Duke (Eds.), *Archaeology and capitalism: from ethics to politics* (pp. 15–40). Walnut Creek, CA: Left Coast.
Hamilakis, Y., & Aitchison, K. (2009). Archaeology in crisis. In making history: BBC 4, radio program, April 4, 2009. http://www.bbc.co.uk/programmes/b00jxfqn. Online resource, accessed 5 May 2009.
Hamilakis, Y., & Duke, P. (Eds.). (2007). *Archaeology and capitalism: from ethics to politics*. Walnut Creek, CA: Left Coast.
Harvey, D. (2003). *The new imperialism*. Oxford: Oxford University Press.
Harvey, D. (2005). *A brief history of neoliberalism*. Oxford: Oxford University Press.
Harvey, D. (2006). *The limits to capital*. London: Verso.
Holtorf, C. (2005). *From Stonehenge to Las Vegas. Archaeology as popular culture*. Lanham: AltaMira.
Joukowsky, M. (1991). Ethics in archaeology. *Berytus, 39*, 11–20.
Kingwell, M. (2011). The language of work. In J. Glenn (Ed.), *The wage slave's glossary*. Emeryville, ON: Bibilosasis.
Lauzanne, S., & Thiébault, S. (2003). Les archéologues contre la privatisation. *Nouveaux Regards, 21*, 24–34.
Little, B., & Shackel, P. (Eds.). (2007). *Archaeology as a tool of civic engagement*. Lanham: AltaMira.
Lord, S. (2011). Les fouilles archéologiques au Québec, c'est 5 M$. Canoe.ca/Argent, July 6, 2011. http://argent.canoe.ca/lca/affaires/quebec/archives/2011/07/20110706-141317.html. Online resource, accessed 13 Jul 2011.
Lowenthal, D. (1999). *The past is a foreign country*. Cambridge: Cambridge University Press.
Lynott, M. (1997). Ethical principles and archaeological practice: development of an ethics policy. *American Antiquity, 62*(4), 589–599.
Marx, K. (1996). *Manuscrits de 1844*. Paris: Garnie Flammarion.
Matthews, C. (2010). *The archaeology of American capitalism*. Gainesville, FL: University of Florida Press.
McGuire, R. (2008). *Archaeology as political action*. Berkeley, CA: University of California Press.
Mészáros, I. (2005). *Marx's theory of alienation*. London: Merlin.
Mizoguchi, K. (2006). *Archaeology, society and identity in modern Japan*. Cambridge: Cambridge University Press.
Moser, S. (2001). Archaeological representation: the visual conventions for constructing knowledge about the past. In I. Hodder (Ed.), *Archaeological theory today* (pp. 262–283). Cambridge: Polity.
Rainbird, P., & Hamilakis, Y. (Eds.). (2001). *Interrogating pedagogies: archaeology in higher education*. Oxford: Archaeopress.
Ralite, Jack M. (2003). Archéologie préventive: deuxième lecture. Groupe Communiste Républicain et Citoyen au Sénat dans le cadre de la discussion et du vote de la loi à la commission des affaires culturelles du Sénat, 22 Juillet 2003.
Regourd, S. (2004). *L'exception culturelle*. Paris: PUF.
Sabloff, J. A. (2008). *Archaeology matters: action archaeology in the modern world*. Walnut Creek, CA: Left Coast.

Scarre, C., & Scarre, G. (Eds.). (2006). *The ethics of archaeology: philosophical perspectives on archaeological practice*. Cambridge: Cambridge University Press.

Shanks, M., & McGuire, R. (1996). The craft of archaeology. *American Antiquity, 61*(1), 75–88.

Stout, A. (2008). *Creating prehistory: druids, Ley hunters and archaeologists in pre-war Britain*. Oxford: Blackwell.

Thomas, J. (2004). Archaeology's place in modernity. *Modernism/Modernity, 11*(1), 17–34.

Vitelli, K. (Ed.). (1996). *Archaeological ethics*. Walnut Creek, CA: AltaMira.

Wylie, A. (1996). Ethical dilemmas in archaeological practice: looting, repatriation, stewardship, and the (trans)formation of disciplinary identity. *Perspectives on Science, 4*(2), 154–194.

Wylie, A. (2003). On ethics. In L. Zimmerman, K. Vitelli, & J. Hollowell-Zimmer (Eds.), *Ethical issues in archaeology*. Walnut Creek, CA: AltaMira.

Zimmerman, L., Vitelli, K., & Hollowell-Zimmer, J. (Eds.). (2003). *Ethical issues in archaeology*. Walnut Creek, CA: AltaMira.

Zorzin, N. (2010). Archéologie au Québec: portrait d'une profession. *Archéologiques, 23*, 1–15.

Zorzin, N. (2011). Contextualising contract archaeology in Quebec: political-economy and economic dependencies. *Archaeological Review from Cambridge, 26*(1), 119–136.

Chapter 10
Trading Archaeology Is Not Just a Matter of Antiquities: Archaeological Practice as a Commodity

Jaime Almansa Sánchez

Is trying to save the world with archaeology what we want to be doing?

Jeppson (2010:63)

Perhaps it is the world of archaeology which needs to be changed in order to be saved.

Little (2010:154–155)

By looking at the history of archaeology and the archaeological record, we are looking at the beginning of the commoditization of archaeology. As Bruce Trigger rightly points out, there is a slight difference between the interest in past remains, and what we make of them to learn more about that past (Trigger 2007:40). Meanwhile, Clive Gamble (2008:3) defined archaeology as "whatever you want it to become". It seems that what we have mostly wanted it to become is a commodity.

With social complexity being rooted in human communities, the artefacts it produces acquire value. And given that classic civilizations also had time for "art" and the expression of beauty—as they understood it—which happened to accord to the tastes of the modern Occident, the remains of this "art" thus became of interest to the new bourgeoisie. And so, *collections* began. But even centuries earlier, artefacts were already venerated: this is evident in the pervasiveness of looting, once powerful rulers decided to bury themselves with artefacts that had (and continue to have) an economic value. While it might seem as if those, which we consider to be archaeological remains, are of more value and interest in the context of scientific practice, we must keep in mind that long before capitalist endeavours and the bourgeoisie thinking beyond the object, "antiquities" were already a commodity (see Bevan and Wengrow 2010).

J. Almansa Sánchez (✉)
JAS Arqueología S.L.U., Plaza de Mondariz 6, 28029 Madrid, Spain
e-mail: almansasanchez@gmail.com

C. Gnecco, D. Lippert (eds.), *Ethics and Archaeological Praxis*, Ethical Archaeologies: The Politics of Social Justice 1,
DOI 10.1007/978-1-4939-1646-7_10

While it may appear as if I am attempting to justify the commoditization of archaeology, the fact that cannot be escaped is that the origins of our discipline brought about a series of concepts and practices that have determined its course since. From the concept of treasure to the development of commercial archaeology in the frame of liberal politics, science remains on the side of a market that goes beyond antiquities, but also partakes in it.

The (Economic) Value of Archaeology

This book aims to approach the varied ethical implications of contemporary archaeological practices. Even though there exists an overwhelming body of literature on the ethics of archaeology (cf. Scarre and Scarre 2006; Vitelli and Colwell-Chanthaphonh 2006; Zimmerman et al. 2003), the economic impact of our profession has not been focused on with the same intensity. It is only in relation to politics and action (Hamilakis and Duke 2007; McGuire 2008) where clearer references to the commoditization of archaeological practice appear.

In 2009, the journal *Present Pasts* opened its first issue with a forum, asking what Public Archaeology was. There, Gabriel Moshenska (2009) directly approached the commoditization of contemporary archaeological practice, by describing five interconnected types of commodity. The last response of the ensuing 2-year debate was a very critical piece by Nikolas Gestrich (2011), who helped to clarify two very important details that are pertinent to the present chapter: a commodity is something with value, and that value is not necessarily monetary (Moshenska and Burtenshaw 2011).

The concept of value has, of course, been extensively analyzed, since the publication of the classic volume edited by Arjun Appadurai, *The social life of things* (1986), and its sequel, *Commodification* (Van Binsbergen and Geschiere 2005). In archaeology, the concept has been most comprehensively discussed by John Carman (1990, 1996, 2005; Carman et al. 1999). Furthermore, in the Southport Report (Southport Group 2011)—probably the most recent and interesting piece on "legality" in archaeology—the word *value* is used heavily throughout. The use of the term is based on two similarly interesting works: Ståle Navrud and Richard C. Ready's *Valuing cultural heritage* (2002), which attempts to assess the value of "public goods" in terms of the market and money, specifically the amount of money someone is willing to pay to use or preserve the "good"; and Gareth Maeer and Isla Campbell's *Values and benefits of heritage* (2008), which compiles a series of real examples where people would actually pay more than asked for items constituting heritage.

What about the "other" values of archaeology? Maybe these can be found in the "universal values" of UNESCO (WHC 2011), such as *uniqueness*, or other similarly outstanding examples that are used to assess the significance of artefacts, even in the United States (Avrami et al. 2000; Hardesty and Little 2009). But what happens outside the Anglo-Saxon sphere? Mediterranean countries adopted a concern for cultural heritage as protection against the systematic looting of "goods", which is why most of the laws in these countries consider cultural heritage to be "public", in the sense of the term used by Charles McGimsey in *Public Archeology* (McGimsey 1972; Almansa 2011a). It is the state that must protect and manage a cultural heritage that belongs to all. And in an interesting article from Iran, archaeology is transformed into an importable commodity for Western archaeologists, with the latter functioning as a sort of administrative office (Papoli and Garazhian 2012). This situation is also present in many African countries, where foreign researchers work on archaeological sites for their own interests, while local communities hardly understand their significance (Almansa et al. 2011; Mapunda and Lane 2004; MacEachern 2010; Schmidt 2009). Moving East, it is interesting to note that what arises from the apparent disinterest of Chinese scholars towards public interest (or values), and from a Maoist national agenda of "letting the past serve the present", is the commercialization of archaeology (Wang 2011). I personally love to mention one of the first public archaeology experiences in Japan (Kondo 1998) where applying the assessing tool of Navrud and Ready (2002), burial mounds in Tsokinawa should probably be the most valuable archaeological site in the world, once a whole community invested their time, resources and money to help completing an archaeological excavation where even the Prince got to participate. Crossing the Pacific Ocean, both Oceania and America offer examples of archaeological practice taking preference over living (or descendant) communities. Although the values exhibited in these cases vary, they do not differ on the basis of scientific or economic grounds, but rather on the grounds of identity, ownership, memory, politics or religion. The only commonality is that we interfere with these notions in our practice (Loosley 2005; Meskell 2009).

The worrying issue in this context is that this identification of values ends up transforming archaeology into a commodity that can be measured in terms of use value and exchange value, or what is worse, marginal utility. Archaeology is not a "cool" activity that enriches our intellect anymore, but a series of values that affect our daily practice from labour (also in academia) to funding (also in the commercial sector), having the current crisis in European commercial companies as a perfect example of loss from the decrease in the consumption of a service—marginal utility. As professionals we assume archaeology has an essential use value for contemporary society—as we cannot define archaeology without people—what transforms it instantly into a social use value. Public consumption of archaeology led to a process of commoditization in which soon money got involved. What does power, identity, development or culture mean in a globalized capitalist world? Whether we like it or not, the commoditization of archaeology has affected every corner of our contemporary practice, beyond the monetary value of the objects themselves and the workings of the traditional market. Can we escape from this market? As a bourgeois modern activity, archaeology has been defined in a context that, if we cannot escape, at least we must be aware of. However, what seems doubtless is our capacity to work besides this capitalist model and to dispute the commoditization of our practice. Do we want to do it?

Archaeology as a Commodity

From traditional academic and administrative jobs, to the commercial sector or popular culture, archaeology is consumed as an everyday commodity. As Cornelius Holtorf's *From Stonehenge to Las Vegas* (2005a) posits, we can tour the world, or our own cities, and experience different forms of archaeology—as officially practiced in a building lot, as enjoyed by tourists, or as consumed as products profiting from the evocation of iconic archaeological imagery. If archaeology is to then mean something, it is that the product of our work—our heritage and knowledge—has an impact, and a price.

Since Mortimer Wheeler's "Theatre of the Past" in the 1930s (Moshenska and Schadla-Hall 2011), archaeology has confronted many economic challenges, such as the organization of large events like the World Archaeological Congress (WAC), keeping in mind Peter Ucko's initial struggles to obtain funding for the UISPP congress (Ucko 1987); the liberal commercialization of archaeological work in the United Kingdom (Aitchison 2012); the rise of alternative archaeologies (Fagan 2006); or even in the austerity cuts in the current economic crisis. In short, the economic aspect of archaeology is incontestable. Unfortunately, however, apart from a number of approaches to the commercial sector in projects such as Archaeology in Contemporary Europe (ACE) and Discovering the Archaeologists of Europe (DISCO), or the increasing concern about sustainable development from heritage—mostly via tourism (Bravo 2003; Comer 2012; Helmy and Cooper 2002)—detailed analyses of this aspect remain scarce.

As such, one of the reasons why Public Archaeology is essential—to use the European understanding of the term (Almansa 2010; Ascherson 2001; Matsuda 2004; Schadla-Hall 1999)—is the way it encompasses the aspects of the conflict between archaeology and the external factors determining its practice (Almansa 2008). At the very least, the analysis of the commoditization of archaeology from this perspective leads to unexpected results (Moshenska 2009:47).

From the Trade of Antiquities to the Trade of Knowledge

Talking about the commoditization of archaeology evokes an image of beautiful artefacts being sold in an auction or on eBay, or being clandestinely shipped to an invidious collector. But although the legal and illegal trade of antiquities and the looting of archaeological heritage have been widely discussed (Brodie and Tubb 2002; Isman 2009; Gibbon 2005; Lazrus and Barker 2012; Pollock 2003; Renfrew 2000; Rodríguez 2012), this is only the tip of the iceberg.

The writing of this very chapter is an example of the commoditization of knowledge. The cost of obtaining the titles referenced in the bibliography would be too great a burden to bear for an independent researcher without access to libraries or digital repositories—like me. And so: if the value of archaeology resides in the price that the public is willing to pay for preservation, or even a visit, can the value of an article be measured by the price of its bibliography? This particular chapter is worth around $3.000 (€2.400), despite a quota of open access of 32 %. In truth, the reasons behind Timothy Gowers' and thousands of other academicians' boycott of Elsevier with The Cost of Knowledge campaign (thecostofknowledge.com) could just as easily be applied to archaeology.

But academic archaeology is commoditized in other ways still. The most obvious is, as politicians are fond of reminding us, the high cost of maintenance. This is why that in times of crisis such as the present, the same two mantras are sounded: "fees must increase" and "knowledge must be transferred". What remains known but largely unsaid, however, is that continuous austerity measures stop ongoing projects in their tracks, and make future research endeavours precarious—which brings the discussion back to the concept of value and the utilitarian "need" of our discipline. Academia has to "sell" something to find funding, signalling a merger between politics and archaeology, and the establishment of knowledge as a commodity (Radder 2010).

From the evaluation of centres and teams in order to obtain "academic excellence", to the widely circulated idea of "publish or perish", researchers—especially those who are young—must write and talk over their natural inclinations and needs, and content themselves on the best possible scenarios within the existing structure. But besides the tangible economic price of these scenarios, there is also a "price" to be paid in terms of knowledge. Unfortunately, however, there are no figures to analyse these tendencies, which begs the need for more investigative studies similar to the ones conducted on British commercial archaeology (Aitchison 1999; Aithchison and Edwards 2003)—or the annual reports of the Institute for Archaeologists (IfA)—, the trials conducted by the aforementioned DISCO or the ongoing Studying Archaeology in Europe (SAE) project (www.studyingarchaeology.eu).

Focusing on the Spanish case, calls for a "different" archaeology have been sounded from some corners of Spanish academia. For instance, García's "Bad times for lyric" (2003)—the title taken from a famous song by *Golpes Bajos*—questions the future of achaeometry in Spain. Even the very creation of an archaeology degree was one of the hardest fought battles in the history of Spanish archaeology (Querol 1997, 2001, 2005); although the Bologna process eventually brought this to fruition, the degree is not without controversy (Comendador, 2012; Ruiz et al. 2009). The future of archaeology, along the lines of it being a valuable/valueless commodity in itself, is still in question, and all the more now with the deepening economic crisis (Almansa 2011b).

But truth be told, what can we argue in our defence if the current system is unable to transfer any new knowledge obtained even to school textbooks? In the end, academic archaeological knowledge is being used to trade in the market of university positions and lucrative European projects, instead of being used to rewrite history and for the education of the public that supports academia with their taxes.

Change *[Spain]* for your country and reflect.

The Market of Dreams

In 1935, Heinrich Himmler, Herman Wirth and Roland Walther Darré founded the society popularly known as Ahnenerbe. Its mission was to conduct archaeological research to nourish the dream of a megalomaniacal, xenophobic movement that ended up triggering one of the worst episodes of our history. This anecdote serves to illustrate that politicians deeply abuse archaeology, with some archaeologists learning to abuse politicians in turn. Archaeology is the market of dreams, in which nationalism, the "being first" syndrome, and empty promises of development are nourished; and in which archaeologists do not play alone, but instead commingle with pseudoarchaeologists to open up the minds and wallets of thousands.

There is an extensive bibliography on nationalism and archaeology (Gathercole and Lowenthal 1991; Kohl and Fawcett 1995; Díaz Andreu and Champion 1996; Meskell 1998; Kane 2003), which analyses the effects of contemporary political identities and geographical borders on the means by which knowledge is obtained and created. Spain is no stranger to this. With the identities of 17 old (and new) autonomous regions at stake, a body of questionable archaeology has emerged, from the nonsensical claim that *madrileños* existed over half a million years ago (Almansa and del Mazo, 2012), the alleged fraud of the Euskera inscriptions in Iruña-Veleia (Canto 2008–2012; Elola 2008), to the existence of the fictional Celts of Asturias (González and Marín 2012; Marín 2005). But dreams also transcend the boundaries of region and country. The wish to claim pride in being the first Europeans has seen the Atapuerca site buzzing with researchers, funded by the millions poured in by over 50 private companies and a dozen administrations and institutions (www.atapuerca.org)—remember the excavation of Çatalhöyük, sponsored by Visa (Hamilakis 1999).

The line between real and unreal turns more blurry still with cases such as Osmanagic's pyramids in Visoko, Bosnia (see Pruitt 2012). Given the impact on the national imaginary—not to mention the millions of dollars—endeavours such as these can generate, it seems impossible to halt the march of the commoditized national dream.

But to not try challenging these endeavours entails eventually accepting as an equal truth astronaut gods from outer space, lost civilisations, and coexistence with dinosaurs, *à la* Raquel Welch. Although Erich von Däniken, Graham Hancock or Zecharia Sitchin may rightly be considered fringe authors, their books are nevertheless bestsellers; as such, they represent one of the major threats not only to archaeological practice, but also to the logical conclusion of the commoditization of the past. It is no accident that the main characters in Ridley Scott's *Prometheus* (2012)—which has, at the time of writing, grossed over 300 million dollars in the box office—are the archaeologists Elizabeth Shaw and Charlie Holloway, who are there to "reinforce" the claim of alien intervention in the birth of mankind. It seems Indiana Jones and Lara Croft are not alone.

It is not so much an issue of the market for pseudoarchaeologies being large; it is the worrying fact that the very same desires and motivations converge upon mainstream archaeological practice. And therefore, the only question left to ask is: what can we do to beat them?

Public "Outrich"

Fighting pseudoarchaeologies is indeed a difficult task (Schadla-Hall 2004; Holtorf 2005b; Almansa 2012), but one of the solutions put forth, which falls within the general fields of communication and public archaeology, is what is commonly known as *public outrich*. Public outrich initiatives in popular media usually differ according to country, but are generally poor aside from the British case (Jordan 1981; Ascherson 2004; Clack and Brittain 2007). Controversial television shows like Spike TV's *American Digger*, for instance, show what the public thinks archaeology is really like, showcasing our impotence in trying to control a message that comes from a large tradition of "treasures" and disinterest in a commoditized world.

Holtorf (2005a:150) uses the term *archaeo-appeal* to describe public consumption of archaeology, but it still remains unclear where this appeal resides. Las Vegas may be a contemporary popular culture example which evokes archaeological images, but is not the only place—see the South African case (Hall and Bombardella 2005) or the failed Gran Scala project in Spain (www.granscalablog.com)—nor is it the only context. The advertising and branding from archaeological activities and sites has become ubiquitous, especially in places with a rich archaeological heritage (MacDonald and Rice 2003; Talalay 2004; Holtorf 2007; Comendador and Almansa 2008–2012).

In the context of community archaeology, sponsored programmes such as the British Young Archaeologists Club (YAC) or the Florida Public Archaeology Network (FPAN) have had some measure of success over the years. With free or low-fee activities, programmes such as these enable archaeology to recover its connection with the community, and even engender innovations in the formats of communication and archaeological work (Gago et al. 2012). But whether through public or private funding, these activities require the hard work of many people that are, in some way or another, integrated in the system. Public outreach is the sale of an archaeological commodity in return for promoting interest in archaeological activity. Does this mean that besides doing our jobs, we are compelled to create an economic or academic profit? Especially in times of crisis such as these, the door is open to speculation and low-level public outreach.

Cultural Resource Madness

As noted above, one notable way in which politics impacts upon archaeology is the management of archaeological heritage. Most countries consider archaeological heritage a public good, but there nevertheless exists huge differences in the ways heritage sites are managed. Factors of land ownership, in addition to the liberal tradition of Anglo-Saxon countries, have made them the leaders in the fields of cultural resource management and commercial archaeology. Public archaeology first arose in these countries as well, stemming from concerns over indigenous and local communities. As much as it can be said that Margaret Thatcher's policies played an essential role in the privatization and commercialization of British archaeology, the Roman legal tradition made Mediterranean countries adopt a (closed) public management model. A vast bibliography of cultural resource management and commercial archaeology exists (King 2002, 2011; Sebastian and Lipe 2009; Everill 2009; Aitchison 2012), and although critics—mainly from within commercial archaeological circles (King 2012)—regularly point out flaws in existing management models, these models are expanding and evolving over time (Demoule 2007; McManamon et al. 2008; Naffé et al. 2008).

However, there is an inherent "madness" in commercial archaeology, best illustrated, I believe, in the rise and fall of the field in Spain. From the late 1970s until the mid 1980s, the 17 autonomous Spanish regions assumed the management of archaeological heritage under their new constitutional roles, as determined by the new national law for the protection of historical heritage and the emerging regional laws (Rodríguez 2004:32). The process was completed in 2007 (Martínez and Querol 1996; Querol 2010). In what I call the "Poncio Pilato Model" the administrations of these autonomous regions, in facing an overwhelming number of encroachments onto heritage sites in the form of new construction developments, decided to "privatize" cultural resource management. What this means is that these administrations kept their "permission giver" roles, but opened the actual execution of the works to contracted companies and freelancers. In addition to already unfavourable laws, the consequences of this deregulation were brutal to the profession: hundreds of subpar new archaeologists were consigned to work in precarious conditions, the number of management companies grew uncontrollably, and prices bottomed out (Parga 2009; Moya 2010).

Employers were more concerned with cheap labour than quality, but with the overloading paperwork to revise by the administration, quality details went unnoticed—in the city of Madrid, a total of 405 expedients were opened in the year of 2007 alone; according to my calculations, this equates to more than 12 thousand expedients for the whole of Spain, for a very limited staff. But with the collapse of the economy in 2008, the unsustainable model fell suit, leaving this swath of companies created in times of false prosperity in ruins. These companies were forced to look for new markets—such as public outreach, in which they have a limited experience—and forgot all the grey literature generated that remains unstudied in the stores of museums (Almansa 2011b).

But the commoditization of archaeology is not only represented by the "free market" model in the execution of archaeological works. This apparently successful model (or at least, easy to manage) is being exported to many countries—including France, pioneer in preventive archaeology and public management (Schlanger and Salas-Rossenbach 2010:71–72). However, the phenomenon of the commoditization of the archaeological labour is probably the most worrying facet of commercial archaeology. Following the descriptions of Karl Marx in *The Capital* (1976), most archaeologists are actually selling their labour as a commodity, as they cannot generate actual commodities themselves (Díaz del Río 2000:15; McGuire and Walker 2008).

With this panorama, the economic crisis and political lurches, it is probably inevitable that stark changes will affect the management of archaeology. This will take the form of either more deregulation, symptom of the value we did not manage to settle (Ansede 2012), more corporatism (Forster 2012), or possibly even a renationalization of archaeological management.

The Crisis and the Expansion

The consequences of the collapse of the American banking system in 2008 lay to waste many welfare states in Western countries. One of the factors in this crisis was the uncontrolled growth of the construction market, which was characterized by opportunism and waste. As we have already seen above, an analogous situation played out in archaeology, and the field is now suffering the consequences of the collapse, especially in European countries (Schlanger and Aitchison 2010). One of the lessons we *are* learning from this crisis is that we are *not* learning anything from the past. It seems that we do not just want archaeology to be a commodity, but we also want its practice to be encapsulated in a deregulated model. Just as the world keeps crumbling around us due to the crisis of liberal deregulated capitalism, we are doing the same with this ineffective model.

Etymologically, *crisis* denotes change, but we are not changing. Countries that kept archaeology within the public sphere are not suffering from the same problems. Others who adopted archaeology as an "imported commodity" face a challenge in keeping their local projects from being trampled upon by outside forces. This dependence on funding needs to be reconsidered in light of the way every sector associated with archaeological practice is mismanaged. The growth of private-managed archaeology, operating on the maxim of "the polluter pays", is unsustainable, and requires greater political and public commitment—especially given the fact that money is now itself a commodity (Keen 2011:360), which makes funding more "expensive".

How Ethical Can We Be?

Every professional association has a code of practice. From the WAC, the SAA, or the EAA, to the dozens of international, national and local associations worldwide, professional associations share some principles of practice based on what we all agree to be the "good" way of doing archaeology. These codes are problematic, however, because the claim of respect for local laws and international recommendations is often spurious, and they only offer a vague framework for archaeological practice instead of serving as a strict guideline for daily practice (Meskell and Pels 2005). One of the reasons for this is the changing norms of society, where things that were perfectly "ethical" 50 years ago are regrettable today.

But taken to its logical conclusion, what if there were a new law stating that archaeology shall not be practiced? Should we "ethically" respect that law? In 2011 and 2012, the *Asociación Madrileña de Trabajadoras y Trabajadores en Arqueología* (AMTTA), a professional association in Madrid, lobbied political parties for deeper regulation of archaeological practice, which will reduce many of the inherent (ethical) flaws of the current model. Although all the political parties approached recognized the seriousness of the situation, which they did not know anything about before, AMTTA's efforts only culminated in a negligent law crafted by the regional government (AMTTA 2012; Pain 2012). If this law happens to be promulgated as is, I for one will be opposing the first principle of conduct for archaeologists involved in contract archaeological work commissioned by the EAA—of which I am a member, in addition to being a part of WAC, SAA, IfA, AMTTA, SAfA and CDL. Is this ethical? I believe so, as through my opposition to this first principle I am supportive of the basic principles of protection, research and divulgation of archaeology.

Why is there a need for an ethical code if it does not have to be adhered to, especially since there are no consequences, at least in Spain, for "light" infractions, and the terrible difficultly of prosecuting negligence? For example, in CDL meetings—the "official" collegiate association in Spain—many members clamoured in calling for the establishment of a code of ethics they did not know had already been ratified by all the regions in 2001, suggesting that they do not really care about a code of ethics in the first place. Self-control is and should be the basis of sane professional practice, and there must be clear standards and assumed ethical principles. A deregulated model of management does not permit equal standards because there is no punishment for those who fail to abide by them.

In current general codes, references to the commoditization of archaeology are so vague that the focus is on the trade and exploitation of heritage (artefacts) only. *The EAA Principles of Conduct for Archaeologists Involved in Contract Archaeological Work* changed the word *commercial* for *contract* during the 1998 Gothenburg meeting, stating that archaeology is not a commercial activity (a commodity), which alludes to the larger never-ending discussion of labels for every miniscule detail in the profession of archaeology. But however much the labels can change, the facts cannot: once there are private companies contracted for profit by developers, there is a commercial relation. And once those companies have to contract professionals to carry out work, there is commoditization of labour.

Coming back to the codes, it is in professional associations related to cultural resource management and commercial archaeology where we find clear principles—for example, in the IfA, the ACRA, or even the CDLs in Spain. All of these associations seem to recognize a situation in which the archaeologist must act as a scientist—in other words, more than just a professional—in order to conduct proper archaeological works under the highest standards, even if their clients attempt to hinder these efforts. It must be noted that apart from the deregulation, the Spanish code is probably one of the most committed in this sense; the lack of an applicable disciplinary code, however, makes it useless. This is not true of the IfA, who have clear codes and standards that all members must fulfil. I am unaware of the consequences of breaching the IfA code, but on paper at least, there seem to exist tools for ensuring ethical practice.

As long as there is a field for commercial archaeology, professionals have just as much right to be paid for their work as an academic is. The profit a professional archaeologist can make from this work is a secondary matter; what is of more import is that he/she fulfils the ethical standards of the profession. Professionals related to the commercial sector also attend congresses, need time to publish, and even undertake traditional research. All of this is paid for by the profits of their work; in this sense, the ethics involved are related not only to the larger commoditization of archaeological practice, but also to the practice itself.

I am referring to the "ethical standard" as a practice that fulfils the basic roles of archaeology; research, protection and divulgation. Those have been defined in the different codes of practice available today and set what we can consider as "good". However, all these codes answer to a bourgeois ethical frame that accommodates the commoditization of archaeology and its perversions.

There have been too many flaws in the structural model of archaeological heritage management. These flaws have led to situations in which the unethical behaviour of some archaeologists has sullied the image of our profession. For the most part, these flaws correspond to areas of archaeological practice that have been commoditized—the need to publish, struggle for funding, political comfort, corporate stability, greed, etc. All we appear to see, however, are the artefacts. For some reason, we are afraid to admit that our practice has become a commodity, as archaeology has been since the beginning. And so it would seem that the first step to get over this problem is to admit that it is a problem. This is why I question how ethical can we be—it is not merely a problem of codes, or commodities, but rather a problem of personal standards in the ethical practice of archaeology. In this sense, the critique should not only be in our ethical stand, but also in the social context of our practice.

Conclusions: Archaeology Does (Not) Have a Price

As soon as archaeology became a profession, archaeological practice had a price. From salaries to any other expense, archaeology has been responsible for the moving of billions of dollars worldwide. Most professionals seemingly choose, however, to not see the commoditization of many aspects of our daily practice:

Commercial: In the practice of commercial archaeology, companies and individuals get an economic profit from their work. This can be open to discussion if the price is fair—that it is not, for cheap—but insofar as the execution of the works fulfil current standards of practice (like the IfA one), it is perfectly ethical. However, it is this sphere in which the most abuses of the profession occur, either pertaining to the contract or working conditions of employees, or the deregulation (and breach) of existing ethical standards.

Academic: academia has evolved to an extremely competitive environment in which knowledge has acquired the status of commodity. Either in the search for project funding, publishing or contracts, unethical behaviour happens to correspond to a commoditized archaeology, in which university positions, peer-reviewed publications, projects, etc. are not always predicated upon purely scientific or academic reasons.

Political: In the largely discussed political impact of our work, we use, or let archaeology be used, as a political commodity in order to get funding for ourselves, or to indirectly assist politicians to win elections.

Social: Society consumes archaeology in many forms. In our daily practice, we usually forget the misconceptions of the social commoditization of archaeology products. It is not our direct mistake, but it is our direct responsibility—which we regularly fail to fulfil—to protect heritage from the indiscriminate misuse and abuse that it suffers. Archaeology and archaeological heritage can be great tools for local economic development and advertising, but we should become more involved in calling for its responsible use. Also, the social and economic success of pseudoarchaeologies is a threat to archaeology as a commodity, as it encourages looting and disrespectful behaviour towards heritage, not to mention the money that these pseudoarchaeologists make from it.

Final 1

Once we recognize the commoditization of archaeological practice, it is time to approach it ethically. We need to solve what I believe is an individual problem that management models have thus far failed to control. We should take our cue from Alcoholics Anonymous, and follow a *Ten-step Program for Recovery from Problematic Ethical Behaviour in Archaeological Practice*:

1. Admit archaeological practice is a commodity.
2. Recognize there are ethical codes that can regulate it.
3. Make a decision to actually fulfil these ethical codes.
4. Examine past errors and possible unethical behaviours.
5. Try to amend those that can still be amended.
6. Ensure this does not ever happen again.
7. Recognise the professional associations that affect our practice.
8. Fight with those associations over the effective regulation of archaeological standards and practice.
9. Fight with those associations against those that still breach the standards.
10. If it comes to it, accept the sanctions for your unethical behaviour and start over.

But first task as a collective is to be united for the ethical practice of archaeology.

Final 2

Assuming that we live in a commoditized world and the complexity of our social, political and economical context, the problem is not in the practice of archaeology per se, but in the failure to fulfil current ethical codes. This is an individual problem that needs to be solved from the collective. Now we have been able to establish and recognize dozens of ethical codes, we need to make sure these codes are useful; but first of all, we need to make sure the basic principles of protection, research and divulgation are respected. I believe we fail as individuals because the model is generally unready to effectively protect heritage and control archaeological practice. There is no place for economical neoliberalism in archaeology—if we still recognize it as a public concern—just as there is no place for dreaming and nepotism in academia. The difference is that we already have codes for commercial practice, but not for academia. Everything else is a matter of common sense already reflected in current codes, but we must put our professional liabilities before our personal interest in the practice of archaeology. In order to achieve this, professional associations are a basic tool for self-control and regulation. It is possible to ethically practice a commoditized archaeology. All we need is commitment. It is also possible to dispute the commoditization of archaeology. Do we want to commit?

References

Aitchison, K. (1999). *Profiling the profession: A survey of archaeological jobs in the UK*. York: CBA-EH-IfA.

Aitchison, K. (2012). *Breaking new ground. How professional archaeology works*. Sheffield: Landwark Research Ltd.

Aithchison, K., & Edwards, R. (2003). *Archaeology labour market intelligence: Profiling the profession 2002/03*. Bradford: CHNTO-IfA.

Almansa, J. (2008). Arqueología pública, o de cómo todo nos afecta. In *Actas de las I Jornadas de Jóvenes en Investigación Arqueológica* (pp. 529–534). Madrid: OrJIA.

Almansa, J. (2010). Pre-editorial: Towards a public archaeology. *AP: Online Journal in Public Archaeology*, *0*, 1–3.

Almansa, J. (2011a). Arqueología para todos los públicos. Hacia una definición de la arqueología pública "a la española". *ArqueoWeb*, *13*, 87–107.

Almansa, J. (Ed.). (2011b). *El futuro de la arqueología en España*. Madrid: JAS Arqueología Editorial.

Almansa, J. (2012). No news is better than evil news. Clearing up the way to face alternative archaeologies. *AP: Online Journal in Public Archaeology*, *2*, 122–136.

Almansa, J., Belay, G., Tibebu, D., Fernández, V., de Torres, J., Charro, C., & Cañete, C. (2011). The Azazo project. Archaeology and the community in Ethiopia. *Public Archaeology*, *10*(3), 159–179.

Almansa, J. & del Mazo, B. (2012). Tesoros, política y otros demonios. La arqueología madrileña en la prensa. *Actas de las VI Jornadas de Patrimonio Arqueológico de la CAM*, Madrid 2009, 419–426.

AMTTA (2012). *Alegaciones de AMTTA al Borrador del Anteproyecto de Ley de Patrimonio Histórico de la Comunidad de Madrid (8 de junio de 2012)*. Madrid, AMTTA. Retrieved from http://es.scribd.com/

Ansede, M. (2012, June 26). Arqueólogos denuncian que Madrid facilitará la destrucción de yacimientos para atraer Eurovegas. *Materia*. Retrieved from http://esmateria.com/

Appadurai, A. (Ed.). (1986). *The social life of things: Commodities in cultural perspective*. Cambridge: Cambridge University Press.

Ascherson, N. (2001). Editorial. *Public Archaeology, 1*(1), 1–3.

Ascherson, N. (2004). Archaeology and the British media. In N. Merriman (Ed.), *Public archaeology* (pp. 145–158). London: Routledge.

Avrami, E., Mason, R., & de la Torre, M. (2000). *Values and heritage conservation. Research report*. Los Angeles: The Getty Conservation Institute.

Bevan, A., & Wengrow, D. (Eds.). (2010). *Cultures of commodity branding*. Walnut Creek: Left Coast Press.

Bravo, Á. (2003). Arqueología aplicada al desarrollo de comunidades atacameñas. *Chungará, 35*(2), 287–293.

Brodie, N., & Tubb, K. (Eds.). (2002). *Illicit antiquities. The theft of culture and the extinction of archaeology*. London: Routledge.

Canto, A. M. (2008–2012). Iruña Veleia y sus "revolucionarios" grafitos I-VIII. *Terrae Antiqvae*. Retrieved from http://terraeantiqvae.com/

Carman, J. (1990). Commodities, rubbish and treasure: Valuing archaeological objects. *Archaeological Review from Cambridge, 9*(2), 195–207.

Carman, J. (1996). *Valuing ancient things: Archaeology and law*. London: Leicester University Press.

Carman, J. (2005). *Against cultural property. Archaeology, heritage and ownership*. London: Duckworth.

Carman, J., Carnegie, G., & Wolnizer, P. (1999). Is archaeological valuation an accounting matter? *Antiquity, 73*(1), 143–148.

Clack, T., & Brittain, M. (Eds.). (2007). *Archaeology and the media*. Walnut Creek: Left Coast Press.

Comendador, B. (2012). La actual formación en arqueología en el marco del EEES: El caso de Galicia. *Minius, 20*, 157–185.

Comendador, B., & Almansa, J. (2008–2012). *Pasado reciclado* (Blog). http://pasadoreciclado.blogspot.com

Comer, D. (2012). *Driver to development or destruction? Tourism and archaeological heritage management at Petra*. New York: Springer.

Demoule, J.-P. (Ed.). (2007). *L'archéologie préventive dans le monde. Apports de l'archéologie préventive à la connaisance du passé*. Paris: La Decouverte.

Díaz Andreu, M., & Champion, T. (Eds.). (1996). *Nationalism and archaeology in Europe*. London: UCL Press.

Díaz del Río, P. (2000). Arqueología Comercial y Estructura de Clase. In M.M. Bóveda López (Ed.), Gestión Patrimonial y Desarrollo Social. CAPA 12 (pp. 7–18). Santiago de Compostela: Universidad de Santiago de Compostela.

Elola, J. (2008). Iruña-Veleia, culebrón arqueológico. *El País*, December 6.

Everill, P. (2009). *The invisible diggers. A study of British commercial archaeology*. Oxford: Oxbow Books.

Fagan, G. (2006). Diagnosing pseudoarchaeology. In G. G. Fagan (Ed.), *Archaeological fantasies* (pp. 23–46). London: Routledge.

Forster, A. (Ed.). (2012). Southport: Gateway to the world? *The Archaeologist, 83*, 2–17.

Gago, M., Malde, A., & Ayán, X. (2012). A Torre dos Mouros (Lira, Carnota): una experiencia de ciencia en comunidad y en directo. In J. Almansa (Ed.), *Arqueología pública en España*. Madrid: JAS Arqueología Editorial.

Gamble, C. (2008). *Archaeology. The basics*. London: Routledge.

García, M. (2003). Malos tiempos para la lírica. ¿Hay todavía futuro para la arqueología científica en la universidad española? *Complutum, 14*, 7–18.

Gathercole, P., & Lowenthal, D. (Eds.). (1991). *The politics of the past*. London: Unwin Hyman.

Gestrich, N. (2011). Putting a price on the past: The ethics and economics of archaeology in the marketplace. A reply to "What is public archaeology". *Present Pasts, 3*(2), 80–82.
Gibbon, K. (2005). *Who owns the past? Cultural policy, cultural property and the law*. New Brunswick: Rutgers University Press.
González, D., & Marín, C. (2012). Celts, collective identity and archaeological responsibility: Asturias (North of Spain) as case study. In R. Karl, J. Leskovar, & S. Moser (Eds.), *Interpretierte eisenzeiten. Die erfundenen Kelten—mythologie eines begriffes und seine verwendung in archäologie, tourismus und esoterik* (pp. 173–184). Hallein: Oberösterreichischen Landesmuseum.
Hall, M., & Bombardella, P. (2005). Las Vegas in Africa. *Journal of Social Archaeology, 5*(1), 5–24.
Hamilakis, Y. (1999). La trahison des archeologues? Archaeological practice as intellectual activity in postmodernity. *Journal of Mediterranean Archaeology, 12*(1), 60–79.
Hamilakis, Y., & Duke, P. (Eds.). (2007). *Archaeology and capitalism. From ethics to politics*. Walnut Creek: Left Coast Press.
Hardesty, D., & Little, B. (2009). *Assessing site significance. A guide for archaeologists and historians*. Lanham: AltaMira Press.
Helmy, E., & Cooper, C. (2002). An assessment of sustainable tourism planning for the archaeological heritage: The case of Egypt. *Journal of Sustainable Tourism, 10*(6), 514–535.
Holtorf, C. (2005a). *From Stonehenge to Las Vegas. Archaeology as popular culture*. Walnut Creek: AltaMira Press.
Holtorf, C. (2005b). Beyond crusades: How (not) to engage with alternative archaeologies. *World Archaeology, 37*(4), 544–551.
Holtorf, C. (2007). *Archaeology is a brand. The meaning of archaeology in contemporary popular culture*. Walnut Creek: Left Coast Press.
Isman, F. (2009). *I predatori dell'arte perduta. Il saccheggio dell'archeologia in Italia*. Milan: Skira.
Jeppson, P. (2010). Doing our homework: Reconsidering what archaeology has to offer schools. In J. Stottman (Ed.), *Archaeologists as activists. Can archaeologists change the world?* (pp. 63–79). Tuscaloosa: University of Alabama Press.
Jordan, P. (1981). Archaeology and television. In J. D. Evans, B. Cunliffe, & C. Renfrew (Eds.), *Antiquity and man: Essays in honour of Glynn Daniel* (pp. 207–213). London: Times and Hudson.
Kane, S. (Ed.). (2003). *The politics of archaeology and identity in a global context*. Boston: Archaeological Institute of America.
Keen, S. (2011). *Debunking economics. The naked emperor dethroned?* London: Zed Books.
King, T. (2002). *Thinking about cultural resource management. Essays from the edge*. Lanham: AltaMira Press.
King, T. (Ed.). (2011). *A companion to cultural resource management*. Malden: Wiley-Blackwell.
King, T. (2012). Public archaeology is a menace to the public—and to archaeology. In Forum: Is public archaeology a menace? *AP: Online Journal in Public Archaeology, 2*, 5–9.
Kohl, P., & Fawcett, C. (Eds.). (1995). *Nationalism, politics and the practice of archaeology*. Cambridge: Cambridge University Press.
Kondo, Y. (1998). *Tsokinawa Kofun*. Okayama: Kibito Shuppan.
Lazrus, P., & Barker, A. (Eds.). (2012). *All the King's horses. Essays on the impact of looting and the illicit antiquities trade on our knowledge of the past*. Washington: SAA.
Little, B. (2010). Epilogue: Changing the world with archaeology. In J. Stottman (Ed.), *Archaeologists as activists. Can archaeologists change the world?* (pp. 154–158). Tuscaloosa: University of Alabama Press.
Loosley, E. (2005). Archaeology and cultural belonging in contemporary Syria: The value of archaeology to religious minorities. *World Archaeology, 37*(4), 589–596.
MacDonald, S., & Rice, M. (Eds.). (2003). *Consuming ancient Egypt*. London: UCL Press.

MacEachern, S. (2010). Seeing like an oil company's CHM programme. Exxon and archaeology on the Chad Export Project. *Journal of Social Archaeology, 10*(3), 347–366.
Maeer, G., & Campbell, I. (2008). *Values and benefits of heritage. A research review*. London: Heritage Lottery Fund.
Mapunda, B., & Lane, P. (2004). Archaeology for whose interest—Archaeologists or the locals? In N. Merriman (Ed.), *Public archaeology* (pp. 211–223). London: Routledge.
Marín, C. (2005). El celtismo asturiano. Una perspectiva arqueológica. *Gallaecia, 24*, 309–333.
Martínez, B., & Querol, M. Á. (1996). *La gestión del patrimonio arqueológico*. Madrid: Alianza.
Marx, K. (1976). *Capital. A critique of political economy*. London: Pelican Books.
Matsuda, A. (2004). The concept of "the public" and the aims of public archaeology. *Papers from the Institute of Archaeology, 15*, 66–76.
McGimsey, C., III. (1972). *Public archeology*. New York: Seminar Press.
McGuire, R. (2008). *Archaeology as political action*. Berkeley: University of California Press.
McGuire, R., & Walker, M. (2008). Class (Chapter 3). In R. H. McGuire (Ed.), *Archaeology as political action* (pp. 98–139). Berkeley: University of California Press.
McManamon, F., Stout, A., & Barnes, J. (Eds.). (2008). *Managing archaeological resources*. Walnut Creek: Left Coast Press.
Meskell, L. (Ed.). (1998). *Archaeology under fire. Nationalism, politics and heritage in the East Mediterranean and Middle East*. London: Routledge.
Meskell, L. (Ed.). (2009). *Cosmopolitan Archaeologies*. Durham: Duke University Press.
Meskell, L., & Pels, P. (Eds.). (2005). *Embedding ethics*. New York: Berg.
Moshenska, G. (2009). What is public archaeology? *Present Pasts, 1*(1), 46–48.
Moshenska, G., & Burtenshaw, P. (2011). Commodity forms and levels of value in archaeology: A response to Gestrich. *Present Pasts, 3*(2), 83–84.
Moshenska, G., & Schadla-Hall, T. (2011). Mortimer Wheeler's theatre of the past. *Public Archaeology, 10*(1), 46–55.
Moya, P. (2010). Grandezas y miserias de la arqueología de empresa en la España del siglo XXI. *Complutum, 21*(1), 6–26.
Naffé, B. O. M., Lanfranchi, R., & Schlanger, N. (Eds.). (2008). *L'archéologie préventive en Afrique. Enjeux et perspectives*. Saint-Maur-des-Fossés: Éditions Sépia.
Navrud, S., & Ready, R. (Eds.). (2002). *Valuing cultural heritage. Applying environmental valuation techniques to historic buildings, monuments and artefacts*. Cheltenham: Edward Elgar Publishing.
Pain, E. (2012, August 24). Economic crisis forces Spanish archaeology to rethink its roots. *Science*. Retrieved from http://www.sciencemag.org/
Papoli Yazdi, L., & Garazhian, O. (2012). Archaeology as an imported commodity. A critical approach to the position of archaeology in Iran. *Forum Kritische Archäeologie, 1*, 24–29.
Parga, E. (2009). *El mercado del patrimonio: nacimiento, estructura y desarrollo de las empresas que gestionan el patrimonio arqueológico*. Santiago de Compostela: LaPa-CSIC.
Pollock, S. (2003). The looting of the Iraq museum. Thoughts on archaeology in a time of crisis. *Public Archaeology, 3*, 117–124.
Pruitt, T. (2012). Pyramids, performance and pseudoscience in Visoko, Bosnia. *AP: Online Journal in Public Archaeology, 2*, 26–34.
Querol, M. Á. (1997). La arqueología en las universidades españolas. *Boletín del Instituto Andaluz de Patrimonio Histórico, 22*, 15–18.
Querol, M. Á. (2001). La formación arqueológica universitaria: Un futuro por el que luchar. *Boletín del Instituto Andaluz de Patrimonio Histórico, 37*, 32–34.
Querol, M. Á. (2005). La génesis del título universitario de arqueología: desde mi ángulo. *Complutum, 16*, 213–219.
Querol, M. Á. (2010). *Manual de gestión del patrimonio cultural*. Madrid: Akal.
Radder, H. (Ed.). (2010). *The commodification of academic research*. Pittsburg: University of Pittsburg Press.
Renfrew, C. (2000). *Loot, legitimacy and ownership*. London: Duckworth.

Rodríguez, I. (2004). *Arqueología urbana en España*. Barcelona: Ariel.
Rodríguez, I. (2012). *Indianas Jones sin futuro. La lucha contra el expolio del patrimonio arqueológico*. Madrid: JAS Arqueología Editorial.
Ruiz, G., Fernández, V., Álvarez-Sanchís, J., & Armasa, X.-L. (2009). Foro: ¿qué arqueología enseñar en la universidad del siglo XXI? *Complutum, 20*(2), 225–254.
Scarre, C., & Scarre, G. (Eds.). (2006). *The ethics of archaeology. Philosophical perspectives on archaeological practice*. Cambridge: Cambridge University Press.
Schadla-Hall, T. (1999). Editorial: Public archaeology. *European Journal of Archaeology, 2*(2), 147–158.
Schadla-Hall, T. (2004). The comforts of unreason: The importance and relevance of alternative archaeology. In N. Merriman (Ed.), *Public archaeology* (pp. 255–271). London: Routledge.
Schlanger, N., & Aitchison, K. (Eds.). (2010). *Archaeology and the global economic crisis. Multiple impacts, possible solutions*. Tervuren: Culture Lab.
Schlanger, N., & Salas-Rossenbach, K. (2010). One crisis too many? French archaeology between reform and relaunch. In N. Schlanger & K. Aitchison (Eds.), *Archaeology and the global economic crisis. Multiple impacts, possible solutions* (pp. 69–80). Tervuren: Culture Lab.
Schmidt, P. R. (2009). What is postcolonial about archaeologies in Africa? In P. R. Schmidt (Ed.), *Postcolonial archaeologies in Africa* (pp. 1–20). Santa Fe: SAR Press.
Sebastian, L., & Lipe, W. (Eds.). (2009). *Archaeology and cultural resource management. Visions for the future*. Santa Fe: SAR Press.
Southport Group. (2011). *Realising the benefits of planning-led investigation in the historic environment: A framework for delivery*. Southport: Southport Group.
Talalay, L. (2004). The past as commodity. Achaeological images in modern advertising. *Public Archaeology, 3*, 205–216.
Trigger, B. (2007). *A history of archaeological thought*. Cambridge: Cambridge University Press.
Ucko, P. (1987). *Academic freedom and apartheid. The story of the World Archaeological Congress*. London: Duckworth.
Van Binsbergen, W., & Geschiere, P. (Eds.). (2005). *Commodification: Things, agency and identities ("The social life of things" revisited)*. Berlin: LIT.
Vitelli, K., & Colwell-Chanthaphonh, C. (Eds.). (2006). *Archaeological ethics*. Lanham: AltaMira Press.
Wang, T. (2011). "Public archaeology" in China: A preliminary investigation. In K. Okmura & A. Matsuda (Eds.), *New perspectives in global public archaeology* (pp. 43–56). New York: Springer.
World Heritage Centre. (2011). *Operational guidelines for the implementation of the World Heritage Convention*. Paris: UNESCO.
Zimmerman, L., Vitelli, K., & Hollowell-Zimmer, J. (Eds.). (2003). *Ethical issues in archaeology*. Lanham: AltaMira Press.

Chapter 11
The Differing Forms of Public Archaeology: Where We Have Been, Where We Are Now, and Thoughts for the Future

Carol McDavid and Terry P. Brock

Introduction: A Contingent (and Pragmatic) View of Contemporary Public Archaeology

Over the course of the past century, public archaeology (however defined) and archaeological ethics have been mutually constituted. Public archaeology is the arena in which archaeologists and multiple publics enact existing ethical assumptions and (as laws and ideas shift) experiment with new ways of working together. These experiments are best seen as contingent and context-specific—what is ethically desirable in one situation may not work for any other. Even so, for years, professional archaeology associations have written formal codes for archaeologists to follow when making ethical decisions, and there are many volumes (including this one) which have explored both the codes and the decisions.

Unfortunately, these codes frequently do not reflect or account for the contingency of what actually happens when archaeologists and publics work together. What matters more, in our view, are the pragmatic ideas that archaeological work is best evaluated by looking at its results, and that these evaluations should be made by those who are directly concerned (on both sides of the archaeology/public exchange). Why does our work matter? What does it matter to any community, person, or descendant? To any agency or any client? To any archaeologist? Or, even, to people with whom we may disagree (subsistence "looters," for example Hollowell 2006). As William James put it over a century ago, our "work" is never a solution; it is always a program for more work (James 1995:7).

C. McDavid (✉)
Department of Anthropology, Rice University, 1638 Branard, Houston, TX 77006, USA
e-mail: mcdavid@publicarchaeology.org

T.P. Brock
The Montpelier Foundation, 2306 Park Avenue Apt B, Richmond, VA 23220, USA
e-mail: brockter@msu.edu

C. Gnecco, D. Lippert (eds.), *Ethics and Archaeological Praxis*,
Ethical Archaeologies: The Politics of Social Justice 1,
DOI 10.1007/978-1-4939-1646-7_11

In archaeology itself, we are used to this idea—the best science never reaches full closure, and the best questions lead to more questions. This is just as true in public archaeology. Archaeology's engagements with publics are best seen as starting points to make mutual discoveries and decisions about what should happen next in any situation. There are usually thorny issues to deal with during this process—differential power being perhaps the most obvious—but having predetermined codes does not eliminate or even mitigate them. With or without codes, it is within the decision-making process that people can, working together, avoid the pitfalls of either relativism or absolutism. One truth is not as good as another, but the best truths are found within the process of looking for them (McDavid 2000).

In our view, then, public archaeology is what happens when different people and communities (including archaeological ones) attempt to make decisions about archaeology (ethical and otherwise) that are tolerable to all. As this occurs, archaeological ethics emerge within certain practices, methods, and approaches (Meskell and Pels 2005a), which are themselves experimental and contingent.

Here, after covering some historical ground, we will propose a definition of public archaeology that covers the broad scope of public archaeology that exists today. We will then discuss four of the most prominent approaches used in contemporary public archaeology practice: activism, multivocality, collaboration, and community engagement. Indeed, in our view, all of these practices also define what ethical archaeology practice is, in 2013. We will then discuss these approaches as they relate to an important new venue for public archaeology practice, new social media. Finally, we will close with some questions for the future.

We should make it clear that we do not feel, as do some, that ethical codes are obsolete (Pels 1999; Tarlow 2000); they have their purposes (Schrader 1999; Shore 1999; Sluka 1999). We do, agree, however, with the same writers who view ethical practice as the result of negotiation—as "a set of moral agreements composed contingently, perhaps inconsistently, but at least appropriate for the situation at hand" (Pels 1999:114); see also Agier (1999) and Meskell and Pels (2005b).

Some provisos apply to this text. First, we work within the Americanist tradition of anthropological historical archaeology, and this bias will likely emerge, even though we will provide pointers to the wider literature. Second, the approaches we discuss in historical terms still operate within current practice: temporal boundaries are not absolute. Third, our proposed categories of practice are themselves contingent: individual projects we mention here could easily fall into multiple groupings at one time.

Public Archaeology in the Past

Ethical issues in archaeology have always been, and continue to be, conditioned on the context within which they are situated. Therefore, in order to understand what is known today as public archaeology, and to define current ethical practice, we must first briefly trace its history.

What is seen as public archaeology today is often traced to various pieces of legislation in this century (the Antiquities Act of 1906, Historic Sites Act of 1935, and the National Historic Preservation Act of 1966). Over the course of US history, however, many members of the public—indigenous, diasporic, and otherwise—have had a variety of intersections with archaeology (not all positive), and one short paper cannot begin to cover this history properly. Therefore, our brief historical review will begin in the 1970s, when McGimsey (1972) first used the term "public archaeology."

At that point, the term referred to the growing field of Cultural Resource Management, or CRM, the roots of which were planted by the National Historic Preservation Act of 1966 (building on the earlier legislation noted above) (Green and Doershuk 1998; Little 2012). The years after this act witnessed an explosion of CRM public archaeology projects, in which the word "public" referred to the rationale driving the work (public laws enacted with public support) and to the way that it was (and is) regulated and reviewed (by public agencies funded by public dollars). The rapid growth of CRM reflected a growing ethical recognition that there is cultural value in the past for the present, and CRM was seen as a means to ensure that this value could be preserved and protected—or at least mitigated. We should note that the term "CRM" subsumes a wide array of practices and places (King 2002:1), of which archaeology is only one.

Over time, two often-overlapping forms of CRM emerged. The first is archaeology conducted by private commercial firms, often referred to as "contract archaeology." Even though this work is mandated by public law and reviewed by public agencies, and even though specific members of the public are often designated as "interested parties," the process itself is still controlled by professional archaeologists (King 2009). By the 1980s, at least 80 % of archaeology done worldwide was taking place as commercial CRM archaeology (Neumann and Sanford 2001:1) and by then CRM had "achieved de facto recognition as the principal form of archaeology in the United States" (Green and Doershuk 1998:124).

The second form of CRM refers to archaeology conducted by or at the behest of public agencies, usually (though not always) on public land. Examples include the National Parks Service, the Bureau of Land Management, Tribal Preservation Offices (TPOs), and State Historic Preservation Offices (SHPOs). These and similar agencies conduct a wide array of avocational archaeology programs and support archaeology projects in the nonprofit sector (e.g., Marcom et al. 2011). In these sorts of projects, the public-at-large sometimes has a very large role, at least with respect to site tours, outreach activities, and the like.

Also by the mid-1980s, two additional and distinct threads of public archaeology practice had begun to take form. One of these, "public archaeology as archaeology education," emerged as the archaeological community in the United States became alarmed about the numbers of archaeological sites that were being destroyed by widespread looting. Discipline-wide efforts began to educate the public that saving archaeological sites was important—and that scientific archaeological research was vital to this process; for examples see Gelburd (1989) and Rogge and Montgomery (1989); for an historical perspective see Friedman (2000). Because this work directly involved the public, it also began to be referred to by many as "public archaeology," even though the earlier definition of the term (as CRM) was still common. Archaeology education programs were initiated at all levels of archaeology, and were seen as "a strategy to combat the rampant vandalism that was destroying the nation's archaeological resources" (Friedman 2000:13).

This approach to archaeology developed hand-in-hand with the "stewardship" ethos that is now embedded in most professional archaeology ethics statements (Lynott and Wylie 1995a, b); for a critical review of such statements see Tarlow (2000); for an historical one see Wylie (2005). The implicit assumption in the wording of these statements was that professional archaeologists were the persons best suited to perform the stewardship function. The same assumption was also evident in archaeology education materials, most of which promoted scientific methods as the best way to understand the material past (e.g., Smith and McManahon 1991). This related directly to the positivist approaches to archaeology that were dominant at the time. Although archaeologists during this period seem to have supported the idea of doing educational work very little of it appeared in professional journals, despite advocacy from some (Goldstein 1998:529).

Archaeology education case studies, from both indigenous and historical archaeology, continued to appear in numerous edited volumes throughout the 1990s and early 2000s (Jameson 1997; Smardz 2000). It must be said, however, that regardless of its substantive and positive impact on the field, "public archaeology as education" (as it was originally envisioned) represented a form of public archaeology that was for archaeology's needs. It was not aimed at the needs of the "public at large." Instead, the main idea was to convince people that archaeological priorities—conservation, preservation, scientific methods, etc.—should be theirs as well. This was recognized as problematic by some at the time (Zimmerman et al. 1994) and later (Mouer 2000:235).

In the late 1990s and into this century, archaeology education began to embrace broader agendas, even though preservation and stewardship were (and are) still internal disciplinary concerns. Practitioners started to analyze archaeology education as well as to practice it, and to articulate some of its benefits to the wider public (Bartoy 2012; Davis 2005; Jeppson and Brauer 2003, 2008; Jeppson 2010, 2012; Zimmerman et al. 1994). The current emphasis of much archaeology education is now aimed at using archaeology to:

> …help people to appreciate diversity in the past and present and thereby to practice living more tolerantly in a multicultural society…[and to help] students of any age learn teamwork, critical thinking, and a perspective on their own lives within the time and space of human life (Little 2012:396).

A second thread in public archaeology, which also emerged in the 1980s, came primarily from the academy—what we will refer to as "critical public archaeology." This thread was more allied with the "postprocessual" theoretical approaches that developed as critiques of positivistic archaeology. Indeed, it sprang directly from one of them, critical archaeology, as developed by Mark Leone (Leone et al. 1987), his students (e.g., Potter 1994), and others (Handsman 1984; Wylie 1985). This work provided new frameworks for thinking about the ways that "publics" and "public interests" are integral to contemporary archaeological practice, and for understanding the political role of archaeology in the present. As was occurring in archaeology education, critical public archaeology also broadened as the 1990s progressed, as archaeologists began to work more with the public, listening to them and their agendas (Brown 1997; Leone 1995), and as writers from other strands of post-processual archaeology began to advocate more direct public interaction (Hodder 1996; Hodder et al. 1995).

Before moving to the present, it is necessary to understand two specific events in the early 1990s that drove significant changes in the culture of archaeology—without either, the way that public archaeology is practiced today would be much different. The first occurred in the United States with the 1990 passage of NAGPRA (the Native American Graves Protection and Repatriation Act). Because of this legislation, archaeologists working with indigenous remains became legally obligated to consult with living descendants. After a period of adjustment, archaeologists across the discipline began to accept the benefits of sharing power with living people in the present (Stutz 2011; Swidler et al. 1997; Zimmerman 1994). We will not discuss NAGPRA in detail, other than to note that it marks a period in which the assumptions behind the word "public," in "public archaeology" began to shift. It no longer referred to "public" in the sense of law, funding, land, etc., but also began referring to specific living publics. This shift took place within both indigenous archaeology and historical archaeology as they were practiced in the United States.

The next event was the African Burial Ground Project (ABG), which took place in New York City from the early to mid-1990s. As is well known, in 1991 hundreds of previously undisturbed graves were discovered in Lower Manhattan during the construction of a new federal office building. The salient point here is that after their discovery and a period of much public debate, African American descendant communities in New York (self-defined as cultural, not lineal, descendants) wrested control of the project from the building planners and archaeologists. They insisted on having substantive input into decisions about the research design, the researchers themselves, and the subsequent public interpretation of the site (LaRoche and Blakey 1997:100). As a result, the ABG team proposed a new ethical framework for CRM projects: that there are two types of clients. The first is the ethical client (usually the self-identified descendant community most affected by the research) and the second is the business client (the agency funding the research and the contract archaeology implementing it) (Blakey 2004:10, 103).

The strategies archaeologists have used since then to operationalize this distinction vary widely, in part because African American sites (or those occupied by similarly disempowered groups) do not necessarily have the legal mandates for "consultation" that are required when the archaeology takes place on public land—there is no NAGPRA for non-Native groups. Even so, archaeologists can, if they wish, advocate voluntary consultation with ethical clients as an archaeological "best practice"—just as they might advocate certain scientific best practices (McDavid et al. 2012). For example, the archaeologist and business client, working with the ethical client, could create an Advisory Group (or something similar) to review the preliminary research design (e.g., Feit and Jones 2007). The ethical client's input could then be sought in that design—voluntarily. Likewise, all clients can be asked to review relevant reports before they are finalized—and if there is a disagreement, the ethical client's input could be included in the report as an "alternate" view.

It is true that being voluntarily multivocal, collaborative, etc. would not necessarily require business clients to cede any real power (and some disputes between the two types of clients will not be resolved easily, if at all). It would also run counter to the impulse, in most corporate quarters, to keep potentially controversial projects "under the radar." Nevertheless, small shifts in practice could still give descendant groups and other ethical clients a formal and recognized voice in the documentation of archaeological research, and would add some transparency to a process which is extremely opaque to most "everyday" citizens (King 2009). In this framework, ethical clients would also have obligations—for example to provide their input by whatever timetable, and whatever format, that everyone agrees upon ahead of time. The point with respect to ethical practice is that archaeologists are already empowered to seek input from ethical clients and to take that input seriously.

Some are already doing so—although the ABG project was not the only, or earliest, African American archaeology project to involve descendants (in CRM or otherwise), both NAGPRA and the ABG project marked a shift in archaeological culture. As Leone et al. (2005:587–588) put it:

> Sites such as the burial ground mirror the lessons of NAGPRA in ways that have fundamentally changed how archaeologists think about the role and power of public reactions to our work, as well as how the public engages with sites or projects they identify as critically important. The burial ground is just one of several sites at which the public, deeply invested in the outcome, forced the sharing of power and access to information.

Despite legislative and regulatory limits (which still privilege documented, usually lineal descendancy) many archaeologists now accept the idea that a descendant community is a "self-defined group of people in the present that link themselves—socially, politically, and economically—to a group of people in the past". Although this view is still uncommon in most "everyday" CRM, that too is slowly changing (see Boyd et al. 2011; LaRoche 2012; Levin 2012).

During the same long period, slightly different, often non-anthropological, discourses about public archaeology were emerging in global contexts. Some of these sprang from "heritage" (both practice and research) as it was framed by universities in Europe and elsewhere, and by nongovernmental organizations involved in heritage conservation. One major event in the global arena was the 1985 creation of the World Archaeological Congress (WAC), founded in part as a response to South African apartheid. Over time, WAC has attracted a truly global attendance in which public archaeology topics are seen as an integral part of professional practice (see Carman 2002; Funari 2000; Funari and Bezerra 2012; Schmidt and Patterson 1995; Smith 2004 for examples of global approaches).

By the late 1990s, public archaeology was broadly understood to encompass three areas of practice: CRM (mandated by public law); archaeology education (aimed at preserving archaeological sites and developing a public appreciation for archaeology); and, most recently, work that attempts to understand archaeology's place in the world and to use archaeology as a locus for reform and critique (Little 2012). By the turn of the twentieth century, across the discipline, archaeological discussions had "broadened appropriately to include the rights and responsibilities of descendant *communities* to control, protect, and share aspects of tangible and intangible cultural heritage *on their own terms*". By this time, archaeologists of all kinds had expanded their "public" priorities far beyond the original goal of promoting positivist archaeology (even if they did not necessarily call themselves public archaeologists).

Public Archaeology Today

Public archaeology in 2013 is best defined broadly, as any practice in which "the public" (however defined) and archaeology (as an academic discipline) intersect. Put another way, public archaeology is any endeavor in which archaeologists interact with the public, and any research (practical or theoretical) that examines or analyzes the public dimensions of doing archaeology. Before we continue, some unpacking of this proposed definition may be useful.

Framed along these lines, public archaeology can include publicly mandated or funded archaeology, archaeology education, interpretation, outreach, writing for/with the public, tours, lesson plans, talks, brochures, and web sites. It can also include policy work, political advocacy, applied anthropology, community organizing, participatory action research, oral history (formal and informal), ethnographic research, participant observation, and participatory GIS. It can include research about the intersections between publics and archaeology—histories and historiographies about how archaeology has developed in different parts of the world, attempts to understand how the past is understood in the present (including social memory research), and research about archaeological laws and norms in different areas. It can include writing about research methods and strategies, and research about the ways that artifacts and archaeology are deployed by various publics (the antiquities market, for example). It can focus on managing archaeological resources—such as heritage management of archaeological landscapes, sites, and collections, issues surrounding sustainability and stewardship, and public engagements with that work. Last, but not least, it can include working with the public for the larger benefit of society. This would include the more recent work that casts itself as "activist" or geared towards various global justice issues. We will discuss specific examples below.

Our proposed definition may seem broad, but it is similar in scope to others, such as that used by the international journal *Public Archaeology*, which began publication in 2000. The masthead states that it provides "an arena for the growing debate surrounding archaeological and heritage issues as they relate to the wider world of politics, ethics, government, social questions, education, management, economics, and philosophy." This is similar to the definition proposed by an even newer (2011) international online journal, *arqueologiapublica*, which defines public archaeology as "the study of the relations between… archaeology and society in every aspect of daily life (social, economical, and political)." This journal's web site provides a long list of potential topics, similar to those covered by *Public Archaeology*. Because of this conceptual expansion of what public archaeology "is," it is now possible for public archaeologists in the United States to participate in worldwide conversations about the interaction between archaeology as a closed discipline and archaeology in public practice.

Moving to the Present: Activism, Multivocality, Collaboration, and Community

Writing about the most recent public archaeology tends to cross the "usual" disciplinary lines more than earlier writing, which tended to be situated within the traditional geographic and temporal discourses (such as "prehistoric" archaeology, classical archaeology, and historical archaeology). In our view, this only started to occur as North American public archaeology began to expand beyond the original scope described early in this paper. WAC, as noted earlier, is no doubt playing a role in this, as are efforts by North American and international scholars to expand the scope of conferences, publications, etc. to participants worldwide (see Skeates et al. 2012) for a recent example.

In this context, what is "ethical" (or not) has emerged within a number of contingent, situated practices as archaeologists have engaged with multiple, diverse publics. The practices themselves are the starting points for mutual decision-making about what is ethical and what is not. We will examine four of these, all of which underpin contemporary practice: activism, multivocality, collaboration, and community engagement.

Public Archaeology as Activism

For the past several years, archaeologists and public archaeologists have been exploring how, and whether, archaeology can help to resolve inequities in society (Little 2009; McGuire 2008; Stottman 2010). Whether this work has been successful is open for analysis and critique (Dawdy 2009), and it is by no means certain whether archaeology itself (a fairly limited field of engagement) can inform some of the most serious and troubling contemporary issues (e.g., human trafficking, and using rape as a weapon of war). Even so, much recent work does illustrate that many archaeologists are keenly aware of social and political contexts in which they work, and willing to use their work to create change within those contexts. This is not totally new, of course; earlier writers critiqued the political use and/or abuse of archaeology (Gathercole and Lowenthal 1994; Leone 1995; Trigger 1984), but the newer writing is more frontal with respect to specific societal issues and struggles, and situated more firmly in public, not necessarily academic, arenas (McDavid 2011b). Some of these archaeologists have proposed that societal change could be an important result of working with professional educators, in both the classroom (Jeppson 2004; Stone 2000) and in community service learning projects (Nassaney and Levine 2009). Others have sought ways for archaeology to be more democratic, or for this democracy, if achieved, to make society itself more open and democratic (Jeppson 2001, 2012; McDavid 2002a). Some have focused on specific social issues, such as racism and white privilege (Babiarz 2011; McDavid 2005), class struggle (Gadsby and Chidester 2012; McGuire 2008), poverty (Matthews and Spencer-Wood 2011), environmental issues (Derry 2003), and cultural violence (Gonzalez-Tennant 2007, 2010; Meskell 1998). Still others examined how archaeology can benefit wider society in broader terms (Little 2002, 2007; Sabloff 2008).

Public Archaeology as Multivocality

In archaeology, multivocality refers to both the differences between professional archaeologists (so-called "experts") and the publics they work with, and the differences between the publics themselves. It also refers to the ways that these different people and groups value, interpret, and find meaning in any given archaeological site, as well as the narratives they create about places and objects. These differences do not necessarily fall into predictable, seemingly simple categories of ethnicity, training, gender, and the like. Although the realities of "standpoint" and individual perspective are critical when considering multivocality, how it plays out in practice varies from situation to situation, project to project, and person to person.

In projects which aim for multivocality, both archaeologists and publics (or, to use a currently popular term, stakeholders) attempt to find ways for different points of view about history, meaning, and physical remains to be expressed, at the same time. The ideal scenario is that they do this together, that power (to "own," control, interpret, assign meaning, etc.) is shared among different players, and that one group does not have power at the expense of another.

Multivocality can operate, and be analyzed, both locally and globally—although it is important to understand that these arenas constitute and influence each other, and the categories "local" and "global" should not be seen as rigid, simple, or non-permeable. On local levels, multivocality can refer to the idea that different (often previously marginalized) groups should have a voice in interpreting archaeological findings—or in interpreting history in ways that may include archaeology but is not limited to it. There are many examples of this across the discipline, in which a variety of people with different skillsets and interests have collaborated in planning museum displays, interpretive centers, web sites, and the like.

Multivocality is often seen as one way to dismantle larger forces of colonialism, and is often enacted in the work that archaeologists and others do with international organizations such as UNESCO and the World Archaeological Congress. Therefore, there are important differences of scale as different archaeologists engage with the idea of multivocality. Some focus mostly on local practice, while others situate their work in broader arenas. Some of the scales are temporal, in which the focus is on past practices, and the complicity of archaeology (and in some contexts, anthropology) in maintaining dominant hegemonies and imperialist power structures. Put simply, those who have been oppressed in the past, or who are still oppressed today, often see archaeology as part of that oppression, and thus suspect. Much of the recent work framed as "archaeological ethnography" attempts to address this (Castañeda and Matthews 2008; Meskell 2005; Mortensen and Hollowell 2009) as does work positioned explicitly as "postcolonial" (Habu et al. 2008; Rizvi and Lydon 2010).

Another focus of multivocality has to do with relativism. How does any person, or group, evaluate differing truth claims? Although most archaeologists are willing to engage respectfully with those whose epistemological and ontological perspectives are widely different from their own, few archaeologists are willing to reject empiricism altogether. Despite this, many have found ways to have positive and multivocal conversations with those who have different perspectives, and to conduct archaeology in ways which incorporates those perspectives (Colwell-Chanthaphonh and Ferguson 2006; Hodder 2008; Kim 2008; McDavid 2002b; Silberman 2008; Silliman 2008; Stutz 2011; Wylie 2008). Most recently, archaeologists who are, themselves, members of indigenous groups have explored strategies that neither reject or privilege Western mainstream approaches, but instead are hybrids which allow different "truths" to be equally true, even if they are not commensurable in a scientific sense (Atalay 2008a, b, 2010; Watkins 2001).

Multivocal work would also include that done by countless agency, academic, nonprofit, and museum archaeologists who acknowledge (and sometimes seek) multiple voices to engage with, even when they do not (or sometimes cannot) write about this aspect of their practice. Some of these operate in the CRM field, where opening up their practices in an explicit way can be difficult, given the push-pull of client interests and politics. In these cases, multivocality often exists, but in a more hidden way that is seldom written about in public forums (but see LaRoche 2011 for an important example where it is).

In all of these approaches to multivocality, the ideal scenario is usually defined as one where there is mutual empowerment between different groups. Obviously, this is difficult to achieve. In a global context, multivocality has mostly to do with eliminating the power imbalances caused by centuries of domination by "the West." In commercial archaeology contexts worldwide, power is almost always weighted towards professionals, policy makers, and private property advocates, who are in turn subject to (and support) the power held by politicians. In other contexts, especially over the last couple of decades, some tribal/indigenous groups now have real power with respect to some issues (although some groups do not). In addition, issues surrounding class, race, and gender, as well the legislative and cultural specifics that emerge from different legal, governmental, and geographical contexts complicate and influence who has the "real" power in any given situation. Despite these realities, many archaeologists across the globe have attempted to create situations in which multiple voices and narratives can at least be expressed, and where there is genuine, reciprocal dialogue between various people and roles.

Public Archaeology as Collaboration

The sorts of projects described above are sometimes enacted as "collaborations," not as multivocality per se—in practice and in writing, the terms and ideas are often conflated. That is, archaeologists who seek multivocal strategies usually hope that their work will be collaborative (and reflexive, open, relevant, etc.). A useful idea to take on board, if one is attempting to develop strategies along these lines, is the "collaborative continuum" suggested by Chip Colwell-Chanthaphonh and T.J. Ferguson. Here one accepts that even though all projects will fall at one point or another along a continuum of collaboration, or multivocality, or mutual empowerment (etc.), it is still worthwhile to make an effort that works towards these things. Therefore, one may find, at one end of the spectrum, projects in which publics actively resist archaeology. Near the other, one would find projects that are truly multivocal and mutually empowered in all stages of the project—from planning to implementation to interpretation and public interpretation. Simply "sharing" archaeological information might fall somewhere in the middle.

In these sorts of attempts, sharing "real" power is important, but how this is defined, and the degree to which it can be achieved, are extremely context-specific. Power can be shared in small acts, such as deleting a family name from public materials about a site, if the family desires (Brown 1997). It can be informing a local descendant community that a site—say, a small sharecropper cabin—has been located, rather than avoiding public knowledge about it (a common practice in commercial archaeology that is not subject to consultation regulations—that is, almost any African American archaeology). It can be more challenging with respect to current norms, such as inviting members of the public to comment on archaeological finding, and including their comments in published reports. In such scenarios, the archaeologists do not "lose" power; they simply share it. Scientific and other ways of understanding the past are provided equal standing; if the archaeologist or business client disagree with whatever the ethical clients have to say (often, there is no disagreement at all), the ethical clients' input could be included as an alternate view. Alternatively, that view might be expressed elsewhere—such as web site for example, or in new social media contexts (to be described below).

It is also important to realize that even when archaeologists attempt to create collaborative projects at the mutually empowered end of the spectrum, the result is not always positive. As noted above, each party has to evaluate the truth claims of other parties, and to accept—even if only "for the sake of argument"—that multiple, even contradictory, truths can exist in any given project or any social or political context. One only has to look at the fraught and bloodstained histories that exist in many parts of the world to know that this is often difficult (Meskell 1998). In many indigenous and African American contexts, long-term suspicion springing from past wrongs can prevent successful collaboration (McGhee 2008). At the same time, these dark pasts can provide an "ethical foundation and moral motivation" to conduct more collaborative projects.

What can be even more game changing, however, is when individuals (members of the public and archaeologists) attempt to push past business-as-usual practices to create new forms of cooperation. Because, as noted earlier, the majority of commercial CRM practice today often marginalizes actual publics (King 2009), thinking about collaborative practices as falling along a continuum can encourage any archaeologist to include them in their practice, to the degree they feel able—whether that practice be CRM, academic, or somewhere in between. Cheryl LaRoche put it this way in an article describing the effect of public involvement in CRM work at African American sites:

> …members of the public… have been able to force agencies, cities, and even our own colleagues to figure out ways to do archaeology *anyway*—to take important but previously avoided histories seriously, to study them properly, and to give them the recognition they deserve. *There are many people inside the "system" who also work, often sub rosa, as allies of this…* (LaRoche 2011:652–654; italics added).

Public Archaeology as Community Archaeology

Some multivocal and collaborative public archaeology has been described as "community archaeology," which has been traditionally defined as public archaeology situated in specific, geographically contiguous communities, organized around a variety of overlapping and often fluid interests—family, descendant, ethnic, intellectual, political, cultural, and more. Community archaeologists have attempted to understand these community interests and to incorporate them into their archaeological work in various ways (e.g., see contributions to Marshall 2002 and Mullins 2007; Paz 2010; Tully 2007).

Some archaeologists are, however, questioning earlier taken-for-granted definitions of the word "community" (e.g., Agbe-Davies 2010): not all communities fall into easy categories. Recently the idea of "stakeholders"—borrowed from legalese—has been applied to definitions of community, with stakeholders loosely defined as any entity (person or group) which sees itself as having a stake in any particular site or project.

Seen in this way, stakeholder communities are not necessarily defined either by professional archaeology, or by its supporters—or for that matter by geography, as will be discussed more below. For example, commercial developers usually claim a stake in what they are allowed to build or not build on any given property, and some developer "communities" have caused the destruction of archaeological sites, even when neighborhood communities have emerged to resist this destruction. Likewise, antiquity dealers have a stake (Kersel 2012), as do "looters", (bearing in mind that this negative term sometimes includes descendants who see archaeological remains as a legitimate cash crop that they have a moral right to exploit) (Hollowell 2006; Velzen 1996). In all of these self-defined and other-defined communities, context-specific tropes about power, property ownership, culture, and politics are at play. Therefore, the best community archaeology research (and practice) does not take any definition of community, stakeholders, or descendants for granted. A critical, reflexive perspective is essential.

Outside the United States, in the United Kingdom and Australia, the idea of "community archaeology" is a bit different, and refers mostly to the practice of archaeology by communities (see Faulkner 2000; Simpson and Williams 2008; Thomas 2011). Although the projects defined in this way are often (though not always) field-directed by professional archaeologists, the overall direction and work force is community and/or amateur-driven. The main thrust is to involve local communities in archaeology and to promote "the appreciation and care of the historic environment for the benefit of present and future generations" (http://www.britarch.ac.uk/). This echoes the idea of "stewardship" discussed above, but the work itself tends to be somewhat more bottom-up with respect to community involvement in various phases of archaeological research. This idea is roughly equivalent to the idea of "avocational archaeology" in the United States, in which projects are conducted with large numbers of volunteers who have varying degrees of training. In many cases, avocational archaeologists are extremely skilled, especially with respect to field methods and material culture analysis (metals, ceramics, glass, etc.).

It is also important to remember that archaeologists themselves are embedded in professional communities as well as academic, national, political, epistemological, and ontological communities of practice. The question in these contexts is not whether to engage, it is to look at how engagement itself helps to define what archaeology is and what it accomplishes. Community archaeology, seen in this way, is not work that archaeologists choose to do, but is inherent to how archaeology is practiced.

In all of these contexts, it is necessary to consider the desired results for community archaeology projects. Are they conducted so that archaeologists can better understand the communities they work with? Or, are they meant mainly as a way to share archaeological research? Or, do they provide ways for a community to better understand itself?

If someone from a community has a seat at the archaeological table—what are that person's responsibilities? What is the potential for community archaeology to be actively dialogic? Can archaeological community engagement reveal and address "community-building"? How, or do, the communities formed through archaeology projects create new knowledge that is relevant to archaeologists and communities alike? Do they add to an informed understanding of the archaeological past? Do imagined and actual intersections between archaeology and communities speak to the relationships between community members and other outside interests such as nonprofits/NGOs, interests in education and business, or deeper social and cultural interests of national and global capitalism? In practice, all of these sorts of understanding are developed, but not all are given priority in archaeological writing. One future goal would be to find better collaborative and open ways to write about the particular types of knowledge that emerge in community work.

Both archaeologists and communities are only starting to understand the roles that community members can play in long-term collaborative archaeology projects. Even so, community archaeology has come of age in the last decade as one important form of collaborative public archaeology, and community archaeology projects are now at the vanguard of creating a multivocal, inclusive knowledge-building process in which archaeology as it is traditionally practiced is just one of many routes to knowing the past.

The Web and Social Media: New Practices for a Digital Public Archaeology

In the Internet age, definitions are a moving target, but it is safe to say that social media can, for a while, be defined as any form of online communication in which content is "continuously modified by all users in a participatory and collaborative fashion" (Kaplan and Haenlein 2010:60). As such, it can also create a new form of public archaeology practice.

At this writing, the most popular forms of social media would include platforms such as Facebook, Twitter, YouTube, Wikipedia, and blogs. These forms of communication, and many others, are part of the Web 2.0 "evolution" that has enabled the World Wide Web to accomplish what was originally envisioned by early hypertext theorists—to be a platform allowing user-generated content, and thus the free exchange of information. What some archaeologists began to experiment with late in the last century (Hodder 1999:178–187; McDavid 1999) is now closer to reality in the current world of social media.

In addition to social media, but beyond our scope here, there are many other arenas in which digital technologies, archaeology, and publics now intersect.

In addition to a number of social media platforms not examined here (the landscape shifts constantly) other examples would include using virtual reality as a form of public archaeology (González-Tennant 2010; Morgan 2009, 2011) and using Participatory Global Information Systems (PGIS) to create collaborative community projects (Purser 2012). They would also include the increasing availability of online journals, as well as experiments with digital archives that make archaeological information freely available to the public (Freeman 2012; Kansa et al. 2011; Merriman and Swain 2002; Richards 2001). Because a full treatment of the current technological landscape would exceed the bounds of this paper (and be outdated almost immediately) our focus here is narrow: to comment briefly on certain aspects of social media with respect to how it does, and sometimes does not, enact the ethical modes of practice described above (activism, multivocality and collaboration, and building/supporting communities).

Signal Versus Noise

Many users are not aware how the most recent technologies limit the information they actually see when they use the Internet. First, most information is now validated through contests of popularity. Newer search engines rank pages not only by user-defined keywords, but also by the volume of site traffic, thus equating a site's popularity with its importance or accuracy (Graham 2011). Second, social media is vetted by self-selected social networks, which obviously can limit the user's exposure to alternate views. In these contexts, a few loud voices can sometimes have a dampening effect on meaningful "multivocal" communication. On the other hand, even self-selected networks can advocate for and sometimes achieve certain levels of social and political change.

Building Online Communities?

The notion that social media networks can create communities has received much popular attention of late, especially with the recent "Arab Spring" events in the Middle East, in which they proved to be powerful political tools. On the other hand, Sherry Turkle, an early and enthusiastic scholar of the relationships between people and computers (Turkle 1984, 1995), has recently taken a more cautious view and questioned whether one can call the associations that exist in social media "communities," pointing out that in online networks:

> ...people can just leave when they wish; the friended is not a friend ... when we decided to call these online connections "communities" and "relationships," we chose the words we had available to us, and we confused ourselves... (Nolan 2012:60–61).

Can public archaeologists use the digital world as a means for building community? Or is the type of commonality produced more akin to an "imagined community" (Anderson 1991; Gruzd et al. 2011)? To what degree does physical proximity matter? We do know that when used by local communities, social media can reinforce commonalities that already exist in a physical space (see http://digventures.com for one example). Some of these experiments have gone farther, to create dialogue among those with differing viewpoints, which could conceivably lead to "community-type" conversations and negotiations.

When McDavid analyzed the Web 1.0 Levi Jordan Plantation web site in 1999, the Internet had a limited role in building communities, even though it clearly provided a way to collaborate with an already-existing community (McDavid 2002b). However, recent research using Web 2.0 social media is more promising (Brock 2011; Brock and Goldstein 2010; Freeman 2012; Graham 2011; Kansa et al. 2011; Lowe 2011; Nohe and Brock 2011; Normark 2011; and the papers presented in).

Access

In terms of available technology, skill, and cost, it is now possible for most people to build a web site, join a social media network, or write a blog—especially in this age of smartphones and computer tablets. Social media platforms continue to evolve as well. Just as web sites created in the past now seem downright archaic current public archaeology experiments in social media will also be supplanted, and probably a lot faster.

Access intersects with these experiments in two arenas. The first is the so-called digital divide—that is, how do real-world differences (such as race, ability, class, gender, urban-ness/rural-ness, and others) operate in the online world? Some data suggests that different cultural groups use social media in different ways (Richardson 2012), so effort should be invested at the front end of any particular project to identify the ways in which any given community uses (or in many cases may not use) the Internet.

Related to this, although simply participating in digital conversation is an important first step, it is just as important to participate well. To this end, several training programs have emerged which focus on practicing public archaeology in digital space. These have incorporated digital training into archaeological field schools and other educational programs (Brock and Goldstein 2010; Brock 2011; Watrall 2012). Having a web site, Facebook page, or blog does not mean that meaningful multivocal engagement takes place (McDavid 2002b; Richardson 2012)—some digital divides still exist.

The second intersection has to do with transparency and openness. Can social media help archaeologists to share our decision-making process in ways that enable others to draw their own conclusions from archaeological data (McDavid 2004a)? Can they enable us to expose "the processes of creating knowledge, not just the products of those processes" (Joyce and Tringham 2007)? Preliminary data suggests that using social media with real-time feedback can communicate openness (Brandon 2010; Brock and Goldstein 2010), but doing this can require a great deal of on-site attention by staff dedicated to that purpose.

We are still in the infancy of Web 2.0. Even so, it is clear that some archaeologists have begun to take the practical and ethical implications of Web 2.0 seriously, and learned how to participate effectively in this arena. The successes experienced so far (only touched on here) are due, at least in part, to the training and institutional support that some of the archaeologists involved have received. This allowed them develop methodologies that work with respect to the practices outlined here as critical to contemporary ethical archaeology practice.

Conclusion: Sustainability and the Long Term

In this paper, we first reviewed different forms of public archaeology that existed in the past. Next, we discussed some practices that are embedded within, and emerge from, the ethical practice of public archaeology today: activism, multivocality, collaboration, and community. We then discussed new forms of digital communication, keeping the same practices in mind. Underpinning all of this has been the idea that formal ethical codes, while sometimes useful for internal purposes, are insufficient tools for creating ethically thoughtful and enlightened public archaeologies. These can only come about through mutually empowered, continually renewed, contingent and reflexive communication between those who have a stake in archaeology and those who practice it. We will close by asking a few final questions about how this plays forward—questions about public archaeology and the long term, for which we have no ready answers.

Traditionally, archaeologists have tended to think of their work in terms of projects that have a beginning, middle, and an end. This is usually assumed by public archaeologists as well—most assume that at some point we will "finish" with one project and move on to the next. In our experience, however, this rarely happens, even when the original archaeological project is complete.

In projects which are truly "engaged," there are ongoing responsibilities both to the data itself (or, one might say, to the past) and to the publics involved. With regard to archaeological data, once a project moves past the excavation/research stage the archaeologist's role can either disappear (the usual scenario), or shift, from primary investigator/researcher to public interpreter (that is, to help create museums, displays, etc.). What voice should the archaeologist claim in helping to create those interpretations over the long haul? What happens when other actors (master planners, curators, etc.) enter the process? The point is that many of the interpretive and other decisions made while doing "publicly engaged archaeology" are never static—what is negotiated once, as part of a multivocal process, may (will) change later. Archaeologists, publicly engaged or not, are seldom in a position to predict or control what will happen with the data they so conscientiously "engage" the public in collaboratively interpreting.

Things also become complicated when, as often happens, new communities form around the archaeological process. Friendships are formed and alliances are built, often aimed at solving community-wide concerns, not only archaeological ones. What is an archaeologist's responsibility to a community over the long haul? This is especially problematic when archaeologists work with publics that are disempowered—for example, when a community is fighting the gentrification destroying the "historical" landscape, or split in half by a new highway project. Often archaeologists are called upon to advocate for causes that have nothing to do with archaeology, and it is easy to find one's activist inclinations tested.

In addition, there are often fundraising and administrative duties that the archaeologist is used to expediting, which communities sometimes find difficult to take on alone. It is probably true that oral history, outreach and education programs, archaeology displays, site tours, etc. are the most meaningful aspects of archaeological work to communities. When this work is done by the archaeologists (who do it as part of the "collaboration," and, frankly, to gather data for their own purposes—these are not mutually exclusive), the process keeps moving forward. If the archaeologist leaves the project, local communities often have few resources to fund this sort of activity as continued, paid work.

The question then becomes: do public/community/collaborative archaeology projects have a life cycle? Should capacity-building and sustainability be factored into the public archaeology practices described here? If so, what would this look like—would archaeologists provide (or procure) training, workshops, or something else? Where does the archaeology end and something else (altogether different) begin?

At this point, how do (or should) archaeologists devise ethical exit strategies from projects that have reached either a natural (or unnatural) end? What would an ethical exit strategy look like in any particular context? That is, if collaboration is a key component of an ethical archaeology practice, can one leave "collaboratively"?

To some degree, the practices and ideas described in this paper have been dealt with too abstractly—space does not permit detailed examples of the many ways that "the public" has broadened and deepened archaeological practice over the past few decades. Although it took many years, as noted earlier, for public archaeology to be seen as a legitimate subfield of archaeology, it is now past time for it to be recognized as a recognized component of any ethical archaeology practice. That is, all archaeology is public archaeology.

We began by suggesting that the best public archaeology embraces contingency and experimentation, and we end with questions about the future of those efforts. As archaeologists, we use the best, most advanced methods we can afford to understand the past. As public archaeologists, we seek open, contingent, mutually empowered conversations with multiple publics, in the hope that the pasts we study can have meaning and use in the present. Both are essential, because it is within these meanings where the past matters—and where archaeology counts.

References

Agbe-Davies, A. (2010). Concepts of community in the pursuit of an inclusive archaeology. *International Journal of Heritage Studies, 16*(6), 371–387.

Agier, M. (1999). Comment on Pels. *Current Anthropology, 40*(9), 114–115.

Anderson, B. (1991). *Imagined communities: Reflections on the origin and spread of nationalism*. London: Verso.

Atalay, S. (2006). Introduction: Decolonizing archaeology. *American Indian Quarterly, 30*(3).

Atalay, S. (2008a). Multivocality and Indigenous archaeologies. In J. Habu, C. Fawcett, & J. M. Matsunaga (Eds.), *Evaluating multiple narratives: Beyond natonalist, colonialist, imperialist archaeologies* (pp. 29–44). New York: Springer.

Atalay, S. (2008b). Pedagogy of decolonization: Advancing archaeological practice through education. In S. Silliman (Ed.), *Collaborating at the trowel's edge: Teaching and learning in Indigenous archaeology* (pp. 123–144). Tucson: University of Arizona Press.

Atalay, S. (2010). "Diba Jimooyung"—Telling our story: Colonization and decolonization of archaeological practice from an Anishinabe perspective. In U. Rizvi & J. Lydon (Eds.), *Handbook of postcolonial archaeology* (pp. 61–72). Walnut Creek: Left Coast Press.

Babiarz, J. (2011). White privilege and silencing within the heritage landscape: Race and the practice of cultural resources management. In J. A. Barnes (Ed.), *The materiality of freedom: Archaeologies of post-emancipation life* (p. 47–57). Columbia: University of South Carolina Press.

Bartoy, K. (2012). Teaching through rather than about: Education in the context of public archaeology. In R. Skeates, C. McDavid, & J. Carman (Eds.), *The Oxford handbook of public archaeology* (pp. 552–565). New York: Oxford University Press.

Blakey, M. (2004). Chapter 3: Theory: An ethical epistemology of publicly engaged biocultural research. In M. Blakey & L. Rankin-Hill (Eds.), *Skeletal biology final report* (Vol. I, pp. 98–115). Washington: National Parks Service.

Boyd, D., Franklin, M., & Myers, T. (2011). From slave to landowner: Historic archeology at the Ransom and Sarah Williams Farmstead. *Current Archaeology in Texas, 13*(1), 8–14.

Brandon, J. (2010). Making historical archaeology visible: Community outreach and education. Retrieved from http://www.sha.org/blog/index.php/2012/03/making-historical-archaeology-visible-community-outreach-and-education/

Brock, T. P. (2011). *Teaching archaeology and community engagement through blogging: A public archaeology field school project at Michigan State University*. Paper presented at the Annual Meeting of the Society for American Archaeology, Sacramento.

Brock, T. P., & Goldstein, L. (2010). *Connecting the campus to campus archaeology: Using digital social media for community outreach and engagement*. Paper presented at the Annual Meetings of the Society for Historical Archaeology, Amelia Island.

Brown, K. (1997). Some thoughts on archaeology and public responsibility. *African American Archaeology: Newsletter of the African-American Archaeology Network, Fall*(18), 6–7.

Carman, J. (2002). *Archaeology and heritage: An introduction*. London: Continuum.

Castañeda, Q., & Matthews, C. (Eds.). (2008). *Ethnographic archaeologies: Reflections on stakeholders and archaeological practices*. Lanham: AltaMira Press.

Colwell-Chanthaphonh, C., & Ferguson, T. J. (2006). Memory pieces and footprints: Multivocality and the meanings of ancient times and ancestral places among the Zuni and Hopi. *American Anthropologist, 108*(1), 148–162.

Davis, E. (2005). *How students understand the past: From theory to practice*. New York: AltaMira Press.

Dawdy, S. L. (2009). Millennial archaeology: Locating the discipline in the age of insecurity. *Archaeological Dialogues, 16*(2), 131–142.

Derry, L. (2003). Consequences of involving archaeology in contemporary community issues. In L. Derry & M. Malloy (Eds.), *Archaeologists and local communities: Partners in exploring the past* (pp. 19–30). Washington: Society for American Archaeology.
Faulkner, N. (2000). Archaeology from below. *Public Archaeology, 1*(1), 21–34.
Feit, R., & Jones, B. (2007). *"A lotta people have histories here…": History and archaeology in Houston's Vanishing Freedman's Town. Report prepared for the Texas Historical Commission.* Austin: Texas.
Freeman, M. (2012). Primary archaeology data for non-archaeologists? Retrieved from http://www.sha.org/blog/?p=1617
Friedman, E. (2000). Preface. In K. Smardz & S. J. Smith (Eds.), *The archaeology education handbook: Sharing the past with kids* (pp. 13–16). Walnut Creek: AltaMira Press.
Funari, P. P. (2000). Public archaeology from a Latin American perspective. *Public Archaeology, 1*(4), 239–244.
Funari, P. P., & Bezerra, M. (2012). Public archaeology in Latin America. In R. Skeates, C. McDavid, & J. Carman (Eds.), *The Oxford handbook of public archaeology* (pp. 100–115). New York: Oxford University Press.
Gadsby, D., & Chidester, R. (2012). Class, labour, and the public. In R. Skeates, C. McDavid, & J. Carman (Eds.), *The Oxford handbook of public archaeology* (pp. 513–536). New York: Oxford University Press.
Gathercole, P., & Lowenthal, D. (Eds.). (1994). *The politics of the past*. London: Routledge.
Gelburd, D. (1989). Improving the public's perception of archaeology. In P. S. Miller, D. E. Gelburd, & G. E. Alderton (Eds.), *Cultural Resource Management in the 1990s* (pp. 3–8). American Society for Conservation Archeology: Portales.
Goldstein, L. (1998). Editor's corner. *American Antiquity, 63*(4), 529–530.
Gonzalez-Tennant, E. (2007). *Imperial scholarship in historical archaeology: What critical race praxis can do for/with research into the Chinese diaspora*. Paper presented at the Annual Meetings of the American Anthropological Association, Washington.
Gonzalez-Tennant, E. (2010). Community centered praxis in conflict archaeology: Creating an archaeology of redress with the 1923 race riot in Rosewood, Florida. *SAA Archaeological Record, 10*(4), 60–61.
González-Tennant, E. (2010). Virtual archaeology and digital storytelling: A report from Rosewood, Florida. *African Diaspora Archaeology Network Newsletter.* Retrieved September 2010 from http://www.diaspora.uiuc.edu/news0910/news0910-1.pdf
Graham, S. (2011). *Signal versus noise: Why academic blogging matters*. Posted by author at http://electricarchaeology.ca/2011/04/02/signal-versus-noise-why-academic-blogging-matters-a-structural-argument-saa-2011/. Paper presented at the Annual Meetings of the Society for American Archaeology, Sacramento.
Green, W., & Doershuk, J. (1998). Cultural Resource Management and American archaeology. *Journal of Archaeological Research, 6*(2), 121–167.
Gruzd, A., Wellman, B., & Takhteyev, Y. (2011). Imagining Twitter as an imagined community. *American Behavioral Scientist, 55*(10), 1294–1318.
Habu, J., Fawcett, C., & Matsunaga, J. (Eds.). (2008). *Evaluating multiple narratives: Beyond nationalist, colonialist, imperialist archaeologies*. New York: Springer.
Handsman, R. (1984). Historical archaeology and capitalism, subscriptions and separations: The production of individualism. *North American Archaeologist, 4*(1), 63–86.
Hodder, I. (1996). *Faultlines. The construction of archaeological knowledge at Catalhoyuk in 1996*. Paper presented at the Theoretical Archaeology Group Conference, Liverpool.
Hodder, I. (1999). *The archaeological process: An introduction*. Oxford: Blackwell.
Hodder, I. (2008). Multivocality and social archaeology. In J. Habu, C. Fawcett, & J. M. Matsunaga (Eds.), *Evaluating multiple narratives: Beyond natonalist, colonialist, imperialist archaeologies* (pp. 196–200). New York: Springer.
Hodder, I., Shanks, M., Alexandri, A., Buchli, V., Carman, J., Last, J., & Lucas, G. (Eds.). (1995). *Interpreting archaeology: Finding meaning in the past*. London: Routledge.

Hollowell, J. (2006). Moral arguments in subsistence digging. In C. Scarre & G. Scarre (Eds.), *The ethics of archaeology. Philosophical perspectives on archaeological practice* (pp. 69–96). Cambridge: Cambridge University Press.

James, W. (1995). What pragmatism means. In G. H. Bird (Ed.), *William James: Selected writings*. London: Orion.

Jameson, J. (Ed.). (1997). *Presenting archaeology to the public: Digging for truths*. Walnut Creek: AltaMira Press.

Jeppson, P. (2001). *Pitfalls, pratfalls, and pragmatism in public archaeology*. Paper presented at the Annual Meetings of the Society for Historical and Underwater Archaeology, Long Beach.

Jeppson, P. (2004). *Doing our homework: Rethinking the goals and responsibilities of archaeology outreach to schools*. Paper presented at the Annual Meetings of the Society for Historical Archaeology and Underwater Archaeology, St. Louis.

Jeppson, P. (2010). Doing our homework: Rethinking the goals and responsibilities of archaeology outreach to schools. In J. Stottman (Ed.), *Changing the world with archaeology: Activist archaeology*. Tuscaloosa: University of Alabama Press.

Jeppson, P. (2012). Public archaeology and the US culture wars. In R. Skeates, C. McDavid, & J. Carman (Eds.), *The Oxford handbook of public archaeology* (pp. 581–604). New York: Oxford University Press.

Jeppson, P., & Brauer, G. (2003). Hey, did you hear about the teacher who took the class out to dig a site? Some common misconceptions about archaeology in schools. In L. Derry & M. Malloy (Eds.), *Archaeologists and local communities: Partners in exploring the Past* (pp. 77–96). Washington: Society for American Archaeology.

Jeppson, P., & Brauer, G. (2008). Archaeology for education needs: An archaeology and an educator discuss archaeology in Baltimore. In J. Jameson & S. Baugher (Eds.), *Past meets present* (pp. 231–248). New York: Springer.

Joyce, R., & Tringham, R. (2007). Feminist adventures in hypertext. *Journal of Archaeological Method and Theory, 14*(3), 328–358.

Kansa, E., Kansa, S., & Watrall, E. (Eds.). (2011). *Archaeology 2.0: New approaches to communication and collaboration* (Vol. 1). Los Angeles, CA. http://escholarship.org/uc/item/1r6137tb#page-16

Kaplan, A., & Haenlein, M. (2010). Users of the world, unite! The challenges and opportunities of social media. *Business Horizons, 53*(1), 59–68.

Kersel, M. (2012). The value of a looted object: Stakeholder perceptions in the antiquities trade. In R. Skeates, C. McDavid, & J. Carman (Eds.), *The Oxford handbook of public archaeology* (pp. 253–274). New York: Oxford University Press.

Kim, M. (2008). Multivocality, multifaceted voices, and Korean archaeology. In J. Habu, C. Fawcett, & J. M. Matsunaga (Eds.), *Evaluating multiple narratives: Beyond natonalist, colonialist, imperialist archaeologies* (pp. 118–137). New York: Springer.

King, T. (Ed.). (2002). *Thinking about Cultural Resource Management: Essays from the edge*. Boston: Rowman & Littlefield Publishing.

King, T. (2009). *Our unprotected heritage: Whitewashing the destruction of our cultural and natural environment*. Walnut Creek: Left Coast Press.

LaRoche, C. (2011). Archaeology, the activist community, and the redistribution of power in New York City. In C. Matthews, C. McDavid, & P. Jeppson (Eds.), The dynamics of inclusion [Special issue]. *Archaeologies, 7*(3).

LaRoche, C. (2012). The anthropology of archaeology: The Benefits of public intervention at African-American archaeological sites. In R. Skeates, C. McDavid, & J. Carman (Eds.), *The Oxford handbook of public archaeology* (pp. 629–658). New York: Oxford University Press.

LaRoche, C., & Blakey, M. (1997). Seizing intellectual power: The dialogue at the New York African burial ground. In The Realm of politics: Prospects for public participation in African-American archaeology [Special issue]. *Historical Archaeology, 31*(3), 84–106.

Leone, M. (1995). A historical archaeology of capitalism. *American Anthropologist, 97*(2), 251–268.
Leone, M., LaRoche, C., & Babiarz, J. (2005). The archaeology of black Americans in recent times. *Annual Review of Anthropology, 34*, 575–598.
Leone, M., Potter, P., & Shackel, P. (1987). Toward a critical archaeology. *Current Anthropology, 28*(3), 283–302.
Levin, J. (2012). Activism leads to excavation: The power of place and the power of the people at the president's house in Philadelphia. *Archaeologies, 7*(3), 596–618.
Little, B. (2002). *Public benefits of archaeology*. Gainesville: University Press of Florida.
Little, B. (2007). Archaeology and civic engagement. In B. Little & P. Shackel (Eds.), *Archaeology as a tool of civic engagement* (pp. 1–22). Lanham: AltaMira Press.
Little, B. (2009). Forum: What can archaeology do for justice, peace, community and the earth? *Historical Archaeology, 43*(4), 115–129.
Little, B. (2012). Public benefits of public archaeology. In R. Skeates, C. McDavid, & J. Carman (Eds.), *The Oxford handbook of public archaeology* (pp. 395–413). New York: Oxford University Press.
Lowe, J. (2011). *Blogging as an American CRM professional*. Paper presented at the Annual Meetings of the Society for American Archaeology, Sacramento.
Lynott, M., & Wylie, A. (1995a). Stewardship: The central principle of archaeological ethics. In M. Lynott & A. Wylie (Eds.), *Ethics in American archaeology* (pp. 28–32). Washington: Society for American Archaeology.
Lynott, M., & Wylie, A. (Eds.). (1995b). *Ethics in American archaeology*. Washington: Society for American Archaeology.
Marcom, R., Marcom, R., & McDavid, C. (2011). *Interpreting the Bernardo Plantation: A collaboration between metal detectorists, avocationals, and professionals to study the first plantation in Texas*. Paper presented at the Society for Historical Archaeology 2001 Annual Meetings, Austin.
Marshall, Y. (Ed.). (2002). Community archaeology [Special issue]. *World Archaeology, 34*(2).
Matthews, C., & Spencer-Wood, S. (Eds.). (2011). Archaeologies of poverty [Special issue]. *Historical Archaeology*.
McDavid, C. (1999). From real space to cyberspace: Contemporary conversations about the archaeology of slavery and tenancy [Special theme: Digital publication]. *Internet Archaeology, 6*.
McDavid, C. (2000). Archaeology as cultural critique: Pragmatism and the archaeology of a southern United States plantation. In C. Holtorf & H. Karlsson (Eds.), *Philosophy and archaeological practice: Perspectives for the 21st century* (pp. 221–240). Lindome: Bricoleur Press.
McDavid, C. (2002a). Archaeologies that hurt; descendants that matter: A pragmatic approach to collaboration in the public interpretation of African-American archaeology. *World Archaeology, 34*, 303–314.
McDavid, C. (2002b). *From real space to cyberspace: The Internet and public archaeological practice*. Doctoral dissertation, University of Cambridge, Cambridge.
McDavid, C. (2004a). From "traditional" archaeology to public archaeology to community action: The Levi Jordan Plantation Project. In P. A. Shackel & E. J. Chambers (Eds.), *Places in mind: Public archaeology as applied anthropology* (pp. 35–56). New York: Routledge.
McDavid, C. (2004b). Towards a more democratic archaeology? The Internet and public archaeological practice. In N. Merriman (Ed.), *Public archaeology* (pp. 159–188). London: Routledge.
McDavid, C. (2005). *Beyond strategy and good intentions: Civic engagement, archaeology, race and class*. Paper presented at the Society for Historical Archaeology, York.
McDavid, C. (2011b). From "public archaeologist" to "public intellectual": Seeking engagement opportunities outside traditional archaeological arenas. *Historical Archaeology, 44*(3), 11–25.
McDavid, C., Feit, R., Brown, K., & McGhee, F. (2012). *African American archaeology in Texas: A planning document*. Houston: Community Archaeology Research Institute.

McGhee, F. (2008). African American oral history and archaeology: Perceptional politics, political practice. *Bulletin of the Texas Archaeological Society, 79*, 95–105.
McGimsey, C. (Ed.). (1972). *Public archaeology*. New York: Seminar Press.
McGuire, R. (2008). *Archaeology as political action*. Berkeley: University of California Press.
Merriman, N., & Swain, H. (2002). Archaeological archives: Serving the public interest? *European Journal of Archaeology, 2*(2), 249–267.
Meskell, L. (Ed.). (1998). *Archaeology under fire: Nationalism, politics and heritage in the Eastern Mediterranean and Middle East*. London: Routledge.
Meskell, L. (2005). Archaeological ethnography: Conversations around Kruger National Park. *Archaeologies, 1*(1), 81–100.
Meskell, L., & Pels, P. (2005a). Introduction: Embedding ethics. In L. Meskell & P. Pels (Eds.), *Embedding ethics: Shifting boundaries of the anthropological profession* (pp. 1–26). Oxford: Berg.
Meskell, L., & Pels, P. (Eds.). (2005b). *Embedding ethics: Shifting boundaries of the anthropological profession*. Oxford: Berg.
Morgan, C. (2009). (Re)bulding Çatalhöyük: Changing virtual reality in archaeology. *Archaeologies, 5*(3), 468–488.
Morgan, C. L. (2011). Contextualizing digital archaeology. http://middlesavagery.wordpress.com/2011/12/19/contextualized-digital-archaeology-dissertation-chapter/
Mortensen, L., & Hollowell, J. (Eds.). (2009). *Ethnographies and archaeologies: Iterations of the past*. Gainesville: University Press of Florida.
Mouer, D. (2000). Comment: Can there be a pragmatic archaeology? In C. Holtorf & H. Karlsson (Eds.), *Philosophy and archaeological practice: Perspectives for the 21st century*. Göteborg: Institutionen för arkeologi, Göteborgs Universitet.
Mullins, P. (2007). Politics, inequality, and engaged archaeology: Community archaeology along the color line. In B. J. Little & P. A. Shackel (Eds.), *Archaeology as a tool of civic engagement* (pp. 89–108). Lanham: Alta Mira Press.
Nassaney, M., & Levine, M. A. (Eds.). (2009). *Archaeology and community service learning*. Gainesville: University Press of Florida.
Neumann, T., & Sanford, R. (2001). *Practicing archaeology: A training manual for cultural resources archaeology*. Walnut Creek: Alta Mira Press.
Nohe, S., & Brock, T. (2011). *Social media as public archaeology*. Paper presented at the Annual Meetings of the Society for American Archaeology, Sacramento.
Nolan, J. (2012). A conversation with Sherry Turkle. *The Hedgehog Review: Critical Reflections on Contemporary Culture, 14*(1), 53–64.
Normark, J. (2011). *Dealing with the public view of the Maya*. Paper presented at the Annual Meetings of the Society for American Archaeology, Sacramento.
Paz, Y. (2010). Community archaeology in proto-historical Tel Barequet, Israel: School children and agency for active public engagement in cultural heritage projects. *Public Archaeology, 9*(1), 34–47.
Pels, P. (1999). Professions of duplexity: A prehistory of ethical codes in anthropology. *Current Anthropology, 40*(2), 101–136.
Potter, P. (1994). *Public archaeology in Annapolis: A critical approach to history in Maryland's ancient city*. Washington: Smithsonian.
Purser, M. (2012). Emptying the magician's hat: Participatory GIS-based research in Fiji. In R. Skeates, C. McDavid, & J. Carman (Eds.), *The Oxford handbook of public archaeology* (pp. 496–512). New York: Oxford University Press.
Richards, J. (2001). Digital preservation and access. *European Journal of Archaeology, 5*(3), 343–366.
Richardson, L. (2012). *An Internet delusion? Public archaeology online*. Paper presented at the Annual Meeting of the European Association of Archaeologists, Helsinki.
Rizvi, U., & Lydon, J. (Eds.). (2010). *Handbook of postcolonial archaeology*. Walnut Creek: Left Coast Press.

Rogge, A. E., & Montgomery, J. (Eds.). (1989). *Fighting Indiana Jones in Arizona*. Portales: American Society for Conservation Archaeology.

Sabloff, J. (2008). *Archaeology matters: Action archaeology in the modern world*. Walnut Creek: Left Coast Press.

Schmidt, P., & Patterson, T. (Eds.). (1995). *Making alternative histories: The practice of archaeology and history in non-Western settings*. Santa Fe: School of American Research Press.

Schrader, H. (1999). Comment on Pels. *Current Anthropology, 40*(2), 123.

Shore, C. (1999). Comment on Pels. *Current Anthropology, 40*(2), 124.

Silberman, N. A. (2008). Virtual viewpoints: Multivocality in the marketed past? In J. Habu, C. Fawcett, & J. M. Matsunaga (Eds.), *Evaluating multiple narratives: Beyond nationalist, colonialist, imperialist archaeologies* (pp. 138–143). New York: Springer.

Silliman, S. (Ed.). (2008). *Collaborating at the trowel's edge: Teaching and learning in Indigenous archaeology*. Tucson: University of Arizona Press.

Simpson, F., & Williams, H. (2008). Evaluating community archaeology in the UK. *Public Archaeology, 7*(2), 69–90.

Skeates, R., McDavid, C., & Carman, J. (Eds.). (2012). *The Oxford handbook of public archaeology*. New York: Oxford University Press.

Sluka, J. (1999). Comment on Pels. *Current Anthropology, 40*(2), 125.

Smardz, K. (2000). Digging with kids: Teaching students to touch the past. In K. Smardz & S. Smith (Eds.), *The archaeology education handbook* (pp. 234–248). Walnut Creek: AltaMira Press.

Smith, L. (2004). *Archaeological theory and the politics of cultural heritage*. London: Routledge.

Smith, K. C., & McManahon, F. (Eds.). (1991). *Archaeology and education: The classroom and beyond*. Washington: National Park Service.

Stone, P. (2000). Applying the message to the medium. In K. Smardz & S. Smith (Eds.), *The archaeology education handbook* (pp. 280–287). Walnut Creek: AltaMira Press.

Stottman, J. (Ed.). (2010). *Archaeologists as activists: Can archaeologists change the world?* Tuscaloosa: University of Alabama Press.

Stutz, L. N. (2011). Legislating multivocality: Drawing on the NAGPRA experience. In A. Olafssoon (Ed.), *Archaeology of Indigenous people's in the north*. Umea: Umea University.

Swidler, N., Dongoske, K., Anyon, R., & Downer, A. (Eds.). (1997). *Native Americans and archaeologists: Stepping stones to common ground*. Walnut Creek: AltaMira Press.

Tarlow, S. (2000). Decoding ethics. *Public Archaeology, 1*(4), 245–260.

Thomas, S. (2011). F. Simpson "Values of community archaeology: A comparative Assessment between the UK and US". *Public Archaeology, 10*(1), 59–62.

Trigger, B. (1984). Alternative archaeologies: Nationalistic, colonialist, imperialist. *Man, 19*(3), 355–370.

Tully, G. (2007). Community archaeology: General methods and standards of practice. *Public Archaeology, 6*(3), 155–187.

Turkle, S. (1984). *The second self: Computers and the human spirit*. New York: Simon and Schuster.

Turkle, S. (1995). *Life on the screen: Identity in the age of the Internet*. New York: Simon and Schuster.

van Velzen, D. T. (1996). The world of Tuscan tomb robbers: Living with the local community and the ancestors. *International Journal of Cultural Property, 5*, 111–126.

Watkins, J. (2001). *Indigenous archaeology: American Indian values and scientific practice*. Walnut Creek: AltaMira Press.

Watrall, E. (2012). *Michigan State University's Cultural heritage informatics initiative: Developing a model for training and capacity building in digital cultural heritage*. Paper presented at the High-Tech Heritage, University of Massachusetts.

Wylie, A. (1985). Putting Shakertown back together. *Journal of Anthropological Archaeology, 4*, 133–147.

Wylie, A. (2005). The promise and perils of an ethic of stewardship. In L. Meskell & P. Pels (Eds.), *Embedding ethics* (pp. 47–68). Oxford: Berg.

Wylie, A. (2008). The integrity of narratives: Deliberative practice, pluralism, and multivocality. In J. Habu, C. Fawcett, & J. M. Matsunaga (Eds.), *Evaluating multiple narratives: Beyond nationalist, colonialist, imperialist archaeologies* (pp. 201–212). New York: Springer.

Zimmerman, L. (1994). Sharing control of the past. *Archaeology, 47*(6), 65–67. 68.

Zimmerman, L., Dasovich, S., Engstrom, M., & Bradley, L. (1994). Listening to the teachers: Warnings about the use of archaeological agendas in classrooms in the United States. In P. Stone & B. Molyneaux (Eds.), *The presented past: Archaeology, museums and public education* (pp. 359–374). London: Routledge.

Chapter 12
Ethics in the Publishing of Archaeology

Mitchell Allen

Dennis Stanford can be considered a serious archaeologist. Head of the division of archaeology at the Smithsonian, he is author or editor of half a dozen books and many research articles. Bruce Bradley is an equally serious archaeologist. Associate Professor of Archaeology at University of Exeter, his list of publications stretches as long as Stanford's. These are two archaeologists whose ideas can and should be taken seriously. Yet, the professional credentials and ethical positions of the two have faced challenge from their colleagues. The problem: they proposed the hypothesis that migrants from Solutrean Europe traveled across the Atlantic Ocean at the end of the Pleistocene and left their technology—called Clovis west of the Atlantic—in the Americas. A radical theory, certainly, but backed with the best data two respected researchers could muster. Why is this an ethical issue?

The Solutrean Hypothesis, summarized in a recent popular book (Stanford and Bradley 2012) and a documentary featuring the two scholars, has had social and political ramifications far beyond the world of Paleoindian studies. If the Americas were settled originally by Europeans, what does this do to the legacy of European colonization and genocide of those same populations? The hypothesis has been picked up in white power and white supremacist circles and is now part of their dogma. One blogger, claiming to be part of the Solutrean Liberation Front, rewrites history as:

> The truth is, most Americans are descended from the indigenous White people of the Americans; the Solutreans. The Solutreans are the descendants of a prehistoric people who sailed across the Atlantic and populated the Americas, but mostly settled in North America. The Red Indians were an Asiatic people who crossed the Bering Strait and settled in North America, however, this was not until after the Solutrean population has already been established… For a time, the Solutreans continued to defend their thriving civilization against these threats. However, around 770 CE, the Red Indians, aided by their aliies (sic), the

M. Allen (✉)
Left Coast Press, Inc, 1630 N Main St #400, Walnut Creek, CA 94596, USA
e-mail: mitch@lcoastpress.com

C. Gnecco, D. Lippert (eds.), *Ethics and Archaeological Praxis*,
Ethical Archaeologies: The Politics of Social Justice 1,
DOI 10.1007/978-1-4939-1646-7_12

> Mongols and the South American Indians, launched a massive war against the Solutrean Republic, and by 1000 CE brought the continent under their dominion. The freedom and prosperity established on the continent by the White Solutreans was no more (American Wayyy 2011).

The hypothesis is also source of at least one white supremacist novel, *White apocalypse*. The cover copy describes the book as

> In White Apocalypse, a rogue anthropologist teams up with a proponent of the Solutrean Hypothesis and a fiery lawyer in order to reveal to the world the shocking truth that carries immense cultural, political, and racial significance: 17,000 years ago, white people immigrated to North and South America from Europe, and when the Amerindians arrived by crossing the Bering Strait roughly 12,000 years ago, the latter subsequently and systematically murdered the former (Bristow 2010).

Though neither Stanford nor Bradley should be considered racist and their hypothesis is far more nuanced than the simplistic pronouncements of the Solutrean Liberation Front, those who would revise prehistory to include only white people have latched onto this as evidence to forward their racist agendas. Whether Stanford and Bradley are correct or not in their interpretation of the late Pleistocene evidence, which Stanford himself claims to be "off the wall kind of idea," (Stanford 1997) was the publication of this theory ethical? Stanford and Bradley are professionals who brought substantial expertise and decades of research on this subject to bear. But what of University of California Press editorial staff responsible for publishing their book *Across Atlantic ice*: *the origin of America's Clovis culture*? Though a highly skilled and highly reputable group of people noted for publications which support cross-cultural understanding, the editors at UC Press are not expert on Paleolithic Europe or preClovis America. Nonetheless, they were asked to make the judgments on the merits of a theory that contained much potential for fostering racism and justifying colonialism. Should they have published *Across Atlantic ice*? Was the publication decision ethical? And how does anyone who is not an archaeologist specializing in the specific content of a research area make that kind of judgment when the specialists themselves have been arguing about it for a decade?

This is only one example, only the tip of the iceberg, of ethical issues involved in archaeological publishing. These issues are legion and cover every medium of dissemination, every possible source of authorship, all parts of the world, and almost every contested major issue in the discipline. Each becomes more contentious with the threat of taking the discussion beyond the realm of the professional community and making them available to the general population through the publications process. These issues—including maintaining secrecy of archaeological sites to prevent looting, publication of human skeletal remains and sacred objects, intellectual property rights over a community's heritage, and the validity of traditional knowledge and oral history as evidence of the past—mirror the general ethical issues facing the discipline, topics covered in depth in other chapters of this volume.

In the case of each of these issues, ethical hotspots arise among professional archaeologists, local communities, and forces representing economic development and political power. Publishers of books, websites, or periodicals are generally not active players in the decision-making process of what constitutes ethical archaeological behavior in these cases, but need to decide whether to bring this work to a wider world. Similarly, journal and book series editors, while having adequate credentials in the field, cannot be expected to be experts on each topic generating controversial material. As outsiders to the debates but gatekeepers in the publication decision process, publishers and editors need to make complex ethical judgments of the appropriateness of publishing ideas about which they are not always fully versed.

The ethics of archaeological publications therefore mirrors the quagmire of ethical questions that bedevils other parts of the discipline. The general ethical principles relating to publications that publishers, editors, and authors need to follow should generally mirror those in other parts of the discipline. This chapter will attempt to outline five key principles of ethical archaeological publishing in the context of these larger ethical issues.

Archaeological Research Needs to Be Published

We'll start with a "tree in the forest" question: If an archaeological project's data and findings never see the light of day, was it ethical to begin the project at all? In any scholarly research endeavor, publication is considered the final, inescapable phase of the project. No matter how good the research methodology, without publication in some format colleagues are unable to vet, reexamine, or critique the conclusions of the researcher. In many ways, the act of publication of archaeological evidence is what separates the archaeologist from the pseudoarchaeologist. We are willing to open ourselves up for criticism, for alternative interpretations of our data, for the embarrassment of unexplained outliers, and for careful scrutiny of our work. In contrast, the pseudoarchaeologist presents an iron-clad case designed to prove their cherished theory and carefully hides whatever doesn't fit well (Fagan 2006). The firewall between science and pseudoscience vanishes in the absence of archaeological publication.

Delays in publication while scholars can fully analyze their data are not unique to archaeology. How archaeology is unusual in the world of scholarship revolves around the multiyear research projects involving dozens of scholars addressing many different facets of the site or region, a complexity of content and players that might cause long delays in publication. To wait for the last piece to be completed before beginning to issue field reports is a guarantee of unacceptable delays in making the bulk of the data available to the research community. Many projects never get published, with the field data resting on dusty shelves or in outmoded computer databases in university offices. The major Palestine site of Tel en-Nasbeh, excavated in the 1920s and 1930s, was not published until it became the dissertation topic of Jeffrey R. Zorn (n.d.) in the 1990s. Alfred Kroeber's important 1926 field project in Nazca, Peru, which included the first scientific description of the Nazca Lines, saw the light of day only 70 years later (Kroeber et al. 1998).[1] The list of projects unpublished a decade or more after the fieldwork ended is long. There are even grants offered to support publication of long delayed reports, such as from The Shelby White-Leon Levy Program for Archaeological Publications administered by Harvard University (http://www.fas.harvard.edu/~semitic/wl/).

One cause of this is "interpretive primogeniture," the understood right of a project's principal investigator to be the first to offer an interpretation of the meaning of the mounds of data collected (Allen and Joyce 2010). Only by divesting the process of making available the data of a project from the researchers' interpretation of this data will this barrier be overcome. If the data were available to all, it would create an incentive for the principal investigator to offer an initial interpretation more quickly and will allow others to assess that interpretation and make their own more quickly.

Even in cases where the archaeological work is designed to effect social change or enhance community solidarity and heritage, knowledge transmission is still an essential element of the process. This "publication" may take place in a variety of ways—through site interpretation, local newsletters, public meetings, websites, or tours—but the transfer of the archaeologist's knowledge of the heritage project is as much an ethical obligation in conducting community archaeology as in any traditional research project. Withholding or delaying the archaeologist's contribution to the community's knowledge of its heritage has the same net effect as delays in academic publication.

While this principle of "you gotta publish" seems to be something that no archaeologist would disagree with and is embodied in the Society for American Archaeology code of ethics, it has its own nuances. The intent to publish—even if the follow through does not occur for decades—is one of the items that separates professional archaeology from treasure hunting. But ethical quicksand lies in all directions: Does publication of CRM projects not made available to the public or to other archaeologists because of developer, government, or local community privacy concerns meet the test described above, that of allowing other scholars to review your work? Is this an ethical conclusion to a project? The requirement to deposit these publications in a state historical preservation archive is a partial, but not complete, solution to this quandary.

Should an archaeologist present her considered findings to a descendant community group if it conflicts with traditional oral history or challenges community values? What about those who do archaeology for profit, but who undertake to publish their work as justification for conducting that work? Does careful recording and publication make a project ethical of its own accord? For example, Odyssey Marine Exploration, infamous for its discovery of high value shipwrecks and sale of its contents, has posted 25 scholarly papers on its website documenting its shipwreck

---

[1] I was responsible for its publication at AltaMira Press. The manuscript languished in the files of the Field Museum at Kroeber's death in 1962 and a combination of politics, funds, and priorities left it there for a quarter century until David Collier, son of the late Field Museum South American curator Donald Collier, brought it to my attention. Without that accidental network connection it might still be there today.

excavations. Does this meet the test of ethical archaeology publishing? Odyssey justifies its work as archaeology:

> Odyssey Marine Exploration has pioneered a new branch of archaeology, which we call "commercial marine archaeology," defined as the pursuit of deep-ocean archaeological research and exploration as a "for profit" venture. This model is currently the only practical way of sustaining highly expensive research and archaeological operations in the long-term and has enabled us to actually explore more shipwrecks than any university or institute in the world (Odyssey Marine Exploration 2012).

As with every ethical question addressed in this volume, this one has no simple solution.

Publication Decisions Should Usually, But Can't Always, Rely on Peer Review

Peer review is a cornerstone of the process of assessing the academic worth of publications, but not the sole determinate of a publication's worthiness. But from Thomas Kuhn onwards, scholars recognized that the peer review process is a socially constructed, value-laden activity. As paradigms change, interpretations of archaeological data change with it. The untenable archaeological theory of one era can become the dogma of the next generation only to be overturned again by the succeeding one.

Publishers and editors are caught in the middle of these paradigm wars. While reviewers might consider a new idea to be outside the ideological mainstream, does that exclude it from getting a hearing? Will the next generation of scholars applaud the publisher who went against conventional wisdom and took a chance on a plausible idea against the bulk of scholarly thinking of the day? Or will the ideas seem even more silly in subsequent years? Given that publishers are rarely specialists in the topic, how are we to discern forward thinking from the lunatic fringe. The Solutrean Hypothesis question described above is a prime example of this. Several additional personal examples might serve to highlight this dilemma.

As publisher of AltaMira Press, I was offered the opportunity to publish Steven Lekson's (1999) *The Chaco Meridian*. This volume, now familiar to most southwestern US archaeologists, proposed a radical thesis that the central place of the Ancestral Pueblo peoples moved from Chaco Canyon to Aztec Ruin to Paquime, Mexico over the span of a century and that those locations were chosen as central places because they were located on a single longitudinal meridian. *Chaco Meridian* caused a firestorm of argument after publication that still has not died down (Phillips, n.d.). It could have been—and might still be—a form of voodoo archaeoastronomy. Yet Lekson's theory has been endorsed by as many southwestern archaeologists as those who have denigrated it. Whether Lekson is right or wrong, publication of his work was important for the field in challenging the conventional wisdom about the astronomical expertise of ancient southwest cultures.

I was offered the opportunity 20 years ago to publish the work of Maureen Clemmons, an independent researcher with a Ph.D. and MBA, who worked with a team of Caltech engineers to demonstrate the possibility that the huge blocks that comprise the Egyptian pyramids were lifted into place using kites (Cray and Clemmons 2011). Clemmons theory, backed by the successful raising of an obelisk by her Caltech partners, led to a lot of press in 2001 and a subsequent book and History Channel documentary film. Clemmons is a scholar with good credentials, though not in archaeology, supported by data from one of the top engineering schools in the world. It presented a believable case. I passed up that opportunity. More recent work in Egypt has produced far more plausible interpretations for pyramid building, supported by much more sensible data than Clemmons used (Lehner 2008). Was Clemmons' theory wrong? Did she deserve a hearing anyway? While she had academic credentials and her research partners did as well, she lacked knowledge of archaeological research traditions and stood outside the corpus of research on Egyptology, which made it easy to reject her proposal.[2]

I didn't hesitate to publish Alice Kehoe's (2007) *Controversies in archaeology*, which included her radical contention of significant prehistoric contact across the Pacific. Kehoe has been suggesting this for many years and built an entire chapter around the idea that transoceanic contact was the norm in prehistory, generally relegated to the world of pseudoarchaeologists from Thor Heyerdahl to Graham Hancock. It has only been in recent years that researchers have pushed the date of human sailing expertise back to the Pleistocene in places like the Pacific northwest, Crete, and Australia, though acceptance of regular prehistoric transoceanic contact is by no means accepted canon.

What differentiates Lekson's work from Clemmons's from Kehoe's? And how is a publisher or journal editor, not a specialist in Ancestral Pueblo astronomy nor Egyptian engineering nor prehistoric sailing technology, supposed to identify which claims about the past are worth promoting and which to ignore. The peer review process provides the proper filter for most of this, but even that is highly dependent on the choice of peer reviewers and the publisher's knowledge of the reviewers' expertise in the topic. As an archaeologist as well as publisher, I've had better than average training to make independent judgments on some of these topics. Much harder are the choices made by other publishers whose background may be in French literature or organizational management. Yet, the decision to publish one of these works advances or discourages certain theories. Many of these theories deserve to be aired and discussed. Some do not. Professional careers often hang in the balance.

Like most publishers, I use the peer review process in book decisions, but also scholarly plausibility. Does the scholar have adequate credentials? Does the idea seem to have support with reasonable archaeological data? Does the theory deserve to be aired and discussed, whether right or wrong? Like all publishers, I've been wrong on occasion. But, like my counterparts at UC Press, I would have taken a

[2] She ended up self-publishing and coauthoring with a professional writer. The amount of popular press for her theory was inversely proportional to how little solid research lay behind it.

chance on Stanford and Bradley's *Across Atlantic ice*. The theory needs to be aired in the discipline, despite the willful misappropriation of its content.

The process is the same when it comes to scholarly articles. Journal editors are the ultimate decision makers in these case and many have taken risks on ideas that have drawn flak from the parts of the discipline and cheers from other parts. It comes with the territory. But, in every case, the presentation and adoption of a radical new interpretation of the past has come from the willingness of a journal editor to buck the conventional wisdom that permeates the peer review process and take a chance on someone's ideas that fall outside the mainstream.

Archaeological Publications Must Address Its Multiple Audiences, Constituents, and Stakeholders Using Language and Media Appropriate for Them

Archaeology can no longer considered to be a guild craft in which its arcane practitioners speak to each other with a firewall buffering them from the rest of the world. It has become increasingly important to justify archaeological work to the many stakeholders and publics who make use of the past (Little 2002). Beyond questions of self-interest—making sure that the money and jobs are open to the next generation of archaeologists—heritage is a key value in many cultures (Smith et al. 2010). Archaeologists are crucial participants in understanding and preserving this value.

The range of stakeholders and publics include local communities, scholars in other disciplines, policymakers, research funders, and the general public seeking to connect identity to their heritage. The relationship between archaeology and these publics is better explored elsewhere, including in this volume. But from a publication standpoint, they create the need for archaeologists to become far more skilled in their ability to speak to many audiences using media the audiences will respond to.

Distributing at a townhall meeting the 326 page CRM report that presents the research on a parcel destined for development is nonsensical. The plumbers and architects and teachers and retirees in the audience won't read the document. Nor do they need to. Most of it is irrelevant to their world. But they would read a single sheet that summarizes findings and links those findings to the decisions needing to be made. If the archaeologist is to make an impact on community decision making, it needs to be in the language and medium that the audience can use.

Opening a local archaeological site for tourism is not the occasion for making available your journal articles about the site on their website for viewing by the general public. A brief, glossy brochure with limited text and good photos based on your work will go much further to educate the hordes of tourists. For audiences with limited reading capability, a brief video or public lecture might be the right answer. For elementary students, a hands-on exhibit might do the trick. A document for an indigenous community should include the community's voices and their perspectives on the heritage question you've been asked to research, not just your stratigraphic sections and lithic seriation. In short, the method by which the archaeologist communicates to her many publics needs to be in the medium and the language that that audience can understand (Allen and Joyce 2010:279–281).

All of these groups are audiences for archaeological information. The farmer with a Mississippian mound in his plowed field. The fourth graders in an urban school district whose teachers instruct in "local history." The townspeople on the indigenous reserve where the houses are interwoven with the fragmentary structures inhabited their great grandparents. The legislative analyst negotiating with the corporate lobbyist who wants to turn a historic downtown into a shopping mall. Can archaeologists communicate well enough to reach all these audiences? Can anyone?

Not likely. Certainly not the archaeologists. Grad school is about Binford, GIS technology, trimmed balks, and theories of materiality. Learning how to write for fifth graders seems pretty low on the very long priority list of things to master. Fortunately, there are those who are communications experts at reaching certain audiences: science journalists, documentary filmmakers, tour guides, public relations officers, video game makers, novelists. These experts can often do a better job at communicating to diverse audiences than the archaeologist, who is trained in a different skill set. But these experts do not have the expertise at the content that the archaeologist has. Partnerships between the two seem to be the most effective way to solve that problem. This requires the archaeologist to rely on the expertise of the communications specialists, ceding some of the authority for explaining the past to someone who might not fully understand the message but better understands how to present that message. A good partnership, or set of partnerships, seems to be the most effective way for archaeologists to include these publics into their publication universe.

If an ethical stance in archaeology includes contributions to the public good, to the wealth of human knowledge, to the building of community heritage and solidarity, then archaeologists need to pay more attention to how to effectively provide their information to many publics beyond their small coterie of colleagues.

Archaeological Publication Requires Sensitivity to, and Collaboration with, the Communities from Which the Research Was Drawn

The challenge by communities of origin to the claim of ownership of archaeological information as intellectual property of the researcher has been on the radar screen of most archaeologists over the past two decades. Most of us have recognized the hubris of viewing ourselves as dispensing the wisdom of the past to the world from our elevated position as scientists. Knowledge and its presentations represent a form of power. Taken from the hands of a community and dispensed like Pez bits to the rest of the world through our publications, they may have an impact on a community's ability to maintain its power, to preserve its world view, and to steward its intangible heritage for the future.

Who should have control of the publication of research on a community, the individual author/scholar or the community in which she works? Claire Smith (2004:527) notes that much archaeological research includes contributions by both the researcher and the community, whether in the form of local wisdom offered to the research, ethnoarchaeological parallels, or direct engagement in the archaeological project. Thus, she writes, both parties have a stake and intellectual property rights in the project that require consideration. This ethical question begs for the development of partnerships between communities of interest and the scholarly and publishing communities.

Negotiations between western researchers, their institutions, and indigenous communities over the rights to the intellectual property of a community's past are a complex one. The norms of western scholarly, legal, and economic systems allow for scientist's ownership of her research findings and the commodification of that intangible cultural knowledge into publications (Nicholas and Bannister 2004:328). The indigenous world view generally uses group consensus as the norm and views knowledge systems as embedded in culture, not separable into tangible goods, such as publications, to be packaged and shipped to a journal or a publisher.

I've foundered on this shoal before. A young anthropologist returns from the field after several years living with a Canadian First Nations community, dissertation in hand, written by him and illustrated by his key informant, a community member. The nation's history and foundational stories are the subject of this work, along with the scholar's analysis and interpretation of these stories. The anthropologist signs my publishing contract and sends it to his indigenous partner for signature. The partner goes to his nation's council for approval—to people who helped this scholar gather his data for years and knew of his intentions to have it published. Faced with the possibility of their heritage being broadcast internationally, the council cools to the idea and refuses the artist permission to sign the publishing contract. Without his partner's contributions, the scholar's work is only half complete. The project dies an untimely death.

The issues here are highly complex and have been discussed in greater depth elsewhere (Brown 1998; Hollowell and Nicholas 1998). They involve both strategic uses by indigenous communities of western legal concepts for their own advantage, the importance of collaboration and consultation, shared decision making, and an archaeological sensitivity to the broader long-term societal impacts of their work.

One way out of this conundrum is in the support of indigenous-based publishing initiatives. Many museums, electronic publications, and official websites belonging to indigenous communities support book services that promote publications about the nation, often written by community members. Some communities maintain their own publications program. The Blackfoot official website, http://www.blackfoot.org, features a dozen books from Spirit Talk Press, owned by the nation, some available as e-books. The Malki Museum in Banning, California, not only publishes material relevant to the Cahuilla people who own the museum, but is one of the key publishers of California archaeology and indigenous research in general (http://www.malkimuseum.org/index.html). In Australia, the Institute for Aboriginal Development (IAD) Press in Alice Springs (www.iad.edu.au/press/iadpresshome.htm) has been publishing books of both popular and academic interest for over 40 years.

There are also ample examples of partnerships that have bridged the gap between indigenous knowledge and scholarly publication. Many American university presses have publication series in indigenous studies guided by series editors who are both scholars and members of indigenous communities. These scholars can provide the necessary bridge between western and indigenous world views. WAC sponsors its own a series on indigenous archaeology, published by Left Coast, and including several American Indian scholars on the editorial committee (http://www.lcoast-press.com/books_series.php?id=21). Heyday Books, a nonprofit publisher in Berkeley, is now in its 25th year of publishing News from Native California, which includes research, literature, and information on California's native peoples (http://www.heydaybooks.com/news/).

At the theoretical, legal, policy, and scholarly levels, issues of indigenous intellectual property are being explored in many places including Australian Institute of Aboriginal and Torres Strait Islander Studies (IATSIS), Alaska Native Knowledge Network, and the World Intellectual Property Organization. Specific to archaeology and heritage studies, the Intellectual Property in Cultural Heritage Project (IPinCH), housed at Simon Fraser University and funded by the Canadian Social Sciences and Humanities Research Council, is a multiyear, multidisciplinary research, policy, and advocacy effort involving over 50 researchers and 25 partner organizations. The IPinCH website is developing resource materials for archaeologists, other scholars, policy makers, and community members. Among their projected products is a sourcebook and toolkit for communities to help them better negotiating intellectual property issues (http://www.sfu.ca/ipinch/working-group/sct-relating-to-culturally-important-ip).

Global Capitalism Is Not Going Away Anytime Soon: Accommodations Should Be Expected, But Creative Thought Should Be Given to How to Make These Accommodations Ethically

The issue in publishing ethics that riles archaeologists the most is the link between publication and capitalism. Scholarly writing is sold by global media conglomerates at high prices with little benefit going back to the researcher. Scholarly ideas become commodities, assessed for their commercial potential as much as for their intellectual contributions, under a capitalist-controlled publishing model. Unfortunately, global capitalism is likely to be here for a while, probably for our collective lifetimes. Get over it.

Most key outlets for scholars—journals and books—rest in the hands of for-profit publishing companies. Some of these companies who control a significant amount of the published literature—Springer, Taylor and Francis, Elsevier—rank among the larger media companies in the world. And, as global commercial institutions, they often rake in profits that seem outsized to their role as conveyors of scholarly knowledge. Elsevier, for example, reported a 36 % net profit in 2011 on sales volume of $3.2 billion (The Economist 2011). Even the not-for-profit publishing institution Oxford University Press reported sales of $1 billion in 2010–2011 with a surplus of 19 % (OUP 2011, p 5). Impressive. Smaller academic presses don't command anywhere close to this rate of profitability, if any, so scale seems to matter. In the global flow of scholarly information, big is more sustainable than small.

The tension between producers and owners of texts goes back to the very beginnings of writing. From ancient Mesopotamian royal and temple archives, to Greco-Roman libraries, to medieval monasteries, those who wrote usually did so beholden to those in power, whether it was the temple, palace, or church. Most authors in medieval and early modern times were sponsored by a patron, who commissioned, protected, encouraged, and usually controlled the nature of their work (Finkelstein and McCleery 2006:72). It was only with the development of mass produced texts afforded by Gutenberg's invention of the printing press that the concept of a printer/bookseller was invented, as someone who both produced books and marketed them to buyers (Hellinga 2007:217). They became the patron of the author and, as before, controlled their work. Attempts to limit and control flow of information by large commercial institutions—assisted by government regulation—reach back to the establishment of the Stationers' Company by London book sellers in the seventeenth century England (Feather 2007a:241). Some of these booksellers morphed into the earliest publishers in the nineteenth century (Finkelstein and McCleery 2006:86). Significant tensions existed between this incipient capitalism and the reins of state, which had traditionally controlled the flow of information. The actions of early European printers/publishers were often restricted by state regulations and censorship, such as the British Licensing Act of 1662 (Feather 2007b:524). That tension between the publishing industry and the state over control of publications has carried forward to this day. The producers of the contested commodities, the authors, were rarely considered in the conflicts between power and commerce. It was only with the advent of author copyright in the eighteenth century that rights of the author to their works finally began to be considered (Finkelstein and McCleery 2006:75–76). But even then, control of publication usually still rested in the hands of the publisher.

As the distribution of archaeological publications went from local to regional to national to global, the need for large global systems to advertise availability became crucial to the success of published work. These mechanisms exist within the current commercial publishing infrastructure. Publication of a new book in English anywhere on the globe is routed through the databases of RR Bowker in the USA or Nielsen in the UK to bookstores, academic libraries, and library wholesalers worldwide. Journal articles are similarly publicized through systems such as Thomson-Reuters Web of Science or EBSCO Discovery. These systems connect with search engines to make availability of these ideas known to scholars everywhere. The lone scholar wishing to reach colleagues in Mali, Myanmar, and Minnesota could not possibly duplicate this system. The global information flow favors large-scale media institutions.

Even the idea of a publishing "industry" in archaeology is a misnomer. Publication outlets range from the lone scholar posting her latest data or musings on the web, to university-based publication outlets for faculty and students,[3] to not-for-profit professional publishers including university presses and other not-for-profit organizations.[4] For-profit presses range from the miniscule Wormwood Press, the brainchild of the late UCLA archaeologist Clem Meighan and run by his widow and children, to the archaeological publishing arms of global conglomerates Springer, Routledge, and Elsevier.[5] A similar panoply of publishing establishments exist that produce scholarly journals, newsletters, and other periodicals. More recently, there has been the emergence of a group of digital archives to house raw archaeological data and scholarly analysis.[6]

In addition to the diversity of types and sizes of publishing establishments, archaeology is one of the few fields in which publications range from STEM (Science, Technology, Engineering, Medicine) models to purely humanistic ones. DNA or radiocarbon studies done by archaeologists (as well as by biologists and physicists) populate the literature of the discipline as thickly as postprocessual essays on materiality and human agency. Professional publishers of STEM information are accustomed to much more expensive publishing models—costs are considerably higher for more technically-driven publishing—and corresponding sales prices much higher. But, the STEM professional often has more resources to obtain publications through research grants to support these costs and pricing. Not so the humanistic, interpretivist wing of archaeological writing and publishing. This is a quandary for the full-range archaeological publisher who might publish both DNA studies and postprocessual essays. What is the ethical way to price archaeological materials? What can be done with data and ideas that are important but not financially self-supporting? How do we create a publishing system for archaeology that allows for the free flow of ideas in a sustainable way, and allows all voices to be heard?

This commodification of scholarly output in archaeology has, as elsewhere in the academy, raised the shining beacon of the open access movement as a solution. After all, should not the output of scholarly information be free and available to all? This is certainly an ideal to work toward. But several problems crop up in trying to liberate archaeology from the grip of modern capitalism. Open access may be open, but it's not free.

The web is not a financially free system, unless you discount the batteries of large-scale computers owned and operated by governments, university, and businesses. There are huge costs to maintain this system, but they are hidden from the small producer and recipients of information. An open access system for

[3] Such as the Archaeological Research Facility publication program at UC Berkeley or UCLA's Cotsen Institute Press.

[4] Like the University of Arizona Press or British Archaeological Reports.

[5] Only English speaking publishing world is discussed here, though this range of publication outlets exists in other languages as well.

[6] Including the Alexandrina Archive and Digital Antiquity.

scholarship places much of the burden on university technology departments and libraries. With the wild fluctuations in university budgets, can these institutions be trusted to maintain the scholarship system 24/7 in perpetuity? When the next budget crunch comes, will a savvy university administrator ensure that the cancer database and electrical engineering publications are preserved, but dump such financially unrewarding projects such as the Global Archaeological Site Database (just after he ditches the Complete Works of Every Living Poet in Wisconsin)?

The open web is not a politically free system either. The limitations placed by the Chinese government on the flow of information to its citizens are the most visible current example. But future nation states might use this power of control over interpretation of heritage as well as contemporary politics. What would stop China from limiting access to archaeological information suggesting that Tibet possessed an independent, vital culture prior to the Chinese takeover? Knowing the political nature of interpretations of the past, as expressed in other chapters of this volume, that specter is not necessarily dystopian fiction.

The open web is also not an even playing field for promotion of information. In the current configuration, to the huckster go the spoils. The best recent example was the media splash around the discovery of a tomb in Jerusalem purported to be the burial complex of Jesus's family by Simcha Jacobvici (who bills himself as the Naked Archaeologist), Biblical scholar James Tabor, and producer James Cameron of Titanic fame. Most scholars swiftly rejected their interpretation of the Jerusalem tombs. But the amount of publicity associated with this find, brought about by the showmanship of Jacobvici and the money and power of Cameron, made this discovery front page news (Discovery Channel 2007). To the general public, who won't follow the details of peer debates over the validity of this very shaky evidence, the last word was "they found Jesus's family." Contrast this to dozens of very real, but equally important discoveries about the past that don't have a well-funded documentary or Hollywood-based publicity machine behind them. Truth goes to the scholar with the best public relations office.

Given that there are costs to any system of archaeological communication—whether commercial or open access—how can this wide range of publishing institutions produce archaeological information for an admittedly small audience in a sustainable way? The ethical answer seems to lie in the sustainable maximalization of audience. Each publication has its audience, whether a few specialists, or a mass public. Producers of these publications should strive to maximize readership. Yet, if the costs of preparing, disseminating, and announcing their publications must be recovered to allow for publication of a second volume, a third, and more. Any economic model must produce ample income to sustain itself. This can happen in a variety of ways. Currently the most reliable source of funds is book buyers and journal subscribers, largely college and university libraries. Libraries might be willing to shift some of their expenditures to open access models, provided that support can be secured for the long term. Publication subsidies from granting agencies, universities, or authors themselves are a traditional method of offsetting the costs of scholarly publication for a small audience. Many commercial publishers are beginning to experiment with author-subsidized open access: for a fee, you can make your article openly available on the web. Whatever the model used, the goal is to reach the maximal audience at the minimal price to maintain sustainability. That might vary enormously between global media companies and university-based archaeology institutes. But it seems the most ethical way to build a long-term system for producing and sustaining archaeological publications.

How archaeologists are going to influence global media companies to maintain prices at affordable, yet sustainable, levels? They are already doing so, through competitive pressure. The World Archaeological Congress, for example, sponsors series with three different commercial publishers. As part of this arrangement, WAC members are given discounts on other books from those publishers. A series of textbooks from SAA Press, run by Society for American Archaeology, are priced at a level below most other publishers, which provides downward pressure on other textbook publishers' prices. More scholarly works published by Archaeological Research Facility at Berkeley, Cotsen Institute at UCLA, or British Archaeological Reports also serve to cap prices for all publishers. Individual scholars can help through the decisions they make as to where to send their own scholarly writing for publication.

Conclusion

There are few issues raised here that are not addressed in other parts of this volume. But that point is important. The publications function of the archaeological enterprise—whether to scholarly, general public, or community audiences—is embedded in the general ethical questions that face the discipline. The battles over control of the past that are featured in other aspects of this enterprise are exacerbated when brought to the public. And, as also demonstrated here, archaeologists have agency through their funding, publishing, and purchasing decisions toward enacting a more ethical profession.

References

Allen, M., & Joyce, R. (2010). Communicating archaeology in the 21st century. In W. Ashmore, D. Lippert, & B. Mills (Eds.), *Voices in American archaeology* (pp. 270–290). Washington: SAA Press.

American Wayyy (2011). The founding of America, published August 16. Retrieved September 3, 2012 from http://americanwayyy.blogspot.com/

Bristow, K. (2010). *The white apocalypse*. Charleston: CreateSpace Independent Publishing.

Brown, M. (1998). Can culture be copyrighted? *Current Anthropology, 39*(2), 193–206.

Cray, D., & Clemmons, M. (2011). *Soaring stones: A kite-powered approach to building Egypt's pyramids*. Los Angeles: Delcominy Creations.

Discovery Channel (2007). The lost tomb of Jesus. Retrieved September 4, 2012 from http://dsc.discovery.com/convergence/tomb/tomb.html

Fagan, G. (2006). Diagnosing pseudoarchaeology. In G. Fagan (Ed.), *Archaeological fantasies* (pp. 23–46). Abingdon: Routledge.

Feather, J. (2007a). The British book market 1600-1800. In S. Eliot & J. Rose (Eds.), *A companion to the history of the book* (pp. 232–246). Oxford: Blackwell.

Feather, J. (2007b). Copyright and literary property. In S. Eliot & J. Rose (Eds.), *A companion to the history of the book* (pp. 520–530). Oxford: Blackwell.

Finkelstein, D., & McCleery, A. (2006). *An introduction to book history*. New York: Routledge.

Hellinga, L. (2007). The Gutenberg revolutions. In S. Eliot & J. Rose (Eds.), *A companion to the history of the book* (pp. 207–219). Oxford: Blackwell.

Hollowell, J., & Nicholas, G. (1998). Intellectual property issues in archaeological publication: Some considerations. *Archaeologies, 4*(2), 208–217.

Kehoe, A. (2007). *Controversies in archaeology*. Walnut Creek: Left Coast.

Kroeber, A., Collier, D., & Schreiber, K. J. (1998). *The archaeology and pottery of Nazca, Peru: Alfred Kroeber's 1926 expedition*. Walnut Creek: AltaMira.

Lehner, M. (2008). *The complete pyramids*. London: Thames & Hudson.

Lekson, S. (1999). *The Chaco meridian: Centers of political power in the Ancient Southwest*. Walnut Creek: AltaMira Press.

Little, B. (Ed.). (2002). *Pubic benefits of archaeology*. Gainesville: University Press of Florida.

Nicholas, G.P., & Bannister, K. P. (2004) Copyrighting the past? Emerging intellectual property rights issues in archaeology, *Current Anthropology, 45*(3), 327–350.

Odyssey Marine Exploration (2012). Retrieved September 8, 2012 from http://www.shipwreck.net/archaeology.php

Oxford University Press (2011). Annual report of the delegates of the University Press, 2010–2011. Retrieved September 3, 2012 from http://fds.oup.com/www.oup.com/pdf/OUP_Annual_Report_2010-11.pdf

Phillips, D. (n.d.). The Chaco Meridian: A skeptical analysis. Retrieved January 1, 2012 from http://www.unm.edu/~dap/meridian/meridian-text.html

Smith, C. (2004) On intellectual property rights in archaeology, *Current Anthropology,* 45(4), 527.

Smith, G., Messenger, P. M., & Soderland, H. (Eds.). (2010). *Heritage values in contemporary society*. Walnut Creek: Left Coast.

Stanford, D. (1997). Interview with Dennis Stanford. Retrieved January 1, 2013 from http://www.oocities.org/latrinchera2000/articulos/stanford.html

Stanford, D., & Bradley, B. (2012). *Across Atlantic ice: The origin of America's Clovis culture*. Berkeley: University of California Press.

The Economist (2011). Of goats and headaches, published 5/26/11. Retrieved September 3, 2012 from http://www.economist.com/node/18744177

Zorn, J. (n.d.). Tel en-Nasbeh: Biblical Mizpah of Benjamin. Retrieved September 8, 2012 from http://www.arts.cornell.edu/jrz3/frames2.htm

Chapter 13
Patrimonial Ethics and the Field of Heritage Production

Michael A. Di Giovine

Introduction

In December 2011, I was invited by Vietnam National University and the Quang Ninh provincial government to conduct a superficial assessment of Yên Tử Mountain, a Vietnamese Buddhist pilgrimage site that has great religious and nationalistic significance in the northern part of the country. They were in the early stages of preparing the Nomination File for submission to UNESCO's World Heritage Committee, and solicited my input on the viability of their plan to inscribe this destination on the World Heritage List. It is never an easy task to take an affective site of national importance and craft a universalizing narrative around it.[1] Like most religious sites, the Yên Tử mountain complex is, in a word, complex. Regarded as the *axis mundi* of the "land of happiness" in the Chinese hinterland during the T'ang and Song dynasty, Yên Tử was a symbol of Vietnamese Taoist, Buddhist, and Confucian cosmologies before the powerful emperor Trần Nhân Tông (1258–1308) renounced his throne, was ordained a Buddhist monk, and retreated to the top of the mountain in 1299. It was here that he founded a particularly indigenous Zen Buddhist sect called Trúc Lâm (Bamboo Grove School), which fused together Zen teachings from three non-Vietnamese sages: Vinitaruci from India, Wu Yan Tong from Guangzhou, China, and Tsao T'ang from Champa. Eager to forge a unifying

---

[1] UNESCO (2008:5) alludes to this in its official *Information Kit*: "How does a World Heritage site differ from a national heritage site? The key lies in the words 'outstanding universal value'. All countries have sites of local or national interest, which are quite justifiably a source of national pride, and the *Convention* encourages them to identify and protect their heritage whether or not it is placed on the World Heritage List."

M.A. Di Giovine (✉)
Department of Anthropology & Sociology, West Chester University,
775 S. Church Street - Old Library, West Chester, PA 19383, USA
e-mail: michael@michaeldigiovine.com

C. Gnecco, D. Lippert (eds.), *Ethics and Archaeological Praxis*,
Ethical Archaeologies: The Politics of Social Justice 1,
DOI 10.1007/978-1-4939-1646-7_13

nationalist narrative free of colonial overtones, in 1974 North Vietnam recognized Yên Tử as a national heritage site, since Trúc Lâm seems to be the only non-imported form of Zen Buddhism in Vietnam (Dao 2008:99–103).

Though it boasts an archaeological legacy that is relatively untapped, Yên Tử is also a living site: since the 1980s and 1990s, pilgrimage here has become increasingly popular for Vietnamese Buddhists, many of whom espouse animist tendencies and other elements of "popular" piety that conflict with the official State religion (Dao 2008). Each spring pilgrims flock to this place to make an arduous pilgrimage up the sacred mount, scrambling over rocks and fallen trees slick with lichen and moss, past Buddhist effigies and the tranquil tombs of monks and hermits, and cutting through fir and bamboo forests inhabited by a variety of fauna—including humans living in a small shantytown hugging a steep bluff halfway up the tall mountain. These residents lease land from the government for 20 years at a time and make their living serving weary pilgrims fortifying local delicacies midway through their journey.

I traveled off-season and was accompanied by a young local scholar who had a graduate degree from Harvard. Before taking the new French-constructed funicular up to the timberline—where we would be greeted by an immense, yet-unfinished seated bronze Buddha that could (and probably is meant to) rival those in Hong Kong or Nara—we stopped to admire the sweeping verdant landscape, interrupted only by a thin strip of those brilliantly colored homes, their rusted, corrugated metal roofs glinting in the sunlight. "We should move these people off the mountain, right?" he asked me. After all, the land wasn't theirs to lose. The question was actually intended to be more innocent than it might sound to Western academics and reflected a long-standing problem in the popular conceptualization of "heritage" as something located exclusively in the past, and sullied—or made less authentic—by the present. My concern for these people piqued in my meetings with the government officials, who attempted to get me to endorse the management plan that they had already drawn up but were not prepared to show me. Although the site itself boasted new means of facilitating contemporary pilgrimage to the sacred mount not surprisingly they also talked very little about the current-day pilgrims who visit the site and any potential impact (positive or negative) they had on it; rather, they focused alternatively on how the archaeological-historical record revealed Yên Tử's past importance for the country and how such material culture could draw new kinds of (primarily foreign) visitors to the site, given Yên Tử's proximity to the province's star tourist attraction, the UNESCO World Heritage site of Ha Long Bay.

As this episode at Yên Tử reveals there are not only many different uses of heritage (cf. Smith 2006) but also many different meanings espoused by many different stakeholders; indeed, the onetime head of the British National Trust famously commented that heritage can mean "whatever you want" (qtd. Hewison 1989:15). All definitions, however, are in some way based on the notion of an ongoing link between the past, present and future. Stemming from earlier legal usage as a bequest of familial patrimony from one generation to another, as in a will (cf. McCrone et al. 1995:1; Harvey 2001:322), heritage thus includes a notion of ownership-through-descent, marking an "in" group (those who "own" it) and an "out" group (those who don't).

Although heritage claims are often localized in an object, monument or cultural practice, heritage is not a thing but a value-creating, ideological narrative—one that is, as Harrison (2005:3) points out, performed often to those who are "not us." Part of this performance is through preservation; it is imperative to preserve heritage sites (and other forms of tangible and intangible heritage) for perpetuating the present society (or "in" group) into future generations. Heritage therefore operates primarily through affective means, often stirring up strong emotions among individuals and groups, particularly when they feel they have a stake in its (and therefore their) preservation—or, conversely, when they feel threatened by another group's contrasting heritage claims. As my experience with Yên Tử reveals, heritage is not created through authorized discourse alone (cf. Smith 2006); it is constantly formed and reformed in a dialectical fashion through the interactions, negotiations, and struggles between diverse groups of stakeholders or "epistemic" groups (see Knorr-Cetina 1999)—within what I have elsewhere called the Bourdieuian "field of heritage production" (Di Giovine 2009b:9–15; see Bourdieu 1993).

Bourdieu is, of course, ultimately concerned with power (social, economic, political) exercised through the "consecration" of particular class-based distinctions (Rey 2007:8); heritage "properties" can certainly be counted among the almost sanctified, moralized objects used to exert socioeconomic domination (cf. Silverman and Ruggles 2008). The field of heritage production is a structured, totalizing set of relationships, often in conflict, that order a diversity of these groups who struggle to stake their claim to, define, and ultimately utilize, a particular heritage site. These groups include, but are not limited to, site managers, preservationists, development workers, conservation-minded donors, local communities, (local, regional, national, transnational) politicians, academic researchers, museum professionals, tourists, and travel industry professionals (including tour operators, local service providers, transportation professionals, guides, hoteliers, restaurateurs, etc.), and sometimes religious institutions. Rarely are these epistemic groups solely focused on the one site per se but rather have specific uses for it in their broader objectives; when their interests fall within the field of production these groups will stake out claims, or positions, regarding the site in relation to the other groups. The multilayered, simultaneous acts of positioning and position-taking are dialectically dependent on one another; the internal struggles within each group depend on the correspondence they have with the external struggles within the broader field and, likewise, these macroscopic struggles often find their protagonists in certain dominant individuals within the various groups who put a public face to their group's position. Although these groups are in near-constant conflict (though to various degrees) they can also become "adversaries in collusion" (Bourdieu 1993:79) when they align against the positions of other groups, which so often happens among anthropologists and archaeologists who find themselves alternatively working alongside other stakeholder groups that have their own, divergent interests, for designating, preserving and managing a heritage site. Often marked by a clash of moralities, it is precisely during such alignments that we are made to act within certain historically and culturally contingent ethical paradigms—what I call here "paternalistic" and "multicultural" ethics.

In this chapter, I will examine some of the major types of situations that cause those of us, archaeologists and anthropologists, who are engaged in the field of heritage production, to act in accordance with one of these ethical paradigms. In the most general sense, which I use here, "ethics" denotes right or wrong action, the "moral correctness of specific conduct" (Oxford Dictionaries 2013), with that conduct being the "production" (designation, preservation, valorization) and management of cultural property. It is important to note, however, that ethics is not descriptive but rather prescriptive; future-oriented, it is a "rational procedure by which we determine what human beings 'ought'—or what is right for them—to do or to seek to realize by voluntary action" (Sidgwick 1981:1). As Preston (2007:16) eloquently puts it:

> In general, ethics is concerned about what *is right, fair, just, or good*; about what we *ought* to do, not just about what *is* the case or what is most acceptable or expedient. This distinction between "ought" and "is" signals the need to distinguish ethical claims from factual ones. … Ethical claims *prescribe*, rather than describe. They are concerned with how people *ought* to behave and suggest how social and behavior can be improved (italics in the original).

Preston's definition is salient for my discussion on two levels. First, ethics is future-oriented and, often, ultimately valorizes the ethically minded actor, as invoked by the word "improved." Indeed, Herbert McCabe (2005:49) argues that ethics "is not simply about how to talk about being good but is intended to make people good as well." When we act ethically in regard to heritage designation and preservation we are asserting—voluntarily, rationally, yet often through making difficult decisions—a moral "goodness" towards ourselves and our epistemic community, those who also use or identify with the heritage object and, even ostensibly, the heritage object itself. And we seek to change—to improve—the social relations surrounding us. Along with this is the second consideration: this definition indexes the very social, and relational, aspect of our actions; though valorizing our own moral positions within the field of heritage production these actions impact not only us but the entire field of actors. Indeed, it is for this reason that I employ the terms "paternalistic" and "multicultural" ethics.

While I will discuss my definitions of these terms in greater depth later on, I wish to emphasize here that these adjective modifiers of the term "ethics" denotes our (social) position (in the Bourdieuian sense) vis-a-vis other groups within this field of heritage production. On the one hand, "paternalistic ethics" sees archaeologists and anthropologists assume an explicitly dominant position as both "experts" and self-defined stewards of cultural property over other epistemic groups that may lay claim to it; indeed, paternalism in general denotes behavior by individuals, organizations or political entities that limits the activities of other groups ostensibly because the latter will be "better off" or protected by harm (Dworkin 2010). "Multicultural ethics," on the other hand, posits a distinctively explicit openness (if only superficially) to incorporating alternative or "minority" voices in acts of designating and preserving objects of cultural heritage—voices that specifically come from equally alternative epistemic "cultures." Thus, for example, multicultural ethics would theoretically purport to take into consideration, if not privilege, a different understanding of the value of a heritage object if it came from a distinctively diverse "culture"—most often thought to be "indigenous"—but it would not necessarily privilege a different conception of its value if it came from, say, an alternative epistemic community equally rooted in Western culture, such as the tourism industry—though, as I will argue later on, the tourism industry itself comprises at least one epistemic group with its own "epistemic culture" (Knorr-Cetina 1999). Importantly, what will become evident is that the right or wrong action—the ethics here—pertains less explicitly to the heritage object itself and more to the ways in which our epistemic community deals with others within this field.

Yet what I argue here is that both of these dominant forms of ethics are problematic when we consider ourselves as but one community within a field of heritage production that is veritably constituted by struggles and contestation between the field's epistemic groups, which are at least normatively centered on the preservation and/or use of a heritage object itself. As it will become clear, the notion of doing what is "right, fair, just or good" towards other social groups is antithetical to the field of production, predicated as it is on its epistemic groups' explicit espousal of alterative dispositions and relational acts of "positioning and position-taking" against each other (see Bourdieu 1993:30). Thus, in this chapter, particular focus will be given to those situations that emerge when we find ourselves as "adversaries in collusion" with other epistemic groups who often attribute radically different use-values to heritage objects, yet whose short-term goals align with ours; it is in these situations that tensions between paternalistic and multicultural ethics are brought to the fore. Yên Tử is an appropriate jumping-off-point because, like most heritage sites, it exists on many different planes and scales (local, regional, national, transnational), is valued by different groups for different reasons and, particularly as it is an active pilgrimage site, is imbued with a number of different and conflicting ideologies. From such an examination it becomes evident that a new ethical paradigm should be adopted: one that focuses both on the multivocality of all stakeholders (including "indigenous" and "Westerners," or "insiders" and "outsiders") as well as on the heritage object itself, pregnant as it is with myriad meanings. That is, if one can say that a heritage site's significance cuts across, and transcends, the oft-conflicting epistemic groups within the field of production then the ethical paradigm involved in how those meanings condition heritage-related practices by anthropologists and archaeologists must also cut across these diverse moralities. With this in mind, I call this paradigm "patrimonial ethics" to indicate our moral potential to do "what is right, fair, just or good" not only to other stakeholders within the field of heritage production but to ensure the constructive present and future utilization of the heritage object (or patrimony) itself.

Paternalistic Ethics, Archaeology, and the Field of Heritage Production: A Concise History

The emergence of the field of heritage production coincided with the development of archaeology and anthropology as scientific disciplines in the nineteenth century. Although archaeological records indicate that humanity entertained some distinctive conceptualization of what we would call heritage at least as early as ancient

Egypt (Di Giovine 2009b:48–51), the term "heritage" as we use it today only entered the lexicon proper during the age of imperialism—and with it, the modern-day heritage industry. According to Penny Edwards, the term first appeared in 1830s France as *patrimoine* in the official title of the national office created to protect and manage the nation's historic monuments (*monument historique*, a term which appeared only 40 years earlier); this was both a process of recovery (as in excavating and preserving monuments from antiquity) and discovery (as in figuring out the roots and composition of the modern French empire). It was soon expanded to encompass all of the natural and cultural artifacts collected in the far-flung protectorates, which were displayed in museums and World's Fair exhibitions back at home, and which helped to enrich and diversify the concept of what constituted French nationhood (Edwards 2007:27–28; see also Smith 1991:6–7, 19; Chastel 1986:424). Likewise in the UK, the other great nineteenth century colonial power, it is commonly claimed that term heritage became diffuse with the ratification of the 1882 Ancient Monuments Act and the creation of the British National Trust in 1895 (cf. Harvey 2001:320, 2008:20–21). Here, too, "heritage" emerged from both fin-de-siècle fears of societal decadence and transience at the hands of modernization and industrialization (cf. Freud 1950:35) and the imperial imperative to order an increasingly expanding world into enlarging national boundaries. Marked, as it was, with the broad colonial idea of the "white man's burden" (Kipling 1899) in which Western imperialists played a paternal and civilizing role among the natives who were perceived to be anthropologically behind in some universal evolutionary trajectory (see, for example, Tylor 1871), heritage endeavors were strongly permeated with a paternalistic ethic. The temples at Angkor, for example, were "discovered" by French naturalist Henri Mouhot (despite the fact that ethnic Khmer lived in the region), then cleared from the forest's stranglehold, cleaned, documented, studied, and preserved; importantly, early archaeologists sought an outside explanation for the construction of these impressive structures, believing that the current population could not possibly have been able to construct such complex material culture (see Dagens 1995:60).

While a cultural artifact-based understanding of heritage may not have been as prominent on the other side of the Atlantic, the turn of the century also ushered in a similar movement to preserve natural areas from what was perceived as nature's inevitable transience at the hands of US political expansion, industrialization, and societal transformation. Just as the colonial explorers charting uncharted areas of Southeast Asia, Africa, and Oceana broadened their empire's understanding of the complexity of the natural world, so too did the American purveyors of Manifest Destiny "discover" a natural world to claim as their own—a claim about the past's future (destiny) with implications for the present. Significantly, the creation of the National Parks Service in 1872 was one of the earliest of its kind, and became a model for UNESCO's World Heritage program (see USNPS, n.d.). Both the discipline of archaeology and the heritage field underwent tremendous growth following World War II, when transformations in the global political economy and global mobilities brought several new groups into contact. This period marked the true birth of cultural resource management in the West and in emerging countries that were in the process of rebuilding after the devastation of the war; and, in the USA at least, a new generation of archaeologists—their ranks enlarged by the GI Bill—were able to assume these new duties. In response to more robust legislation concerning heritage management, by the 1970s, more than half of all American archaeologists worked in applied capacities outside of academia (McGimsey 1995:11).

These changes also impacted developing countries. On the one hand, the creation (and ostensibly the safeguarding) of heritage sites was adopted by newly created, postcolonial nation-states as a means of constructing a new national identity. While previously the ideology of heritage, coupled with imaginaries of past civilizational grandeur, had been employed as an imperialist means of subjugation, it was now adopted by the formerly subjugated (albeit often foreign-educated elites) to assert their own claims of sovereignty and civilizational greatness (Edwards 2007; cf. Said 1994).

On the other hand, furthermore, the post-war world also saw the emergence of the modern tourism industry—organized through an international marketing association, the International Union of Official Travel Organizations (IUOTO), and facilitated by swifter forms of communication and transportation technologies. When a worldwide petroleum crisis threatened developing countries' modernization initiatives in the 1970s, they turned to the "extraction" of their cultural resources—their own "heritage," artifactually conceived—for consumption by foreign tourists. Paradoxically, their means of development was the very underdevelopment they wished to transcend. It is not a chance occurrence that in 1974 IUOTO was reformed under the aegis of the United Nations (UN) as the World Tourism Organization (UNWTO), whose "fundamental aim … [would] be the promotion and development of tourism with a view to contributing to economic development, … pay[ing] particular attention to the interests of the developing countries in the field of tourism" (UNWTO 1974:83).

UNESCO's 1972 World Heritage Convention was also born out of post-war reconstruction, contemporary globalization, and political economic factors, yet as I have argued elsewhere, its impetus transcended purely political and economic concerns (Di Giovine 2014). Rather than focusing exclusively on economic development, UNESCO was created with the lofty understanding that "a peace based exclusively upon the political and economic arrangements of governments would not be a peace which could secure the unanimous, lasting and sincere support of the peoples of the world, and that the peace must therefore be founded, if it is not to fail, upon the intellectual and moral solidarity of mankind" (UNESCO 1945:1). Such solidarity had manifested itself in the 1960s when UNESCO successfully spearheaded an ambitious plan to move the Nubian temples of pharaoh Ramses II (1303–1213 BCE) out of the way of floodwaters from Gamal Nassar's Aswan High Dam—a daring, $42 million project that involved cutting the temples into 20-ton blocks and relocating them atop a man-made mountain overlooking the original site. Over 40 member-states raised $80 million, nearly double the amount needed. In addition, for 6 years an international team of archaeologists excavated the Egyptian and Sudanese countryside threatened by the reservoir; it was the first time archaeological excavations were undertaken in the Sudan's "practically virgin land"

(UNESCO 1982:30). The episode of Abu Simbel had a profound effect on the future of World Heritage, and UNESCO proclaimed it "a triumph of international solidarity" (UNESCO 1982). It revealed the strong emotional relationship that such heritage properties—and the prospect of their transience—could exert on the international community, irrespective of national origins, and brought nations and experts (especially archaeologists) together for the common goal of researching, and preserving, these monuments.

Following Abu Simbel, a White House conference in 1965 called for the creation of a "World Heritage Trust" to engage the international community in the preservation of exemplary sites "for the present and the future of the entire world citizenry" (qtd. UNESCO 2008b:7). It should be noted that this was not solely linked to the global heritage preservation, but marked the development of federal interest in domestic cultural resources management (see McGimsey 1995:11). A plan was adopted which was similar to that of the US National Parks service (see USNPS, n.d.); in 1968, the International Union for the Conservation of Nature (IUCN) adopted a similar framework for its membership. These proposals were combined in 1972, when delegates to the United Nations Conference on Human Environment in Stockholm called for a new Convention that could better ensure the safeguarding and management of cultural and natural properties. Later that year, it became the World Heritage Convention spearheaded by UNESCO; IUCN and two cultural heritage preservation organizations present at the conference, ICOMOS and ICCROM, were made expert "Advisory Bodies." Signatories to the World Heritage Convention would be eligible to inscribe "their" properties into an elite List of sites deemed to be of "universal value" and would pledge to safeguard them. For UNESCO, such an activity seems to alter the very significance of heritage as something that is owned by an "in" group through descent; now all of humanity becomes the "in" group, for they are to recognize in each disparate site a common narrative claim, "unity in diversity" (Di Giovine 2009b:119–144). Whether or not this is actually the case in practice, since 1974 the World Heritage Committee—elected every 4 years from among the signatories—meets annually to inscribe an average of 30 new sites on the World Heritage List; to date the list is nearly 1,000 entries long. They also evaluate management plans and safeguarding efforts of these sites, monitor those places inscribed on a List of World Heritage in Danger, and also debate critical issues the Convention faces in light of changing notions of what constitutes "heritage" (see Di Giovine 2014). Lastly, in response to growing dissatisfaction among non-Western and minority groups that the World Heritage Convention's criteria was too exclusive and did not adequately address their alternative cultural practices, after a decade-long process, UNESCO ratified the Convention for the Safeguarding of the World's Intangible Cultural Heritage and its associated List of Intangible Heritage in Danger in 2003 (see Hafstein 2009).

While certainly UNESCO's World Heritage Convention, with its emphasis on peacemaking rather than conflict, marked a radical shift in the meanings and potentialities ascribed to objects of "heritage," it is important to note that it did not change the fundamental ethical paradigm associated with heritage preservation. Although it explicitly speaks against neocolonialism, providing more voice to nation-states in designating and determining the significance and value of heritage properties—the hallmark of multiculturalism, as I will explain below—it assumes the role of the parental guardian in an explicitly paternalistic ethical paradigm. While the nation-state must "offer up" its cultural property as a World Heritage site, creating its own narrative of how the site reveals "outstanding universal value" that is the "common heritage of mankind" (see UNESCO 1972, 2008), it still is ultimately a UNESCO-affiliated advisory body that provides the definitive expert assessment of the nation-state's nominated site before the site's inscription is voted upon; it is UNESCO's World Heritage Committee who votes to inscribe the site on the World Heritage List; and it is UNESCO who keeps a fatherly eye on the management of the site by both sending its Advisory Bodies to undertake periodic assessments, as well as soliciting—again like a paradigmatic father figure—the nation-states to update the World Heritage Committee on recent developments, problems, and issues associated with the integrity of the site. Finally, it is UNESCO—and not the nation-state, as has been proven recently when Thailand threatened to pull out of the World Heritage Convention[2]—that can take away a designation as well by de-listing a site when the nation-state has failed to adequately preserve those qualities for which the property was designated. In the ultimate form of chastisement, UNESCO does not delete the de-listed site from its list but rather crosses it off, as if to publically show that it was, at one time, a World Heritage site until the nation-state failed to uphold its end of the bargain.

Furthermore, as in the past, the unit of measurement of this ethical paradigm—the focus of this moral imperative—continues to be the preservation not of an indigenous community or of diverse cultural groups per se but of a hegemonic community modeled in the likeness of UNESCO. This community is not a traditional empire or sovereign nation-state but what I have elsewhere called a global *heritage-scape* (Di Giovine 2009): a dynamic and ever-changing "worldwide imagined community" predicated on the ritual re-appropriation and juxtaposition of tangible monuments, objects, and natural features (Di Giovine 2010:67).

Paradoxes of Multicultural Ethics

In recent decades, anthropologists and archaeologists have become increasingly aware of their historical role in the colonial endeavor and the paternalistic forms of ethics marking their work (see Wylie 1999, 2005). As a result, the disciplines have embraced what Cristóbal Gnecco has called "multicultural" ethics, which guide

[2] In June 2011, the governing regime in Thailand publically announced that it would withdraw from the World Heritage Convention in protest over Cambodia's designation of the Khmer monastery of Preah Vihear; UNESCO responded that the Thai sites that were already deemed to have "outstanding universal value" (and thus which were inscribed on the World Heritage List) would remain on the List, even if Thailand withdrew. Fortunately, a regime change shifted the country's position towards UNESCO, and the organization never had to follow through with enforcing the ambiguous status of a non-member state with World Heritage listings. See a sympathetic article in *The Nation* (Ganjanakhundee 2011), written in the midst of the crisis, for an interesting analysis from the Thai perspective.

more inclusive archaeological and museological practices—at least purportedly (Gnecco 2009, 2014). In particular, archaeologists guided by multicultural ethics include local actors in their projects, open local museums for the benefit of making their finds more accessible to the surrounding population and integrate alternative historical understandings in their interpretations. Yet Gnecco argues that such multiculturalism, while expanding the reach of archaeologists' work and the breadth of their hermeneutics, continues to privilege the hegemonies in the *status quo*—the patriarchs, so to speak, in the paternalistic ethical paradigm.

This is not simply a peculiarity of our epistemic community but marks multicultural politics in general, as Talal Asad (1993) argues rather forcefully in his analysis of the British government's famed reaction towards its Muslim citizens' outcry against the publication of Salmon Rushdie's *Satanic Verses*. As both Gnecco (2003) and Asad (1993) point out, multiculturalism—like the discipline of archaeology and the heritage industry themselves—traces its historical trajectory to the colonial era, in which diverse "others" were "clearly defined, delimited, separated" and stereotyped so as to facilitate their assimilation into the dominant culture under the rubric of "diversity," which "masked its ideology of assimilation" (Gnecco 2003:20). This traditionalist or "conservative multiculturalism" (Gnecco 2003:20) stands in stark contrast to the ideologically utopian multiculturalism offered by practitioners in various fields, which see this as a means of fostering cross-cultural interaction and even the empowerment or "promotion of minority intellectual contributions as a counter to the dominant, majority culture" (Walker and Staton 2000:451; see Faulkner et al. 1994; Lewis and Ford 1990; Pinderhughes 1997; Weinrach and Thomas 1996). And just as postcolonial peoples have begun to appropriate notions of, and practices surrounding, cultural heritage for the purpose of identity politics, anthropologist Terry Turner (1993:411–412) points out that multiculturalism "has also assumed more general connotations as an ideological stance towards participation by such minorities in national 'cultures' and societies," and, particularly in what he calls "critical multiculturalism" it is conceived as "a movement for change… a conceptual framework for challenging the cultural hegemony of the dominant ethnic group." Yet, such processes eliding culture and the cultural construct of ethnicity often serve more to entrench separations between groups rather than blurring the boundaries between *us* and *them* aspired to in the American metaphor of multiculturalism, the so-called "melting pot." It creates, as Barth (1969) would say, not only fixed stereotypes of a particular group but the impetus for boundary maintenance—both by the minority and majority cultures, sometimes leading to the augmentation of disparities between the minority and the hegemonic groups.[3] Gnecco goes further to assert that such ideological discourses and practices concerning multiculturalism are dangerous for the minority groups, particularly in the heritage field, because it merely veils true problems of equality and representation; it "postpones" the resolution of the very tensions that it helped create and "does so by treating different

[3] This is especially the case in what Turner (1993:414) calls "difference multiculturalism," in which cultural distinctions are reified by "cultural nationalists and fetishists of difference, for whom culture reduces to a tag for ethnic identity and a licence for political and intellectual separatism."

conceptions of history as a mere isolated diversity" to be exploited by the heritage industry (Gnecco 2014; see also Martín-Barbero 2000). This occurs largely despite the good intentions of certain epistemic groups within the field of heritage production, including our own.

The problem with multiculturalism in general, therefore, is not that it is necessarily intended to be a thinly veiled excuse for maintaining the ruling power's hegemony but that it simply cannot truly unify divergent cultural practices when diverse cultures entertain fundamentally different—and often contradictory—understandings and traditions. To ensure a basic form of multiculturalism these conflicting practices, discourses and—in the case of heritage—uses must therefore be interleaved into an over-arching schema that totalizes, reifies and regulates them. These non-dominant groups, Asad (1993:254) argues, are therefore "not simply importers [or, in the case of the field of heritage production, espousers] of 'cultural differences' which they are free to synthesize and develop as they please in their new social environment;" rather, they must be "inserted into very specific economic, political, and ideological conditions." Thus, the hegemonic power "extends itself by treating them as norms to be incorporated and coordinated" (Asad 1993:261) and reduces minority cultural practices to a knowledge base to be competently negotiated, rather than actually valued and practiced (Walker and Staton 2000). In short, it perpetuates the very paternalistic ethical position against which multicultural ethics self-reflexively seeks to push back. This is not to say, however, that we anthropologists and archaeologists *wish* to act in a postcolonial, paternalistic fashion; indeed, many of us are highly sensitive to our ambiguous position as both advocates for, and also sometimes privileged experts over, our indigenous interlocutors.[4] Along with this, we run the risk of imposing, through our hegemony, our own well-intentioned "multicultural" values on other groups. As Pyburn and Wilk (1995:72–73) stated quite a while ago:

> Give *them* back their history, ask for *their* input on research design, make sure that all *relevant* groups are contacted, ensure that our research *benefits* the public—much current literature by archaeologists is alarmingly packed with these types of statements. While all these dicta are motivated by the highest of western values—well, that is exactly the problem. The new awareness of the rights of local groups has startled us into forgetting that we are anthropologists, and we are about to get caught foisting our value system rather thoughtlessly onto others under the guise of good deeds.

Particularly in certain situations when the designation and preservation of heritage objects are concerned, such ambiguity creates marked tensions when deciding the ethical path—the "right action"—one should take; these decisions are often—though, I argue, erroneously—couched as choosing between a "paternalistic" or "multicultural" ethic.

[4] To wit, one can read the essays in a now-dated special report of the Society for American Archaeology on ethics (Lynott and Wylie 1995), in which the contributors argue vociferously for the inclusion of indigenous interlocutors in their work. Tellingly, these same concerns continue to be voiced today.

Identity Politics, Archaeological Expertise, and Multicultural Ethics

This paradox is most clearly expressed when archaeologists' and anthropologists' work with heritage sites is implicated in different groups' struggle to construct and represent their own identities. Their relational acts of position-taking concerning a heritage site involves decontextualizing and recontextualizing it—a semiotic process built around acts of naming, framing and marking. Social scientists are particularly implicated in this activity for our professional practices also consist in pulling objects out of the context in which they were found and placing them in another context in which they can be analyzed, discussed, and presented to a broader public. Archaeology does this quite literally and something similar can be said of ethnography, no matter how "thick" the description of cultural practices may be (see Geertz 1973). Furthermore, as Hodder (2010:864) points out, excavation physically "destroys the very contextual information that it seeks to explore." Yet he reminds us that these actions are not simply destructive; they are also productive. They produce "a material outcome that has a public place;" they insert the object into broader social life, into more public discourse and, therefore, create new social relations in the world around it.

While UNESCO expanded the arena of social relations into a global "heritage-scape" (Di Giovine 2009b, 2010b, 2011) not all social groups are included and World Heritage discourses continue to prove contentious and destructive as certain groups stake alternative positions to UNESCO's meta-narrative of "unity in diversity." As Hodder (2010:870; see also Jacobs 2009) argues "The notion that the past is owned by someone is also necessarily conflictual. To claim an origin is always to exclude others, it is always to determine in-groups and out-groups. It is always about dividing populations." In constructing a World Heritage narrative, as with other heritage claims, certain aspects of the object's total life history are emphasized and others are forgotten in accordance with the needs and ideologies of the dominant social group (see Zerubavel 1995; Abu El-Haj 2001; cf. Bourdieu 1987); Smith (2006:11) in particular argues that this necessarily "undermines alternative and subaltern ideas about heritage." More tangibly, such heritage discourses often intentionally or unintentionally marginalize these subaltern groups. Since nation-states ultimately "offer up" their property to the heritage-scape they are the ones who shape the universalizing narrative—often (if not always) in a way that valorizes the nation with respect to other groups. Thus, while the World Heritage site of Ha Long Bay has been occupied by floating villagers for hundreds of years UNESCO's official narrative leaves out any reference to them, reflecting their long-standing social, legal, and political marginalization by mainland Vietnamese. This then translates into policy: while the Vietnamese government continues to build coal mines that seriously threaten the bay's delicate ecosystem and allows for more tourist junks that further pollute the water it was praised for its environmentally conscious efforts to instruct the floating villages to respect their own heritage by installing floating trash receptacles and immense signs telling them that "protecting Ha Long Bay is everyone's duty" (Di Giovine 2009b:253). Perhaps more nefariously, Meskell (2010:845) describes several South African cases in which the nation-state wrested land from indigenous groups, called it a national heritage site and then issued lucrative contracts to foreign companies to develop the areas into luxurious tourist resorts.

My fears for Yên Tử followed a similar vein: In addition to denying the multiplicity of "popular" religious meanings attributed to the site by diverse groups of pilgrims, contextualizing Yên Tử in terms of the historical significance of Buddhism for the nation-state will necessarily involve "forgetting" the quotidian importance of the place for those who presently make their living on the mountain. This will inevitably have material outcomes: the people (and their homes-cum-pilgrim restaurants) will be removed to ensure pristine natural vistas, and modern restaurant facilities will be erected nearby in a UNESCO-approved tourist center. Archaeologists and anthropologists therefore walk a fine line when carrying out such practices of decontextualization and recontextualization. It is clearly within the purview of archaeological practice to construct narratives about the past in relation to the material cultural remains in the site—but must we think about how such narratives of the past will then be employed to marginalize subaltern groups? As members of an "epistemic community" authorized to construct such "objective" narratives, are we necessarily part of the elite exponents of "authorized heritage discourse" (Smith 2006)? Can we speak for the subaltern? Can we be trusted to speak in their best interests?

Furthermore, this expert discourse often translates into practice. As Dingli (2006) acutely notes, universalized heritage sites (whether inscribed on UNESCO's list or not) are often managed through the principle of subsidiarity—that is, by outside experts rather than the local communities—and indeed, Pacifico and Vogel (2012) point out that archaeologists often attempt to play the role of expert advisors or consultants to local communities contemplating tourism and preservation initiatives. Of course, the most obvious of these authoritative practices is the role that UNESCO and its Advisory Bodies play in assessing, evaluating, and ultimately passing judgment on the "universal value" of, and local management plans for, on each potential World Heritage site. These Advisory Bodies are composed of scholars from relevant disciplines who are experts in evaluating individual properties' supposedly intrinsic value, while at the same time taking macroscopic view of how it can fit in with the ever-growing World Heritage List, something that is difficult for local experts to do. The fact that the government officials of Quang Ninh province felt it necessary to gain my own endorsement for their locally drafted management plans points to the importance postcolonial states continue to attribute (or are compelled to attribute) to the judgments of Western experts within the heritage field.

Recent events indicate that historically marginalized groups are beginning to push back on the "expert" authority of professional (Western) archaeologists and preservationists, particularly those from UNESCO's Advisory Bodies. For example, Meskell (2012) recounts how the recommendations by ICOMOS and IUCN at the 2011 World Heritage Committee meeting were disregarded by the majority of committee members, who came from the "global South"—thereby challenging their expertise and authority in an unprecedented fashion. Despite well-grounded objections towards inscribing a number of sites on the World Heritage List that year—including inadequate management plans that may have an adverse effect on the properties' future states of conservation—members of this bloc challenged the experts' authority by based on their subjective "feelings" concerning the site's importance. Such contestation must have stemmed from these groups' long-standing marginalization on the World Heritage List, which traditionally skewed towards Western conceptions of beauty, value, and monumentality (see UNESCO 1994)—and the Advisory Bodies who made their recommendations based on these notions. Similarly, Meskell and Masuku Van Damme (2007) and Shepherd (2003) discussed the polarizing effects of post-apartheid archaeologists and historians in mediating between tribal groups struggling over issues of repatriation, ownership, and reburial customs at the Iron Age site of Thulamela in Kruger National Park. Despite their comparative knowledge and experience with these issues the tribes viewed these experts skeptically, given the historical complicacy of the scientific community in perpetuating apartheid in South Africa (Meskell 2010:852).

As this last example shows the way in which archaeologists' expertise is utilized in the larger heritage field also has political implications that may produce unintended outcomes. For example, by inscribing in 2012 Nazareth's Church of the Nativity on the World Heritage List and the List in Danger under Palestine—which was not recognized by the United Nations as a legitimate state—UNESCO lost the financial support of the USA and Israel, which accounted for 22 % of its annual operating budget. Furthermore, the USA's sanctions might actually work against its best interests; China and Qatar may have gained power and diplomatic goodwill among UNESCO member-states when they assumed the USA's financial responsibilities (Anonymous 2012). And sometimes UNESCO's activities have had adverse material impacts on the very sites themselves. For example, when at their 2012 meeting in St. Petersburg the World Heritage Committee began to discuss inscribing Timbuktu's tombs of Sufi saints on the List of World Heritage in Danger in light of a fundamentalist coup in Mali the Islamist group promptly destroyed the monuments in an act of public iconoclasm; while UNESCO's actions were meant to mobilize the global community to protect this World Heritage site it really produced a public platform with which the group could both gain global prominence and conduct an effective act of psychological warfare against the (Muslim) citizens of Timbuktu who venerated the saints—in much the same way the Taliban did in the 2001 destruction of Afghanistan's Bamiyan Buddhas. A few years earlier UNESCO sparked a different sort of negative reaction when it designated the Khmer temple of Preah Vihear as a World Heritage site. Though straddling a border with Cambodia that Thailand has disputed for a century and at the time accessible only through Thailand Preah Vihear was listed only as Cambodia's, which seemed to lend tacit approval to the disputed geopolitical boundary. Riots soon broke out which ushered in a series of coups in Bangkok; Thailand closed access to the site and armies amassed on both sides of the site. To date there have been several skirmishes and more than a dozen soldiers' deaths on both sides.

However, like all players in the field of heritage production, academics and practitioners do push back by undertaking new practices relative to the position-taking acts of these other groups. For example, capitalizing on the aforementioned treatment of Ha Long Bay's floating villagers by the (terrestrial) Vietnamese government Amareswar Galla—a museologist, heritage scholar, and "intangible heritage" advocate, who is himself a member of a South Asian minority group—helped create the Ha Long Ecomuseum, essentially designating an entire floating village as an open-air museum. Like the government's billboard initiative his stated purpose was to educate the floating villagers in conservation and preservation (Galla 2002) and while the colonial notion of considering living humans alternatively as museum "objects" and as primitives to be educated has been criticized (see Di Giovine 2009b:256–258) this project should also be read as a way of co-opting prevailing prejudices concerning the villagers (as well as the government's desire to diversify tourist offerings at the site) to empower them—to involve them in some way with the burgeoning heritage tourism market from which the government explicitly marginalized them.

Tourism, Commodification, and Development

Many of the decisions affecting our position within the broader field of heritage production cannot be boiled down solely to identity politics between majority and minority groups—the hallmark of both paternalistic and multicultural ethics. Rather, our actions transcend these binaries, and indeed transcend these groups, to include other, often peripheral global epistemic communities that nevertheless have a stake in the ways in which the heritage property is signified, used and preserved—even if the primary objective of their involvement is not directly related to the property itself. Furthermore, these two ethical paradigms—focused, as they are, on this binary—also lacks a clear understanding and conceptualization of the site itself as a social actor, around which a variety of other players utilize, value, and make meaning of these places. The global, yet multifaceted, tourism industry provides an exemplary illustration of this: it involves a number of different groups, with varying understandings of, and values attributed to, a particular heritage object. Their goals certainly are incumbent on the preservation and valorization of a heritage property to a certain degree but are not necessarily explicitly centered on it: on the one hand, the primary objectives of for-profit tourism service providers are often economic. On the other hand, the satisfaction of this goal involves capitalizing on more elements than one discrete heritage object; it is achieved by delivering a successful experience of the total destination—which includes, yet transcends, that singular heritage site. Indeed, such an experience even transcends the mere visitation of "heritage sites" (or other tourist sites) themselves and is dependent on the satisfaction of other intangible issues such as creating and managing touristic expectations, providing appropriate (and often quite comfortable) lodging and efficient services and offering culinary experiences that meet clients' varied tastes and desires. Yet, importantly, these groups' needs and dispositions will impact the total meaning, use and value of the particular heritage site as much (if not more) than the interventions of archaeological experts or local stakeholders (Di Giovine 2009:145–185).

Nevertheless, the promotion of heritage tourism counts among the primary activities of the heritage field, since it is both the primary vehicle for diffusing heritage-centered narrative claims and also perceived to generate economic benefits; as tourism is the largest and fastest-growing industry in the world (UNWTO 2011) it also enables broader interaction among individual, locally based members of global epistemic groups. From the visitor's perspective heritage tourism can be considered "travel-related identity seeking where they visit monuments, historic sites and other places of interest in an effort to get a glimpse of where they came from and an understanding of how they define themselves" (Finley 2001). To cultivate processes of identity formation the "heritage" toured here does not have to be thought of as the tourist's own—though of course domestic tourism factors considerably in national cultural heritage management plans since the first European heritage legislations in the nineteenth century; indeed, engagement with alterity creates and reinforces cultural boundaries and stereotypes integral to identity formation (cf. Barth 1969).

Heritage tourism is not monolithic. Closely related to the Grand Tour one subcategory is archaeotourism, which involves the visitation of archaeological ruins and other tangible heritage sites (Giraudo and Porter 2010; Pacifico and Vogel 2012). Another, "roots" tourism often makes use of the archaeological record to present visitors from diasporic communities the opportunity to "return" to the "motherland," "home," or their imagined points of origin (see Basu 2007). Most popular examples include "birthright" tours of Israel for North American Jewish youths—which are often paid for by Israeli or American nonprofit organizations and juxtaposes tours of pre-Diaspora archaeological sites (the Wailing Wall, Masada) with stays at *kibbutzim* in which these students relive the difficult early twentieth century Zionist experience—and "roots" tours by African-Americans to West African destinations, in which travelers (including US President Barack Obama) visit, among other places, the UNESCO World Heritage site of Gorée Island and its "door of no return" through which slaves were loaded onto ships bound for the Americas (Schramm 2007; Sharpley and Stone 2009). Another notable form is thana-tourism or "dark" tourism—in which travelers encounter "heritage that hurts" (Sather-Wagstaff 2011; see also Seaton 2009). These are sites of war, death and genocide, and destruction—revealing man's inhumanity to man, and, morbid curiosity aside, reminding tourists of the extreme consequences when one group's sociocultural, political, or economic interests irreparably clash with that of another's. Battlefields (Normandy beach), prisons (Robben Island, Gorée Island), concentration camps (Auschwitz), sites of terrorist attacks (N.Y.'s "Ground Zero"), mass graves (Cambodia's Killing Fields), and ruins from natural or manmade disasters (tsunami-affected areas, Hiroshima, Chernobyl), are all examples of thana-tourism destinations. Furthermore, some of these (Hiroshima, Auschwitz, Gorée Island, and the empty spaces where the Bamiyan Buddhas used to stand) are inscribed on UNESCO's World Heritage List. I have elsewhere termed these "negative" heritage sites since their heritage narratives are the mirror image of traditional heritage claims; that is, they all seem to emphasize the transience of humanity, the divisiveness of human nature and the eradication of social groups—rather than their perpetuation—to promote UNESCO's meta-narrative of "unity in diversity" (Di Giovine 2009b:124–129).

Thana-tourism elicits many of the ethical critiques leveled against tourism in general by scholars from the social sciences, particularly those concerning the objectification and commodification of sensitive cultural materials—and of other peoples themselves. This is not necessarily a new issue, nor one from which archaeologists and anthropologists have been immune: private objects and material remains of the deceased have long found a place in the halls of museums and other tourist destinations without the consent of the cultural "owners," though laws such as the USA's Native American Graves Protection and Repatriation Act (NAGPRA) and new museologists' heightened sensitivity have begun to significantly change this practice—even though other tourist venues, such as Catholic Churches (with their relics) and science museums hosting exhibits such as Gunther von Hagens' *Bodyworlds* (see Di Giovine 2009a) more-or-less continue this practice. Tensions emerge when deciding on whose heritage is displayed at these "dark" sites and who is allowed to speak for, utilize, and profit from them: locals, the nation-state, foreign professionals or the affected groups for whom "dark" sites mark individual or collective suffering. As debates concerning NAGPRA showed what constitutes "safeguarding" also is an issue and traditional museological means of preserving and displaying may be in conflict with certain groups' notions.

Even when the heritage site itself does not generate direct material profit heritage tourism is often connected to larger economic development goals and, particularly, can reinforce—or create new forms of—public-private collaborations. Winter (2010) points out that new wealth and mobility in East Asian countries, primarily China and Korea, have created new forms of heritage travel and spurred new local-international partnerships in protecting and facilitating visitation to these countries' heritage sites. However non-Western these forms of travel and collaboration are Nash's early critiques of tourism as inherently imperialistic (1977)—another mode in which certain groups exert their hegemony over others—continues to hold sway. Indeed, while heritage sites in Southeast Asia had previously been restored and preserved through the intervention of former colonial powers in the region—particularly France, Japan, and the USA—today new restoration efforts and improved touristic infrastructures (such as a paved roadway leading to Preah Vihear) are being built through "gifts" and public-private joint ventures from China and Korea. Though many development practitioners continue to believe in tourism's economic benefits (see, for example, Wong et al. 2009) since the 1980s it has become clear that the tourism industry is inclined towards vertical integration, causing notable "leakages" of money and expertise out of the country and often enriching only select groups of elite locals who have the political or educational ability to interface with foreign tourism entities embedded in the area (de Kadt 1979; see also Di Giovine 2009c, 2010a).

Lastly, tourism development practices are often at odds with preservation. This is made clear by UNESCO's silence towards tourism in the early years of the World Heritage Convention; "tourism" is only mentioned once in the Convention and it is cited as a possible threat (UNESCO 1972:6). While "tourist pressures" such as wear-and-tear, graffiti and pollution are often cited broader environmental and social issues are often at stake as well. Building and maintaining hotels, golf courses, restaurants and resorts drastically consume limited natural resources, further limiting locals' access to fresh water, hunting and foraging grounds and may even displace them—thereby exacerbating class divides between locals, elites and tourists. For example, archaeologists who work at the Angkor Archaeological Park have complained privately that the construction of lush touristic resorts in the nearby town of Siem Reap has contributed to the deforestation of the surrounding forest and also is quickly draining the water table underneath the temples, putting the stability of their foundations at considerable risk—more so than any pressures millions of tourists exert on individual monuments by touching or walking through them.

Valorization and the Contribution to "Heritage Wars"

Direct economic gain in the long-term (either through tourism or economic assistance for historic preservation initiatives) is not the only reason that groups may incur economic expense and losses in managerial autonomy to open up sites of local or national import to the global heritage-scape. The valorization of the property's acknowledged "owner" is also a strong motivating factor for gaining broader recognition from outside authorities.

One perceived benefit is a country's legitimization on the world stage through the adoption of common models of what a nation-state should be (Anderson 2003; Meyer et al. 1997:163). While promoting a meta-narrative of worldwide "unity in diversity" UNESCO both relies on the nation-state to identify, nominate and protect its "universalized" sites as well as to sustain the World Heritage Convention (Omland 2006:250–251). Possessing World Heritage sites suggests that the developing country is a member of the international community and shares similar values (Labadi 2007; UNESCO 2008:9); of course, the nation's heritage-values may also be contested among national groups (e.g., Scham 2009). More practically, it also necessitates the construction of "global infrastructures," bureaucratic entities and other forms of state apparatuses that correspond with those in other nation-states, despite their diverse sociopolitical compositions. These offices are at once mediators linking the local to a broader network of global nation-states as well as translators that help outsiders—such as other groups in the global heritage field—"understand," support and sustain the country (Meyer et al. 1997:145). In short, UNESCO works with nation-states to enhance both the local and global contexts simultaneously through a now-diffuse phenomenon that Robertson (1994, 1995; see also Salazar 2005; Omland 2006:251) has termed *glocalization*.

Along with this, another perceived benefit is prestige (UNESCO 2008:9, 2011; cf. Dore 1974); like all Lists, the World Heritage List is exclusive, thereby indexing a particular value-based hierarchy (Schuster 2002). This often creates a high level of competition and in formal and informal talks with heritage professionals (and reading literature produced by tourism authorities) it is clear that many implicitly understand that the more sites a state possesses, the higher the value and legitimacy of that nation (see Di Giovine 2009b, 2014). Competition may occur when one group succeeds in designating its site while another fails in its effort to designate a similar property. Archaeologists and heritage professionals therefore may unintentionally contribute to what can become veritable "heritage wars," helping to perpetuate broader political competition between nation-states as they work to amass heritage in an almost museological practice of collecting sites for the sake of collecting (and status), sometimes without adequate regard for, or ability to, protect them—as what occurred during the 2011 World Heritage Committee meeting.

The Threat of Destruction: Illness or Symptom?

As the heritage field continues to produce heritage sites more potentially endangered places to safeguard and preserve will emerge, perpetuating the very system and our involvement in it. UNESCO frames these dual creating-and-saving actions as moral obligations on the part of local and national actors, on the one hand, and for the world community as a whole, on the other (Omland 2006), and the early successes of such initiatives reveal, at the very least, that this appeal is emotionally understood by different groups around the world. Preservation is a social issue that appeals in particular to archaeologists and anthropologists, concerned as we are with documenting, studying and preserving culture in its material and immaterial forms. Yet it is often decontextualized—like heritage-designating practices do to the sites themselves—from the broader social, political and historical contexts in which they are inserted. Like other social issues this creates further gray areas between the paternalistic and multicultural ethical paradigms as the call for preserving these highly valued natural and cultural sites could advertently or inadvertently mask deeper problems and larger issues; that is, the case for preservation—the very need for preservation—is often the symptom, not the result, of larger social and political issues.

Associated with both "salvage archaeology" and preservation initiatives this problem has certainly accompanied the World Heritage program from its earliest moments, beginning with the Aswan High Dam; focus was on the need to excavate and preserve, rather than on concerns for the displacement of people, poverty alleviation, despotism, and the broader Cold War dynamics that Nasser was playing.[5] As Kleinitz and Näser (2011) show in their discussion of Merowe Dam archaeological salvage project at Sudan's fourth Nile cataract locals may also work against the interests of preserving their cultural "property" in order to address deeper problems and inequities in their treatment by the government. Corruption, human rights violations, political instability, even civil or religious war also can be masked or, at least, de-emphasized by the call to save heritage properties. It should be noted that UNESCO (through its World Heritage Committee) did not call on the international

[5] Particularly salient is a *Time* article (1963) decrying the USA's early disengagement with the plan to "save" the temples; this inaction was, of course, a response to Nassar's acceptance of the Soviet Union's assistance in constructing the Dam!

community to assist in peacekeeping in Mali, to limit terrorist attacks on civilians or work towards eradicating the terrorist network supporting the Islamist uprising or even to alleviate the poverty and despotism that were at the root of the coup—but rather to save the ill-fated Sufi tombs. Another example of this is in Cambodia, where poverty, malnutrition and lack of medical care had historically led some locals to contribute to the black market looting of their prized temples in the Angkor Archaeological Park (cf. French 1999). In his scathing critique of development practice and corruption in the country Brinkley (2011) points out that foreign donors continue to give 1.1 billion dollars annually—of which millions are earmarked for conservation and tourism development projects at the Angkor Archaeological Park (see Winter 2007)—despite acknowledging that very little of it actually goes to its destination. While Brinkley (2011:299) argues that expat aid workers' greed is largely to blame (and surprisingly does not mention Angkor development projects at all) more telling is the refrain informants would repeat (a "popular rationalization," he calls it) that "some [help]…is better than nothing." With many stakeholders, many interests and many ways of profiting in doing the business of heritage, does doing a little immediate good justify perpetuating the very system that underlies these problems? What are the consequences of withholding funding and expertise in the short term? In the long term?

Conclusion: Towards an Understanding of Patrimonial Ethics

This chapter examined several areas in which archaeologists and anthropologists working in the field of heritage production find themselves delicately negotiating two different paradigms informing "right, fair, just or good" action: what I have called paternalistic and multicultural ethics. In these situations, their actions tend to moralize preservation and thus valorize the preservationists and, at the same time, call into question the morals of preservation practices themselves, particularly as they affect others. Multicultural ethics in particular attempt to elide these two Manichean concerns by "inserting" or otherwise "including" other stakeholder groups (particularly indigenous ones) into their overall preservation initiatives. Yet it is precisely for this reason that I have argued that multicultural ethics, while frequently well-intentioned, create or perpetuate the very tensions it seeks to resolve. I propose here a slightly different ethical paradigm, one that is centered both on a more robust understanding of the totality of stakeholder groups involved in the designation, preservation and management of a particular heritage property, their specific histories and, especially, the specific history of their interactions, as well as on the site itself. Indeed, for this latter point it is clear that both ethical paradigms, in their focus on relations between archaeologist and non-archaeologist, foreign and local, expert and non-expert, the focus on the heritage object itself tends to be obscured, if not lost. It is for this reason that I call this new ethical paradigm "patrimonial ethics."

Patrimonial ethics is concerned, first and foremost, with the heritage object itself. Indeed, while paternalistic or multicultural ethics largely inform many disparate anthropological and archaeological practices, my notion of patrimonial ethics is intended only to speak to our work within the heritage field—that is, when we are concerned with the issue of cultural resource management and the creation, identification, valorization and preservation of cultural "patrimony." This does not mean, of course, that we must privilege our own "expert" values, ideas and understandings of heritage preservation but it does underscore the need to shift our ethical focus—that is, what constitutes "right, fair, just or good" action—from other stakeholders to the heritage object itself or, at the very least, to conceptualize the object as one of the many discrete stakeholders with whom we are interacting and, indeed, towards whom our interactions are—or *ought* to be—focused. This means that we treat it as the social actor that it is (see Di Giovine 2009b), complete with its own "social life" (Appadurai 2005). We must therefore understand and be sensitive to the fact that any intervention we make will inevitably impact that object's life, its meaning and its relationship with other actors.

The first step in developing patrimonial ethics is to more fully understand the history and social structure of our engagement with the heritage object as taking place within a field of production (Bourdieu 1993) in which a variety of stakeholders (or "epistemic groups") are involved in nearly constant struggles, negotiations and acts of position-taking regarding the meanings, values and usages of particular heritage sites. We must understand that the so-called heritage industry (Lowenthal 1998) is not a monolithic entity whose priorities are exclusively economic nor that it is simply a political interaction between "indigenous" yet inexpert groups and foreign professionals but a field in which various stakeholders assign different uses and values to heritage and stake out various positions regarding heritage that are in relation to the positions of others. It is not simply that we concede that "nonarchaeologists may have different and valid ways of knowing the past" (Zimmerman 1995:65) but that there are nearly always a number of disparate and valid ways of knowing, understanding and valuing the past—historically and culturally situated within a variety of epistemic groups—that will impact the total significance of the heritage object. And that we must adjust our own "position," our own actions, accordingly.

Indeed, the second step is to recognize that we comprise one of these groups in the field, whether we want to be or not. Archaeologists and anthropologists therefore may wish to assess the entire situation of our engagement before involving ourselves: who are the key players and what are their positions? How are these positions constructed and against which other groups' positions? Who seem to be waiting on the sidelines (or relegated to the margins) and what stake do they have in it as well? For whose voices are we helping the heritage site to speak and whose are we helping to silence? We must assess the short-term effects as well as the long-term, keeping in mind the proclivity of the field to produce unintended consequences, composed as it is of nearly constant conflict between epistemic groups. But we must also be realistic: even if these questions elicit unfavorable answers, will they trump our desire to identify, study, preserve and safeguard these objects for posterity? Indeed, anthropologists and archaeologists have been historically involved in these activities: of extracting, possessing and exhibiting material remains, of examining intangible cultural practices and of advocating for the preservation of heritage objects to which we often ascribe a universalized set of values (whether or not they are termed "world heritage"). We are significant players in this field of heritage production, at times defining the very rules of the game (cf. Mahar et al. 1990:7). We do the business of heritage and we all are, to a certain extent, a significant part of the heritage business. Patrimonial ethics does not deny this; if anything, it forces us to recognize our position within the field, thereby allowing us a greater understanding of the complex entanglements in which we are involved.

Importantly, the third step is to also remember that the field of heritage production is not monolithic, global or universal—that is, it will not impact different sites in the same way. Rather, it is simply a model for understanding how diverse epistemic groups interact with one another to determine a particular heritage object's ultimate significance. That is, discrete heritage objects are individually "created" through the very specific composition of interactions of epistemic groups within a specific field of production at whose center it lies. Depending on the type, geographic location, political and economic history, past interventions, current management challenges, and level of global awareness of a particular object, different groups will coalesce around a heritage property with different intensities. Top global tour operators, for example, may devote a significant amount of resources to a particular site that is well-known, well-valued (perhaps designated a World Heritage site), well-located and well-embedded in the collective imaginaries of their biggest clients—such as Rome, Florence, or Venice—but less (or none) to a primarily locally valued, relatively unknown (to Western tourists) place with low accessibility and poor infrastructure. Conversely, local groups may stake a greater claim to a small, globally unknown local temple than to a nearby World Heritage site. In both of these cases we should not presume that these groups attribute the same value or significance to the site than we do, let alone to use it, share the same kinds of knowledge about it or ensure its preservation in the same way. In short, they might even share some idea that the site is a cultural "resource" or "property" of value to be passed onto future generations—a form of "patrimony," as Western a conception as it may be—but we should not presume that "patrimony" even means the same thing to them. Yet through the particular interaction between epistemic groups—with such disparate ideological understandings of the meanings, values, and practices attributed to the site—the heritage property will take on new significance and will be valorized in a unique way.

Thus, patrimonial ethics also recognizes that, since a heritage object's significance is individually determined by the particular configuration of epistemic groups within a specific field of production there can be no one guiding ethical principle for every heritage site nor one form of value that a site should possess. Rather, having a more robust conceptualization of the total field of production we can make better decisions on what specific actions are "right, fair, just or good" in the specific context. These decisions, therefore, begin not with the assumption that alternative voices concerning a heritage object must be integrated into our own conceptual framework but that there are multiple architectures of significances that will inevitably overlap, forming the specific field of heritage production. It is through teasing out these frameworks, through schematizing these architectures, which leads to understanding the specific patrimonial ethical action that is appropriate in the context. If this seems semantic, it may be; but it is also necessary to release the potential not only of the various epistemic groups coalescing around a heritage object but of the very object itself. And, as the aforementioned definitions of ethics make clear, unlocking the true potential of actors—bringing us all towards moral "goodness" and "improvement" by understanding what we *ought* to do rather than what is most obvious or convenient—is an integral quality of any ethical paradigm.

Acknowledgements This paper was written, in part, with the support of an Honorary Fellowship in the Department of Anthropology at the University of Wisconsin-Madison and the author would especially like to thank his research assistant at Madison, Avery Check, for her help during the final stages of writing this paper. Special thanks also are extended to David Pacifico and Raja Halwani who read and commented productively on an earlier version of this chapter.

References

Abu El-Haj, N. (2001). *Facts on the ground*. Chicago: University of Chicago Press.

Anderson, B. (2003). *Imagined communities*. New York: Verso.

Anonymous (2012, July 4). U.S. needs wiggle room to escape UNESCO trap. *Bloomberg View*. Retrieved August 31, 2012 from http://www.bloomberg.com/news/2012-07-04/u-s-needs-wiggle-room-to-escape-unesco-trap.html

Appadurai, A. (Ed.). (2005). *The social life of things. Commodities in cultural perspective*. Cambridge: Cambridge University Press.

Asad, T. (1993). *Genealogies of religion*. Baltimore: Johns Hopkins Press.

Barth, F. (1969). *Ethnic groups and boundaries*. Boston: Little, Brown and Co.

Basu, P. (2007). *Highland homecoming: Genealogy and heritage tourism in the Scottish diaspora*. London: Routledge.

Bourdieu, P. (1987). *The biographical illusion*. Working Papers and Proceedings of the Center for Psychosocial Studies 14, 1–7.

Bourdieu, P. (1993). *The field of cultural production*. New York: Columbia University Press.

Brinkley, J. (2011). *Cambodia's curse: The modern history of a troubled land*. New York: Public Affairs.

Chastel, A. (1986). La notion de patrimoine. In P. Nora (Ed.), *Les lieux de mémoire. Tome II: La Nation (II)* (pp. 416–445). Paris: Gallimard.

Dagens, B. (1995). *Angkor: Heart of an Asian empire*. New York: Harry N. Abrams, Inc.

Dao, D. T. (2008). *Buddhist pilgrimage and religious resurgence in contemporary Vietnam*. Doctoral dissertation, University of Washington, Seattle.

de Kadt, E. (1979). *Tourism: Passport to development?* Oxford: Oxford University Press.

Di Giovine, M. (2009a). Bodyworlds and Bodyworlds 2: Towards the construction of an instructive museum of man. *Museum Anthropology Review, 3*(1), 25–86.

Di Giovine, M. (2009b). *The heritage-scape: UNESCO, world heritage, and tourism*. Lanham: Lexington Books.

Di Giovine, M. (2009c). Revitalization and counter-revitalization: Tourism, heritage and the Lantern Festival as catalysts for regeneration in Hội An, Việt Nam. *Journal of Policy Research in Tourism, Leisure, and Events, 1*(3), 208–230.

Di Giovine, M. (2010). UNESCO's heritagescape: A global endeavour to produce 'Peace in the Minds of Men' through tourism and preservation. In R. P. B. Singh (Ed.), Heritagescapes and cultural lanscapes (pp. 57–86). New Delhi: Subhi Publications.
Di Giovine, M. (2010a). Rethinking development: Religious tourism to St. Padre Pio as material and cultural revitalization in Pietrelcina. *Tourism: An International, Interdisciplinary Journal, 58*(3), 271–288.
Di Giovine, M. (2010b). World heritage tourism: UNESCO's vehicle for peace? *Anthropology News, November*, 8–9.
Di Giovine, M. (2011). UNESCO's heritage-scape: A global endeavour to produce "peace in the minds of men" through tourism and preservation. In R. Singh (Ed.), *Heritagescapes and cultural landscapes* (pp. 57–86). Delhi: Shubhi Publications.
Di Giovine, M. (2014). World Heritage objectives and outcomes. In C. Smith (Ed.), *Encyclopedia of global archaeology* (pp. 7894–7903). New York: Springer.
Dingli, S. (2006). A plea for responsibility towards the common heritage of mankind. In C. Scarre & G. Scarre (Eds.), *The ethics of archaeology: Philosophical perspectives on archaeological practice* (pp. 219–241). Cambridge: Cambridge University Press.
Dore, R. (1974). *The prestige factor in international affairs*. Proceedings from the 23rd Stevenson Lecture. London: London School of Economics.
Dworkin, G. (2010). Paternalism. In E. Zalta (Ed.), *The Stanford encyclopedia of philosophy*. Retrieved April 26, 2013 from http://plato.stanford.edu/archives/sum2010/entries/paternalism/
Edwards, P. (2007). *Cambodge: The cultivation of a nation (1860–1945)*. Honolulu: University of Hawaii Press.
Faulkner, A., Roberts-DeGennaro, M., & Weil, M. (1994). Introduction: Diversity and development. *Journal of Community Practice, 1*(1), 1–8.
Finley, C. (2001). The door of (no) return. *Common-Place*, 1(4). Retrieved August 31, 2012 from www.common-place.org/vol-01/no-04/finley/
French, L. (1999). Hierarchies of value at Angkor Wat. *Ethnos, 64*(2), 170–191.
Freud, S. (1950). *The standard edition of the complete psychological works of Sigmund Freud* (Vol. XIV). London: The Hogarth Press.
Galla, A. (2002). Culture and heritage in development: Halong Ecomuseum, a case from Vietnam. *Humanities Research, 9*(1), 63–76.
Ganjanakhundee, S. (2011). Walkout: More loss than gain. *The Nation*, June 28. Accessed from http://www.nationmultimedia.com/2011/06/28/national/Walkout-More-loss-than-gain-30158865.html. on August 26, 2014.
Geertz, C. (1973). *The interpretation of cultures*. New York: Basic Books.
Giraudo, R., & Porter, B. (2010). Archaeotourism and the crux of development. *Anthropology News, 51*(8), 7–8.
Gnecco, C. (2003). El erotismo de la desnudez arqueológica. In C. Gnecco & E. Piazzini (Eds.), *Arqueología al desnudo. Reflexiones sobre le práctica disciplinaria* (pp. 5–24). Popayán: Universidad del Cauca.
Gnecco, C. (2009). Archaeology and multiculturalism. Paper presented at the American Anthropological Association annual meeting, Philadelphia.
Gnecco, C. (2014). Multicultural archaeology. In C. Smith (Ed.), *Encyclopedia of global archaeology* (pp. 5074–5082). New York: Springer.
Hafstein, V. (2009). Intangible heritage as a list: From masterpieces to representation. In L. Smith & N. Akagawa (Eds.), *Intangible heritage* (pp. 93–111). London: Routledge.
Harrison, D. (2005). Introduction: Contested narratives in the domain of World Heritage. In D. Harrison & M. Hitchcock (Eds.), *The politics of World Heritage: Negotiating tourism and conservation* (pp. 1–10). Bristol: Channel View Publications.
Harvey, D. (2001). Heritage pasts and heritage presents: Temporality, meaning, and the scope of heritage studies. *International Journal of Heritage Studies, 7*(4), 319–338.
Harvey, D. (2008). The history of heritage. In B. Graham & P. Howard (Eds.), *The Ashgate research companion to heritage and identity* (pp. 19–36). Aldershot: Ashgate.

Hewison, R. (1989). Heritage: An interpretation. In D. Uzzell (Ed.), *Heritage interpretation* (The natural & built environment, Vol. I, pp. 15–23). London: Belhaven Press.
Hodder, I. (2010). Cultural heritage rights: From ownership and descent to justice and well-being. *Anthropological Quarterly, 83*(4), 861–882.
Jacobs, J. (2009). Repatriation and the reconstruction of identity. *Museum Anthropology, 32*(2), 83–98.
Kipling, R. (1899). The white man's burden. *McClure's Magazine.*
Kleinitz, C., & Näser, C. (2011). The loss of innocence: Political and ethical dimensions of the Merowe Dam Archaeological Salvage Project at the fourth Nile cataract (Sudan). *Conservation and Management of Archaeological Sites, 13*(2–3), 253–280.
Knorr-Cetina, K. (1999). *Epistemic cultures: How the sciences make knowledge.* Cambridge: Harvard University Press.
Labadi, S. (2007). Representations of the national and cultural diversity in discourses on World Heritage. *Journal of Social Archaeology, 7*, 147–170.
Lewis, E., & Ford, B. (1990). The network utilization project: Incorporating traditional strengths of African-American families into group work practice. *Social Work with Groups, 13*(4), 7–22.
Lowenthal, D. (1998). *The heritage crusade and the spoils of history.* Cambridge: Cambridge University Press.
Lynott, M., & Wylie, A. (Eds.). (1995). *Ethics in American archaeology: Challenges for the 1990s.* Washington: Society for American Archaeology.
Mahar, C., Harker, R., & Wilkes, C. (1990). The basic theoretical position. In R. Harker, C. Mahar, & C. Wilkes (Eds.), *Introduction to the work of Pierre Bourdieu: The practice of theory* (pp. 1–25). New York: St. Martin's Press.
Martín-Barbero, J. (2000). El futuro que habita la memoria. In G. Sánchez & M. E. Wills (Eds.), *Museo, memoria y nación* (pp. 33–63). Museo Nacional: Bogotá.
McCabe, H. (2005). *The good life: Ethics and the pursuit of happiness.* New York: Continuum.
McCrone, D., Morris, A., & Kiely, R. (1995). *Scotland—The brand. The making of Scottish heritage.* Polygon: Edinburgh.
McGimsey, C. R., III. (1995). Standards, ethics, and archaeology: A brief history. In M. Lynott & A. Wylie (Eds.), *Ethics in American archaeology: Challenges for the 1990s.* Washington: Society for American Archaeology.
Meskell, L. (2010). Human rights and heritage ethics. *Anthropological Quarterly, 83*(4), 839–860.
Meskell, L. (2012). The rush to inscribe: Reflections on the 35th Session of the World Heritage Committee, UNESCO Paris, 2011. *Journal of Field Archaeology, 37*(2), 145–151.
Meskell, L., & Masuku Van Damme, L. S. (2007). Heritage ethics and descendant communities. In C. Colwell-Chanthaphonh & T. Ferguson (Eds.), *The collaborative continuum: Archaeological engagements with descendent communities* (pp. 131–150). Thousand Oaks: AltaMira Press.
Meyer, J., Boli, J., Thomas, G., & Ramírez, F. (1997). World society and the nation-state. *The American Journal of Sociology, 103*(1), 144–181.
Nash, D. (1977). Tourism as a form of imperialism. In V. Smith (Ed.), *Hosts and guests: The anthropology of tourism* (pp. 37–52). Philadelphia: University of Pennsylvania Press.
Omland, A. (2006). The ethics of the world heritage concept. In C. Scarre & G. Scarre (Eds.), *The ethics of archaeology: Philosophical perspectives on archaeological practice* (pp. 242–259). Cambridge: Cambridge University Press.
Oxford Dictionaries (2013). *Ethics.* Oxford: Oxford University Press. Retrieved April 22, 2013 from http://oxforddictionaries.com/us/definition/american_english/ethics
Pacifico, D., & Vogel, M. (2012). Archaeological sites, modern communities, and tourism. *Annals of Tourism Research, 39*(3), 1588–1611.
Pinderhughes, E. (1997). The interaction of difference and power as a basic framework for understanding work with African-Americans: Family theory, empowerment and educational approaches. *Smith College Studies in Social Work, 67*(3), 322–347.
Preston, N. (2007). *Understanding ethics.* Leichhardt: The Federation Press.
Pyburn, K. A., & Wilk, R. (1995). Responsible archaeology is applied anthropology. In M. Lynott & A. Wylie (Eds.), *Ethics in American archaeology: Challenges for the 1990s* (pp. 71–76). Washington: Society for American Archaeology.

Rey, T. (2007). *Bourdieu on religion: Imposing faith and legitimacy*. London: Equinox Publishing.
Robertson, R. (1994). Globalization or glocalization? *Journal of International Communication, 1*(1), 33–52.
Robertson, R. (1995). Glocalization: Time-space and homogeneity-heterogeneity. In M. Featherstone, S. Lash, & R. Robertson (Eds.), *Global modernities* (pp. 25–44). London: Sage.
Said, E. (1994). *Orientalism*. New York: Vintage Books.
Salazar, N. (2005). Tourism and glocalization. "Local" tour guiding. *Annals of Tourism Research, 32*(3), 628–646.
Sather-Wagstaff, J. (2011). *Heritage that hurts. Tourists in the memoryscapes of September 11*. Walnut Creek: Left Coast Press.
Scham, S. (2009). Diplomacy and desired pasts. *Journal of Social Archaeology, 9*, 163–199.
Schramm, K. (2007). Slave route projects: Tracing the heritage of slavery in Ghana. In F. de Jong & M. Rowlands (Eds.), *Reclaiming heritage: Alternative imaginaries of memory in West Africa* (pp. 71–98). Walnut Creek: Left Coast Press.
Schuster, M. (2002). *Making a list and checking it twice: The list as a tool of historic preservation*. Chicago: University of Chicago.
Seaton, T. (2009). Thanatourism and its discontents: An appraisal of a decade's work with some future issues and directions. In J. Tazim & M. Robinson (Eds.), *The Sage handbook of tourism studies* (pp. 521–542). London: Sage.
Sharpley, R., & Stone, P. (2009). *The darker side of travel: Theory and practice of dark tourism*. Bristol: Channel View Publications.
Shepherd, N. (2003). State of the discipline: Science, culture and identity in South African Archaeology 1870–2003. *Journal of Southern African Studies, 29*, 823–844.
Sidgwick, H. (1981). *The methods of ethics*. Indianapolis: Hackett Publishing Co.
Silverman, H., & Ruggles, F. (2008). Cultural heritage and human rights. In H. Silverman & F. Ruggles (Eds.), *Cultural heritage and human rights* (pp. 3–22). New York: Springer.
Smith, C. (1991). Museums, artefacts and meanings. In P. Vergo (Ed.), *The new museology* (pp. 57–72). London: Reaktion Books.
Smith, L. (2006). *Uses of heritage*. London: Routledge.
Time Magazine (1963, April 12). The pharaoh and the flood. *Time Magazine online*. Retrieved September 4, 2011 from www.time.com/time/magazine/article/0,9171,828111-1,00.html
Turner, T. (1993). Anthropology and multiculturalism: What is anthropology that multiculturalists should be mindful of it? *Cultural Anthropology, 8*(4), 411–429.
Tylor, E. B. (1871). *Primitive culture*. London: John Murray.
UNESCO (1945). *Constitution of the United Nations Educational, Scientific and Cultural Organization*. London, November 16, 1945.
UNESCO. (1972). *Convention concerning the protection of the world cultural and natural heritage*. Paris: UNESCO.
UNESCO. (1982). *Nubia: A triumph of international solidarity*. Paris: UNESCO.
UNESCO (1994). Expert meeting on the "Global Strategy" and thematic studies for a representative world heritage list. (WHC-94/CONF.003/INF.6). Paris: UNESCO, 20–22 June 1994.
UNESCO. (2003). *Convention for the safeguarding of the intangible cultural heritage*. Paris: UNESCO.
UNESCO. (2008). *World heritage information kit*. Paris: World Heritage Centre.
UNESCO. (2011). *65 ways UNESCO benefits countries all over the world*. Paris: UNESCO.
UNWTO. (1974). Establishment of the World Tourism Organization. *Annals of Tourism Research, 2*(2), 83–88.
UNWTO. (2011). *UNWTO tourism highlights*. Madrid: UNWTO.
USNPS (n.d.). World heritage. Retrieved August 31, 2012 from http://www.nps.gov/oia/topics/worldheritage/worldheritage.htm
Walker, R., & Staton, M. (2000). Multiculturalism in social world Ethics. *Journal of Social Work Education, 36*(3), 449–463.

Weinrach, S., & Thomas, K. (1996). The counseling profession's commitment to diversity-sensitive counseling: A cultural reassessment. *Journal of Counseling and Development, 74*, 472–477.
Winter, T. (2007). *Post-conflict heritage, postcolonial tourism: Culture, politics, and development at Angkor*. London: Routledge.
Winter, T. (2010). Heritage tourism: Dawn of a new era? In S. Labadi & C. Long (Eds.), *Heritage and globalization* (pp. 117–129). London: Routledge.
Wong, M., Christie, I., & Al Rowais, S. (2009). *Tourism in South Asia. Benefits and opportunities*. Washington: The World Bank.
Wylie, A. (1999). Science, conservation, and stewardship: Evolving codes of conduct in archaeology. *Science and Engineering Ethics, 5*, 319–336.
Wylie, A. (2005). The promise and perils of an ethic of stewardship. In L. Meskell & P. Pels (Eds.), *Embedding ethics* (pp. 47–68). London: Berg.
Zerubavel, Y. (1995). *Recovered roots*. Chicago: University of Chicago Press.
Zimmerman, L. (1995). Regaining our nerve: Ethics, values, and the transformation of archaeology. In M. Lynott & A. Wylie (Eds.), *Ethics in American archaeology: Challenges for the 1990s* (pp. 71–74). Washington: Society for American Archaeology.

Chapter 14
Archaeologies of Intellectual Heritage?

Lesley Green

"A *sambaqui?* The holy grail of archaeological debates here... and you aren't pursuing it?" The moment was as awkward as the question. It was being posed by a leading public intellectual on a hot, muggy evening at an outdoor restaurant table in Oiapoque, at an impromptu dinner of academics and researchers whose paths had converged in this town to which the *Lonely Planet Guide to Brazil* had said not to go. I had no idea how to begin an answer. Persuading my interlocutor would have required trying to defend the instinct of the field researcher: the kind of hunch that is the embryo of an argument which has yet to find its words. A sip of beer provided a few seconds to choose battle or retreat. I chose retreat and passed the salad, trying to prevent the wan grin of the idiot from appearing on my sunburnt face.

I am not an archaeologist, but an anthropologist with an interest in the relationship between states, sciences, and publics. At the time, the project of which I was part (Fordred-Green et al. 2003) was trying to identify possible archaeological sites, based on a careful study of Amerindian narratives in the Palikur language, within a participatory project (Green and Green 2013).

The site in question is a mound of shells: a "monte", in Portuguese: bigger than what can be conveyed by the word "mound" but smaller than the derivative "mountain". The sheer scale of it, surrounded by forest, is what is surprising: about 30 m

This article is dedicated to the memory of Ivanildo Gomes, Palikur school principal, field guide, and challenger-in-chief to intellectual charity in any form, who passed away in tragic circumstances in August 2012. Much of my thinking here is informed by the memory of dialogues that were so difficult for both of us. Research was supported by the Wenner Gren Foundation, the South African National Research Foundation, the World Archaeological Congress and the University of Cape Town. I thank David Green for facilitating the fieldwork and translating the stories included here

L. Green (✉)
School of African and Gender Studies, Anthropology and Linguistics, University of Cape Town, Private Bag x3, Rondebosch, 7701 Cape Town, South Africa
e-mail: lesley.green@uct.ac.za

C. Gnecco, D. Lippert (eds.), *Ethics and Archaeological Praxis*,
Ethical Archaeologies: The Politics of Social Justice 1,
DOI 10.1007/978-1-4939-1646-7_14

by 16 m, and deep, with surface shells being younger and more whole, and deeper shells being darker and more fragile, and more likely to be crushed. A colleague who specialised in shell mounds had put one of the larger shells under a lab microscope, and shown us the unmistakeable evidence of filing, rather than accidental breakage, around the edges of the two holes in it. The implication was that a long time ago, human hands had probably made it into a necklace. We (David Green and I) did not do any excavations there, nor did we plan to: not being archaeologists, all we could do was to find the place mentioned in the stories of Waramwi (Fig. 14.4), the Cobra Grande, which is a large, mythical anaconda (see Vidal 2007). But much as the site itself was automatically protected by Brazilian laws on heritage and patrimony, it was also a place that, more than any other, was under the protection of the kind of strong feelings that cause a site to be labelled as "sensitive". Understanding what that was or why it should be so, would take more than a few interviews or story recordings. It was not that we needed "initiation" into some kind of "sacred knowledge", but more that there were a lot of basics that we did not understand, so people struggled to talk with us about what we could not grasp.

From the beginning, the project had struggled with the gradual realisation that a participatory research ethic was stretching our basic assumptions. The first concerned the possibilities offered by multiculturalism and a social construction of knowledge, with a growing sense that a sociocultural politics of knowledge—our view; their view—was inadequate to capture the complex processes at work in dialogues about sites and places. The second concerned the assumption that archaeological and anthropological researchers had any right to produce knowledge about the sites. This did not make the project or us or locals somehow "anti-science": far from it. The issue was much more complex than any readily available set of positions might allow for, since what was at issue was knowledge itself, in its ontology and episteme, and in the history of the assumption that there is one ontology and one episteme that produces only one truth about the past. An identity-based relativism seemed too quick and easy a backstop to discussion, for its assumption was that ethnicity—or DNA itself—shaped knowledge, when clearly we were surrounded by thinking people who were as keen to critique received ideas as we were, and it was more and more apparent that writing off new local ideas as cultural pollution was an insult to our hosts.

Of all the places we looked at, the shell mound at Ivegepket offered a particular challenge to the anthropology of knowledge. It forced a confrontation with the idea that animism and reason were the two opposite poles that defined what "we" did and what "they" did. In this paper, I want to make a (virtual) return to this site in relation to some ideas about the politics of intellectual heritage, in order to try to find that elusive "line of flight" from the assumption that we are trapped into a choice between declaring accounts of places to be either myth or knowledge. In attempting to open up a different place from which to speak about the heap of shells of Ivegepket, this chapter addresses questions of ethics, politics, and rationality in anthropological and archaeological practice (Fig. 14.1).

Waramwi-givin (Waramwi's home) is on the island called Ivegepket, or Lookout Place. Somewhat higher than the surrounding landscape, it offers a good view of a length of the Arukwa river, otherwise known as the Rio Urucauá, which winds its

Fig. 14.1 Xoni Batista at Ivegepket. Photo: David Green

way through the flooded grasslands and islands of coastal rainforest on the Brazilian section of the Guianas, in the north-eastern quadrant of South America. Home to remnant clans of Arawakans and associates who had been decimated by wars with Caribs and explorers in the era of the European expansion, Arukwa is a *pantanal* that offers an abundance of freshwater and forest hunting, as well as access to mangrove life and soils rich enough for agriculture.

Waramwi-givin was, the story said, marked by a mound of seashells on Ivegepket that was known as Waramwi-giyubi (leftovers or garbage). From various hunters' anecdotal descriptions, we suspected might be a shell midden or sambaqui, similar to other sambaquis along the coast of French Guiana and northern Brazil. That one man had shown us an alligator carved from stone that he said he had long before found there, made the island even more interesting, as zoomorphic lithics are associated, in this region, with very early settlement.

To get to Ivegepket we had gone downriver by motorboat with a dugout canoe precariously balanced across the gunwales, then paddled for most of a day through the flooded grasslands. By the time we had reached the point of land where hunters usually made camp, it was late afternoon. As before, within an hour our team had set up a structure for hanging all the hammocks, using our tarpaulin for a roof where usually they would have cut palm leaves to make a thick thatch. When it was complete, three of the group went out to explore the surrounds, and we heard a shot close by. Apparently a jaguar had been on a rocky outcrop and was about to spring, and a shot from a small calibre revolver had wounded it. It had disappeared, leaving a trail marked with drops of blood. It was the first time that any of us had been threatened by a predator, and that combined with the knowledge that there was a wounded jaguar in the area made all of us edgy. To add to the difficulties, I became violently ill in the night. In the morning, Ivailto set off to get me some plant medicine—some sap from a vine, and some shavings from the bark of a tree. They made a huge difference to my strength, but I was in no condition to walk and spent the day in a hammock at the camp while the rest of the group searched for the shell mound. Late that afternoon, the group came back carrying the carcass of a deer: the most prized of all wild meat. It was carefully carved up and salted, and people were anxious to return home to take it to their families. David and I were unwilling to leave so soon, however, and pointed out that we had not come here on a hunting trip. It was a point of difficulty: one that was vested in the difference between our respective economies, and our senses of self in them. We were there to hunt knowledge, secure in the assumption that the inherent value of the work paid for our enormous cans of tuna and that in not hunting here ourselves, we were being appropriately environmentally responsible, and they were coming along to assist. But it was not so simple. They were well paid, certainly, but were not employees in the sense that David or I could "call the shots". Moreover, they were under no obligation to participate in our moral economy, with all the contradictions that attend a global trade in canned tuna, or slabs of meat sold under clingfilm on polystyrene from a local supermarket. In the emerging tensions, I began to glimpse the different "cogitos" in play: my "cogito" was the "cogito ergo sum" variety, in which research paid my bills and gave me a place in the knowledge economy that was paradoxical in its remove from the environment it sought to protect. In that context, theirs was more of a *cogito ergo como*—I think therefore I eat. For the first time, we found ourselves on a jungle trip where there was a sense of the team actively pulling in different directions. I felt vulnerable; acutely aware that I had very few of the skills necessary to surviving in the swamp or the forest on my own.

We searched the island the next day, split in two groups, and again found nothing. We went out onto the water to look at the island from further away, to try to get a sense of the lie of the land. The island itself was low and it curved around our canoe, almost like a giant anaconda. Huge clouds rolled in, followed by a deluge. Supper that night was quiet; the meat of the deer sweet and delicious, but the timeframe of rotting was upon us. Piranhas had devoured the remaining flesh on the bones and entrails in the swamp water where they had been left. The canoe in which the meat had been prepared, reeked. Clearly, the salt on the meat itself would stave off rotting only another day at best.

The third morning, we again split into two groups, and it was clear that happiness was not the dominant emotion. Separate conversations in low tones were something we were not familiar with, in this team we felt we knew so well. In late morning the familiar "puggghhhh" sounded—someone blowing through his shotgun like a trumpet—and the groups converged in that direction, to find a long, low shell mound, much bigger in scale than I could possibly have imagined, with an unpleasant smell and, all over it, an unfamiliar vegetation. But people were silent and tense, talking quietly in a small group apart from us. I was puzzled and a little offended. David and I measured the length and breadth of the mound and took a few samples for testing and made our way back to base camp with Xoni, while the others walked separately. We packed up quickly, leaving behind piles of stinking deer meat. Only a few pieces were still good. Poling and heaving the canoe through the grassland took a long time, and in the ensuing hours we passed through six or seven cloudbursts. When we got to the river, Kiyavwiye Nenelio was waiting for us in a motorboat. He said he had been there all of the day before, as he had been anxious about us, and was just about to depart a second time. I realised only much later that his concern was about our wellbeing in the space of Waramwi.

Many days later, Ivailto apologised for the tension. He had, he said, been affected by the smell of the shell mound, and it had affected his thinking.

The tension was unusual within the group of five normally genial Palikur men who had accompanied us on many similar trips. The response to our return was equally unusual. From an article written shortly after that trip:

> On our return to Kumenê, people were amazed that we had found Waramwi-givin—and in contrast to the relative disinterest that had characterised our return from prior jungle trips, there was intense interest in the small bags of shells that we had gathered for the laboratory. Everyone wanted some. People came to visit our house especially to see them. That we had found "Waramwi's garbage" was, paradoxically, confirming the myth for some, but for those with whom we had worked closely, it gave the lie to it. A day later, from [my] notebook:
>
> I got back to the house an hour or so after feasting on pakig [wild pig] at the church festival. Found Nenel (Ivanildo's step-father) and Ivanildo in quite an earnest conversation. Couldn't understand exactly what was being said but they were talking about Waramwi and the ancestors (amekenegben) and their stories. The feeling of the conversation was of consternation. Nenel sighed, "Yuma Waramwi!" (No Waramwi). His tone indicated the conclusion of the conversation; the summary; the finding. A sense of surprise and dismay. I asked—pivewken henewa yuma Waramwi? (Do you truly think there was no Waramwi?). Yuma (none) he said. Mmahki? I asked (why?). Ivanildo started to explain. When he got to the shell mound yesterday and saw there was no hole (i.e. cavern, or route into the underworld), he was intensely disappointed. There was no Waramwi hole at the shell mound at all. So how could it be true? It is a myth, he said, "like the story that the whites discovered Brazil 500 years ago." So the stories that the old ones tell, are just myths, with no truth in them at all.

The discussion in that paper concluded with the following:

> If heritage is ultimately a cultural construction, one route for public archaeology here would be to prioritise local versions of history over professional assessment of the material record. Yet such an answer is unsatisfactory given the importance of the historical realities to which sambaqui sites in the region attest… Is it possible to proceed on such a site with as much caution over narratives and sensibilities as artefacts? Such questions are pertinent to several sites that mark mythical and sacred stories about the past… Unthinking excavation can bury these meanings.
>
> M]ultiple histories attend [a site like Ivegepket], of which the authorised archaeological version is but one. Recognising this forces one to accept one of two conclusions. The first possible conclusion is that where radically opposed understandings of the past surround a particular site or series of sites, one should retreat from further work there. The second is more delicate: to explore the values of opposed historiographies. This entails recognising that archaeological scholarship is a valid enquiry into past human activity on a landscape, yet a more powerful one because it is more readily accepted in the wider public sphere. Ethnohistory is equally valid in that it is grounded spatio-temporally rather than chronologically and memorialises the skills that continue to enable the mastery of a landscape. In this sense, the Waramwi narrative marks something of great importance.

Reading these lines now, a number of lines of critique are apparent.

First, I am not surprised at my inability then (as primary author) to understand the cosmological significance of the site. Almost a decade later, only after David had translated almost 4,000 min of Palikur narratives that he and I had recorded as part of the larger project (1997–2008), did I begin to glimpse the importance of Waramwi as not only a participant in life here along the Urucauá, but also as a teacher of how to think, in order to eat, and in order to survive.

Second, I am surprised that I could not see that artefacts themselves are not given, but emerge in relation to particular interests and narratives and technologies. What appears as a piece of dirt or garbage to one, is a vital carbon sample or domestic fragment to another. Artefacts, in other words, emerged in relation to the narratives we brought in to the situation, and the wider networks in which we told them. For this reason, I am enormously grateful to Brazilian anthropologist Lux Vidal for her thoughtful counsel to consider avoiding the site, as I am to Eduardo Góes Neves, the archaeologist who directed the excavations elsewhere in the area some months later, for not forcing the issue at all. With hindsight, it was the right decision not to proceed to work there, for reducing the site to a set of material artefacts defined in spatial and temporal relationship to one another would have dismembered the very memories we would have hoped to engage.

Third, in the text, the idea of mythical and sacred stories reiterated the belief-knowledge divide: we had knowledge; they had belief. Such a binary was the quickest of shorthands: an idea that occluded other ideas and insights about what it is to know or to have knowledge about the past. It made it impossible to work with partial connections and local critical thinking. It resolved different versions of nature into an argument that we had different cultures. Putting that binary aside does not mean dissolving knowledge and belief into one thing, for that would make impossible any critical thinking at all. But rushing to characterise as belief all different ways of knowing, makes impossible any conversation about what it is to know; how one knows, or why one knows, or what it is to be someone that knows.

Fourth, the related dualism of indigenous knowledge and science that I was imposing pays little attention to the history of the rise of the idea of "indigenous knowledge" as an opposition to "science". The problem here is that those categorisations of difference are deeply rooted in the history of coloniality, race, and power (Green 2012). To take them as real, in the sense of being ontological givens, is deeply problematic. Moreover, one of the consequences of taking them as givens is that the categories themselves "occult" (in the sense used in astronomy, when one body occludes another) what Marilyn Strathern would call partial connections. For example: the account notes that Ivailto had said that there was no hole at the shell heap, as the stories had specified that there would be, and that this was provoking consternation and rethinking. If that moment is read (as it was then) as an instance of "indigenous knowledge being challenged", the consequence is a moral panic about the ethics of scholarly enquiry; about positionality and social construction and power and imposition. It is easy, in such a scenario, for archaeology to be "bad" and "polluting" where indigenous knowledge is held to be "good" and "pure". There are several problems with the approach. First, these are moral positions more than they are scholarly arguments. Second, a multiculturalist tolerance[1] can be insulting, as the same logic would, for example, ask an Amerindian why he builds with bricks and corrugated iron instead of wood and palm thatch. Third, it denies indigenous people the space in which to think critically about received wisdoms.[2] The ontology of "IK vs. Science" in the 2003 paper made me so anxious about my own (apparent) power as a researcher to impose a hegemonic idea, that I missed the partial connection: that both Ivailto and I were asking questions about what it means to know what has gone before.

[1] For a discussion of tolerance and multiculturalism see Stengers (2011).

[2] In the context of a very different argument to mine, Meera Nanda (2003) calls this "epistemic charity."

By contrast, an anthropology of knowledge that does not take "indigenous knowledge" as a given, fixed category, is able to work with this along a different grain: to think about how Ivailto was asking questions, and producing knowledge. It allows a very different engagement with regional knowledge: instead of my taking on a rather patronising responsibility to protect and conserve his knowledge (on the assumption that it is fixed) from my way of making knowledge (on the assumption that my way was uniquely inquisitive, open to critique and revision), a more promising way of working is to open a discussion about what is to know, and how one makes knowledge (Verran 2013). That approach works with intellectual heritage per se, which includes asking questions of all the knowledge in play, including the knowledge (or at least, the idea) about how we make sense of difference. This is not to assume there is no difference, as to impose sameness would be to go to the opposite extreme. Rather, the question is how do different ways of seeing bring different aspects of reality to the fore, and what critiques are possible of each.

These kinds of questions emerge from a shift in theorisation of knowledge that moves on a different track to that proposed by multiculturalism. In working with knowledge, multiculturalism proposes that the reason for difference is "culture". That version of culture sees it as given object; a social whole that the critical humanities have long since abandoned (see Sharp and Boonzaier 1988; Latour 2005). Rethinking the analytic and explanatory value of culture confronts one with a different set of questions: about the intellectual heritage of modernist thought, and the argument that nature is universal and given, while difference is simply cultural. In working with these questions, anthropological research on narratives and landscapes and knowledge in an archaeological work can widen its terms of reference to include intellectual heritages on all sides of the table. The implication is that the modernist version of nature that undergirds archaeological work is not the only "naturing" that is possible in the world. Such an argument sits on the interstices of science and technology studies, on postcolonial and decolonial thinking, and research on indigenous movements (see Blaser 2009, 2010; De la Cadena 2010, 2013; Escobar 2008; Viveiros de Castro 2004a, b). Most importantly, the debates open up different possibilities for thinking about the ethical in archaeological field research. Why this should be so, is the focus of the remainder of this paper. For if "nature" is not limited to the scientific account of "natural objects", then it might be possible to think with different kinds of ontologies or "naturings". In this regard, the section that follows here explores what the Waramwi site might mean (Figs. 14.2 and 14.3).

Waramwi is a significant figure among the creatures of the landscape[3]: someone in whom people are genuinely interested—precisely because he is an ambivalent figure. He is a person and an anaconda; he is a predator that had to be outwitted; he is part of the land and also the ocean, and his pathways extend to the upper worlds and under world. He is immensely strong, yet was outwitted by an ill, old and ailing Palikur man: a common theme in Palikur narratives, where almost always the smaller and weaker beat the strong. Waramwi is a person who puts on the cloak of an ana-

[3] For a full version of the story of Waramwi with an extended discussion see Dos Santos et al. (2013).

Fig. 14.2 Ivanildo Gomes. Photo: David Green

Fig. 14.3 The *Waramwi Giyubu* or sambaqui at Ivegepket, along the Rio Urucaua. Photo: David Green

conda and becomes one, and as such, the story of Waramwi is in many senses a story about how to work with a person when they take on different perspectives. As an anaconda, for example, Waramwi and his wife Wanese see children as parrots. In the story of Waramwi, the old man who outwits him has to understand how Waramwi and Wanese are seeing the world: he has to take on their consciousness. Waramwi is invested in the landscape in the shell mounds at Ivegepket, and he is also invested in pathways through this landscape to other worlds. The shell mound, for that reason, is a rich resource and a challenge, for it teaches a range of ways of thinking.

Foremost among these is the principle of *perspectivism*[4]: learning to understand the way of thinking of a creature with a different body. Uwet explains: "He saw so many parrots here! Plop! In the water. But he did not see them as if they were in the water. He saw them as if they were way up in the tree tops. He saw them, as if we would see them, way up in the trees." Waramwi is looking at children playing in the water, but he sees parrots as if they were squawking in the trees. Similarly, Waramwi's fishing net is made of many small anacondas: "He threw out his fishing net. There were lots of fishing nets. He threw them onboard, but they were [actually] little anacondas. A fair size. Anacondas, like this." His rifle is his tongue: "He shot amongst the children but it was with his tongue! It. They say it was with a rifle, because he splashed down so forcefully. He made [a sound] like a rifle with his tongue amongst the children." Most important is to understand that a different way of seeing the world, and a different body, go together. So while Waramwi is at times a person, he can put on the body of an anaconda: "It was a large cloak. The anaconda [had] such a huge cloak. He took it. Zip! Plop! Inside of it. "Farewell!" He left. Because Waramwi, he was also like a person." But Waramwi can also take on the body of the predator by taking on the thoughts and ways of seeing of a predator: "He arrived there. He took a good look. He looked [at their bodies?] well. He returned. When he returned then. He came [back] then. He did not come as a person any longer. Now he came as a complete axtig [predator, eater]!"

Part of the skill of knowing how to survive in this landscape is the skill of being able to understand the world as another creature would, and to act accordingly. A central dramatic tension in this story is that of the old man who goes to live with Waramwi in order to try to rescue the children. Named Tunamri, the old man becomes the guardian of Waramwi's child. Having become "one of the Waramwi family", he is faced with the awful dilemma of having to kill his own people. This aspect of the story exemplifies the moral and practical dilemma of perspectivism: how to inhabit another's world, but still be ethical in one's own. In the following extract, Waneseg, Waramwi's wife, hears the children (as parrots) and tells the man to go and catch them for supper: "She heard the squawking of parrots. She said, "Young man! Go quickly [and shoot for me] the parrots! I do not want to send your father… He is [cross; grumpy?]. You go quickly!" He observed this. He went. He arrived there. He saw only his relatives swimming in the water! He stood up there. He looked on! He saw his relatives. He saw that one. His nephew. He saw that other one. His uncle. He was all alone in the water! He said, "What shall I do now?" He observed [them, above, all gathered together?] He shot. Bang! [Pale smoke rose

---

[4] For discussion on perspectivism see Lima (2005), Vilaça (2005) and Viveiros de Castro (2004a, b, 2012).

up?] Scatter! ["Was it where they climbed ashore?"] He looked. [He hit] not a single one! Then he left. He arrived up to his mother. She said, "And did [you hit any]?" He said, "I shot. I did not hit them." Now his mother said to his father, "Come and take a look at older brother. Why can he not hit those [parrots]? Look at his arms." "So be it then." He brought his arms there, to his father. "Stretch out your arms, this way." He poked his arms. Poke! He [Waramwi] pounded [massaged] there. He said, "It is better than mine. (Why) are you a bad shot with that one? Why can you not hit anything? Because you [are letting too many escape]!" Now he pounded him well."[5]

Waramwi's massaging of the man's arms brings about a partial transformation, echoing an idea noted elsewhere in Amazonian literature that massage transforms a person, potentially transforming their body into the likeness of the person who is doing the massaging (see Viveiros de Castro 1987; Rival 1998; Oakdale 2007; Gow 2000; Lagrou 2000). In Uwet's story, the effect of the massage is clear:

> Then he pounded [the other arm], this way, again. Now he poked the [other arm]. He pounded it also. He said, "Good! It will not make you a bad shot. [How can you possibly be a bad shot?]! [Everything should be on target]!" Now when he was fivnished the massage then. Afterwards, he sent him out. [There was] loud squawking! "Go now!" He went. He arrived there. He found two of them. Different people, who were not his relatives… He caught two young men. Bang!

The message is clear: in becoming another, you are still yourself: both "not I" and "not not-I".[6] Waramwi, in other words, is a figure who exemplifies Amerindian right to the land in general, and Palikur right to it in particular. Yet that right is not a right in the sense of universal law (although it does not exclude such a right), but in the sense that one who understands the landscape, is one who can survive. The knowledge Waramwi offers is not a collection of knowledge (in the sense that an Encyclopaedia might offer) but an approach to making knowledge. As such, Waramwi could be said to be an archetypal figure who teaches what it is to know the world from multiple perspectives—that is, from multiple bodies, for the world is made of multiple bodies all of whom are interacting with each other. That body includes the body of the landscape itself, for the river is a creature that acts in the world, and a place has (and offers) a way of seeing. In order to act in the world effectively you need to be able to anticipate how other bodies are going to act and in order to be able to do that you need to be able to see as they see, to inhabit another's body, to transform oneself into that body. Amazonian literature has many examples of predation as a way of taking on another's perspective and in this sense an anaconda is an iconic creature for it alone among predators can take another's body whole into itself. Waramwi, then, stands as a figure that crosses between species and worlds—and, importantly for the purpose of an essay such as this, is one whose story proposes an ethics of multiple perspectives. In this sense, perhaps an indigenous archaeology on a site such as this is literally about re-membering: taking on a different body. By contrast, an objectivist account of

[5] The Waramwi story cited here is excerpted from Dos Santos et al. (2013). Translation from the Palikur into English by David Green.

[6] The phrase is from Willerslev (2007).

the site would indeed have dis-membered local knowledge, in the sense that objective science specifically seeks to avoid any form of embodiment.

It took many years to begin to grasp the implications of the site at Ivegepket for what it is to know the world and make knowledge of it. Only then could I begin to grasp—perhaps—why it was that our trip to that site had been fractious and difficult. There was, throughout that trip, a real sense that an anthropological and archaeological project was something of a blunderbuss and it was the first time that I encountered serious questions about the ethics of defining archaeological sites in the area. My sense at the time was that there were too many moments of consternation around the site to justify further site visits. After a long discussion with Brazilian anthropologist Lux Vidal, who cautioned that the story of Waramwi was too important to risk the imposition of a narrative of archaeological truth, I made the decision to recommend that any further archaeological enquiry here be pursued on less sensitive sites. It was around that moment—amid what Helen Verran calls "a vulnerable dialogue"—that the dinner guest in Oiapoque had asked the questions about what it was that we thought we were doing.

Verran's argument about working across epistemic difference in a discussion on conservation biology in Aboriginal Australia places great value on the figure of the idiot in philosophy. Citing Deleuze and Guattari (1994:61) she writes:

> The term idiot… refers to one of philosophy's conceptual personas, a shadowy, mysterious "something else… that appears from time to time or that shows through and seems to have a hazy existence halfway between concept and preconceptual plane, passing from one to the other…The [old rationalist] Idiot says "I" and sets up the *cogito* [and] also lays out the plane [in which concepts appear]". The poser of questions about knowledge practices, the new idiot, has no wish for the indubitable truths of singularism, the simplifications of rationalism, but insists on ineluctable and irresolvable complexity (Verran 2013).

Such insights are welcome in finding words for those moments, like the one with which I opened in this paper, in which fieldwork experiences begin to yield insights that at times make it difficult, if not impossible, to speak to established scholarly authority. Isabelle Stengers (2010) speaks of the ecology of ideas: the recognition that in any science (in this case, formal archaeology) the conceptualisation of a situation as an evidentiary requires it to be framed as a set of particular objects. Scientific nature, in other words, is not pre-given; its objects are generated by a particular way of thinking about evidence as objects, as matter set in space and time. The work of Bruno Latour (1999a) with soil scientists in the Amazon is compelling; it offers for archaeologists and indigenous people an alternative mediation: rather than setting scientific nature in opposition with indigenous culture it begins to be possible to think about different ways of making nature into a particular set of representations, as reality. This does not assert at all that there is no reality, rather, that there are multiple "naturings". A way of thinking based in movement, for example, attends to flows and motion in ways that integrates space, time, and bodies; it is a way of "naturing" that does not, in my view, need to be disaggregated and reassembled into the Cartesian view of nature as matter set in space and time. There is nothing inherently wrong or untrue with Cartesian "naturing"—other than the claim that it is the only way of "naturing". The implication for archaeologies and anthropologies that

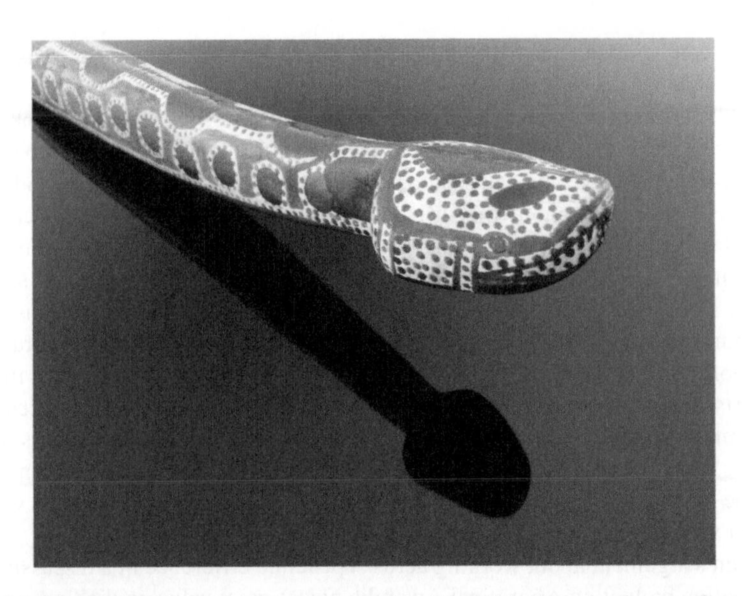

Fig. 14.4 *Waramwi* the anaconda: the carving by Uwet Manoel Antônio dos Santos, afloat. Photo: David Green

struggle towards a different ethics in their engagements with publics of all kinds is that it opens possibilities for what Eduardo Viveiros de Castro calls "a symmetrical anthropology"—a way of working that includes both the researched community and the research community in its field research. Moreover, rather than assuming that true nature will emerge in the application of rigorous research methods it asks questions about its own research methods (epistemology) and its assumptions about nature itself (ontology). Rather than taking scientific nature as a given set of facts that must (or ought to guiltily) overlay "myth" or "belief" it becomes possible to approach "myth" and "belief" and "animism" from a different angle: that of the history that renders some ideas "nature" or "theory" and others "mythic", "sacred" or "other". The issue is not simply one of a politics of epistemology. Rather, it goes to the history of ideas in modernist thought, in which the ontological divide between objects and subjects establishes scientific objects as facts that lie outside of the realm of human relationships and networks (Fig. 14.4).

The implications of the possibility of multiple conceptualisations of nature—or what I would call "naturings"—for ethical archaeological engagements with indigenous communities are significant, as the discussion is no longer limited to "dealing ethically with different culture" and can begin to engage different intellectual heritages themselves. Isabelle Stengers calls for a "slow science" that is able to take the time to rework received understandings, ready ideas, available narratives, given objects. Following Deleuze and Guattari on the value of the idiot one can begin to recognise the value of "idiot moments" and to see in them the moment at which the basic tenets of agreement no longer provide the certainty of truth or what to do next. Thinking back to my awkward moment at the dinner table so many years back I can recognise now the value of the moment in which an extensive period of field research had caused me to no longer be able to speak to scholarly company about a particular issue. The moment was a rude confrontation with the reality that ways of thinking about the site were so different and that none of the tools of my own training had equipped me to make sense of the experience that very different ethical obligations were in play, in response to very different naturings. Perhaps one might begin to think of moments like that as moments of partial connection, in which the divide between scholarship and what we have termed "the indigenous" begins to break down[7] and one begins to comprehend the incomprehensible.

The project we had designed had been forged in dialogue with WAC's proposals for an ethical and participatory archaeology, which asked for different social and cultural versions of the past to be part of archaeology. Yet what the Waramwi site brought us up against was that if only "culture" or "social construction" are to be admitted to the debate about different versions of historical reality we were left holding all the cards of truth, for true nature remained in the hands of scientific techniques: cartography, geometrics, emplacement, chemical analyses, technologies for studying the traces of movement in wear and use. The Waramwi site proposes that knowing the world is about understanding that there are many ways in which nature comes to appear real and that what appears as one thing to someone in a lab coat or with a funding grant might appear to another person (or creature) as something else. Such an approach—which has a great deal in common with what others have called a relational ontology[8]—provides the beginnings of a different conversation about an ethical archaeology for it does not insist on a single version of nature. That is not because there is no real reality (Latour 1999b) but because it recognises that ways of making the world begin with the *cogito*—that is, with who one understands oneself to be and what it might mean to survive—whether at a dinner table of competitive academics or a forest full of predators. The irony: the concepts that make the story of Waramwi meaningful are very close to this set of insights. It makes the point that a hunter learns: that in order to understand and predict another's behaviour one must grasp that the world appears differently to different people, bodies, species. It proposes that when one takes on the body of another—as a hunter might do or a thinker—one responds to the world differently. There is not one singular nature that appears true to all in the same way nor need it to be so in order for different creatures, species, beings or people to operate effectively in the world.

What does this mean for archaeologies and anthropologies of places like Ivegepket? Ivegepket has not been excavated. Perhaps one day it might be and perhaps the necessary dialogue could be facilitated by archaeologists. But I think that the ethical choice not to excavate there, right then, gave us time and opportunity to do a different kind of archaeology. This is not the kind of work that maps objects in

[7] The argument about intellectual heritage that I am exploring here also calls into question the categories "indigenous" and "scholarship" themselves as concepts that come to have meaning, are enacted and historically generated.

[8] For a lucid exposition see Lien and Law (2011).

space and time but a kind of archaeology that engages the intellectual heritages that counter modernity. Whether we call the shells *waramwi-giyubi* or a *sambaqui* they speak to different concerns and different rationales for being a person-who-knows. The challenge is to move beyond matching perspectives, theirs to ours, to an engagement with the real challenges that are the challenges of "the real": the possibility of different empiricisms; different "cogitos". There is perhaps a different archaeology to be done on sites like this: not an archaeology of nature (materials) or of culture (cultural ideas) but an archaeology of the ecologies of knowledge and knowing, an archaeology of intellectual heritages and their value in grasping multiple ways of knowing and making, ecologies of knowledge.

References

Blaser, M. (2009). Political ontology: Cultural studies without "cultures"? *Cultural Studies, 23*(5–6), 873–896.

Blaser, M. (2010). *Storytelling globalization from the Chaco and Beyond*. Durham: Duke University Press.

De la Cadena, M. (2010). Indigenous cosmopolitics in the Andes: Conceptual reflections beyond "politics". *Cultural Anthropology, 25*(2), 334–370.

De la Cadena, M. (2013). About "Mariano's archive": Ecologies of stories in contested ecologies. Nature and knowledge: Local theory and vulnerable dialogues in southern Africa, Latin America and Australia. In L. Green (Ed.), *Dialogues on nature and knowledge in the south*. Cape Town: HSRC Press.

Deleuze, G., & Guattari, F. (1994). *What is Philosophy?* London: Verso.

Dos Santos, U. M. A., Green, D., & Green, L. (2013). *Waramwi: A cobra grande*. Sao Paulo: IEPE.

Escobar, A. (2008). *Territories of difference: Place, movement, life, redes*. Durham: Duke University Press.

Fordred-Green, L., Green, D. R., & Neves, E. G. (2003). Indigenous knowledge and archeological science: The challenges of public archeology in the Reserva Uaçá. *Journal of Social Archaeology, 3*(2), 366–397.

Gow, P. (2000). Helpless. The affective preconditions of Piro social life. In J. Overing & A. Passes (Eds.), *The anthropology of love and anger* (pp. 46–63). London: Routledge.

Green, L. (2012). Beyond South Africa's "indigenous knowledge" versus "science" wars. *South African Journal of Science, 108*(7/8), Art. #631.

Green, L., & Green, D. R. (2013). *Knowing the day, knowing the world: Engaging Amerindian thought in public archaeology*. Tucson: Arizona University Press.

Lagrou, E. (2000). Homesickness and the Cashinahua self: A reflection on the embodied condition of relatedness. In J. Overing & A. Passes (Eds.), *The anthropology of love and anger* (pp. 152–169). London: Routledge.

Latour, B. (1999a). *Pandora's hope: Essays on the reality of science studies*. Cambridge: Harvard University Press.

Latour, B. (1999b). Do you believe in reality? In *Pandora's hope: Essays on the reality of science studies* (pp. 1–23). Cambridge: Harvard University Press.

Latour, B. (2005). *Reassembling the social: An introduction to actor-network theory*. Oxford: Oxford University Press.

Lien, M., & Law, J. (2011). Emergent aliens: On salmon, nature and their enactment. *Ethnos, 76*(1), 65–87.

Lima, T. S. (2005). *Um peixe olhou pra mim: o povo Yudjá e a perspectiva*. São Paulo: Editora UNESP, Instituto Socioambiental e NUTI.

Nanda, M. (2003). *Prophets facing backwards*. New Brunswick: Rutgers University Press.
Oakdale, S. (2007). Anchoring "the symbolic economy of alterity" with autobiography. *Tipiti: Journal of the Society for the Anthropology of Lowland South America, 5*(1), 59–78.
Rival, L. (1998). Androgynous parents and guest children: The Huaorani couvade. *Journal of the Royal Anthropological Institute, 4*(4), 619–642.
Sharp, J., & Boonzaier, E. (1988). *South African keywords*. Cape Town: David Philip.
Stengers, I. (2010). *Cosmopolitics I*. Minneapolis: Minnesota University Press.
Stengers, I. (2011). *Cosmopolitics II*. Minneapolis: Minnesota University Press.
Verran, H. (2013). Engagements between disparate knowledge traditions: Toward doing difference generatively and in good faith in contested ecologies. In L. Green (Ed.), *Dialogues on nature and knowledge in the south*. Cape Town: HSRC Press.
Vidal, L. B. (2007). *A cobra grande: uma introdução à cosmologia dos povos indígenas do Uaçá e Baixo Oiapoque, Amapá*. Rio de Janeiro: Museu do Índio.
Vilaça, A. (2005). Chronically unstable bodies: Reflections on Amazonian corporalities. *Journal of the Royal Anthropological Institute, 11*, 445–464.
Viveiros de Castro, E. (1987). A fabricação do corpo na sociedade Xinguana. In João Pacheco de Oliveira Filho (Ed.), *Sociedades indígenas e indigenismo no Brasil* (pp. 31–41). Rio de Janeiro: UFRJ/Editora Marco Zero.
Viveiros de Castro, E. (2004a). Perspectival anthropology and the method of controlled equivocation. *Tipití: Journal of the Society for the Anthropology of Lowland South America, 2*(1), 3–22.
Viveiros de Castro, E. (2004b). Exchanging perspectives: The transformation of objects into subjects in Amerindian perspectives. *Common Knowledge, 10*(3), 463–484.
Viveiros de Castro, E. (2012). Cosmological perspectivism in Amazonia and elsewhere. Four lectures given in the Department of Social Anthropology, Cambridge University, February–March 1998. *Hau Masterclass Series*, Vol. 1. HAU Network of Ethnographic Theory, Manchester.
Willerslev, R. (2007). *Soul hunters: Hunting, animism and personhood among the Siberian Yukaghirs*. Berkeley: University of California Press.

Chapter 15
Just Methods, No Madness: Historical Archaeology on the Piikani First Nation

Eldon Yellowhorn

Introduction

I doubt I would have chosen this career if it led me down nefarious paths. Instead I write this chapter because I am an ardent supporter of archaeological work. The analogy I would cite to make sense of it is in regard to my personal estate. I possess real and portable property, some of which I could liquidate and some that I can only describe as memento that I keep because of their significance to my family. Thus, this heirloom effect is the motive that compels me to do archaeological research. I begin with the premise that Aboriginal people possess a duty of stewardship for the heritage sites they have inherited from their ancestors. Therefore, we have to be advocates for them and use any means to advance this ideal. I feel I am doing a service to my community by appropriating the methods I need to pursue internally defined objectives. This internalist approach to archaeology places me in charge of the research agenda and my professional training informs my practice.

The search for guidance to animate ethics in archaeology takes place at a very high level of abstraction. Statements developed by professional organisations rely on global declarations that attempt to provide direction for their members and they typically contain monolithic principles that their membership agrees to uphold. Although exclusive to a specific association, they do filter to our broader constituency because of public interest in the work we do and how we do it. Thus, practice occurs at a low level of abstraction so the methods we deploy in our fieldwork and in the laboratory create the fascia of our discipline that the world sees. Connecting them becomes necessary when provenance jostles up against perspective and creates the friction that sparks discord. The ensuing discourse on ethics and praxis emerges

E. Yellowhorn (✉)
Department of First Nations Studies, Simon Fraser University,
8888 University Drive, SWH9083, Burnaby, BC, Canada V5A 1S6
e-mail: ecy@sfu.ca

C. Gnecco, D. Lippert (eds.), *Ethics and Archaeological Praxis*,
Ethical Archaeologies: The Politics of Social Justice 1,
DOI 10.1007/978-1-4939-1646-7_15

independent from any inherent qualities that methods possess. Here I discuss my own experience with historical archaeology, and in particular the programme I carry out with the endorsement of the Piikani First Nation, using techniques that are basic for the task.

Anyone trained in field methods, would recognise my survey strategy because I rely on remote sensing techniques, such as air photographs, and recording way points with a global positioning system (GPS) and storing them using software that is designed to handle large masses of data typical of landscape archaeology. As with any dig, I began by establishing a local datum and then I determine where to place the several 1×1 m units before proceeding to excavate them in 10 cm levels. Artefacts unearthed in this manner were the raw data that we cleaned, measured, described, catalogued and packed away. Back on campus my student assistants and I employed analytical methods such as spreadsheet software to organise data on charts and tables to aid our interpretations. We used laboratory methods, such as microscopy, to make detailed observations and photography to put together an image bank. Due to the shallow time depth of these artefacts we could research trademarks, media or any distinguishing traits, such as colour, to identify them.

Historical archaeology is all about inferring a narrative about the places we study and by triangulating the data from the three-cornered constellation of archival documents, material culture and oral history. Therefore, since Piikani history from the early reserve days is so poorly documented the artefacts and features I find provide an opportunity to elicit details from tangible sources that might otherwise elude notice. While my internalist approach to archaeology is pragmatic in its insistence on appropriating the methods to aid this exploration, it is also about mediating the dialogues between the local and the global explanations for the human experience. In searching for the roots of our identity, and introducing our history to a modern generation through my studies, I am trying to better understand the prevailing conditions of those generations that made the transition to reserve life. The Piikani internal dialogue about the past is a self-reflexive chronicle of how today's conditions became our reality. Internalist archaeology places a community's unique history at the centre of the investigation and applies standard methods to generate new knowledge about seminal events and the built environment (Yellowhorn 2006a).

Historical Archaeology in Canada

When practitioners of historical archaeology first began to ply their trade in Canada, they worked within a very narrow definition, which was the identifiable presence of Europeans at a site (Kidd 1969:5). Helge Ingstad had already discovered the earliest historic site when he unearthed the Viking outpost at L'Anse aux Meadow in the province of Newfoundland. In the scheme then in vogue, there would be no more historic sites made for several centuries after the abandonment of Vinland, whereas those labeled "aboriginal sites" would continue to proliferate. Given the perception that history and a European presence were synonymous, implying that it started up again when they returned, the complaint that "American historical archaeology's emphasis on the colonial and immigrant experience has been 'ethnified'" (Rubertone 2000:425) is easy to grasp.

Colonial history in Canada is all about the fur trade and the sites associated with that era, so these were typically the loci of research for historical archaeologists. Right from the start, they grappled with the empirical methods they contrived to control their database. Unaware that the biases implied by their model could only generate inadequate definition that frequently identified anomalous sites. For example, sustaining that concept ignored some aspects of indigenous trading networks that brought aspects of European culture, such as horses, into regions where no white person had visited. Horses had a transformative effect on plains cultures long before they had direct contact with the fur trade. Blurring the borders between categories caused the next generation of historical archaeologists to wonder whether those neat tables and charts were implying a doubtful dichotomy, especially since the range of sites kept expanding.

Since the 1960s, historical archaeology has moved past the strict distinction based on fur trade material culture. Native people had been excluded from those early sites to the extent that one archaeologist (Kennedy 1997:xviii) stated:

> I am well aware that we know far more about the archaeological record of Euroamericans than we do of the native people who formed the other half of the trade equation. With that realization, my own research over the past few years has been directed towards the identification of native archaeological sites of the fur trade era, so a more equitable picture of culture contact can be gained.

She expressed a sentiment common to her generation because they understood that two settlements of Aboriginal people existing coeval to each other could not be classified separately based on the presence of material culture from Europe. Archaeologists trained in innovative methods, such as isotope analysis, learned to elicit history from unwritten sources, so the occurrence of textual artefacts was no longer mandatory. Such data have proven so reliable that they routinely form part of the repertoire of methods used in field and laboratory work.

By the time I entered the fray in 1993 historical archaeology was already breaking free of its ties to the fur trade. Various places received formal recognition as heritage sites, particularly the built environment that contained architectural genres from specific times, and the expectation of time-depth became more flexible. I had just completed my MA degree and I was about to learn what Margaret Kennedy meant when she wrote of "the other half of the equation".

Fresh out of graduate school and gainfully unemployed, I jumped at the opportunity offered by the McLeod Lake Indian Band, a Tsek'ehne community north of Prince George, British Columbia. There along the shore of McLeod Lake was an old fur trading post, founded by Simon Fraser in 1805, that was the nucleus of the mission and village their ancestors built. The band's immediate interest was an archaeological dig to explore the potential for cultural tourism to generate employment in their community.

As a supervisor of a crew of five students, I organised our activities around standard methods of excavation. Given the overarching objective, and the multiple occupations, anywhere I selected to dig would produce results. I outfitted my troop with trowels, dustpans, buckets and whiskbrooms, all the while assuring them that ours was a scientific endeavour. We set up a station for sifting the matrix through screens so as to be thorough in our examination. We dutifully made notes of our finds, wrapped the artefacts in lunch bags and catalogued them for later analysis. However, there was a narrative associated with the material culture that complemented the written accounts of fur traders. I discovered how interrogating antiques from any age elicited insights about their particular time and place. Moreover, that was where we would find traces of Tsek'ehne ancestors and the conditions they encountered when they left behind their traplines to take on village life and a wage economy.

Knowledge dissemination figured prominently in our public communications strategy, but people began visiting our digs simply because they were interested in what we were finding. So in the waning days of that summer we hosted a 2-day open house and invited tourist to attend and sample customary Tsek'ehne hospitality. We constructed a campsite with the habitations typical of their traditional culture. Elders participated by demonstrating skill for bush life and living off country foods. Although our invitation was extended to the travelling public, there was an equal level of interest among village residents because they had never seen exhibitions dedicated to their culture.

As 1994 rolled along, the band concentrated on restoring the factor's residence, which had fallen into disrepair due to neglect. Once the log building was renovated and the exhibition was installed, it became the anchor for the heritage park. Interpretive signage related to visitors the story of the post and the cemetery we reclaimed from under a crown of vegetation. Opening day arrived and the small crowd eagerly awaited the invitation to enter after the ribbon cutting. Local residents mixed with visitors to view the old photographs on display and read the signs explaining the artefacts in the showcases. Since there was a huge gap in the local historical record, the exhibit was enthralling for a Tsek'ehne audience that was unaccustomed to hearing about their ancestors' contributions to the fur trade.

From my experience I demonstrated that the archaeological record was a valuable, albeit undiscovered, source for information about Tsek'ehne people and their presence in local history. And that archaeology provides a bundle of methods that we deploy to help us gain insights about those days. If we have some about ourselves, that is a bonus. Whether they are useful for field surveys, or analysis, such as taxonomies, or bring us to the laboratory, for example, to radiocarbon date a specimen, methods exist to accrue and organise data (Yellowhorn 2006b). Our analytical tools help us bring order to the confusion of artefacts, features and sites we encounter in our searches. Even the scientific method is just that, a systematic method for gathering in observations. I learned that archaeology is most effective as a vehicle that helps us reach a goal. I came to the conclusion that getting public allies is essential because that support was in archaeology's best interest. While unearthing fascinating stuff that might lead to publications that benefit my career, I became aware that I had to bestow some real advantage for my hosts. Therefore, leaving a legacy that enriches the local community from the research I do became crucial for generating an atmosphere of collaboration. In this case, the final product was a museum and heritage park around the theme of the fur trade in Tsek'ehne history. However, creating meaningful work for local residents was just as fulfilling.

Internalising Historical Archaeology

When I decided to take the archaeology career path, it had no analogue in the Piikani world even though its focus was on the ancient manifestations of plains cultures. Research questions skipped over contemporary peoples and focused on the Ice Free Corridor, regional chronologies, environmental variation and technological changes. Plains archaeologists organised their data using taxonomies that deflected any connection to Piikani or other Aboriginal people. Interest in local archaeology did foster a vibrant tourist economy when Head-Smashed-In Buffalo Jump was recognised as a World Heritage Site. Exhibitions that attract travelers to the site extol the challenge of a technique for communal hunting that disappeared with the arrival of the horse in Blackfoot culture (Ewers 1955). Given its prominence in plains antiquity, it also figured large in my own training. When I started conducting my own field research, I would regularly spend days scouring the landscape looking for evidence of bison kill sites or stone tools (Brink 2005). I studied the way modern land use jostled against them and suggested legal remedies for heritage protection on reserve lands and how to mitigate the impact (Yellowhorn 1999). I overlooked historic sites due to my own bias because my interest had always been directed to those with an older provenance.

While growing my experience as a consultant on impact assessments I routinely encountered historic sites that did not fit conventional definitions I learned in my courses. Gradually I came to the realisation that each era made unique contributions to the archaeological record and my objective was to understand the narrative embedded in the sites and artefacts. Knowing how all history is local and that a sporadic collection of documents could relate only a partial image, I came to regard material culture as a supplementary record that held its own stories. Once I started visiting the archives to increase the strands of evidence I could consult, and interviewing witnesses to past events, I discovered that historic sites were no less interesting than stone tools and butchered bones. There is no greater thrill for me than finding ancient artefacts, but now I find purpose in searching through the leavings at not-so-old settlements.

In graduate school I returned to my interest in antiquity on the northern plains, but the tack I followed led me to Piikani mythology to find an explanation for the archaeological mystery about the origins of large-scale communal hunting. I surmised that myths were a spoken record of lived experience and therefore were vulnerable to my inquiry using archaeological data as proxy evidence for our customs. In this manner I was able to organise our folklore into chronological order and so I could state confidently when certain traditions, such as tobacco cultivation and the ensuing ritualism, entered Piikani culture (Yellowhorn 2002). I also shed new light to the accuracy of messages contained in old stories, which is one of the criticisms that sceptics use to disparage oral narratives (Mason 2006). I also contradicted the idea that Piikani ancestors only arrived on the northern plains circa 1790 by demonstrating great time-depth to our occupation of our homeland.

My professional career brought me back to my roots. I returned to the reserve where I grew up to pursue my active research programme. Although it was familiar, I knew little about its beginning and its early history. I had decided to apply my skills toward the goal of understanding that era of my community and to fill in a blank page in local history. When I proposed a study that emphasised historical archaeology I expected that its novelty would be a tough sell to the band council. Instead they supported my request and so I began my examination of the material culture record left over from the early reserve era of the Piikani people in Canada, c. 1880–1920. My objectives included examining the adjustments to Piikani culture brought about by settling on a reserve.

When I first became a student of my ancestors, the influential sources recommended to me were the written works of authors such as Clark Wissler (1909), Willard Schultz (1907) and Walter McClintock (1910). Without question I absorbed these nostalgic depictions based on the memories of elders whose first-person accounts of the old days fuelled my own interest. As I continued to research further, I discovered that these publications substituted for historical treatments of Piikani and their kinfolk. Anthropological writing during the twentieth century invariably started in this ethnographic present and paid minor attention to reserve conditions (Ewers 1958). This oeuvre still represents the starting point for studies of Piikani history, whether looking back to the recent or ancient past. However, this outlook has its mirror in the modern community because the people esteem the old culture as the authentic one.

Piikani culture is replete with imagery from our ancient connection to the northern plains, where our ancestors practiced the mobile lifeways of bison hunters. Our nation's flag features a stylized warrior's shield emblazoned with a bison motif and fringed with eagle feathers. Ubiquitous emblems of those olden days appear everywhere on the items of modern domesticity and inspire the annual community celebration called the Indian Days. The nostalgia on display recalls an identity unfettered by reserve boundaries and expressed in its own terms. Less importance falls on the history when farming became the prominent mode of existence. There are no fairs commemorating a lifestyle synonymous with hardship and poverty and which recalls a time of control from afar. This early reserve history simply does not enter the equation, yet it was a transformative time for Piikani culture because that is when it took on its modern dimensions.

My ancestors, who settled on lands reserved for them in 1880, never had a chance to record their own story for themselves. Since this internalist perspective is missing, I wanted to explore an alternative point of departure for Piikani studies that did not depend solely on the ethnographic present. My search for documentary evidence led me to the national, provincial and local archives that curated letters, reports, dispatches and photographs. I learned to interrogate textual artefacts and to reveal the story concealed with the words and paper. I noticed, for example, the stylistic change accompanying the move from hand-written to typewritten reports that seemed to suggest an entrenched bureaucracy.

I commenced my research in the archives but I augmented these data with oral history interviews. I queried a cross section of residents about their impressions of Piikani community and culture, being cautious not to privilege one generation's perspective at the expense of another. The questions posed to the interviewees had them reflect on their own experience of the dynamic nature of the village and its environs. Our discussions were captured on videotape for a documentary I am making about the project and its results. Of course, since their stories were personal reminiscences we had to get approval from the Office of Research Ethics at our institution and have the subjects agree to be interviewed on camera.

Field archaeology tends to be my pleasant seasonal activity, so when summer arrived in 2006 I was happy to initiate the final component that concentrated on material culture studies. Selecting a family farmstead, built circa 1911, allowed me to examine the domestic geography of this cabin and compare it to the use of space around a tipi, the original mobile home of the plains. It's located in an isolated part of the reserve, which had no terrain alterations after it was abandoned so the in situ artefact preservation was excellent. With assistance from a graduate student we did an initial sweep around the cabin foundation with a metal detector. In this manner we could ascertain the main activity areas, which were mainly where the front side of the house was. Indeed there were a lot of metal artefact such as a thimble, some buttons and many nails, but there were also non-metal objects. Glass shards from broken windows were common too, but mixed in were fragments of medicine bottles and product jars bearing distinguishing marks, colours and designs. Although Piikani ancestors did make their own earthenware for about two millennia, the ceramic pieces we found were manufactured in England and brandished a flamboyant floral design with lettering on the bottom side. Plastic items, such as a ladies' comb, a child's toy and buttons, were perhaps the most surprising historical objects we found. We augmented our dig with archival photographs and interviews with elders whose lived experience included time at this farmstead as children.

Unlike the ethnographic portrait of Piikani communities in the early reserve era our excavations revealed that they were very engaged with the modern world. Rather than being isolated from the society growing around them, they were willing to acquire those items that made sense to their lives. Whether that was the vernacular architecture of their neighbours or gardening techniques, they were intent on making adjustments to their culture when needed. Despite switching from circular to four-sided housing, within the walls of their one-room log cabins they preserved the domestic geography of their tipi habitations. Customary dwellings align on an east-west axis with the door facing to the east. Before electricity was common, log houses were oriented so the doors and windows opened to the south to maximise sunlight. The stove in the centre was like the hearth in a lodge. The interior space maintained the custom of gender division, wherein the man's side, to the right of the door, is equivalent to the family area and the woman's side is for entertaining visitors. Piikani households were like a microcosm of their reserve, and each family had to accommodate change so that the whole community could survive.

In contrast to the domesticity of farm life, I spent the summers of 2008 and 2009 examining the imprint left behind by an old residential school that stood at the site before being decommissioned and physically dismantled. Church of England missionaries built it in 1897 and activated their government-sanctioned objective of bringing Christian civilization to the Piikani. In addition to religious training, they taught children the basics of numeracy and literacy, but mostly the vocation of farming. Geography had much to do with the school's demise because the terrace in the river valley where it was built did not escape the flood when heavy rains poured down in the spring of 1925. The infrastructure sustained heavy damage that led to its abandonment and leveling 2 years later. Whereas the wood frame buildings no longer stood, our first challenge was to determine where in the school grounds we were digging. A search through the archives yielded one photograph showing some of the buildings intact and from it we could ascertain that we were digging in the assembly space in front of the schoolhouse.

My initial sweep with a metal detector proved indeterminate because nails of all sorts were ubiquitous so every square inch registered a signal. Prior to beginning my excavation I assessed the terrain with a gradiometer, a near-surface remote sensing technique that is effective for identifying hot spots of disturbance in the matrix. I then followed up with a test pit sampling strategy to ground truth the readings before selecting an area for excavation. Immediately upon breaking soil we began to unearth an assortment of artefacts. In addition to nails, the items made of metal included plates, cutlery and other utensils, suggesting a deliberate selection for longevity. The ceramic artefacts were mass-produced and displayed no sign of decoration; perhaps not a surprise given the institutional setting. What did bewilder us was the complete absence of material culture attributable to children, even though many students lived there during its 30 years. Correspondence and reports written by the staff reveal that parents brought presents to their children during visits. Since no pupils survive who can give first hand descriptions, the place had passed out of living memory so oral history can only convey a vicarious familiarity.

Considering the school's goals, we could put family lore side by side with material culture to infer an austere backdrop to the students' school days.

Three graduate students worked with me and each led a project that examined a discrete topic within the overall research agenda that was also the basis for a thesis. Our excavations garnered much interest in the community so we reached out with a public communication strategy. The first event we targeted was the annual Treaty Day celebration where we reserved a table to put our research activities on display. We set out the artefacts we found and invited people to inspect them and ask questions. To profit from transparency, we put up posters to inform Piikani residents about the projects and their objectives. While this type of contact is immediate and popular, it is of short duration. I wanted to build on their interest and ensure that the project left a legacy that would benefit them in some real and tangible manner. Toward this end I compiled the historical documents I discovered and made copies to establish a village archive. Certainly the theses produced from this project will contribute detailed analysis of the trends that shaped the early years of reserve life. Using video footage of the land, the village and the interviews I conducted, I began work on a documentary about local history that disseminates the results of our work. I produced a preview video that I posted on the YouTube channel hosted by the Canadian Archaeological Association (Yellowhorn 2012).

I could assess the impact of my research by its results. I demonstrated that the archaeological record is a potent option for researching local history that adds an interesting new complement to the ethnographic literature. I established that, rather than the isolation implied by ethnographers, the folks settling on reserves were very attuned to the tastes that influenced their choices. They wanted what their white neighbours had and they were actively engaging the world. However, recent history represents a legacy of loss for Piikani. Whether we refer to our language, our culture, or our identity, we are always on the verge of losing something. On the other hand, archaeology offers up the promise of finding some part of their history.

Discussion

Today the landscape is dotted with so many tributes to ethics as to trivialise the whole concept. Perhaps the most dubious example being the beauty products I saw marketed with "ethical pricing", instead of just being on sale. Whether they are about consuming coffee, chocolate or water, or curious claims of oil and global geopolitics, the world seems to be awash in them. As consumers we use our debit cards and the products we purchase to measure our commitment to fairly traded goods. We wish to make right with ourselves, or at least do no harm. Sustaining all the loose talk is a genuine search for social justice, especially in the case of dispossessed, marginalised people. So the search for an ethical standard in the practice of archaeology mirrors a broader trend in contemporary popular culture exemplified by publications such as *Be good: how to navigate the ethics of everything* (Cohen 2012) that purport to contain advice on how to attain your ideal conduct.

Prior to 1990 the topic of ethics in archaeology did not occupy a great deal of space in the published literature, but we cannot conclude that we worked in a moral vacuum. Researchers pursued their own interest without thought to the social inequality imposed on the descendants of the cultures they were studying because it was not a regular part of their profession's discourse. That changed when Indigenous peoples began questioning the motives of archaeologists excavating their burial grounds and sacred sites. This accepted practice was foundational to the discipline. The father of American anthropology, Franz Boas, thought grave robbing was just another day of fieldwork on the northwest coast of America (Cole 1999). Despite his haunted dreams, and his friendly relations with the Indians, he carried on his task because it was a scientific endeavour. In the process, he brought disrepute for his discipline that lingers in the minds of first nations to this day. As late as the 1970s, Aboriginal people expressed dismay with the methods deployed as fieldwork. At a symposium on emerging trends in Canadian archaeology in 1975, Basil

Johnston (1976), an Ojibway man himself, articulated a sentiment opposed to excavating human remains that came to prominence the next decade. While grave robbing still finds an audience in the entertainment industry of popular culture, it has no place in the repertoire of contemporary field methods. Instead, we can readily observe the milestones leading to our present discussion, such as the Native American Graves Protection and Repatriation Act (NAGPRA) that is routinely cited in our lexicon by its acronym.

After 1990 there was a swift sea change as demonstrated by the sudden appearance of ethical statements adopted by professional umbrella organisations. When Thomas (1996) published his review of his discipline's relationship with Native Americans, he could only reference four major groups with formal positions on ethics. Scarcely a decade later, Joe Watkins (2005) contributed his own appraisal of those conjoined twins and cited seven more additions to this oeuvre. Each in its own way arrived at the same conclusion that parity between archaeologists and Indigenous peoples was a prerequisite for future archaeological work. My career in archaeology began before there was much attention paid to ethics in our profession, but that changed for me personally when I co-chaired the task force created by the Canadian Archaeological Association (1997) to develop a statement of ethics for its members. Tim Murray, an Australian archaeologist writing too about constructive engagement, described the change wrought so far as transformative, but sounded a cautious note about the ties that bind when he observed:

> These socially and politically engaged archaeologies are still maturing rather than matured. As a result, much of the writing on these matters is still abstract and programmatic, and focuses on possibilities and the future rather than a welter of thoroughly worked examples (Murray 2011:372).

My self-selected livelihood grew from my interest in earth sciences and an insatiable curiosity about my ancestors and their lifeways. In this regard I thought I was on my own but over the years I have noticed that Aboriginal people possess a strong interest in a secular antiquity they are just discovering. With my own historical archaeology programme in partnership with the Piikani First Nation, I am making a contribution to maturing this relationship. I developed my internalist perspective to situate my research in a context that emanates from the internal dialogue that Piikani people have about their past. I long ago left behind the notion that I, as a Piikani, could not opt for a career in archaeology because it was implicated in colonial history. Instead, I regard archaeology as an instrument of society that can be wielded by anyone to pursue internally defined goals. In doing so I have been able to appreciate our folklore for the insights I have gained through my research and to demonstrate that Piikani mythology can be a source of explanation for archaeological manifestations on the northern plains.

Questions of ethics arose when considering the merits of collecting objects or leaving them in situ, especially when there is no local repository to house them. Moreover, Piikani custom holds that offerings represent someone's troubles left at a site and to collect them is to accept the misfortune attached to them. Even today community leaders are reluctant to make requests for repatriation and instead prefer the relics be returned to their original provenance. Of course, that is anathema to archaeologists who see the same offerings as artefacts to be curated. Between these two positions is the spectrum of contingency that confronts me as I travel my career path. Although letting go the habit to collect strains against my training, sometimes that might be the accepted option.

Ethical discourse and archaeological practice intersect around the basic principle that we care about our profession and the legacy we leave in our wake. We care that people should perceive our actions in the best light possible. When we engage in sensitive work, such as excavating human remains, we do our best to display our humanity. Unlike the Boasian rationale, that looting graves was in the best interest of science, we take pains to preserve the dignity of the perpetual act of burial. It is perhaps the most controversial work for me personally since I am breaking all the Piikani taboos about avoiding the dead. However, I recognise that since I possess specialised skills I have a duty to advocate on behalf of ancestors disturbed of their rest, be they my own or someone else's. I assuage any misgivings by understanding that exhuming the deceased may be the last best option or that it may bring resolution to an old injustice. Also, there are conditions that make the task easier. For example, if a native community is involved, if the site is threatened, if there is allowance for scientific inquiry and if the ultimate intention is reburial.

Archaeological work does not always entail the same level of discord featured in the debate surrounding human remains. While embedding a standard ethical practice in the discipline may not be achievable, the search for a respectful relationship with descendant communities must continue. This was a typical response on the part of students working with me on my historical archaeology project. They did not want to be isolated from the community and took every opportunity to interact with local residents. My crew was certainly grateful that I invited some Piikani elders to the site to conduct a smudge ceremony and bring tranquility to our work place. When we were out surveying the forests we routinely left tobacco offerings at the sites we discovered in order to express our respect. Such practices do not dilute the scientific nature of our work; rather, it is an opportunity to put our humanity on display.

I enjoy fieldwork and interacting with my community by deploying archaeological methods to examine our ancient and recent histories. When I first started down this career path, I assumed that methods and theory constituted an indivisible pair. As I have proceeded to learn the nuances of each I now understand that to appropriate the methods for my research does not mean I am obligated to accept the theories of earlier researchers. In fact I have a duty as a scholar to construct my own theories based on the observations I make, knowing full well that they will be judged on their own merit. However, this takes place at a level of abstraction higher than the practical applications of methods.

Acknowledgements The Piikani Chief and Council endorsed this project and provided logistical support for my crew and I. This research was made possible by a grant from the Social Sciences and Humanities Research Council, Ottawa.

References

Brink, J. (2005). *Imagining Head-Smashed-In: Aboriginal buffalo hunting on the northern plains*. Edmonton: AU Press.

Canadian Archaeological Association. (1997). Statement of principles for ethical conduct pertaining to Aboriginal peoples. *Canadian Journal of Archaeology, 21*(1), 5–8.

Cohen, R. (2012). *Be good: How to navigate the ethics of everything*. San Francisco: Chronicle Books.

Cole, D. (1999). *Franz Boas: The early years, 1858–1906*. Vancouver: Douglas & McIntyre.

Ewers, J. (1955). *The horse in Blackfoot Indian culture: With comparative material from other western tribes*. Washington: Smithsonian Institution.

Ewers, J. (1958). *The Blackfeet: Raiders of the northwestern plains*. Norman: University of Oklahoma Press.

Ferguson, T. J. (1996). Native Americans and the practice of archaeology. *Annual Review of Anthropology, 25*, 63–79.

Johnston, B. (1976). The cultural and ethical aspects of archaeology in Canada: An Indian point of view. In A. G. McKay (Ed.), *Symposium on New Perspectives in Canadian Archaeology: Proceedings of a Symposium Sponsored by the Royal Society of Canada* (pp. 173–175). Toronto: Royal Society of Canada.

Kennedy, M. A. (1997). *The whiskey trade of the northwestern plains*. New York: Peter Lang.

Kidd, K. E. (1969). *Historic site archaeology in Canada*. Ottawa: National Museum of Canada.

Mason, R. J. (2006). *Inconstant companions: Archaeology and North American Indian oral traditions*. Tuscaloosa: University of Alabama Press.

McClintock, W. (1910). *The old north trail; or, life, legends and religion of the Blackfeet Indians*. London: Macmillan.

Murray, T. (2011). Archaeologists and Indigenous people: A maturing relationship? *Annual Review of Anthropology, 40*, 363–378.

Rubertone, P. (2000). The historical archaeology of Native Americans. *Annual Review of Anthropology, 29*, 425–446.

Schultz, W. (1907). *My life as an Indian: The story of a red woman and a white man in the lodges of the Black-feet*. London: J. Murray.

Watkins, J. (2005). Through wary eyes: Indigenous perspectives on archaeology. *Annual Review of Anthropology, 34*, 429–449.

Wissler, C., & Duvall, D. (1909). *Mythology of the Blackfoot Indians*. New York: American Museum of Natural History.

Yellowhorn, E. (1999). Heritage protection on Indian reserve lands in Canada. *Plains Anthropologist, 44*(170), 107–116.

Yellowhorn, E. (2002). *Awakening internalist archaeology in the aboriginal world*. Unpublished PhD dissertation, Montréal, Canada.

Yellowhorn, E. (2006a). Understanding antiquity: Bruce Trigger on his life's work in archaeology—An interview. *Journal of Social Archaeology, 6*(3), 307–327.

Yellowhorn, E. (2006b). The awakening of internalist archaeology in the aboriginal world. In R. Williamson & M. Bisson (Eds.), *The archaeology of Bruce Trigger: Theoretical empiricism* (pp. 194–209). Montréal: McGill-Queen's University Press.

Yellowhorn, E. (2012). Encountering modernity: The Piikani historical archaeology project. 6:33 minutes. Retrieved from http://www.youtube.com/user/canadianarchaeology?feature=results_main

Index

C. Gnecco, D. Lippert (eds.), *Ethics and Archaeological Praxis*,
Ethical Archaeologies: The Politics of Social Justice 1,
DOI 10.1007/978-1-4939-1646-7

CPSIA information can be obtained at www.ICGtesting.com
Printed in the USA
BVOW10*0812201114

375984BV00001B/2/P

9 781493 916450